MEASURES OF OCCUPATIONAL ATTITUDES
AND OCCUPATIONAL CHARACTERISTICS

(APPENDIX A TO
MEASURES OF POLITICAL ATTITUDES)

JOHN P. ROBINSON
ROBERT ATHANASIOU
KENDRA B. HEAD

Survey Research Center
Institute for Social Research

February 1969

Supported by grant MH 10809-02 of the
United States Public Health Service

Fourth Printing

Library of Congress Number 0-87944-051-1

PREFACE

The purpose of this monograph is to provide researchers with a systematic review and evaluation of the major empirical measures relevant to the study of variables related to a person's occupation. Particular attention is focused on measurement scales, that is, series of attitude items that attempt to measure the same attitude content.

A preliminary form of this monograph was printed in May, 1967. The few copies that were made available were for review purposes only. The present volume differs in only minor ways from this preliminary volume. This is due not to the fact that our reviewers made so few suggestions for revision but that they made so many. It was apparent that to upgrade this volume to suitable professional standards would require more resources than we had available. It is our fervent hope that the limited value of this volume will inspire someone in the field to produce a more satisfactory volume of this type in the future.

We are particularly grateful for the suggestions made by Professor Stanley Seashore. Unfortunately, we were unable to carry out all of them, especially those dealing with major revision and updating of certain chapters.

We are also indebted to Lois Huang and Virginia Nye for their patient typing of this manuscript.

John P. Robinson
Robert Athanasiou
Kendra B. Head

February 1969

WHAT IS CONTAINED IN THIS VOLUME

A brief summary of the 18 chapters of this handbook may prove helpful to the reader. The introductory chapter touches on the background of this project and lays out in brief, the major criteria to be used in evaluating the 77 scales reviewed in this volume. These evaluative criteria fall into three groups:

1) Item construction criteria (sampling of relevant content, simplicity of item wording, and performing item analyses on the data.

2) Response set criteria (controlling spurious effects of acquiescence and social desirability on responses to items).

3) Psychometric criteria (representative sampling, presentation of proper normative data on the instrument, test-retest reliability, item homogeneity, discrimination of known groups, cross-validation and other statistical procedures).

Of course, the meeting of these criteria does not alone determine the value of a scale. For example, one can construct a scale with high item homogeneity merely by including items which express the same idea in a number of different ways; again, one can ensure significant discrimination of known groups merely by sampling groups which are so divergent that they are unlikely to agree on anything. For this reason, we recommend that the choice of a scale from this volume be placed as much as possible within a decision-theoretic framework.

The subsequent three chapters--chapters 2,3, and 4--deal with reviews of three important facets of research on job satisfaction: historical perspective, cross-sectional studies, and predictability. An historical perspective of research on job attitudes is crucial in understanding how the instruments reviewed in this volume came to exist and why they have the particular advantages and drawbacks that they do. Paul Kimmel of the Office of Manpower and Training of the Department of Labor traces the social and economic conditions which have influenced the directions which social scientists have taken in their pursuit of explaining work behavior. Kimmel concludes that the scientific study of work as it is experienced and evaluated by the worker is in its infancy. Research on job attitudes in America since the turn of the century has been dominated by perspectives other than those of the worker. Industrial and counseling psychologists have looked at work from management's perspective, focusing on the development of tests, techniques, procedures, and conditions that will promote productivity and cut costs. Occupational sociologists and critics of the management approach have looked at work from the humanitarian perspective, focusing on those procedures and conditions which impede the self-expression, development, and self-actualization of the worker. Available research on the worker's view of work indicates that these two perspectives are over-simplified generalizations. Dimensions of work that have been shown to be relevant to the worker vary with a number of work place, job, and worker characteristics, and their interactions. Further study focusing directly on the worker's concerns about the conceptions of his work is needed to clarify these dimensions and to establish their relationship to the worker's attitudes under a wide variety of organizational, interpersonal, and individual conditions. Such a "research approach" should serve to bring studies of work out of the realm of social engineering and moral philosophy into the era of science.

Certainly, there has been far from satisfactory interplay between the results of representative national surveys and the rest of the literature on job attitudes. Most job attitude research is based on studies of single organizations or departments, and usually on managerial or other white-collar professions. Even more questionable is research based on college students who are extremely likely to be headed into higher-status occupations and who, in addition, usually have no work experience anyway. The review by John Robinson (Chapter 3) makes explicit the very real gaps in the work attitudes of various occupational groups. Of particular interest to those interested in devising scales which will adequately cover the factors that can affect job satisfaction are the responses given to open-ended questions on the things people find pleasing or displeasing about their job. Because of the complexity of the topic and the diversity of research findings, Robinson is able to discover few generalizations in a literature which has not previously been pulled together. Nevertheless, those generalizations that do appear, appear consistently, so that much literature in this area of job satisfaction wastefully covers ground already clearly charted from cross-section samples. There do exist dramatic differences between occupational groups in the degree and types of satisfaction they derive from their work. The researcher dealing with a particular segment of the occupational domain would be well advised to see how his segment differs from other workers in work expectations.

The following chapter, by Robert Athanasiou, summarizes the literature dealing with job attitudes and occupational performance. The conflicting and disappoinging results of studies on the relation between attitude and per-formance are given special consideration, as are the writings of Vroom, Brayfield and Crockett, and Herzberg, et al. on this topic. Athanasiou gives a brief review of some representative literature concerning the effects of wages, supervisory styles, group cohesion, job content and organizational structure variables on job satisfaction, and then turns his attention to the equally important topic of the effects of job satisfaction on worker turnover and absenteeism. It appears that from these two behavioral manifestations of discontent one can predict job satisfaction better than one can predict work performance. Athanasiou's ideas imply that one may ensure higher levels of job satisfaction through matching the interests and needs of the person with those of the job.

From this article, we proceed to the detailed chapters dealing with the scales themselves. In Chapter 5, we first consider the general job satisfaction inventories, of which 14 are reviewed. Some of these are competent research instruments and are worthy of recommendation for future use. Under a separate heading in the following chapter are some recommended scales devised for particular high-level groups--managers, scientists--that deserve consideration if one is dealing strictly with such samples. Then in Chapter 7 are scales dealing with limited areas of the job--satisfaction with supervisors, working conditions, etc.--that could have certain merit for particular measurement situations. In Chapter 8 Peay and Wernander have reviewed in summary fashion a large number of factor analytic studies extant in the literature to perhaps cover any factors of important missed in the preceding chapters.

There are a number of concepts which contain the same flavor as satisfaction but deal with it from a unique theoretical or substantive viewpoint. In this category are instruments reflecting the meaning of work, alienation from work, worker motivation and role conflicts or work tension, and these are covered in Chapter 9. Occupational values (inner-other directed, achievement, status) also fall under this rubric but there are so many of them they are covered separately in Chapter 10; also included here are analogues to the "local-cosmopolitan" scale used in political behavior studies.

A major movement has been underway for many years in the social sciences to show the crucial way in which leadership styles (authoritarian, democratic, etc.) affect job performance and satisfaction. There are currently a few instruments available which may help the researcher measure leadership qualities, especially from a human relations point of view, and these are reviewed in Chapter 11. In addition, we review some measures which are organizational in focus: closeness of supervision, decentralization of decision-making, degree of control.

One organizational measure--job performance--was not covered because of the complexity of the topic although this is one of the fruitful and necessary fields of occupational measurement. There is opportunity in this area for true Guttman scale measurement where attendance at work constitutes the lowest step in the scale progressing through meeting the minimum role requirements of one's job up through ego-involvement in one's job and attempts at innovation. Nonetheless, other measurement rating methods are more prevalent (see for example in Whisler and Harper's Performance Appraisal: Research and Practice, Harper and Row, 1962). A competent review of the intricacies of measuring job performance is given in Vroom's Work and Motivation (Wiley, 1964).

In Chapter 12 we consider a number of assorted job attitude areas. The most prevalent instruments here are the measures of union-management perceptions, including the clever (but seldom used) error-choice scales. Also reviewed are scales devised to measure attitudes toward working for the government, as well as scales assessing one's orientation to his profession, career or institution. Then there are the miscellaneous attitude scales: attitudes toward automation, attitudes toward employing older people, work attitudes of the mentally ill.

As Athanasiou has pointed out at the end of his chapter, occupational interest inventories may be useful in the determination of job satisfaction. They are, of course, most often used as job selection devices and are reviewed from this angle in Chapter 13. One particular selection technique we find most intriguing--the Selective Word Memory Test. This test is based on the assumption that people who are likely to be successful in a field become attuned to particular kinds of words; it requires that examinees be able to recall which words were used in sentences which they had read a few minutes before. Another recent vocational measure of some promise is the Job Analysis and Interest Measure which attempts to match the person with the job to which he is best suited.

The importance of the background facts of occupational status is stressed throughout this volume and scales to measure this characteristic are reviewed in Chapter 14. Some scales are seen to be restricted to just a few occupations, some contain very little occupational differentiation while others require too much differentiation to be practicable. The most often used scale, devised by Duncan, is more than adequate for aggregative purposes but has certain short-comings for individual level or small sample analyses. It is recommended that status measures incorporate the individual's education and income, as well as his occupation, in assigning status scores for such analyses.

For many people, however, income, occupation and educational background are out of balance. These people are said to be in a state of "status-incongruence" or "status-ambiguity," a leading predictor of "relative deprivation" and general dissatisfaction for those who make less money or have a lower status position than their education would indicate, but which may lead to mild euphoria for those who are doing better than their educational background would indicate. These findings on status-incongruence, indices to measure it and their advantages and shortcomings, are discussed by Stanislav Kasl in Chapter 15.

Occupational status, however, does not exhaust the supply of inherent sources of variance within the occupational spectrum. In addition to the "vertical" dimension of status, some sociologists have located interesting sources of variance on the "horizontal" dimension of situs. In Chapter 16, we consider five occupational situs category systems; for the most part these are based on the type of industry in which the person works or on whether the worker deals with people, data or things.

The occupational background of a person is to a certain extent dependent on the occupation of his father. The area of study of the extent of this father-son relationship (and other relations in the person's occupational history) is called occupational mobility. A method of measuring this characteristic and a few major findings in this field are discussed in Chapter 17.

In the final chapter, Chapter 18, we attempt to summarize the evidence of the previous four chapters and certain portions of Robinson's earlier chapter under the general heading of occupational similarity. We feel the study of occupational similarity is vital to research into occupational attitudes and behavior because people in various occupations have been found to vary widely in the expectation, interests and orientations they bring to their work. As yet, however, no attempt has been made to construct an easily comprehensible occupational code which incorporates the major sources of such variance within it. To this end, we examine three bodies of data through which it is possible to compare the similarity of members of a number of occupational categories across a wide range of variables. First considered are sociological data on the occupational similarity of friends, neighbors and family members. These data all point to occupational status as the major basis of occupational similarity, as do further data on the attitudes and behaviors toward work and leisure of various occupational groups. The second broad body of data examined is normative information on various vocational interest inventories used in psychological research. These data point to the type of work dealt with (specifically, whether the worker deals with data, people or things) as the crucial source of occupational similarity; however, these interest tests seldom scan the entire occupational spectrum so that the effects of status may be suppressed. The data-people-things distinction forms a primary basis of work done on the Dictionary of Occupational Titles (DOT), probably the largest concerted effort into assessing occupational similarity. Analysis of DOT data forms the third and final body of data examined. The DOT data suggest far greater differentiation within the higher level white-collar occupations than in the lower white-collar or blue-collar jobs.

To conclude the volume we present a tentative two-digit occupational code based on the above considerations. The code is constructed so as to reflect differences between working with people vs. working with data or things within the professional domain and other situs differences (in the lack of any other coherent basis) within the blue-collar domain. It is hoped that this code will be useful for future occupational research in which major likely background sources or differences between occupations are sought or in which the researcher wishes to know with what segment of the occupational spectrum he is dealing.

Despite the wide variety of empirical instruments reviewed in this volume, there are undoubtedly many others that some might have wished us to cover. There are two broad areas which come to mind in this respect but which we feel are already covered in other research efforts. Measures of organizational-level variables, for one, are currently being compiled and reviewed by Bernard Indik at Rutgers University. The reader interested in the use of projective techniques in a work context will find a number of research approaches covered and evaluated in Kinslinger's recent article (Psychological Bulletin, 1966, 134-149).

TABLE OF CONTENTS

Page

WHAT IS CONTAINED IN THIS VOLUME   i

CHAPTER

1. INTRODUCTION 1

2. RESEARCH ON WORK AND WORKER IN THE UNITED STATES (Kimmel) 17

3. OCCUPATIONAL NORMS AND DIFFERENCES IN JOB SATISFACTION: A SUMMARY
    OF SURVEY RESEARCH EVIDENCE (Robinson) 25
        Blauner's Review 27
        Gurin, Veroff and Feld Mental Health Study 29
        Kilpatrick, Cummings and Jennings Study 34
        Wilensky's Labor-Leisure Study of Detroit 43
        Converse and Robinson Meaning-of-Time Study 47
        Some Further Data on Related Issues 58
        Summary and Conclusions 65

4. JOB ATTITUDES AND OCCUPATIONAL PERFORMANCE: A REVIEW OF SOME
    IMPORTANT LITERATURE (Athanasiou) 79
        Relation between Attitudes and Performance 79
        Previous Literature Reviews 81
        Effects of Specific Factors on Satisfaction
            as a Dependent Variable 86
        Organizational Structure Variables 88
        Satisfaction as an Independent Variable 91
        The Use of Occupational Interest Inventories 93
        Conclusions 95

5. GENERAL JOB SATISFACTION SCALES 99
        1. Job Description Index (Smith, et al. 1963) 105
        2. Index of Job Satisfaction (Kornhauser 1965) 108
        3. Factors for Job Satisfaction and Job Dissatisfaction
            (Dunnette, et al. 1966) 112
        4. SRA (Employee) Attitude Survey (1951 and 1966) 116
        5. IRC Employee Attitude Scales (Carlson, et al. 1962) 117
        6. Index of Employee Satisfaction (Morse 1953) 120
        7. Job Satisfaction Scale (Johnson 1955) 122
        8. Job Dimensions Blank (Schletzer 1965) 126
        9. Job Satisfaction Index (Brayfield and Rothe 1951) 129

5. GENERAL JOB SATISFACTION SCALES (continued)

   10. Job Satisfaction (Hoppock 1935) 132
   11. Tear Ballot (Kerr 1948) 136
   12. Employee Morale Scale (Woods 1944) 138
   13. Work Satisfaction and Personal Happiness
      (Noll and Bradburn 1968) 142

6. JOB SATISFACTION FOR PARTICULAR OCCUPATIONS 145

   1. Need Fulfillment Questionnaire for Management (Porter 1962) . . 148
   2. Managerial Job Attitudes (Harrison 1960) 152
   3. Job Attitudes and Job Satisfaction of Scientists
      (Hinrichs 1962) 154
   4. Attitudes of Scientists in Organizations
      (Pelz and Andrews 1966) 160
   5. Job Satisfaction Inventory (Twery, et al. 1958) 162

7. SATISFACTION WITH SPECIFIC JOB FEATURES 165

   1. Supervisory Behavior Description (Fleishman 1957) 167
   2. Attitude toward the Supervisor (Nagle 1953) 169
   3. Satisfaction with Supervisor (Draper 1955) 171
   4. Attitudes toward the Supervisor (Schmid, et al. 1957) . . 173
   5. Employee Opinion Survey (Bolda 1958) 175
   6. Need Satisfaction in Work (Schaffer 1953) 179
   7. About Your Company (King 1960) 181
   8. Group Morale Scale (Goldman 1958) 184

8. FACTORS FROM SOME MULTIDIMENSIONAL ANALYSES OF JOB
    SATISFACTION (Peay and Wernander) 187

9. CONCEPTS RELATED TO JOB SATISFACTION 197

   1. Indices of Alienation (Aitkin and Hage 1966) 200
   2. Alienation from Work (Pearlin 1962) 204
   3. Job-Related Tension (Kahn, et al. 1964) 206
   4. Job Motivation Index (Patchen 1965) 209
   5. Identification with the Work Organization (Patchen 1965) . . 212
   6. Defining Dimensions of Occupation (Pearlin and Kohn 1966) . . 217
   7. Meaning of Work Scales (Guion 1965) 219
   8. Meaning of Work (Tausky 1968) 221

10. OCCUPATIONAL VALUES 223

   1. Occupational Values Scales (Kilpatrick, et al. 1964) . . 229
   2. Occupational Values (Rosenberg 1957) 233
   3. Faith-in-People Scale (Rosenberg 1957) 236
   4. Scale of Inner- and Other-Directedness (Bowers 1966) . . 238
   5. Inner-Other Social Preference Scale (Kassarjian 1962) . . 240
   6. Career-Oriented Occupational Values (Marvick 1954) . . . 244
   7. Career Orientation in the Federal Service (Slesinger 1961) . . 247

11. LEADERSHIP STYLES 249

   1. Leadership Opinion Questionnaire (Stogdill and Coons 1957) . . 254
   2. The SRA Supervisory Index (Schwartz 1956) 258

11. LEADERSHIP STYLES (continued)

3. Leadership Practices Inventory (Nelson 1955) 261
4. How Supervise? (File and Remmers 1948) 263
5. A Proverbs Test for Supervisor Selection (Reveal 1960) . . . 267
6. A Managerial Key for the CPI (Goodstein and Schrader 1963) . 272
7. Managerial Scale for Enterprise Improvement 274
8. Organizational Control Graph (Tannenbaum 1966) 275
9. Profile of Organizational Characteristics (Likert 1967) . . . 276

12. OTHER WORK-RELEVANT ATTITUDES 281

1. Union and Management Attitudes toward Each Other
   (Stagner, et al. 1958) 284
2. IRC Union Attitude Scale (Uphoff and Dunnette 1956) 287
3. Index of Pro-Labor Orientation (Kornhauser 1965) 289
4. Pro-Labor Attitude Error-Choice Tests (Hammond 1948) 293
5. Attitudes toward Labor and Management (Weschler 1950) 295
6. Attitudes toward Working for the Government (Aalto 1956) . . 298
7. Attitudes toward Working for the Government
   (Kilpatrick, et al. 1964) 302
8. Attitude toward Automation (Rosenberg 1962) 304
9. Attitude toward Employment of Older Persons
   (Kirchner 1954) 307
10. Opinions about Work of the Mentally Ill
    (Streuning and Efron 1965). 310

13. VOCATIONAL INTEREST MEASURES 313

1. Selective Word Memory Test (Edel and Tiflin 1965) 321
2. Job Analysis and Interest Measure (Walther 1961) 324
3. Sales Attitude Check List (Taylor 1960) 328
4. Work Attitude Key for the MMPI (Tydlaska and Mengel 1953) . . 331

14. OCCUPATIONAL STATUS MEASURES 335

1. Socio-Economic Status Scale (Duncan 1961) 342
2. Socio-Economic Status Scores (Bureau of Census 1963) 357
3. Occupational Ratings (North and Hatt 1947, 1965) 359
4. Index of Status Characteristics (Warner, et al. 1949) 362
5. Index of Social Position (Hollingshead and Redlich 1958) . . 367
6. Index of Class Position (Ellis, et al. 1963) 369
7. Class Identification (Centers and others 1949-1966) 371
8. Facets for Job Evaluation (Guttman 1965) 375

15. STATUS INCONSISTENCY: SOME CONCEPTUAL AND METHODOLOGICAL
    CONSIDERATIONS (Kasl) 377

Types of Status Inconsistency 377
Theoretical Considerations 378
Some Empirical Findings 379
Methodological Considerations 380
Methods of Statistical Analysis 383
Conclusions 385
Some Measures of Status Inconsistency 391

16. OCCUPATIONAL SITUS 397

    1. Situs Categories (Morris and Murphy 1959) 399
    2. Occupational Groups (Roe 1956) 400
    3. Occupational Classification (Super 1957) 401
    4. Census Bureau Industry Groupings (1960) 403
    5. Data, People, Things (Dictionary of Occupational Titles
       1965) 404

17. SOCIAL MOBILITY 407

    Steps for Measuring Occupational Mobility
       (Tumin and Feldman) 410

18. OCCUPATIONAL SIMILARITY 413

    1. Sociological Evidence of Occupational Similarity. 418
    2. Mappings of Occupational Similarity Underlying the Strong
       Kuder, and Minnesota Vocational Interest Measures 422
    3. Some Similarity Assessments Implicit in the Dictionary of
       Occupational Titles 433
    4. A Tentative Revised Occupation Code for Survey Research . . 436

1. INTRODUCTION

The instigation for this handbook goes back to the pioneer efforts of Professor Robert Lane, a political scientist at Yale University. Professor Lane, as many social scientists still are today, was appalled at the proliferation of empirical instruments in fields related to his area of interest. In the summer of 1958, he attempted to pull together those scales that would be of value to researchers in the field of political behavior whose interests ranged from authoritarianism to opinion leadership to internationalism. While Professor Lane was able initially to interest the National Institutes of Health to continue this research, previous commitments on his time forced him to turn to other matters. Subsequently, the availability of personnel at the Survey Research Center ensured that this valuable work would be continued under the general supervision of Professor Philip Converse.

There exist of course many cogent reasons for such an undertaking. Empirical instruments are likely to appear in any one of 15 social science journals (and may appear in 20 others), under surprising book titles, in seldom circulated dissertations, from commercial publishers, as well as in the long undisturbed piles of manuscripts in the offices of social scientists. Surely this is an inefficient grapevine of information for the interested researcher. One must stay in the same area of interest (and few social scientists can) to become aware of the empirical literature and instruments available. Often, the interdisciplinary investigator is interested in the relation of some variable of which he has heard casually to his favorite area of interest. His job of combing the literature to pick a proper instrument consumes needlessly long hours that often just lead to a frustrating decision to forego measuring this or that characteristic. Worse still (perhaps having already learned the frustrations of the above game in a previous research venture), he may resort to rapidly devising his own measure and adding to the already burdensome number of inadequately conceived instruments. In our search through the literature we found an appalling amount of replication of previous discoveries as well as unawareness of related (and usually better) research done in the same area.

Our searching procedure took us back through the earliest issues of Psychological Abstracts (even before 1920), as well as the printed history of the most likely periodical sources of psychological instruments (Journal of Abnormal and Social Psychology, Journal of Applied Psychology, among about ten others) and sociological or political measures (Sociometry, American Sociological Review, American Political Science Review). Doctoral dissertations were combed by examining back issues of Dissertation Abstracts and we are grateful to University Microfilms of Ann Arbor for providing us with pertinent dissertations; still, not all universities (notably Harvard) belong to this service. It is also relatively recent. Contact with the large variety of empirical research being done at the University of Michigan opened our eyes and widened our search, as did conversations with expert researchers we were able to contact at the annual meetings of the American Sociological Association and the American Psychological Association for both 1965 and 1966. These meetings also served to bring a number of other empirical instruments to our attention.

However, we feel there is more to our mission than the mere listing of the wide variety of potential instruments available. This would be evident from a perusal of our predecessors in this field (Miller, 1965, Shaw and Wright, 1967, Miles and Lake, 1967), who have taken pains to include useful statistical data in their scale presentations. However, the casual reader or part-time researcher may find it difficult to interpret comparable data when different authors use different statistical procedures. Thus few researchers are aware that a Guttman Reproducibility Coefficient of .91 may be equivalent to an inter-item correlation coefficient of .30, or that a test-retest reliability correlation of .50 may say more about an instrument than a split-half reliability of .80. Nor are authors often disposed to point out the limitations of their instruments when they are writing articles for publication. Hence, many authors fail to alert their readers to the possible dangers of using restricted samples, failing to guard against response set, writing items that are too complicated for most people to understand, failing to item analyze their scales before further analysis or just not covering adequately the totality of behaviors or attitudes relevant to the problem at hand. We have taken it upon ourselves, where possible, to make such liabilities clearly visible to the reader.

Thus, we have made some attempt to rate the 77 instruments in this volume on their ability to stand up to certain desirable standards. Due to the fact that scale write-ups were handled by a number of reviewers, the careful reader will notice an unevenness in the type and extent of critical comments made on each instrument. If future demand for further handbooks is forthcoming, we hope to control this factor by collecting separate reviews, especially by skilled researchers in each area. For now where the experienced researcher may not agree with our assessments, he is free to supplement them with his own. But we hope he has become aware of a minimum number of considerations that he must keep in mind not only when deciding on which instrument to use but also when interpreting his results. We trust that our assessment will not sway the less-discriminating reader into making a choice any more biased than he would have made anyway. Where possible we have tried to be fair, honest, consistent, and not overly demanding in our evaluations, and have tried to show clearly the merits as well as the limitations of each instrument.

The evaluative criteria which we have chosen are listed in the order which may represent the ideal (but not strict) chronological order in which attitude instruments might be constructed. The first step is, naturally, writing or finding items to include in the scale. It is usually assumed that the author knows enough about the field to construct the instrument so that it will cover an important theoretical construct well enough to be useful to other researchers in the field. If it covers a construct for which instruments are already available, the author should demonstrate sound improvements over previous measures. There are three further considerations which represent the minimum that an adequately constructed scale ought to possess. These are:

Proper Sampling of Content: Proper sampling is not easy to achieve, nor can exact rules be specified for ensuring that it is done properly-- as critics of Guttman's phrase "universe of content" have been quick to point out. Nevertheless, there is little doubt of the critical nature of the general aim in scale construction. Future research may better reveal the population of behaviors, objects and feelings which ought to be covered in any attitude area, but the following examples may suggest ways in which the interested researcher can provide better coverage in designing scales. Investigators of the "authoritarian personality" lifted key sentiments expressed in small group conversations, personal interviews, and written remarks and transformed them into scale items; some of these items in fact consisted of direct verbatim quotations from such materials. In the job satisfaction area, we have given detailed consideration to the analysis of responses to open-ended questions from representative samples which ask the respondent, "What things (do you like best) (don't you like) about your job?" We feel that these responses offer invaluable guidelines to the researcher as to both the universe of factors he should be covering and the weight that should be given to such factors. Other instruments in the job satis- faction area have been built on the basis of previous factor analytic work (Smith, et al., 1966) or responses to questions about critical satisfying or dissatisfying situations at work (Herzberg, et al., 1959), or both of these (Dunnette, et al., 1965).

There remain difficult decisions as to how many questions are needed to cover each factor (probably a minimum of two in any lengthy instrument) but the important first step is to make sure that the waterfront has been covered.

Simplicity of Item Wording: One of the great advantages of securing verbatim comments from group discussions or open-ended questions, as those in advertising have apparently discovered, is that the attitudes are couched in language easily comprehended and recognizable by respondents. One of the most obvious advantages of more recently constructed scales is that item wording has become far less stuffy, lofty, or idealistic. Even today, however, survey researchers still have problems adapting items developed from college samples for use on heterogeneous populations.[1]

There are other item wording practices that are, thankfully, going out of style as well: double-barrelled items which contain so many attitudes that it is hard to tell why the person agrees or disagrees with them (e.g., "The U.S. should pull out of Vietnam because this is a civil war and we cannot win anything anyway"), items which are so vague as to mean all things to all people ("American soldiers should not be killed in Vietnam") or items which depend on knowledge of little-known facts ("The United States should adhere to the Geneva Convention Agreements in Vietnam"). Other considerations about writing items, such as negative vs. positive wording, will be covered under our discussion of response set.

Item Analysis: While item wording is something the investigator can manipulate to ensure coverage of attitudinal areas, there is no guarantee that respondents will reply to the items in the manner intended by the investigator. Item analysis is the most efficient method whereby the investigator can check whether people are responding to the items in the manner intended. We have found too many instances in the literature where authors assume that their a priori division of scale items corresponds to the way their respondents perceive them.

There have been many item analysis methods proposed, and in fact complex multidimensional analyses (which are described below under homogeneity in our detailing of statistical procedures) can be seen as the ultimate item analytic procedure. The researcher need not go so far as factor analyzing his data to pick items to be included or discarded, but an item inter-correlation matrix (on perhaps a small subsample or pretest sample) is certainly the most convenient basis of doing item analysis. If it is hypothesized that five items (say 1, 2, 6, 12 and 17) comprise a scale of authoritarianism, then the majority of the ten inter-item correlations between these five items should be substantial. At the minimum they should be significant at the .05 level. While this minimum may seem a bit low, it is in keeping with the degree to which items in the most reputable scales intercorrelate for heterogeneous populations. If items 1, 2, 12 and 17 intercorrelate well but 6 does not correlate well with any of them, then item 6 should be discarded or rewritten. The degree to which an item correlates with external criteria is a further valuable device for the selection of items.

_____

[1]The process is often referred to as "farmerization," i.e., making items intelligible to the less-sophisticated.

We learned one valuable lesson about writing items from a certain item analysis we performed. A previous study had uncovered four dimensions of value--authoritarianism, expression, individualism and equalitarianism--and we wished to incorporate measures of these factors into a study of political attitudes. One individualism item ("It is the man who starts off bravely on his own who excites our admiration") seemed in particular need of farmerization. Accordingly, the item was reworded, "We should all admire a man who starts out bravely on his own." Item analysis revealed this revamped statement to be more closely associated with authoritarian items than with the other individualism items. It became clear that a seemingly logical wording change can unexpectedly alter the entire implication of an item.

Often a researcher does not have the benefit of pre-test groups in order to eliminate or revise undesirable items. In such a case, the item-analysis phase of scale construction should be incorporated into the determination of the dimensionality, scalability or homogeneity of the test items. This will ensure that there is empirical as well as theoretical rationale for combining the information contained in various items.

The second large area of concern to the scale builder is the avoidance of response set in the items. Only through experience and by constant revision can the researcher rid his scale satisfactorily of this dangerous side effect. As a basic guard against response set, the researcher should try to make the scale as interesting and pleasant for the respondent as possible. If the respondent finds the instrument to be dull or unpleasant, there is a greater chance that he will try to speed through it as quickly as possible. In such a setting, the scale is most liable to response set contamination such as all the answers checked off in the right hand column or boxes checked off at random.

There are three further sources of response set that are more difficult to control:

Acquiescence: Most of us have seen (or been) people whose attitudes change in accord with the situation. These people are said to "acquiesce" in the presence of opposition from others. In the same way, some people are "yea-sayers," willing to go along with anything that sounds good, while others, being optimists, are unwilling to look at the bad side of anything. These dispositions are also reflected in people's responses to attitude questions. How then is it possible to separate their "real" attitudes from their personality dispositions?[2]

There are various levels of attack, all of which involve discarding some simple affirmative items. The first involves at least an occasional switching of response alternatives between positive and negative. For simple "yes-no" alternatives, a few "no-yes" options should be inserted. Similarly, for the "strongly agree-agree-uncertain-disagree-strongly disagree" or Likert format, the five alternatives occasionally should be listed in the opposite order. This practice will offer some possibility of locating people who choose alternatives on the sole basis of the order in which they appear. It can also alert the too casual respondent that he must think about his answers.

It is more difficult to vary the item wording from positive to negative, as those who have tried to reverse authoritarianism items have found. A logician can tell us that the obverse of "Obedience is an important thing for children to learn" is not "Disobedience is an important thing for children to learn" and yet one can hardly blame the respondent for feeling that agreeing with both the first statement and the second is completely contradictory. Again, the practice of inserting a single word in order to reverse an item has produced some pretty silly-sounding items, while changing one word in an unusual context has produced items in which the ordinary respondent will not notice a change. In sum, writing item reversals is a tricky business. The interested researcher would be well advised to check previous competent work on the subject (Christie, et al., 1958) before undertaking such a task. However, the literature is still ambiguous as to the real value of item reversals (e.g., Wrightsman, 1966).

A third and more difficult (yet more popular) approach concerns the construction of "forced-choice" items. Here two (or more) replies to a question are listed and the respondent is told to choose only one: "The most important thing for children to learn is (obedience) (independence)." Equating the alternatives' popularity or "social desirability" requires even more intensive effort for both the scale constructor and the respondent. Since the factor of social desirability is an important response set variable in its own right, we give it individual attention next.

Social desirability: In contrast to the theory that the acquiescent person reveals a certain desire for subservience in his willingness to go along with anything, Edwards (1957) has proposed more positively that these people are just trying to make a good impression. As yet research has been unable to determine clearly whether the overly high incidence of positive correlation among questionnaire items is ultimately due more to bias from acquiescence or to social desirability. The methods of lessening social desirability bias, in any event, usually involve the use of forced-choice

---

[2]Rorer (1965) points out many objections to the attempt to separate the acquiescent response set from item content.

items in which the alternatives have been equated on the basis of social
desirability ratings. In more refined instruments, the items are pre-
tested on social desirability, and alternative-pairings (or item-
pairings) which do not prove to be equated are dropped or revised.[3]

We have mentioned the major sources of scale contamination but there are
others of which the investigator should remain aware. One of the more prevalent sources of contamination is the faking of responses according to some
preconceived image that the respondent wants to convey. On a job satisfaction
scale, for example, the respondent may try to avoid saying anything that might
put his boss in a bad light or might involve changing work procedures. College
students may be aware of the professor's hypothesized relationship between two
variables and try to answer so as to make his prediction work out. Other
undesirable variations of spurious response patterns which the investigator
may want to minimize can result from the respondent's wanting (a) to appear
too consistent, (b) to use few or many categories in his replies, or (c) to
choose extreme alternatives.

Finally, we will evaluate each instrument on various statistical procedures
that were followed in its construction. While each of these considerations is
important (sampling, norms, reliability, homogeneity and validation), an
inadequate rating on any one of them does not make the scale worthless. Nevertheless, a lack of adequate ratings on most of the considerations certainly
indicates that the scale should be used with reservation. Fortunately, scale
constructors in the past few years appear to have paid more heed to these
considerations (both in number and quality) than the vast majority of their
predecessors. Nevertheless, even today few scales rate optimally on all these
factors. It is very seldom indeed that one runs across scales which overcome
(or even attempt to overcome) the distortion due to restricted samples or
inadequate validation procedures.

---

[3]One further method consists of using the respondent's score on the
Crowne-Marlowe social desirability scale as a correction factor. See Smith
(1967).

We have chosen seven areas which we hope will cover minimum important standards for scale constructions:

Representative sample: By now, it is hoped, researchers are aware of the fallacy of generalizing results from samples of college students[4] onto an older and much less well-educated general population. Significant differences are likely to be found even between freshmen and seniors, engineering and psychology students, and college A and college B. In the job satisfaction area, we shall see that there are great dangers in expecting findings from white-collar workers to hold for blue-collar workers (or even in using scales developed on white-collar workers on such samples).

This is not meant to discourage researchers from improving the representativeness of whatever populations they do have available for testing, but rather to caution them against implying that their findings hold for people not represented in their samples. Nor is it meant to imply that samples of college students are a useless basis on which to construct scales. In some areas (foreign affairs, for example), one might well argue that college exposure is probably the best index of whether a person can truly appreciate the intricacies of the issues involved. But an instrument constructed from replies of a random cross-section of all students in a university has much more to offer than the same instrument developed on students in a single class in psychology (even if there are many more students in the class than in the university sample). The prime consideration is the applicability of the scale and scale norms to respondents who are likely to use them in the future.

Normative information: The adequacy of norms is obviously dependent on the adequacy of the sample. The absolute minimum of normative information which should be available for the researcher to be aware of any differences between his sample and the sample on which the scale was developed is the mean scale score and standard deviation for the construction sample. There are further pieces of statistical data which are extremely useful: item means (or percent agreements) and standard deviations, median scores (if the scale scores are skewed) or even more obscure statistics like the inter-quartile range. Even more helpful are means and standard deviations for certain well-defined groups (men or women, Catholics or Baptists) who have high or low scale scores. When such differences were predicted, the results bear on the validity of the scale, which is discussed below. Validity, reliability, and homogeneity also constitute needed normative information, of course, and they are covered below in the detail required by their complexity.

Reliability (Test-Retest): One of the most unfortunately ambiguous terms in psychometry is "reliability." There are at least three major entities to which the term can refer: (1) the correlation between the same person's score on the same items at two separate points in time;

---

[4]Some statisticians contend that a sample of a single class should be treated as having a sample size of one, not the number of students in the class.

(2) the correlation between two different sets of items at the same time (called "parallel-forms" if the items are presented in separate format and "split-half" if the items are all presented together); and (3) the correlation between the scale items for all people who answer the items. The latter two indices refer to the internal structure or homogeneity of the scale items (the next criterion) while the former indicates stability of a person's item responses over time. It is unfortunate that the test-retest index, which requires more effort and sophistication on the part of the scale developer, is available for so few instruments in the literature. While the test-retest reliability level may be approximately estimated from indices of homogeneity, there is no substitute for the actual test-retest data.

Homogeneity: In addition to split-half, parallel forms and inter-item indices of the internal homogeneity of the test items, there exist other measures of this desirable property. Some of these item-test and internal consistency measures, as Scott (1960) has shown, bear known statistical relationships with one another. Included in this collection are certain indices of scalability for Guttman items, although not the most often-used Coefficient of Reproducibility. Even between such "radically" different procedures as the traditional psychometric and Guttman cumulative, however, there likely exist reasonably stable relationships between indices based on inter-item, item-test and total test characteristics; as yet, however, these have not been charted. For now, the major difference between the indices seems to lie in the researcher's preference for large or small numbers. Inter-item correlations and homogeneity indices based on Loevinger's concepts seldom exceed .40; if one prefers larger numbers, a Reproducibility Coefficient or split-half reliability coefficient computed on the same data could easily exceed .90. Thus one is forced back to the imperfect criterion of statistical significance (which does appear presently to be the only way of relating the various indices) to evaluate instruments for which varying indices have been employed. To make the job even more difficult, statistical distributions of these various indices are not always available so that significance can be determined.

Of all the indices that have been proposed, however, none combines simplicity with amount of information contained as well as the inter-item correlation matrix. Computing Pearson r correlation coefficients for more than five items is certainly a time-consuming operation on a hand calculator. However, for the researcher who does not have access to a computer to print out such a matrix, there are some simple rank-order correlation formulas that can be calculated by hand in a few minutes, so that even a ten-item scale inter-item correlation matrix can be put together in a few hours. The job is too lengthy if there are too many alternatives or over 25 subjects, but in the case of dichotomous items, the coefficient Y where

$$Y = \frac{\sqrt{ad} - \sqrt{bc}}{\sqrt{ad} + \sqrt{bc}}$$ and

		Item 1		
		Yes	No	
Item 2	Yes	a	b	a + b
	No	c	d	c + d
		a+c	b+d	N

is quite easy to compute. The significance of $\underline{Y}$ can be computed by calculating its standard error for the case where $\underline{Y}$ is hypothesized to be 0. Thus when $\underline{Y}$ exceeds

$$\sigma_Y = \left(\frac{N\sqrt{N}}{4}\right)\left[\frac{1}{(a+c)(b+d)(a+b)(c+d)}\right]^{\frac{1}{2}}$$

by a factor of 2, the items are significantly related at the .05 level, and when it exceeds $\underline{Y}$ itself by a factor of 2.5 the items are related at the .01 level (assuming the number of respondents is greater than 30). Goodman and Kruskal's (1959) gamma, γ, is a measure that can be called into use when the number of item alternatives is greater than 2. It is our understanding that approximate sampling distributions for this statistic have recently become available. The reader may be interested to know that for the dichotomous case, gamma reduces to the formula for Y with the square root signs removed; hence, gamma tends to take on larger values than $\underline{Y}$ for the same data. In any event, these are only approximate rule-of-thumb procedures for deciding whether a group of items deserves to be added together to form a scale or index. Similarly, the criterion of significance level is proposed only because it is a standard which remains fairly constant across the myriad of measures that are now or have been in vogue. Certainly it is the minimum to be expected before one can talk about an adequately constructed scale. Hopefully more satisfactory norms can be proposed in the future.

When the number of items goes beyond ten, however, the inter-item matrix is indeed quite cumbersome to calculate for any coefficient and the researcher is well advised to look for a computer specialist and a correlation matrix program. Computers have the ability to generate 100 item intercorrelations in less than ten minutes, given a reasonably-sized sample. This does not work out to an overly burdensome cost if the researcher has put much effort into his data collection. At this level of analysis (i.e., more than ten items), the researcher might just as well go ahead and invest in a factor analysis or cluster analysis of his data. This type of analysis will help him locate the groups of items that go together much faster than he could ever do by inspecting the correlation matrix. However, the researcher should not be deceived by what appear to be high factor loadings. Items having factor loadings which reach levels of .50 or .70 are equivalent to correlation coefficients of .25 and .49. There are many kinds of factor analysis programs and options; under most circumstances, however, the differences between them usually do not result in radical changes in the structure which is uncovered.

To say that factor analytic programs do not usually vary greatly in their output is not to imply that structures uncovered by factor analysis may not lead to serious ambiguities in the interpretation of data. There is one type of attitudinal data arrangement in particular for which the factor structure seems indeterminant. This is the case where almost all the items are correlated from say .15 to .45. Sometimes only a single factor will emerge from such a matrix and sometimes a solution will be generated which more clearly reflects item differentiation on a series of factors. There is one instance reviewed in this volume in which an instrument supposedly carefully constructed to reflect a single dimension of inner-other direction (see the chapter on Occupational Values) according to forced-choice response format was found to contain eight factors when analyzed in Likert format. Thus we offer no guarantee that inter-item significance will always yield unidimensional scales. Nor can we offer any better advice or recommend any competent practical literature on the inconsistencies into which factor analysis can lead one. On balance, however, one is further ahead performing such analyses than not.

Judging from the length of this discussion, there is little doubt that we feel the determination of homogeneity to be the crucial step in scale construction. It is only by the procedures mentioned above that the analyst can properly separate the apples, oranges and coconuts from the salad of items he has put together. In a forthcoming volume we hope to be able to go into the detailed rationale for the conclusions and recommendations rather hurriedly made in this section. One word of caution: it is possible to devise a scale with very high internal consistency merely by writing the same item in a number of different ways. Sampling of item content then is an important component in internal consistency.

Discrimination of known groups: This is where the value of a scale is truly tested--the aspect of validity. Nevertheless, group discrimination is not necessarily the most challenging validity hurdle to overcome. It is pretty hard to construct a liberalism-conservatism scale that will not show significant differences between John Birchers and Students for Democratic Society, or a religious attitude scale that will not separate Mormons from Jews or ministerial students from engineers. The more demanding hurdle is the ability of the scale scores reliably to single out those liberals, conservatives, agnostics or believers in heterogeneous groups, or to predict which of them will demonstrate behavior congruent with their hypothesized attitudinal state. A still more definitive test is cross-validation.

Double Cross-Validation: A test of double cross-validation requires two different samples and the same measure of some criterion variable(s). The question to be answered by the test is whether that combination of items for sample A which best correlates with the criterion variable(s) will also work for sample B and whether the best set of sample B items works on sample A. Note that the trick involves picking (and if necessary weighting) the items from the sample A experience which work on sample B and those from B which work on sample A. A simpler method which gives similar results is called cross-validation. It only requires that the scoring key developed on sample A be validated on B. Samples A and B must be independent but may be subsets of a larger sample.

An even more refined method, and so far the ultimate standard available, is the multi-trait multi-method matrix as proposed by Campbell and Fiske (1959). The method requires more than one index of each of the several constructs (say x, y, and z) we are preparing to measure by our instrument. It is best to include as many variables and indices of each construct as possible, as well as to control for such variables as intelligence or social desirability which could be at the root of any apparent relationship. In the resulting correlation matrix, the various indices of the single construct (say x) should correlate higher among themselves than x correlates with any indices of y, z or the control variables. Needless to say, this is a gross oversimplification of the Campbell-Fiske method. The reader should study the authors' article thoroughly before attempting comparable analyses. It is worth noting that the authors find only a couple of personality scales which meet their conditions. To our knowledge, no attitude scales have as yet advanced the claim.

Other Procedures: Since not all scales have been constructed by the above procedure, we have left room here to evaluate alternative methods that may have been employed. Such alternatives may include special precautions taken to ensure better items, better testing conditions or adequate validation--although at times the precautions have had the opposite effect from that intended.

One interesting procedure in which researchers have become increasingly interested involves the use of positive and negative items. Sometimes, as we have noted, negative items (as intended) are responded to as negative correlates of positive items; in other instances this does not work. A procedure which may provide valuable insights into the response patterns of the sample is the separation of the high and low scores on both the positive and negative scales. There are four groups to be examined: yea-sayers (who score high on both the negative and positive items), nay-sayers (who score low on both), assenters who score high on the positive items and low on the negatives, and the dissenters, who follow the opposite pattern. A parallel analysis for Likert scales (or procedures which demand more than a simple dichotomous item response) is the separation of the group at the mean into those who are ambivalent (combining extreme positive responses with extreme negative responses) from those who fall in the middle by taking an extreme position on very few items.

Ratings for each scale on the above twelve considerations are given in Chapters 5 and 13 in which there are a sufficient number of instruments to warrant comparison. If these ratings prove helpful enough, it might be worthwhile compiling them for all the attitude scales in this volume. A scale going from excellent and exemplary (+++) to incompetent (--) was used, with 0 meaning that we lacked enough information on the consideration as given in the description of procedures, that the information seemed inconsistent in quality or that such data were not reported. Needless to say, there are very few studies which rate an excellent on any characteristic and fewer still which can be definitely categorized as incompetent. However, the interested researcher might benefit from paying careful attention to examples at each extreme.

It is very important that the reader realize that even this extensive list of proposed criteria is not exhaustive. The actual choice of an instrument, where possible, should be dictated by decision-theoretic considerations. Thus, the addition of the questionnaire items needs to be balanced against its increased cost, respondent fatigue and non-cooperation. To assess general levels of some attitudes, well-worded single items may do the job just as well as longer scales, no matter how competently devised. For an excellent theoretical exposition of the decision-theoretic approach for psychometric problems, Cronbach and Gleser (1965) is recommended. In this extended version of their earlier volume, a number of examples relevant to ongoing personnel problems are presented.

Subsequent volumes in this series will deal with (a) authoritarianism and alienation plus their psychological and political first cousins and (b) political orientations. Resources permitting, volumes on personality/value scales, marriage/family/religious attitude scales and summary text on general attitude methodology can be added to the series. The general methodology report should be most valuable in making clear the rationale on which our instrument evaluation is based, and explaining why we feel these to be the crucial considerations out of vast numbers that have been proposed. For now we highly recommend the American Psychological Association's publication (1966) as an invaluable guidebook for scale construction and evaluation.

REFERENCES

American Psychological Association. Technical Recommendations for Psychological Tests and Diagnostic Methods, Psychological Bulletin Supplement, 1954, 51, No. 2.
N.B.: Revised editions are available from the APA at 1200 Seventeenth Street, N.W., Washington, D. C. 20036.

Campbell, D. and Fiske, D. "Convergent and discriminant validation by the multi-trait multi-method matrix," Psychological Bulletin, 56, 1959, 81-105.

Christie, R. et al. "Is the F scale irreversible?" Journal of Abnormal and Social Psychology, 1958, 56, 143-159.

Cronbach, L. and Gleser, Goldine. Psychological Tests and Personnel Decisions, Second Edition. Urbana: University of Illinois, 1965.

Dunnette, M. et al. Factors Contributing to Job Satisfaction and Job Dissatisfaction. University of Minnesota, Minneapolis, Minnesota, 1966.

Edwards, A. The Social Desirability Variable in Personality Assessment and Research. New York: Dryden Press, 1957.

Herzberg, F. et al. The Motivation to Work. New York: Wiley, 1959.

Miles, M. and Lake, D. Social Measurement Scales. New York: Columbia Teachers Press, 1967.

Miller, D. Handbook of Research Design and Social Measurement. New York: David McKay Co., 1964.

Rorer, L. "The great response style myth," Psychological Bulletin, 1965, 63, 129-156.

Scott, W. "Measures of test homogeneity," Educational and Psychological Measurement, 1960, 20, 751-757.

Shaw, M. and Wright, J. Scales for the Measurement of Attitudes. New York: McGraw-Hill, 1967.

Smith, D. "Correcting for social desirability response sets in opinion-attitude survey research," Public Opinion Quarterly, 31, Spring 1967, 87-94.

Smith, P. et al. Cornell Studies of Job Satisfaction. Cornell University (Ithaca, New York), 1966.

Wrightsman, L. Characteristics of Positively-Scored and Negatively-Scored Items from Attitude Scales. Peabody Teachers' College (Nashville, Tennessee), 1966.

2. RESEARCH ON WORK AND THE WORKER IN THE UNITED STATES

Paul Kimmel
Office of Manpower and Training
Department of Labor

The topic of work and its meaning in men's lives is one that has intrigued scholars since the beginnings of civilization (Tilgher, 1930). Contemporary social scientists are no exception to this generalization. However, while scholars in the more European intellectual tradition have mainly speculated about work in philosophical and historical terms, the social scientist has been much more pragmatic and empirical in his concern with the subject. This essay will deal with three different research perspectives that social scientists have used to analyze work and the worker in this country. The discussion will be of the broad speculative style of the European scholar. Although there will be many exceptions to our generalizations, it is important to examine the historical trends in research on work and the worker to better understand where the problems and promises that characterize today's study of job attitudes have their roots.

With a few exceptions, the empirical study of work by social scientists in this country began after 1910. It was at about this time that the study of psychology was moving out of the armchair and the laboratory and into the industrial field through the research and theory of pioneers such as Munsterberg and Spearman. (Until this time studies of work had been undertaken mainly by efficiency engineers-- time and motion experts--such as F. W. Taylor and Frank Gilbreth.) America's participation in World War I produced an unprecedented demand for workers in "new jobs" created by the wartime economy. The needs of military administrators for effective screening, training, and assessment techniques provided the industrial psychologist and psychometrician with a rich opportunity for developing and testing their skills (Neff, 1966). Although their efforts at classification and evalua- tion were not always successful (as witness the jokes about the auto mechanic who was made a cook or vice versa), the creation of standardized general intelligence tests, such as the Army Alpha and Army Beta examinations, and the work of the Industrial Fatigue Research Board tremendously enhanced the prestige of industrial psychologists and psychometricians.

This recognition, plus the general development of the discipline, led management to continue the employment of these psychologists when the war came to a conclusion. For the most part, the early researchers hired by industry incorporated management goals through attempting to solve specific problems that employers were having with some of their employees. Research efforts were con- centrated on changing the lower status industrial worker's behavior in order to increase his productivity, maximize his efficiency, and/or cut down his absenteeism and turnover. Many of these researchers also accepted the ideology of the business community of that era, which looked upon the lower status worker as an individual part of the production process who was naturally lazy and primarily motivated by income. Given this orientation--which we feel was more a matter of <u>Weltanschaung</u> than of conscious choice--it is not surprising that these researchers adopted to a large extent the experimental methodology used by the efficiency engineers. That is, they measured the individual worker's output (usually through observation), manipulated some aspect of his working situation, such as lighting, temperature, or noise level, and then measured output again to see if it had increased.

Although some progress was made in the standardization of workers' performance of routine tasks by these researchers, the results of their experiments were frequently unexpected and difficult to interpret. Perhaps the most well-known unexpected results were those found in the Hawthorne studies which took place between 1927 and 1932 in the Western Electric Company in Chicago. In this work, Mayo and his associates were startled to find that almost any manipulation that they undertook with a group of female assembly workers resulted in heightened productivity. Indeed, even a return to the working conditions that existed prior to any manipulation resulted in increased output. After talking with the workers, Mayo came to the conclusion that the primary factor influencing the results was the attitudes of the participants in the experiments toward each other and toward the experiment itself. The management of the Western Electric Company was sufficiently impressed with Mayo's findings and interpretation to initiate one of the first industrial counseling programs in a major industry, and to continue and expand the study of worker attitudes in their organization.[1]

The most important implication of the Hawthorne studies from our perspective is that it changed the focus of a great deal of future industrial psychological research from that of the efficiency engineer to that of the social psychologist. Later research took account of the worker's role in his work groups, rather than focusing exclusively on him as an individual. Motivational theories expanded upon the economic man approach and began to take account of factors such as participation, morale, and group cohesion. Supervision was given a great deal of consideration in studies after this time. In short, the worker was now seen as an active participant in the work process, and researchers felt impelled to take account of his motives and attitudes in attempting to predict and improve productivity, efficiency, and lack of turnover.

Another group of social scientists who were interested in the worker and his behavior were the occupational sociologists. Although their theoretical grounding lies in the work of non-pragmatic European scholars (Marx, Pareto, Weber, and Durkheim), these researchers also were oriented initially toward a problem-solving type of research. In this case the problems were social problems of the worker rather than the industrial problems investigated by the psychologists. The first empirical sociological study of the worker took place in this country at the University of Chicago in the 1920's and 30's. These studies focused on particular occupations and might appropriately be called "occupational biographies." The researchers observed and interacted with the workers they were studying, and then wrote composite vignettes describing the interests and activities of the occupational group (Nosow and Form, 1962).

----

[1] The famous bank wiring room research undertaken by Roethlisberger and Dickson (1939) was a continuation of the work begun by Mayo.

For the most part, these occupational groups were either marginal members of the society, such as "jack-rollers" and taxi dancers, or they occupied lower status positions in the economy such as waitresses, dance band musicians, and railroaders. This emphasis on lower status and marginal occupational groups grew out of the concern of these researchers for the problems of the individual adjusting to an urban living situation. Their ideology was usually that of the humanitarian dedicated to uplifting the downtrodden. This perspective frequently produced somewhat "romanticized" accounts of the workers' attitudes (Gross, 1964).

Although these two research approaches--that of the industrial psychologists and that of the occupational sociologists--were quite different in their emphasis, they were quite similar in that both were situational. Since the researchers were dealing with events and issues rather than concepts, the support they could find, the problems they investigated, the techniques they used, and the results they obtained were very much tied to the time and place in which they carried out the research. We can best illustrate this commonality in the two approaches by considering what happened to both during the Depression and World War II.

An examination of the bibliography in an extensive review of job attitudes done by Herzberg, et al. (1957), indicates that the number of published studies of both kinds declined during the ten year period, 1935 to 1945. It is our hypothesis that the social and economic conditions of this decade were a major factor in reducing the number of such studies.

It seems reasonable that the employer, faced with business difficulties far more critical than increasing productivity or reducing turnover, would have little need for the services of the industrial psychologists in the middle and late 30's. When World War II began, management's situation changed rather dramatically. Given the high level of profit and worker morale created by the "war effort", there would not be a great demand for the services of industrial psychologists, who had migrated to the federal government agencies to repeat their performance from World War I.

The occupational sociologists, on the other hand, probably found that the social problems created by unemployment overrode those of any given occupational group during the Depression era, and therefore turned their attention to the study of broader human needs. Research on industrial, community, and familial disorganization flourished in the late 30's. We would speculate that the internal consistency plus the manpower needs that develop in a society which is engaging in armed conflict, reduced the amount of social disorganization and worker marginality to a very low ebb during World War II. The occupational sociologists again found that the more interesting social problems lay elsewhere than with the study of worker attitudes and life-styles. They, too, went to War to study The American Soldier (1949).

The lack of job attitude studies by occupational sociologists and industrial psychologists during this decade indicates to us that a problem-solving research approach requires a rather stable social and economic context in the realm with which the problem-solver is concerned. In times of economic upheaval or social conflict, the more refined problems to which job attitudes may be related, such as increasing output or reducing marginality, are superceded by the more basic concerns of the problem-solver and those who employ him.

Another research approach adopted by social scientists studying work and the worker appears to be less subject to fluctuations in social and economic conditions. This approach is that of the survey researcher who studies attitudes conceptually, without being particularly concerned with changing work behavior or improving the situation of the individual worker. This approach to the study of work also began in the 1920's and 30's with the principal pioneer being Robert Hoppock (1935). His approach, instruments, analyses, and conclusions have served as a model for studies of job satisfaction to this day.

Hoppock set out to obtain a more representative sample of workers than had been polled in previous research studies of job satisfaction. He interviewed the working population of an entire community using a standardized set of questions and attitude scales (see Chapter 5). He did more intensive research on selected samples of employed and unemployed workers and satisfied and dissatisfied teachers using expanded versions of the scales and questionnaires, plus tests of intelligence, interest, and free associations. Although surveys of job satisfaction have been undertaken by numerous researchers since the Hoppock studies, there are few who have made significant substantive or methodological contributions to his approach. Such refinements as have been made seldom change the findings on job attitudes which have been relatively constant over 30 years of research (Robinson, et al. 1966)

This is not to say that all social scientists are satisfied with this research approach. On the contrary, in recent years, the survey technique of ascertaining job satisfaction has been severely criticized.

The concept of satisfaction, for example, is seen as a very gross measure of job attitudes in light of the numerous dimensions that have been shown to relate to workers perceptions, feelings, and behavior (Vroom, 1964). Also, the approach of asking a person directly to talk about his feelings regarding his job has come under attack for its naivete (Blauner, 1960; Wilensky, 1964). However, these are theoretical and technical criticism that can be dealt with by improving experimental designs, instruments, and sampling and analysis procedures. Because these studies are not conceived as efforts to solve management problems or ameliorate the lot of the worker, their investigators have the time and the perspective to recast the "common sense" concepts of employers and employees into more explanatory social science concepts which are less dependent upon specific situations (Pugh, 1966).

In the decade following the Second World War, the three different research approaches to the study of work began to merge in the research programs carried on at various centers associated with U. S. academic institutions. For example, the emphasis on group cohesion and supervisory styles which began with the Hawthorne studies are seen again in the experimental and survey work of the Survey Research Center at the University of Michigan (Katz, 1951). The emphasis on consideration of workers' ideas stimulated by the Hawthorne project appears in the well-known Harwood Pajama Factory study which demonstrated that worker participation in decision-making is an effective means of promoting greater productivity and lower rates of turnover (Coch and French, 1948). Comparisons of satisfied and dissatisfied and productive and non-productive workers were an important part of most of these studies, as researchers began to take account of some of the methodological criticisms that had been leveled at the early attitudinal measurements of the survey researchers. All of these studies were considerably improved theoretically by their attention to the insights of Kurt Lewin (1951) who worked at Harwood and with the Michigan researchers during World War II.

The occupational sociologists also were becoming somewhat more systematic in their methodology and theory. Rather than merely observing a mixture of individuals within a given occupation and writing about what they saw, researchers such as Walker and Guest (1952), Friedman and Havighurst (1954), and Chinoy (1955) were testing hypotheses about alienation within specific industrial groups by talking directly to samples of workers about their job attitudes. These comparative studies of worker satisfaction and others like them were a major step in the movement from an introspective and ideological orientation to a more systematic and disinterested approach in occupational sociology.

By the middle and late 50's the study of job attitudes and their effects on work performance had become the dominant concern of social science researchers investigating work and the worker. However, the focus in many of these field studies was returning to the earlier style of documenting and "solving" problems rather than utilizing the more scientific method of developing and testing hypotheses. It seemed that now that other researchers had demonstrated that job attitudes could be measured and related to aspects of a worker's experience and/or behavior, these management consultants (or human relations experts as they were called) were determined to solve all of their employers' problems by increasing their workers' job satisfaction. To quote a reviewer writing in 1958, "Few and far between are studies which suggest that morale or happiness or job satisfaction are worthy ends in and of themselves. The passion of the day is to prove that high morale does, in fact, increase productivity". (Ferguson, 1958, 246.)

Since the late 50's there has been a decline in the number of studies employing this problem-solving type of approach. Again we might account for this in terms of the social and economic conditions of the era. However, it appears to us that a more cogent explanation is that the problem solvers and those who purchase their services are becoming increasingly aware of the relative barrenness of their efforts to date. In a recent survey of the literature on a number of studies relating job satisfaction with productivity, Vroom (1964) found that the median correlation between high satisfaction and high productivity was approximately .14. Such a figure is indicative of the complexity of the research problem relative to the time and techniques available to the problem-solving researcher. It appears that management is becoming aware that they can obtain as good or better results from simpler, less expensive research procedures than those of the human relations expert.[2]

The critics of the human relations approach have not fared much better in empirically supporting their theories of worker motivation. The few surveys that are available do not reveal any conscious striving for self-confirmation on the part of the worker, nor do they expose any widespread worker alienation

---

[2]   Some approaches that seem to have a greater cost-benefit ratio for management are those of the engineering psychologist and the vocational counselor.

(Blauner, 1964; Kornhauser, 1965; Robinson, 1967; Wilensky, 1964). This has led some of these theorists to modify their explanations and theories of work motivation while others have been content to continue their criticisms of management and management relations researchers.

This lack of evidence for favored theories and inability to produce clear-cut and inexpensive results has discouraged many of the social scientists who have pursued the problem-solving type of approach. More systematic and disinterested research is being carried out by social scientists who are primarily concerned with understanding and measuring the job attitudes of a variety of workers in a variety of situations. They have frequently gone to the controlled conditions of the experimental laboratory to develop and test their hypotheses. These researchers are paying more attention to individual differences between the characteristics of the workers and the characteristics of their work situation. There have been more studies of the interaction between worker personality and job content or organizational structure, for example, in the past few years than there had been in the preceding three decades.

It is our estimation that this more limited and non-problem solving approach will contribute more to our understanding of work behavior and have a greater practical applicability in the long run than have the efforts of those who engage in combatting directly the economic and social problems of their time. Although the problem-solvers have contributed a number of ideas to the general study of work and the worker, they have not produced any reasonably documented theories or laws that have held up in other contests or in replications of their research. In writing about his review of the job attitude literature, Herzberg said, "The book was a saddening experience, because the major conclusion was that we could document almost any position one wished to take with respect to what affected people at work." (1966, 148).

With an increasing sophistication in methodology and experimental design and more emphasis on the development of theory, we expect considerable advances in the growth of a multi-disciplinary, scientific understanding of job attitudes, their consequences and determinants. However, without suitable tests of this understanding in on-going work situations, these studies will be limited to the descriptive level of surveys or to the type of laboratory and classroom exercise that has characterized a great deal of research in the social sciences. We hope that this book will be a stimulus to the researcher, the businessman, and the union official to help develop a more sophisticated and practical industrial social psychology.

In summary, job attitudes, their determinants and consequences are complex, and as yet relatively unanalyzed, phenomena. Few workers have the clear-cut goals of the social critic or the single (or double) motivational systems of the industrial psychologist. It is unlikely that worker attitudes will be predicted by a general theory dealing with abilities, background, or motivation in any more accurate manner than worker performance has been predicted on the basis of reported job satisfaction. In spite of its rather lengthy and extensive history, the study of job attitudes is really only at the threshold of scientific inquiry.

REFERENCES

Blauner, R. Work satisfaction and industrial trends in modern society. In W. Galenson & S. M. Lipset (Eds.), Labor and trade unionism: an interdisciplinary reader. New York: Wiley, 1960. pp. 339-360.

Blauner, R. Alienation and freedom. Chicago and London: U. of Chicago Press, 1964.

Chinoy, E. Automobile workers and the American dreams. New York: Doubleday & Co., 1955.

Coch, L. & French, J. R. P., Jr. Overcoming resistance to change. Human Relations, 1948, 1, 512-532.

Ferguson, L. W. Industrial psychology. In P. R. Farnsworth (Ed.), Annual review of psychology. Palo Alto, Calif.: Annual Reviews, 1958. pp. 243-266.

Friedman, E. A., & Havighurst, R. J. The meaning of work and retirement. Chicago: U. of Chicago Press, 1954.

Gross, E. The worker and society. In H. Borow (Ed.), Man in a world at work. Boston: Houghton Mifflin, 1964. pp. 67-95.

Herzberg, F., Mausner, B., Peterson, P. O., & Capwell, Dora F. Job attitudes: a review of research and opinion. Pittsburgh: Psychological Service of Pittsburgh, 1957.

Herzberg, F. Work and the nature of man. New York: World Publishing Co., 1966.

Hoppock, R. Job satisfaction. New York: Harper & Bros., 1935.

Katz, D. Survey Research Center: an overview of the human relations program. In Guetzkow, H. (Ed.), Groups, leadership and men. Pittsburgh: Carnegie Press, 1951.

Kornhauser, A. W. Mental health of the industrial worker; a Detroit study. New York: John Wiley, 1965.

Lewin, K. Field theory in social science. New York: Haprer Bros., 1951.

Neff, W. S. Problems of work evaluation. Personnel and Guid. J., 1966, 44, 682-688.

Nosow, S., & Form, W. H. Man, work, and society; a reader in the sociology of occupations. New York: Basic Books, Inc., 1962.

Pugh, D. S. Modern organization theory: A psychological and sociological study. Psychol. Bull., 1966, 4, 235-251.

Robinson, H. A., Connors, R. P. & Whitacre, G. Holly Job satisfaction researches of 1964-65. Personnel and Guid. J., 1966, 45, 371-379.

Robinson, J. Occupational norms and differences in job satisfaction (In the next chapter in this volume, 1967).

Rothlisberger, F. J., & Dickson, W. J. Management and the worker. Cambridge, Mass.: Harvard Univ. Press, 1939.

Stouffer, S. A., Guttmann, L., Suchmann, E. A., Lazarsfeld, P. F., Star, S. A., & Clausen, J. A. The American soldier. Studies in social psychology in World War II. Vols I-IV. Princeton, N.J.: Princeton U. Press, 1949

Tilgher, A. Work: what it has meant to men through the ages. New York: Harcourt, Brace & Co., 1930.

Vroom, V. H. Work and motivation. New York: John Wiley, 1964.

Walker, C. R., & Guest, R. H. The man on the assembly line. Cambridge, Mass.: Harvard U. Press, 1952.

Wilensky, H. L. Varieties of work experience. In H. Borow (Ed.), Man in a world at work. Boston: Houghton Mifflin, 1964. pp. 125-154.

3. OCCUPATIONAL NORMS AND DIFFERENCES IN JOB SATISFACTION:

A SUMMARY OF SURVEY RESEARCH EVIDENCE

John P. Robinson

Like most social scientists, those in industrial research would recognize the need for representative sampling. However, a disturbing amount of industrial research reaches the literature with little apparent awareness of the limitations of conclusions reached on samples of single occupations, single organizations or even single departments. To be sure, in a certain sense, data from single work groups and single companies, where various background and locational variables can be controlled or taken into account, are more satisfactory than data from the highly dispersed people found in a representative national sample. However, if the researcher is interested in making generalizations about his findings, and most investigators ultimately must be, he should find the contents of this chapter useful for making such generalizations.

For the great part, this chapter is concerned with exposing, interpreting, and commenting on the value of questions that have been asked of representative national samples, or other large-scale samples for which considerable variation in occupational structure was incorporated into the study design. It is true that most cross-sectional studies are limited in the flexibility and complexity of questions asked. Analysis of such data is thus dependent on the assumption that holding constant the wording of single attitude questions automatically ensures that its meaning is the same for all respondents and can be so interpreted. The increasing body of multivariate research into work attitudes points out the naivete of this assumption and the use of single global questions to assess job satisfaction.

However, we shall see that there is accumulating evidence from large-scale surveys indicating that much the same kinds of factors emerge from representative studies as from multivariate research into work attitudes, usually performed on more limited samples. Furthermore, this survey evidence points to the importance of occupational status as a correlate, or even determinant, of these differential attitudes towards work. This holds true not only for general satisfaction from work but also for the types of expectations that work will fulfill for those in various occupations. It is usually impossible to accurately detect the effects of status in studies of limited segments of the occupational domain.

Sociologists, by the nature of their discipline, are especially attuned to the dramatic status differentials inherent among various occupational categories. Indeed, occupational differences probably form the most important bases for the empirical study of sociological stratification. Students of social stratification, then, are perhaps the least surprised to find that the social status ranking of an occupation predicts so much variance in the distribution of job satisfaction scores. In fact, many would regard the finding as trivial. After all, it doesn't require a Ph.D. to observe how much more involved and interested the manager is in his work than the bookkeeper, or the bookkeeper is than the machine operator, or the machine operator than the janitor. Even casual observers may note that greater satisfaction with a job is expected of the person who holds a position of higher status; it is a social norm, an expectation of the person who holds such a position.

These considerations have led many sociologists (Blauner, 1965, Wilensky, 1964) to question the interpretation of workers' answers to questions regarding how satisfied they are with their jobs. These authors point out the overly large majorities (80-90 percent) of employed people who over the past 30 years have responded positively rather than negatively to what these authors consider naive and superficial questions. Blauner attributes much of this tendency to the fact that by demeaning his job a respondent is questioning his very competence as a person, while Wilensky points to the general cultural bias toward expressing contentment (the process called "acquiescence" or "social desirability" by the more psychologically oriented).

Blauner and Wilensky's views are given substantial confirmation by Argyris' (1958) study of workers in a "healthy" organization, a company which manufactured products of recognized superior quality, paid high wages, pioneered programs of liberal benefits, and required superiors to be sympathetic and understanding with their workers. A preliminary poll using more simplified questions indicated overwhelmingly that both management and employees concurred that it was a good place to work. Fully 92 percent of the employees were satisfied with their jobs as a whole and had no desire or plans to leave; three out of four agreed that management was understanding and "wonderful"; and almost half the number said that there was nothing that they liked "least" about the company. However, further examination of responses to other questions revealed that 2/3 felt that they experienced no personal (intrinsic) satisfactions from their jobs; 3/4 did not aspire to any positions of responsibility; another 75 percent said they never made close friends at the plant, and only 4 percent had any suggestions for improving their jobs. While some interesting differences on these questions (which we shall discuss later) appeared among various occupational levels, one could hardly picture these employees as being unboundedly happy and involved in their work.

This would appear to constitute a strong argument for developing and using more sophisticated indices of job satisfaction than the usual direct questions. In this chapter, then, we shall review a number of study questions which attempt to get at more meaningful aspects of job satisfaction in representative cross-section samples. In the process we shall comment on some data using less-sophisticated questions (rather complete collections of data using such indicators have been presented annually in the Journal of Personnel and Guidance for the past 30 years); but in the main we will be looking for adequate norms on both sophisticated and unsophisticated questions about job satisfaction for various occupational categories. It is our hope that future investigators, using non-representative samples (the usual case in occupational satisfaction research) will utilize this normative information to see if their samples deviate in any important way from more representative groups of respondents.

The relevant literature consists of five major, mainly independent, studies: 1) Blauner's review of poll questions on job satisfaction as of 1960;[1] 2) a national representative sample conducted in 1958 by Gurin, et al. (1960); 3) a 1960 nation-wide sample of both federal and non-federal employees reported in Kilpatrick, et al. (1964); 4) Wilensky's 1960 study of diverse occupational groups in Detroit; and 5) a 1965-66 national urban sample undertaken by Converse and Robinson (in press). Since the studies show little overlap, we can treat them separately in chronological order.

Following these reviews we present short treatments of four relevant topics that bear on further interpretation of the findings contained in the five studies. The first topic is the variation in work attitudes within the blue-collar domain and its sources, for which only sketchy evidence is available from representative surveys. The next section examines similar differences which have been found in large-scale studies of professional and other college-trained segments of the population. The third topic concerns itself with some child-rearing determinants of work attitudes and the fourth with some cross-cultural differences in work attitudes. In this last section, special attention is given to a comparison of American and Russian worker satisfaction in blue-collar occupations; the analysis seems to suggest that work satisfaction attitudes are quite similar in two societies which place different "official" prestige on the value of blue-collar work.

1. <u>Blauner's review</u>. While Blauner makes a strong point of the methodological weaknesses of the direct question approach, he is satisfied that such questions do reveal meaningful differences <u>between</u> various occupational categories. Indeed such differences, in line with the social status argument raised above, appear consistently in 10 U.S. studies[2] cited by Blauner; these differences show up as well in data from five foreign countries (Russia, Germany, Italy, Sweden and Norway) compared by Inkeles (1960). There appears to be some disagreement in these studies over whether the highest level blue-collar workers (foremen, skilled workers, craftsmen) derive more satisfaction from their work than the lowest white-collar employees (clerks, typists); but there is little doubt that within the two groups the status-satisfaction relation holds quite well.

Probably the most informative among the indices of job satisfaction ("If you had the chance to start your working life over again, would you choose the same kind of work as you are doing now?") has given the distributions of Table 1. These data were brought together by Wilensky (1964)

---

[1]This valuable article has reappeared in the recent second edition of Bendix and Lipset's <u>Class, Status and Power</u>. Glencoe, Illinois: Free Press, 1965.

[2]These studies conducted between 1934 and 1954 used a number of direct and indirect questions.

Table 1

PROPORTIONS AMONG OCCUPATIONAL GROUPS WHO WOULD TRY TO GET
INTO A SIMILAR TYPE OF WORK IF THEY COULD START
OVER AGAIN (Blauner, 1965; Wilensky, 1964)

Professional and Lower White-Collar Occupations	Per Cent	Working-Class Occupations	Per Cent
*Urban university professor	93	Skilled printers	52
Mathematicians	91	Paper workers	42
Physicists	89	Skilled auto workers	41
Biologists	89	Skilled steelworkers	41
Chemists	86	Textile workers	31
*Firm lawyers	85	*Blue-collar workers	24
**School superintendents	85	Unskilled steelworkers	21
Lawyers	83	Unskilled auto workers	16
Journalists (Washington correspondents)	82		
*Church university professors	77		
*Solo lawyers	75		
*White-collar workers	43		

*All probability samples or universes of six professional groups and a cross-section of the "middle mass" (lower middle class and upper working class) in the Detroit area, stratified for comparability with respect to age, income, occupational stratum and other characteristics (Wilensky, 1964).

**From a 1952-53 sample of school superintendents in Massachusetts (Gross, et al., 1958).

and by Blauner. By partialling out the constraints on job dissatisfactions imposed by the fact that a respondent's present job is probably the best he can find, this indirect question produces much more conservative estimates of overall job satisfaction. In addition, by thus allowing the respondent a much broader frame of reference, far greater differences between occupations become apparent (compare the results of Table 1 with those of Table 6).

In conclusion Blauner points to three important factors that lead to the differential job satisfaction across occupations: prestige (e.g., doctors and nurses do certain things in their work which would disgust a laborer or janitor, yet the greater prestige of the former occupations more than compensates); control over various conditions of work (time, pace, technical environment, freedom from supervision), and cohesiveness of the work group (one study showed members of cohesive work groups to be over twice as satisfied as "isolated" workers on the same job in the same company). More recent research allows us not only to extend this list of factors, but to examine the differential importance of these various factors between occupational groups. It is to this literature that we now turn.

2. <u>Gurin, Veroff and Feld Mental Health Study</u>. Gurin, et al. (1960), in a lengthy investigation into the mental health of a national cross-section of 2,460 American adults, included the following six sets of open-ended questions which may be seen as getting at different components of job satisfaction:

1) Taking into consideration all the things about your job, how satisfied or dissatisfied are you with it?

2) Regardless of how much you like your job, is there any other kind of work you'd rather be doing?

3) If you didn't have to work to make a living, do you think you would work anyway?

4) Have you had any problems with your work--times when you couldn't work, or weren't getting along on the job, or didn't know what kind of work you wanted to do?

5) What does it take to do a really good job at the kind of work you do? How much ability do you think it takes to do a really good job at the kind of work you do? How good would you say you are at doing this kind of work--would you say you were <u>very good</u>, <u>a little better than average</u>, <u>just average</u>, or <u>not very good</u>? (Question 5 asked of only a random third of all employed respondents.)

6) What things do you particularly like about the job? What things don't you like about the job?

Key breakdowns of these questions by occupation are given in Table 2 for men only;[3] service workers (policemen, waiters, etc.) were apparently

---

[3]Although the same data were collected for employed women, it was decided to examine the male responses only on the assumption that work seldom holds the importance for women as it does for men. It turns out

Table 2

BREAKDOWN OF 6 QUESTIONS ON JOB SATISFACTION FROM GURIN, ET AL. (1960). See text for question wording.

| Occupational Status | All | White Collar | | | | Blue Collar | | | |
		Professional Technical	Managers Proprietors	Sales Workers	Clerical Workers	Skilled Workers	Semi Skilled Workers	Unskilled Workers	Farmers
N	(911)*	(119)	(127)	(55)	(46)	(202)	(152)	(84)	(77)
Question									
1) % neutral, ambivalent	15%	11%	12%	14%	22%	16%	18%	19%	13%
% dissatisfied	8%	3	6	16	17	7	6	16	7
2) % who prefer same	61%	68	69	53	42	57	55	57	84
3) % who would work anyway	85%	87	89	87	85	83	83	76	94
4) % reporting work problems	29%	36	33	38	37	25	29	21	25
5) % just average or not very good at work	**	14	21	31	25	29	34	40	31
6) % mentioning intrinsic satisfactions	80%	96	88	89	74	82	71	58	75
extrinsic satisfactions	40%	18	29	36	59	42	55	55	34
intrinsic dissatisfactions	30%	40	35	40	39	29	21	23	21
extrinsic dissatisfactions	53%	46	48	58	50	52	60	53	64

*The occupation of 49 respondents did not fit into one of these eight occupational categories.

**Question 5 asked of only 1/3 of respondents.

not classified into any category. Since there are subtleties involved in the interpretation of these data, we shall examine each question separately before stating any general conclusions.

Question 1, while dealing directly with job satisfaction and subject to all the pitfalls described above, does require more than a simple nod of the head from respondents. Here then 23 percent of all the employed males would be classified as not explicitly satisfied with their jobs, an expectedly higher figure compared to responses to the simpler questions asking merely "Are you satisfied or dissatisfied with your job?" and much higher compared to the naive and poor question, "Do you like your job?"[4] Nevertheless, we see that only 8 percent of the 1958 sample actually came right out and said they were dissatisfied with their jobs. Surprisingly, using this reply as an index reveals a notable deviation between blue-and white-collar workers in the status ordering pattern noted by Blauner. Occupants of lower-status white-collar positions show far higher incidences of dissatisfaction than all others except the lowest blue-collar workers. Somewhat the same pattern might have been expected from the replies in Table 1. It appears that there are important exceptions to the status-satisfaction relation in the middle ranges of status which need closer examination. In general, however, the relation holds within the white-collar domain and within the blue-collar domain, a finding with reference group theory implications which is substantiated by blue-collar data presented by Kornhauser (1965) and Argyris (1958).

One final comment is in order regarding the grouping of neutral and ambivalent (some positive feelings expressed with negative feelings) reactions in Table 2. There are, as Gurin, et al. point out, considerably different psychological processes accompanying the two reactions,[5] with ambivalence indicating a far greater degree of ego involvement in one's work as well as a greater degree of formal education. Future investigators will be wise to separate the two groups for many of their analyses.

---

there are good methodological reasons as well: women (especially those with no college exposure), despite the oft-heard complaints about discrimination in hiring, report significantly more satisfaction from their jobs. It also appears that women place far greater reliance on social and personal relations on the job in assessing satisfaction (see Kilpatrick, et al. below). It is uncertain if most of the data presented by Blauner are from samples of men or both men and women.

[4]Of course, this does not mean that less sophisticated questions would not be valuable to the investigator interested in studying trends in job satisfaction over time. Since none of the direct job satisfaction questions reviewed has ever been replicated over time on reasonably representative samples, there is no empirical light to be shed on this interesting point. Some comparisons of indirect questions used in the Gurin, et al. study and the Converse and Robinson (in press) study are presented in Appendix A.

[5]Converse (1963) also points out that the two reactions, often grouped together in attitude and attitude change studies, may well show radically different responses to information expected to change these initial reactions.

Question 2, despite its similarity to the question, "Would you do it again if you had it to do all over?", is obviously imbued with so much of the respondent's present frame of reference that the large and consistent differences in job commitment appearing in Table 1 were not replicated.[6] Although the expected downward trend for the white-collar occupations is present, a relatively high proportion of all blue-collar workers report that there is no other kind of work they would rather be doing--perhaps an indication of their limited occupational horizons or even a lack of present upward mobility aspirations.

The replies to Question 3 show that the proportion of each of the blue-collar levels who would continue working if they didn't have to is only slightly lower than that of each of the white-collar levels. Questions 3 and 4 show farming to be a particularly satisfying line of work for those who have remained on the farm (despite the dramatic urban migration of the past few generations). It will be noted that except for extrinsic factors, farmers appear to be average or above average on the other indicators of positive feelings about their work.

Subsequent inquiries on Question 4 revealed that two out of every three specific work problems reported were of a personal nature. The major problem mentioned was that of finding the right kind of work, with supervisory problems and histories of inadequacy at work also receiving prominent mention. It is not implausible to see that such mainly self-reflective concerns were experienced somewhat more often by each of the white-collar groups in Table 2. Still, report of such problems was related to less work satisfaction: twice as many of the dissatisfied than the satisfied reported some work problem. Thus, people who have a hard time choosing an occupation seem to be less satisfied with the work they do choose to enter.

Satisfied workers were also twice as likely to rate themselves as being "very good" at their work (although the replies to Questions 4 and 5 were only minimally related to each other[7]). Again the orders are maintained between white-collar and blue-collar, except for the disproportionately large number of salesmen who feel that they are "just average" or not very good at their jobs. One of the important features of the Gurin, et al. study was that similar questions were asked of other aspects of the respondent's life; this ensured that certain observed effects are not traceable to methodological artifacts. For example, higher levels of education were related to greater feelings of inadequacy in marriage and parenthood. However, in the work area, those with higher education (and concomitantly higher occupational status) reported lower feelings of inadequacy.

---

[6] Question 2 did uncover a notable age contrast: while 75 percent of those over 55 expressed no desire for some other kind of work, only 48 percent of those between 20 and 35 did. A steady increase in job satisfaction with age was found in Question 1. Older people give achievement and health more as reasons for continuing work even if they didn't have to and they derive less satisfaction from the people they work with.

[7] Feelings of inadequacy and report of problems were found to link when parallel questions were asked for the marriage and parent roles.

Gurin, et al. devised an extremely useful code based on motivational constructs (see Appendix A) for the replies to the open-ended questions dealing with things their respondents particularly liked or disliked about their work. The major distinction in the code was between intrinsic or ego satisfactions (achievement, affiliation,[8] independence, curiosity) and extrinsic satisfactions (wages, security, working conditions). As argued by Herzberg, et al. (1958), extrinsic factors were associated with reported job dissatisfaction (Question 1) rather than job satisfaction. In other words, extrinsic factors (such as money) are mentioned as deficiencies by the dissatisfied but are not mentioned as benefits by the satisfied (see the chapter by Athanasiou for more details).

As expected, these types of satisfaction varied considerably by occupation, with intrinsic satisfaction being experienced most prevalently in the higher white or blue-collar occupations with the opposite being true for extrinsic satisfactions. Note, however, that the pattern of dissatisfactions were not quite what we would at first expect (viz. the pattern where low mention of positive feelings implies high negative feelings) from the satisfaction replies. Extrinsic dissatisfactions are mentioned at a higher, but not much higher, rate by blue-collar workers while intrinsic dissatisfactions were noted equally by all white-collar workers at a level considerably higher than the blue-collar respondents.

The authors interpret these somewhat dissonant findings as follows: people in higher status jobs not only receive more ego gratifications in their work but also seek such gratifications more, and consequently experience frustration when they feel that these needs are not gratified. Blue-collar workers on the other hand come to these jobs originally with lower expectations and desires for self-fulfillment, or they become adjusted to the lack of opportunities for such fulfillment. Evidence by Argyris (1958) would tend to place more support with the first of these propositions. In any event, this is one of the major pieces of evidence we shall review which cautions against trying to understand blue-collar attitudes within a middle-class framework. A related finding from Kahn, et al. (1964) is that white-collar workers as a whole report both more satisfaction and more dissatisfaction than when they began their jobs. Both Gurin, et al. and Kahn, et al. find better mental and physical health among higher status employees.

Veroff and Feld (1967) have recently completed more extensive analyses of these data. For most occupations,[9] relations were found between overall job satisfaction and the mentioning of responses coded as achievement satisfying and with the lack of responses coded as achievement dissatisfying.

---

[8]There is some question as to whether to include the affiliation category, especially relations with supervisory personnel, with intrinsic factors. We shall review evidence from Centers (1966) and others which indicates that concern about one's co-workers behaves more like an extrinsic than an intrinsic factor.

[9]This result did not hold for many white-collar categories and Veroff and Feld offer the following explanation which has methodological implications for this type of question: some men avoided mentioning achievement as it reflected on their own failure, while other men did mention such dissatisfaction as a realistic indication of the lack of achievement and stimulation in the job.

Achievement dissatisfactions were noted in those jobs where the worker is not directly involved in determining the quality of the job. A correlated finding is that job satisfaction decreases with greater amounts of supervision, both findings congruent with Blauner's emphasis on control over the work processes as an essential factor in job satisfaction.

The most interesting phase of these further analyses concerns the relations of TAT measures of achievement, affiliation, and power measures with aspects of job content and the types of satisfaction mentioned. The analyses met with varying degrees of success, too lengthy and complicated to report here. However, certain differences in needs between occupations were clearly apparent. Two of these were easily understandable: farmers were lowest in affiliation need and unskilled workers were lowest in need achievement. Others were not: sales personnel and foremen were low in power motivation; salaried (not self-employed) managers were quite high on need achievement. The suspicion that considerable variation is hidden within occupational categories in all of these analyses will be confirmed in later sections of this chapter. For example, teachers, engineers and technicians show widely differing work attitudes within the professional-technical category, as do insurance salesmen, sales clerks, and newsboys in the sales category. This is not to negate the general findings or to find fault with the Gurin, et al. study which has received far too little attention in the job satisfaction literature.

3. _Kilpatrick, Cummings and Jennings Study_. This investigation into the attitudes and values of federal and non-federal employees is another competent research effort which has suffered a fate of neglect and underuse. In this study, conducted in 1960, 1142 employed respondents from a national cross-section sample were interviewed.[10]

The questionnaire contained 22 open-ended questions and 89 items which the respondent rated on a ten point scale. The four most interesting sets of questions for our present purposes consisted of:

1) work features that the respondent would desire in an "ideal" job or would consider as part of a "worst possible" job;

2) a self-anchoring scale rating of how closely the respondent's present job compared with respect to his definitions of an "ideal" vs. "worst" job;

3) the features of the respondent's present job that prevented him from giving it a higher or lower rating (open-ended question);

---

[10] In addition to this cross-section sample, 283 high school teachers, 359 junior and senior high school students, 404 college seniors, 383 graduate students, 470 college faculty members, 287 business executives, and 248 scientists and engineers in business comprised the non-federal sample. A federal sample consisted of 948 general employees, 273 executives, and 281 scientists and engineers. All samples were carefully drawn by random procedures. The response rates averaged between 85-95 percent for these various groups, certainly a more than acceptable level.

4)   thirty occupational value statements rated on the ten point scale.

The remainder of the questionnaire was devoted to attitudes toward and images of government employment and employees.

The self-anchoring scale (see Cantril, 1965, for a fuller description of the technique as well as a cornucopia of cross-cultural data on its use) is obtained by asking the respondent to describe in detail the kinds of <u>things</u> about an occupation that would make it absolutely ideal for him, and then to describe the kinds of things about an occupation that would make it least satisfying. The respondent is then handed a card with a picture of a ladder with rungs numbered 1 to 10, with 10 representing the ideal occupational description and 1 the worst description. He is then asked to rate his present job on this ladder (as well as his job of 5 years ago and his anticipated job situation 5 years hence).

The procedure has much to recommend it. It allows the respondent to define in his own terms the criteria on which he is making <u>his</u> rating. It taps the respondent's historical frame of reference and his aspiration for the future. Interesting open-ended information is evoked in an ultimately more usable form than the traditional open-ended questions. It engages the respondent's attention more than a usual series of survey questions. There are limitations of course. The statistical assumptions made in adding scores across individuals would certainly stagger most practitioners. In fact, there is some question as to how to interpret a single individual's score based on a single scale which might range between quite incomparable extremes, e.g., "no supervision and good pay" versus "lousy working conditions and no variety in the work," rather than separate scales for each of these four characteristics independently.

Nevertheless, the technique deserves to be and probably will be used more widely making it probably that overall changes in levels of job satis- faction can be reliably traced over time for the student of social change. Mean ratings for respondents in various occupational categories of the Kilpatrick, et al. study are presented in Table 3 which can be used for such a purpose. Again we note that responses are heavily on the "positive" side of the ladder (one and a half rungs above 5.5 which could be considered the arbitrary zero point)--a further indication that few people can be said to be entirely unhappy with their jobs. Again, we see the same ordering of occupational satisfaction with status, although we have already noted the advantages of using more than the five occupational category breakdown used in Table 3.[11]

Thus, we are unable to examine more closely to see whether lower status white-collar workers are more content with their jobs than the higher blue-

---

[11]Unfortunately, only a one digit (12 category) code was used in coding occupation for this study, precluding possible secondary analyses with these data.

Table 3

SELF-ANCHORING SCALE RATINGS OF PRESENT OCCUPATION
Scales run from 1 = worst job to 10 = ideal job.
(from Kilpatrick, et al. 1964; sample sizes in parentheses)

Occupation	Employed Public	Federal Employees	College Teachers
All employees	7.1^b (1063)	7.0^b (896)	8.7^a (297)
Farmers	7.4 (78)		
Unskilled/semiskilled	6.6^b (386)	6.5^b (114)	
Skilled	7.1^a (181)	7.1^b (152)	
Clerical	7.3^{ab} (178)	6.6^b (333)	
Professional/ managerial	7.7^a (297)	7.7^a (294)	
Executives	8.1^a (270)	8.0^a (262)	
Natural scientists	8.0^a (82)	7.9^a (85)	8.8^a (115)
Social scientists	8.0^{ab} (72)	7.7^{ab} (85)	8.3^a (101)
Engineers	8.1^a (86)	7.6^a (89)	8.4 (81)
High school teachers	8.4^a (259)		
Vocational counselors	8.4^a (76)		

[a]Present occupation rated an average of one scale point or better over job five years ago (See Appendix B).

[b]Occupation five years hence rated an average of one scale point or better over present job (See Appendix B).

collar (i.e., skilled) workers. Evidence as given is contradictory on this question since clerical (which includes sales) workers scored high for the public sample and skilled workers scored significantly[12] higher for the federal sample. Government clerical workers also score significantly lower than clerical workers employed in business. A closer examination of these workers reveals that postal employees show up as particularly dissatisfied in this category, with a mean rating of 6.2, by far the lowest of any of the occupational group reported.

Figure 1 contrasts the responses of the occupational groups as to where they have come and to where they think they are headed. All groups appear to have an optimistic sense that they are in the middle of at least a ten year surge of progress and prosperity (see Appendix B for the complete data). Farmers, conversely, are the most pessimistic in this regard, although they are currently quite well satisfied with their jobs. Unskilled and semiskilled workers report little progress over the previous 5 years, but are expectant of greater progress in the next 5 years, enough to make them more satisfied than the skilled workers expect to be. Clerical workers are likewise expectant of a more promising future. To the extent that these hopes are unrealistic, one could well expect these groups to be especially liable to frustration and demoralization. In particular, this reflects the overall impression that Gurin, et al. derived from their interviews with clerical workers: "Mobility oriented, high in aspiration, involved in the job area, and frustrated." There are, of course, large variations to be found within the clerical work force--Morse (1953) found 41 percent of a repetitive clerical work force dissatisfied with the content of their work vs. 21 percent of those doing miscellaneous clerical work. Moreover, men in clerical jobs are more dissatisfied than female clerical workers, as can be seen from the Converse-Robinson data.

Before leaving these self-anchoring ratings, we might also report that certain relations with background characteristics are also consistent with earlier findings. Women and older employees continue to report notably higher satisfaction. These constancies with previous research findings may be taken as an indication that the technique does not appear to introduce any serious methodological differences by imposing a "level of aspiration" frame of reference on the respondent. In addition, Kilpatrick, et al. point out unexpected differences according to geographical region and community size. Southerners score .4 points higher than respondents from other locales, and residents of all cities of over a quarter million population (perhaps predominantly lower working-class) score .5 to .9 scale points lower than other communities.

As mentioned above, a further advantage of the self-anchoring scale procedure is that it provides valuable open-ended material. From this material we can glean a much more accurate picture as to what sort of work

---

[12]The authors report a .5 scale point difference to be significant at the 95 percent confidence level where sample sizes are over 100 and .7 difference where one or both sample sizes are less than 100.

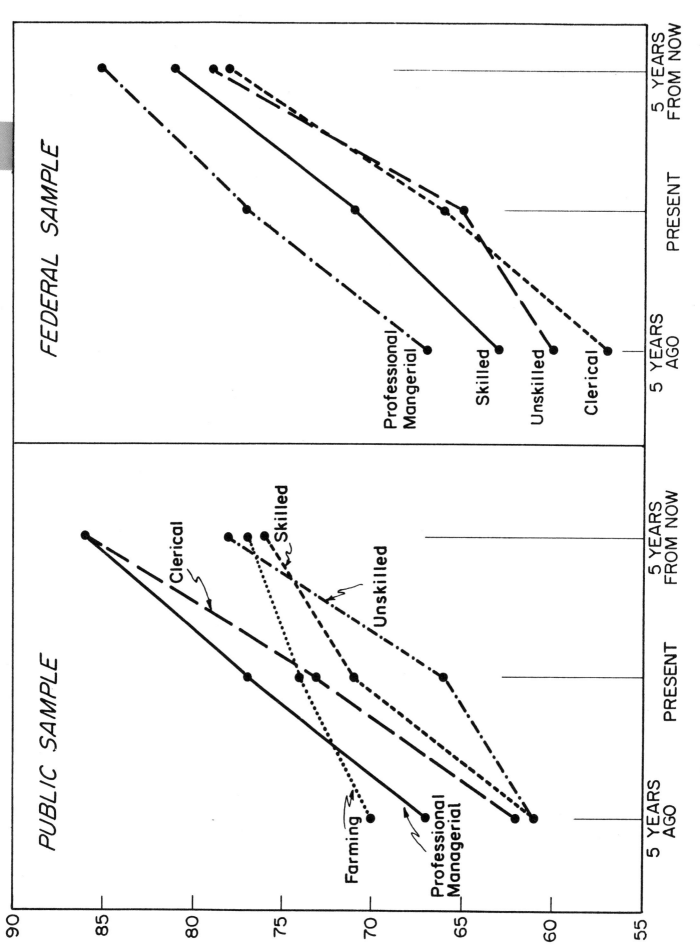

FIGURE 1: SELF-ANCHORING SCALE RATINGS FOR PRESENT JOB, JOB FIVE YEARS AGO AND JOB
FIVE YEARS FROM NOW (Kilpatrick, et al. 1964)

characteristics are salient to individuals in appraising their jobs. Kilpatrick, et al. were able to come up with a far greater number of open-ended replies (an average of 3.5 "ideal" replies and 2.9 "worst" replies) using their technique than Gurin, et al. Further open-ended questions dealing with the reasons the respondent did not rate his job higher or lower on the ladder yielded additional auxiliary information in the realistic context of the respondent's present job. We have taken the liberty of fitting the response categories reported by Kilpatrick, et al. into the general coding scheme devised by Gurin, et al. (Appendix A), which should aid in comparative analysis. The results for both self-anchoring responses and the reasons for not rating the job higher or lower are given in Appendix C.

The most prevalent response to these questions was the rather uninformative reply that the respondent wants to like his work and find it interesting and enjoyable. Other replies are far closer to what we are looking for and appear in this order of frequency for positive features: wages, working conditions (e.g., unpleasant, dirty place to work), self-determination (or independence, "chance to be my own boss"), the chance to fulfill oneself in a job that fits one's talents and training, security and fringe benefits, active personal relations (e.g., talking with and meeting stimulating or interesting people), passive personal relations (e.g., being with or around nice people), and having a good superior or boss. The list of dissatisfiers (in all surveys mentioned less frequently than positive features) is headed by working conditions for the fictionalized "worst" job, and by wages for one's actual present job; perhaps this is an indication that many (48 percent) people have experienced employment that involved bad working conditions and are presently employed in jobs in which satisfactory conditions prevail. Other dissatisfiers in order: too much pressure or a too heavy a work load, too little work variety, trouble with one's boss or superiors, and lack of self-determination. Two factors not mentioned often as determinants of the "worst" job but given prominent mention relative to one's own job were: little or no chance for advancement and lack of job security.

Needless to say, such orderings are practically meaningless until breakdowns by occupational level are examined. Unfortunately, Kilpatrick, et al. give only occupational breakdowns for certain positive features of the ideal job. These are presented in Table 4.

The most obvious differences appear for the "achievement" factors under the intrinsic or ego category. These are in line at a general level with what we noted previously, with the professionals and managers highest and lower blue-collars and farmers lowest. Note, however, that there are only indeterminate differences between the clerical and skilled workers in mention of these factors as desirable qualities in a job--which is somewhat discrepant from what we have been considering as the general distinguishing feature of white- and blue-collar occupations. Further "ideal" features (all ego- or self-oriented), more prevalent as one ascends the occupational structure, do show notable differences between the clerical and skilled workers: pleasant personal relations (both passive and active), doing work that is useful or worthwhile, and having variety in one's work. Only slight differences appear in the other factors. Concern with self-determination is more prevalent among white-collars, but it is a source of considerable

Table 4

BREAKDOWNS OF FACTORS MENTIONED AS ELEMENTS OF IDEAL JOB BY OCCUPATION
(Kilpatrick, et al. 1964; public sample only)

	All	Unskilled Semiskilled	Skilled	Clerical	Professional Managerial	Farmer
EXTRINSIC						
(Economic)						
11 Wages, salary	45%	45%	43%	45%	39%	32%
12 Security						
(Non-Economic)	15	13	20	20	13	4
21 Fringe benefits						
22 Working conditions	41	43	45	53	29	38
INTRINSIC						
(Achievement)						
32 Sense of challenge	7	1	7	7	15	1
33 Self-development	4	5	8	11	17	3
37 Sense of accomplishment	8	4	12	6	13	6
(Affiliation)						
41 Personal relations (active)	12	13	9	19	10	3
42 Personal relations (passive)	19	11	8	33	31	4
44 Superiors, boss	11	14	10	20	4	1
(Influence)						
51 Self-determination	29	24	25	29	35	48
(Curiosity)						
61 Variety in work	10	6	10	15	14	3
GENERAL						
71 Interest, enjoyment	72	72	72	65	72	79
76 Useful worthwhile work	14	10	8	17	24	8
N =	1063	392	185	179	301	79

importance for blue-collar workers as well (as also reflected in the higher complaints among blue-collars about "pressures" and "work loads"), again pointing out the importance of Blauner's "control" variable. On the extrinsic side, the data are at odds with Wilensky's (1964) contention that money is the only thing that the working classes care about. Pleasant working conditions (cited least often by professionals and managers, probably because they already have them) are mentioned just as often as wages by these workers. We noted above, however, that in reference to one's actual job, money does take the prominent position.

It is worth mentioning some interesting if peripheral additional findings: farmers, expectedly, show little concern with affiliative concerns and, not expectedly, with job security. While breakdowns by occupation are not given for the other open-ended replies, differences by educational level are presented in Appendix C. Marked and consistent increases with education for the response in question are indicated by two plus signs (++) while irregular or mild increases are indicated with a single plus sign (+); decreases with educational level are indicated by one or two minus signs, and uneven or flat relations are denoted by a zero (0). The general results are, of course, in line with the occupational differences noted in Table 4. Greatest increases with educational level were found for the chance for self-expression, doing useful-worthwhile work, active personal relations, self-development, sense of challenge, self-determination, variety in work, and sense of accomplishment. Greatest negative relations with education were found for the mention of extrinsic factors--working conditions, job security and fringe benefits, work pressure or work load (only mentioned as a negative feature of both the "worst" job and one's actual job), and wages. The only "intrinsic" factor mentioned more often by the less-educated was relations with one's boss or superior. As suggested by many authors, the reasons better educated people do not mention these factors more often is that satisfactory levels of such factors are practically built-in features of their job. The day when less-educated workers begin plugging for the really intrinsic features of a job does seem a long way off.

A major point of interest is the relation between job satisfaction (as indicated by self-anchoring scale rating for one's present job) and the various types of reasons given for not rating one's job higher or lower on the self-anchoring scale. Of the nine most popular reasons for not rating one's job lower, only two (wages and job security) were not noticeably related to level of job satisfaction. Yet of the five most popular reasons for not rating one's job higher, wages turns out to be the only reason clearly related to job satisfaction (38 percent of those low in satisfaction mentioned wages as a dissatisfier vs. 30 percent of the medium satisfied and 22 percent of the highly satisfied). Again we see wages as the job dissatisfier, not the satisfier.

Strangely enough, the open-ended reply we found most difficult to incorporate into the Gurin, et al. motivational framework[13]--interest,

_____

[13]Two other "non-motivational" replies to these questions also related significantly to job satisfaction: I didn't rate my job lower because "It's a good job in comparison to other jobs" and I didn't rate my job higher because "There's always room for improvement." The former response was given almost entirely by the low or medium satisfaction respondents, the latter was given twice as often by high satisfaction respondents.

enjoyment, pleasure--turned out to be the best differentiator (23 percent low, 31 percent medium, 58 percent high) between levels of job satisfaction. Three other good differentiators were: (active) relations with people at work, self-determination, and sense of fulfillment. Since all of these features were seen to have been related to the more satisfying high status jobs, a more controlled breakdown of these data is clearly required.

Finally, Kilpatrick, et al. supplemented their open-ended materials with ratings of 30 occupational value statements. The results from the two approaches were found to be highly consistent. We have again attempted to arrange these statements into the Gurin, et al. coding scheme in Appendix D to help in comparative analysis. It will be noted that a number of statements involving moral or spiritual statements ("Work is a good builder of character," "Work is a way of being of service to God"), which by nature do not fall into this more motivational framework, are placed in a separate category at the bottom of the table.

While the reader may not agree with certain codings, he is free to place them in separate categories as he wishes. From a sampling point of view, however, it is obvious that achievement values were overrepresented with working conditions and curiosity factors completely neglected in the final list of statements used.

Again the progressive decreases in extrinsic values and increases in intrinsic values (especially preferring opportunity over security, solving hard problems and developing one's own special abilities) for those in higher status positions pervades the Appendix D data. Likewise, the differences between skilled and clerical workers are inconsistent and impossible to interpret, e.g., clerical workers reject more the proposition that "work is nothing more than a way of making a living" but feel no more interested in a job that "offers more opportunity than security."

Pulling together all of their materials, Kilpatrick, et al. make the following conclusions regarding the pattern of work concerns within their various samples:

1) Men stress "breadwinner" and career-related values (job security, self-advancement, self-determination, freedom on the job, and wages); women emphasize personal relationships, good and understanding supervision, and doing work that is worthwhile and constructive. These results generally held up when controlled for type and level of occupation, education, and income. Differences by age were not abundant, although older people did place somewhat greater stress on the inherent goodness and primacy of work.

2) All of the special high-level groups (teachers, executives, natural scientists, social scientists, and engineers) shared the pattern of values common to those at upper levels of attainment. Certain differences, however, were noticed within professions (executive vs. scientist) and within situs of employment (college, business, and federal government), suggesting "numerous stages of self-selection and of being selected, as well as social reinforcement within the groups." Among the more outstanding differences noted were:

a) College teachers: practically no concern about extrinsic factors but with a high degree of concern for occupational involvement and desire to interweave work with other activities in life. Scientists and engineers show even higher concern about self-determination and self-expression.

b) Business: financial reward and status far more salient and social goals somewhat less salient. Within this group, certain members (executives and engineers) show lower ego involvement and more respect for money and status together with more interest in making friends at work, competition, and directing others.

c) Federal employees: greater occupational involvement and subscription to duty and more concern with supervision and personal relationships (especially passive). Less concern with material consideration but an apparent feeling of financial relative deprivation among the upper level federal employees. Federal executives were low in desire to carry out one's own ideas. Natural and social scientists showed lower emphasis on money and competition, making them closer to their college counterparts. Engineers, with more emphasis on money and competition and less on altruism and ego-involvement, are more similar to their business counterparts.

d) Students: Those in high school showed value patterns most similar to the upper-level employees, while college students expected to derive more fun and enjoyment from work, with less dedication and striving for success. Within each group, higher academic grades related to expectations of greater work involvement at a personal level and less concern with extrinsic factors.

Obviously, there is a vast amount of valuable data still unanalyzed from this study. While Kilpatrick does plan to publish (through the Brookings Institute) further occupational value analyses sometime in the the near future, these will not include two vital pieces of information: multivariate inter-relationships between the statements and normative data on the values of more finely differentiated occupational groups.

4. Wilensky's Labor-Leisure Study of Detroit. Through a careful review of the literature and a knowledgeable use of analytic techniques, Wilensky (1964) has proposed certain data which may expose a number of sociological myths and incomplete research findings in the field of occupational sociology. Wilensky began by selecting special contrasting samples in the Detroit area, thereby ensuring that more proper and meaningful comparisons could be made between the various groupings. Essentially Wilensky's sample consisted of professional, clerical, and skilled blue-collar workers only. Within the professional category three groups were picked--lawyers, professors, and engineers; distinct situs categories within each profession were chosen to yield further expected differences--lawyers in firms vs. lawyers in business for themselves; professors in a church-affiliated university vs. professors in an urban public university; engineers employed in a firm making diversified products vs. those in a firm making only one product. Spurious age effects were reduced by taking only respondents between 30 and 55, thus eliminating

those with little experience and those close to retirement. The middle-mass segment of the sample did include respondents aged 21-29, but these were separated for analytic purposes (few of them had their work careers delayed by college, so it would seem safe to include them).

Deftly criticizing previous measures of job satisfaction and job commitment, Wilensky proposed a new index of such content by examining the extent to which the person's job fulfilled certain aspects of his "prized self-image." From what might be viewed as an infinite collection of such aspects, five were selected: sociability, intelligence, conscientiousness, independence, and ambitiousness. While Wilensky is apologetic about the restricted domain of such traits (especially when this index did not reveal as much work alienation as he expected), it can be seen that they overlap with the ego areas of the Gurin, et al. code: more so with achievement (ambitiousness), affiliation (sociability), and moral (conscientiousness) and less so with influence (independence) and curiosity (intelligence).

Wilensky's approach involved a series of open-ended questions through which three measures (alienation, attachment, indifference) were obtained for each self-image aspect. After that portion of a long interview which was likely to affirm positive features of the respondent's life, the following question was asked: "Almost everone has a pretty good idea of the way he is seen by the people he likes and feels comfortable with. How about you--for example, are you known as a good mixer, a person who likes to get together with other people?" (Yes, No, Don't know) If Yes: "Would it make a difference to you if you weren't known as a good mixer?" Then later in the interview (in an effort to avoid a "halo" effect), the respondent was asked, "About how often during an average day do you talk to the people you work with about the things not required by your job--you know, just shooting the breeze? Would it be every few minutes, once or twice an hour, four to five times a day, or less often than that?" If at least four to five times a day: "Would it make much difference to you if you didn't have a good chance to talk that way?" If less often: "Does it bother you a lot that you don't have much of a chance to talk and joke around?"

If the person thinks of himself as a "good mixer" and it makes a difference to him whether others think so or not, and if he has a chance to converse informally at work and it seems to make a difference to him that he does, he receives one point for "Attached." If, on the other hand, this person was in a job which did not afford such opportunity for sociability and it bothered him, he received one point for "Alienated." All other combinations are coded "Indifferent." The remaining four aspects of self were covered by these work characteristics: conscientiousness ("chance to do your work well--do a good careful job" plus "chance to do things you're best at--use the skills that you have"); intelligence ("Plenty of chance to use your own judgment"); independence (doesn't have a boss "who is always breathing down your neck--not watching too closely"); and ambitiousness ("Good chance for promotion where you work"). In all then, each person had six points (two for conscientiousness, one for each of the other self aspects) to be distributed into one of the three categories--alienated, attached, or indifferent.

While the psychometrically-oriented may object to the differential interpretation of a three-category ipsative measure (i.e., if a person is not alienated, he must be either indifferent or attached), there do seem to be complicated relations in the data which are worth examination. For example, restricted sociability is not a source of alienation but plentiful sociability is a source of attachment.

Table 5 contains the distributions of the three measures for the various groups which Wilensky investigated. A major finding is that one professional group, engineers (especially those working for a single product firm), show up as more alienated than the lower white-collar or higher blue-collar groups; it will be remembered that these groups appeared to be the most frustrated in the earlier measures we discussed. Note also certain dramatic situs differences within the professional group: solo lawyers are more indifferent and less attached to their work than firm lawyers, while church university professors are more indifferent, more attached, and more alienated than urban university professors. Lower white-collar workers also show up as less alienated, less indifferent and more attached than upper blue collar workers. The differences, however, are certainly not astounding, and the waters still remain muddied on the question of the respective positions of these groups on the job satisfaction ladder, if such exist.

One of the most welcome features of the Wilensky study was the comparison of how much better occupational status indicators differentiated job alienation, attachment, and indifference than did more concrete aspects of the person's work and life milieu (i.e., organizational structure, control over work processes, previous work history, stage in the life cycle). Clearly, having a chaotic work history was at least as good a predictor as lower social class of alienation, indifference, and lack of attachment. In addition, differences in work alienation (but not in indifference and attachment) were as sharp if not sharper (than those produced by indices of social status) for respondents varying in the control they had over the work pace and the work schedule, those having varying levels of authority over them, those experiencing blocked mobility, and those caught in a life-cycle consumption squeeze (e.g., large numbers of children and small amounts of savings and investments). The "control" variable seemed especially significant: within every occupational level, restricted freedom or control resulted in higher levels of work alienation.

While Wilensky's use of techniques and empirical evidence obviously represent quite significant and needed advances in the study of work attitudes, they do need to be replicated on larger populations to see to what extent the groups selected are representative of what goes on in corresponding situations across the country. By purposely picking groups highly likely to be satisfied or dissatisfied within the professional categories, the effects of occupational status may have been seriously curtailed in relation to what might have been obtained from a truly representative sample. In addition, one might hope for a better distribution on the dimension of work alienation, as 85 percent of the population showed no alienation on any of the self-image items. But then again, it may be that the answers to simple-minded poll questions are a more realistic reflection of the worker's world than the expectations and intrinsically-evaluated projections of social critics and sociologists. As Wilensky opines, people at work may be "playing it cool" and accept their work with

Table 5

DISTRIBUTION OF WORK ALIENATION, INDIFFERENCE AND ATTACHMENT
FOR VARIOUS OCCUPATIONS (Wilensky, 1964)

Group	N	Work Alienated[a]	Work Indifferent[b]	Work Attached		
				High (4,6)	Med. (2,3)	Low (0,1)
Upper-Middle-Class Professionals Age 30-55						
Solo lawyers	100	10%	16%	20%	51%	29%
Firm lawyers	107	8	8	34	49	18
Church university professors	31	10	16	32	45	23
Urban university professors	68	6	9	22	46	32
Diversico engineers	93	19	14	28	45	27
Unico engineers	91	30	15	22	45	33
Middle Mass						
Lower white-collar, age 21-29	69	13	22	20	45	35
Lower white-collar, age 30-55	252	13	25	25	35	40
Upper blue-collar, age 21-29	53	23	22	15	46	39
Upper blue-collar, age 30-55	293	18	36	16	35	49

a Percentage alienated on at least one aspect of prized self-image

b Percentage indifferent on all aspects of prized self-image

what Kornhauser (1965) calls "a kind of mild, passive, somewhat fatalistic contentment."

5. _Converse and Robinson Meaning-of-Time Study_: This is probably the latest available nationwide survey of work attitudes, having been conducted in the Fall of 1965 and the Spring of 1966. We will be going into this study in great detail since this is the first time it has appeared in print; thus the presentation may contain more details than the casual reader is interested in.

In addition to a national probability sample[14] of 1244 adults in urban areas, a survey of 789 adults in Jackson, Michigan was similarly conducted during the same period. The opening part of the hour interview included a 20-minute section on work for the 70 percent of the sample who were employed for pay 10 hours or more a week. The questions included the kinds of things done on the job, the time spent on various aspects of the job, the things the respondent liked best and disliked about his job (as Gurin, et al. had asked), the respondent's rating of seven features of his job, and finally, how satisfied was he with the job, and did he ever think about changing jobs or getting into another line of work.

The responses to these latter two direct questions are presented in Table 6, where the data for residents of Jackson and for the national sample, for both men and women, have been combined. Separate figures for men, given in Appendix F, show that men have less "complete" satisfaction, especially in those occupations predominantly filled by women--school teachers, sales clerks and other clerical. While certain occupational categories are still quite small (artists, professors, other sales, self-employed craftsmen, armed forces), the reader can combine or disregard categories with which he feels uncomfortable. The reader is also warned that there are a number of "grab bag" categories which could use more detailed separation, e.g., service workers, technicians (which includes airline pilots, embalmers and draftsmen) and advisors (including clergymen, lawyers, recreation and social workers). The two indices of job satisfaction are:

a) All things considered, how satisfied would you say you are with your job? Would you say you are _completely_ satisfied, _pretty_ satisfied, _not very_ satisfied, or _not at all_ satisfied?

b) Do you ever think of changing to another job or another type of work?

Responses to the two questions give quite different impressions of the level of job satisfaction in the public. Only 11 percent of all respondents (12 percent of men) chose either of the alternatives "not very satisfied" or

---

[14]The sample was restricted to people between the ages of 19 and 65 living in households where at least one adult member was employed in a non-farm occupation. Only residents of cities qualifying as Standard Metropolitan Statistical Areas were included in the initial sampling frame, which means that the sample represents about two-thirds of the total U.S. population.

Table 6

REPORTED JOB SATISFACTION AND THOUGHTS ABOUT CHANGING JOBS (MEN AND WOMEN)
BY OCCUPATIONS (Converse and Robinson, in press)

| | | Job Satisfaction | | | | |
Occupation	N	Completely	Pretty	Not very Not at all	Interpretation*	Think about changing jobs
Professional- **people oriented**						
Artist, musician	5	80%	20%	0%	Very satisfied	40%
Professor, librarian	8	62	38	0	Very satisfied	25
Advising profession	36	53	41	6	Very satisfied	31
School teacher	54	46	52	2	Very satisfied	26
Nurses, other medical	15	33	67	0	Satisfied	33
Professional- **data oriented**						
Scientist, physician	16	43	50	7	Satisfied	38
Accountant, auditor	13	23	77	0	Ambivalent	54
Engineer	43	23	70	7	Dissatisfied	56
Technician	<u>33</u>	<u>24</u>	<u>67</u>	<u>9</u>	Dissatisfied	<u>61</u>
Professional **technical Total**	223	39	57	4	Satisfied	45
Managerial **Self employed** (large firm)	23	39	57	4	Satisfied	26
Self employed (other)	40	25	73	2	Neutral	40
Salaried	68	50	46	4	Very satisfied	36
Clerical						
Bookkeeper	18	44	56	0	Very satisfied	22
Secretary, typist	70	44	47	9	Satisfied	39
Other clerical	150	31	57	12	Neutral	42
Sales						
High status-goods	11	9	82	9	Neutral	64
High status-services	11	36	46	18	Dissatisfied	55
Sales clerk	28	32	54	14	Neutral	64
Other sales	7	14	86	0	Neutral	42
Skilled						
Self employed	8	50	25	25	Ambivalent	50
Foremen	39	41	54	5	Satisfied	28
Other skilled	151	29	58	13	Dissatisfied	38
Semiskilled						
Operatives	229	27	57	16	Very dissatisfied	42
Service						
Protective,	21	47	48	5	Satisfied	19
Armed forces	9	56	33	11	Satisfied	67
Household	24	46	33	21	Ambivalent	38
Other service	108	32	53	15	Dissatisfied	42
Unskilled Laborer	<u>32</u>	<u>25</u>	<u>56</u>	<u>19</u>	Very dissatisfied	<u>34</u>
TOTAL	1270	34	55	11		40

*To be "satisfied" (or "dissatisfied"), the group must show both more (less) than an average percent of members completely satisfied and less (more) than an average number not very or not at all satisfied. "Ambivalent" means that the percentages completely satisfied and not very/not at all satisfied are contradictory. All other groups are called neutral.

"not at all satisfied," in line with (if not lower than) the earlier estimates given by Blauner. On the other hand, two out of five (44 percent of men) think about changing work. The two questions are, as expected, highly correlated, however.[15] Those who think about changing their jobs or getting into another line of work comprise 17 percent of the completely satisfied, 47 percent of the pretty satisfied, 79 percent of the not very satisfied and 95 percent of the not at all satisfied. This relation is seen very clearly at the group level in Table 6. In only one of the occupational groups--armed forces--where the desire to exit is over 50 percent does the group register essentially positive feelings about their job. Note also, however, that those blue-collar groups which show most dissatisfaction report average or below average thought of other work. Our initial impression--considerably shaken by individual-level analysis which showed practically a constant correlation between the two measures within each occupation--led us to believe that blue-collar workers were resigned to their fate of doing work from which they derived relatively little satisfaction.

Note how finer occupational distinctions lead to dramatic differences within the eight basic census categories. Protective and armed forces with the "service" category, for example, appear far more contented than other service personnel. The same is true of foremen within the "skilled" category, while self-employed heads of smaller firms (i.e., those making less than $10,000 in yearly earnings) show up as relatively discontented managers. The results also corroborate Wilensky's finding (also noticeable in Schletzer, 1966) of relatively high occupational discontent among engineers, one of the occupations currently recording highest membership increases: four times the national average for all occupations and 17 percent over the general professional-technical rate in the 1950-1960 decade (Wattenberg and Scammon, 1965). Table 6 further shows technicians[16] as another dissatisfied group within the professional-technical category.

From these findings it seems that the whole class of what we have labelled "data-oriented" professions is far less contented than workers in the "people-oriented" professions.[17] Whether the "data-oriented" set relatively higher standards or goals for themselves, or are bothered by other displeasing external circumstances (Table 7 shows that they are most satisfied

---

[15]Needless to say, there is a strong age component in both measures. Older men think less about changing jobs ($r = -.37$) and are more satisfied with their job ($r = .17$).

[16]High discontent and status ambiguity were found among technicians in a midwest chemical plant (Clelland, 1966). Although averaging three more years of schooling, they earned $300 a year less than blue-collar workers in the same plant. Despite the rapidly expanding need for people with their skills, they felt that their own chances for success were declining. This was probably due to the fact that, having taken scientists as their reference group, they saw no open channel of mobility to that category within the firm.

[17]Except for social workers, of whom three out of the four in our sample were thinking of leaving. While a small number, to be sure, this proportion stood out among the other small numbers.

Table 7

AVERAGE RATINGS OF VARIOUS ASPECTS OF JOB BY OCCUPATIONS: MEN AND WOMEN
Scores run from 1 = very good to 5 = poor.
(Converse and Robinson, in press)

	Pay	Job Security	Kind of Work Place	Chance to Use Skills	Kind of People	Freedom to Plan	Chance Learn
Professional-people oriented							
Artist, musician	3.40	3.80	1.80	2.00	1.25	1.80	3.00
Professor, librarian	2.75	1.57	1.75	1.25	1.13	1.63	1.6
Adivising profession	2.08	1.63	1.60	1.20	1.37	1.26	1.4
School teachers	2.59	1.74	1.94	1.15	1.65	1.50	1.3
Other medical	2.53	1.73	1.67	1.47	1.71	1.73	2.00
Professional-data oriented							
Scientist, physician	1.75	2.06	1.25	1.56	1.50	1.69	1.5
Accountant, auditor	1.94	1.31	2.25	1.62	1.85	1.62	1.6
Engineer	1.97	1.58	1.84	1.72	1.58	1.58	1.7
Technician	2.73	2.12	1.91	1.79	1.82	2.03	2.0
Managerial							
Self employed (large firm)	2.52	1.83	1.95	1.43	1.64	1.26	1.6
Self employed (other)	2.91	2.47	2.00	1.62	2.03	1.47	1.9
Salaried	2.14	1.57	1.72	1.46	1.68	1.62	1.8
Clerical							
Bookkeeper	3.06	2.06	2.17	1.56	1.56	1.94	2.0
Secretary, typist	2.59	1.87	2.04	1.90	1.66	2.14	2.5
Other clerical	2.61	2.18	2.00	2.46	1.74	2.43	2.7
Sales							
High status (goods)	2.91	1.91	1.78	1.64	1.36	1.64	1.4
High status (services)	2.55	1.82	1.73	1.18	1.73	1.27	2.0
Sales clerk	3.33	2.43	1.93	2.25	1.71	2.64	3.0
Other sales	2.86	2.59	2.50	1.95	1.58	1.59	2.4
Skilled							
Self employed	3.13	3.38	2.50	1.88	1.86	2.25	2.5
Foreman	2.18	2.15	2.28	2.05	2.24	2.13	2.3
Other	2.54	2.41	2.22	1.93	1.95	2.67	2.6
Semiskilled							
Operatives	2.72	2.49	2.32	2.71	1.93	3.34	3.3
Service							
Protective	3.14	1.29	2.19	2.33	1.52	2.85	2.7
Armed forces	3.00	1.33	1.78	2.67	1.89	2.33	2.6
Household	3.50	2.79	2.09	2.75	1.81	1.83	3.5
Other service	3.16	2.12	1.91	2.44	1.83	2.35	3.1
Unskilled							
Laborer	3.10	2.31	2.27	2.72	1.83	2.97	2.9
Overall Average Men	2.63	2.19	2.12	1.53	1.79	2.30	2.5
Overall Average Women	2.73	2.13	1.91	2.11	1.63	2.27	2.7
Standard Deviation	1.33	1.34	1.17	1.36	.90	1.48	1.5

with their pay) cannot be answered conclusively with the limited samples and limited information available from our study. Even though as shown in Table 1, scientists showed the highest desire to stay in their occupation if they had it to do all over again, there does seem to be good reason nevertheless to separate at least these two groups within the professional-technical category.

Of the remaining occupations only the sales group indicated marked interest in other work. This was the case despite the fact that they did not report notable overall job dissatisfaction. In fact, when rating various components of their job (see Table 7 for mean ratings for each group, where a rating of very good was scored 1, good 2, fair 4 and poor 5), the high-status salesmen, such as insurance salesmen or auctioneers, register few complaints about any of them. Foremen, on the other hand, report overall satisfaction despite the very low rating they give the working conditions and the people they work with, plus a low rating to freedom to plan and the chance to learn. Other occupations report overall satisfactions more in line with the pattern of ratings given to the job components. While technicians give about average ratings to the various components, these are nonetheless considerably lower than those given by other professional groups.

The items in Table 7 were chosen as a short global closed-ended assessment of the major content areas of the Gurin, et al. code: pay, job security, and kind of working place (to tap the extrinsic factors), plus "chance to use your skills or abilities" (achievement), "kind of people you work with" (affiliation), "freedom to plan your own work" (influence), and "the chance to learn or try out new things" (curiosity). Lowest ratings went to curiosity (perhaps "creativity" or "variety" is a better term for this item) and pay; however, as will be shown, this is not to be construed to mean that these are the two major predictors of job dissatisfaction. Certain sex differences were significant, with women rating people and working conditions higher than men but rating opportunities for learning and utilization of skills much lower. Older people, as found in earlier studies of overall job satisfaction, tended to give more positive ratings.

Occupational differences were of course much more significant and interesting. Lowest ratings on practically all components clustered heavily in the blue-collar and lower white-collar classes; but this was especially true for the non-affiliative intrinsic factors; for as we have already seen, such factors seem to have at best secondary salience for these workers. Some apparent exceptions to the general pattern are the significance of job security for protective and armed services, pay for craftsmen (especially foremen), operatives and clerical workers, and the chance to use abilities for skilled workers. Clerical, sales and protective service workers have somewhat higher regard for the people with whom they work.

Within the managerial class, salaried managers are more favorable than the self-employed toward the extrinsic factors but not more favorable toward intrinsic factors. Owners of smaller businesses are considerably less satisfied about all factors, as they were on the global questions of Table 6. The plight of technicians has already been mentioned; other differences within the professional category stand out as well. Some "data-oriented" professionals are most contented about their pay and have positive feelings with selected other extrinsic satisfactions as well. The "people-oriented," however, seem to have the better of the intrinsic satisfactions, especially in using achievement and creative skills.

The possibility of correlating these data with the two indices of overall satisfactions constitutes their major source of interest. The correlation matrix for the nine questions is presented in Table 8, along with some test-retest reliability data described in the next paragraph. All coefficients in the matrix are seen to be moderate and positive. Beyond a probable response set bias which should be corrected, it seems safe to say that people's estimates of attributes of their jobs tend to be generally positive or generally negative: those who say they use their skills or abilities like their pay better; those who have the freedom to plan their work say they have the chance to learn or try out new things. Surprisingly, however, the addition of these components contributes nothing to the correlation with job satisfaction (and thoughts of change) beyond the coefficient obtained for the two highest predictors (i.e., .46 and .23). The two major determinants appeared to be wages and using of one's skills, the latter factor relating better to the direct question of satisfaction, while wages were more highly associated with thoughts about other work. The comparable matrix for women differed only slightly, although the best predictor of overall satisfaction turned out to be the chance to learn or try out new things; the use of skills and pay followed close behind. Separate analyses for blue-collar and white-collar males also showed few differences worth discussing. Blue-collar satisfaction was slightly more dependent on good pay and good working conditions.

One of the more fortunate aspects of this study was that test-retest reliability data were collected from a random subsample of 95 respondents from the Jackson area four months after the initial interview. In the initial interview, the overall satisfaction questions directly followed the job components ratings. In the reinterview schedule, these questions preceded the components questions. It appears that asking the more specialized questions first forces the respondent to make his overall responses consistent with the more detailed questions. The reliability (Pearson r) figures for the 41 men and the 17 women who held the same job over the intervening four month period are given at the bottom of Table 6.

The reliability figures for the components (except for two rather low coefficients for women on work place and skills) clearly are superior to the overall measures, especially the more direct question. Such a finding, although based on extremely small samples, give one great cause to wonder about the preferability of global measures over individual component measures. Lest one conclude that the global measures are worthless, however, we did find that they had the redeeming feature of predicting the very useful behavioral feature of job changes. Again the Jackson reliability sample is quite small-- only twelve people had left their jobs, of whom five were women whose employment originally was to overcome temporary company problems or personal financial hurdles. Of the seven men, four were forced to change for external reasons: one was laid off, the company of another moved out of town, one became ill (in the first interview he indicated that he was not at all satisfied with his job), and the fourth, a self-employed feed-mill operator, was forced out of business on financial grounds. Three of these four indicated initial

Table 8

CORRELATIONS BETWEEN COMPONENTS OF JOB, JOB SATISFACTION AND THOUGHTS ABOUT LEAVING: MEN ONLY. RELIABILITY DATA FROM 41 MEN AND 17 WOMEN IN JACKSON, MICHIGAN
(Converse and Robinson, in press)
Decimal points omitted.

	Pay	Security	Work Place	Use Skills	Kind of People	Plan Work	Learn	Satisfied	Change
Pay									
Job security	23								
Kind of working place	21	23							
Use skills or abilities	31	17	29						
Kind of people worked with	14	22	31	17					
Freedom to plan work	23	22	26	22	25				
Learn or try out new things	23	19	28	56	21	44			
How satisfied with job	35	26	26	46	17	22	30		
Ever think of changing	23	15	15	15	09	12	08	41	
Test-retest reliability Men	52	49	70	52	55	50	52	29	41
Women	71	54	-04	05	59	66	68	08	29

satisfaction with their jobs. In contrast, all of the remaining three[18] indicated on the initial interview that they were thinking about changing jobs, and only one gave as high as a "pretty satisfied" response to the direct question. While 11 of the 13 who did change jobs gave negative reactions to their job and 29 of 32 who said they thought about changing never did, the fact that the items successfully singled out those who did voluntarily change in the short time period restores a good deal of faith in the overall measures. Thus, like so many intensively investigated areas in the social sciences, our research (plus others we have reviewed) leaves us with at best quite ambivalent results concerning the utility of single direct measures of job satisfaction.

The Jackson reliability study also afforded us an opportunity to investigate how much increase in job satisfaction could be predicted by weighting the various components as to how important the respondent felt each of these components was to him personally. Accordingly, respondents were asked to pick out the three most important factors from the list of seven used. Weighting the first choice with a 5, the second with a 3, and the third with a 2, we multiplied the ratings on the factor by the appropriate weight and summed them.[19] This score, and a simple unweighted sum of all factors, together with a composite score of both were then correlated with job satisfaction and thoughts of change for both pre- and post-samples and for men and women. The results were remarkably inconsistent as to which of the three scoring procedures was superior. On balance, the use of a simple unweighted index using all components seemed slightly better. From what we have seen of related literature (e.g., Schaffer, 1953), this is simply a further indication that the use of item weights seldom improves overall relationships enough to warrant the extra computation.

Another point of interest in the Converse-Robinson study concerns the answers to the slightly revised Gurin, et al. question about "things you like best" and "things you don't like about your job." The percentages for the entire employed sample of both surveys are presented in Appendix A. It can be seen that, with the exception of affiliation-related differences (which could well be due to different coders or coding procedures), the results for the two surveys are strikingly alike. Since the 1958 survey question was imbedded in the middle part of an interview employing mainly open-ended questions but was the first question for our survey, the difficulty in establishing rapport perhaps accounts for the larger number of "general" responses and

---

[18]The occupational changes and reasons for leaving might be interesting to some readers. One changed from one skilled job to another, indicating promotion and better pay as reasons for leaving. A foreman, indicating dislike for the pressure of working for someone else, opened an ice-cream stand. The third, a young man originally satisfied, found an office job with better pay and bonus than the original job as a grocery clerk.

[19]The most important factors for men were pay and security, for women, the people at work. Centers and Bugental (1966) also found women far more interested in having compatible co-workers on the job; however, interesting work and pay rated somewhat higher for them, as for men. Since Centers had a larger sample for this question, we would put greater trust in his results for factor importance.

the somewhat smaller number of "more concrete" features (especially negative) picked up in the 1966 survey. It is obvious that non-economic extrinsic factors (mainly convenience, work pressure, and hours or working conditions) account for most of the concrete dissatisfactions with work. In the Kilpatrick, et al. study, where a richer fund of replies were obtained, it will be recalled that the economic extrinsic factors were mentioned most often as the source of dissatisfaction. However, an additional piece of information obtained in the 1966 study brings things more into line. When respondents said they thought about changing jobs, we asked them why. Here economic reasons were proposed by 38 percent of those thinking of changing jobs. No other class of reasons received half as many responses, as can be seen in Appendix A. Of these secondary reasons, non-economic, achievement, and general features received about equal overall mention.

Thus a good deal of evidence we have reviewed so far pinpoints wages as a major, if not the major, determinant of job satisfaction. Nor is this concern confined to the lower-income occupations. The available evidence essentially agrees that wage complaints are common to all occupations. In the 1958 and 1966 studies, complaints about wages were voiced most often by sales workers and laborers and least often by engineers and scientists, which is in line with their ratings in Table 7. For the non-economic extrinsic factors, only accountants/auditors and technicians showed consistently low proportions complaining.

The "intrinsic" feature which produced greatest dissatisfaction was bothersome relations with superiors or other particular co-workers. Managers (both self-employed and salaried), school teachers and sales clerks were particularly liable to mention such problems. Intrinsic discontent, as mentioned earlier, was voiced most often by those in white-collar occupations. Achievement complaints were mentioned most often by school teachers, tech- nicians, sales and clerical workers, and foremen. But there is an interesting difference to be noted here: school teachers and foremen are worried about having too much responsibility or influence and too much challenge in their work, while the others complain about having too little. Technicians and public advisors are most likely to be unhappy with curiosity fulfillment in their jobs, yet technicians (and scientists) are far more likely to list such things as positive features of their jobs. Other occupations scoring highly on positive job aspects: operatives and laborers--extrinsic factors; accountants, engi- neers, scientists, salaried managers--achievement; school teachers, public advisors, sales workers and nurses--affiliation; high-status salesmen-- influence.

It is hoped that by now one main point is becoming clear: the factors involved in judging one's satisfaction with his job most certainly vary widely with the respondent's occupation. The most overriding distinction is between intrinsic and extrinsic factors, which yield the major differences between white-collar and blue-collar occupations, with blue collars apparently answering the question in primarily extrinsic terms and the white collars in primarily intrinsic terms (also found in Weiss and Kahn, 1960 and Friedlander, 1965). It is not that the machine operator would not be interested in work that he can become personally involved in or that the scientist is not interested in making more money, but rather that these features are of secondary concern in their respective hierarchies of values.

Corroboration of this contention comes from a cross-section survey by Centers and Bugental (1966) of 692 adults living in Los Angeles. Centers and Bugental asked respondents to choose three of six factors (3 intrinsic, 3 extrinsic) as the most important in keeping them on their present jobs. The results, given in Appendix E, again show all intrinsic factors to be of greater importance to the professional-managerial class and all extrinsic factors as most salient to the blue collars. While concentrating main attention on white-collar vs. blue-collar differences, Centers and Bugental do mention the indeterminant differences in concerns of lower white-collar and upper blue-collar workers which appear in his data and which has been uncovered so often in the evidence we have reviewed thus far. If for the moment we disregard the small differences between these two groups and lump them together, there appear extremely clean and expected decreases in all extrinsic concerns and increases in intrinsic factors as one goes up the socioeconomic ladder.

One further question is worth investigating before leaving the Converse-Robinson investigation. What are the trends in job satisfaction over the past eight years? Are any occupations beginning to show higher or lower rates of satisfaction within their ranks? We plotted the satisfaction scores of 1958 with those of 1966 (Table 5) and looked for occupational points for which deviations around the regression line were maximal. From this analysis, we tentatively suggest that the following trends have been taking place:

Increasing satisfaction: bookkeepers, salaried managers, all salesmen.

Decreasing satisfaction: engineers, technicians, scientists, service personnel.

We have presented a mass of data for the Converse-Robinson study, and undoubtedly some form of summarization would be useful. Rather than isolating all the various and sundry findings, we have enlisted the aid of a computer program which plots the similarity of various objects in relation to each other. The program is called "Smallest Space Analysis" and was developed recently by Guttman (1966) and Lingoes following earlier work of Shepard and Kruskal. We shall have recourse to this valuable program in later parts of this report as well.

The "objects" in this case were 27 occupational categories, and the distances used to separate them were correlation coefficients (more correctly, large correlations indicated small distances). The correlated data consisted of the average ratings of people in these occupations on the seven components of their job, the two overall satisfaction measures, as well as the proportions in each occupation giving each of the open-ended reasons for liking or disliking their job, along with other data regarding total work hours, hours spent on various types of activities, and percentages of women and moonlighters in the occupation.

The results are plotted in Figure 2. The first (horizontal) dimension roughly differentiates occupations by socio-economic status, suggesting the pervasiveness of this factor in the total body of complex data collected in the Converse-Robinson study. The second dimension appears to be based on a data vs. people distinction, but people-oriented in a "manipulative" sense since the groups are comprised mainly of salesmen and self-employed. There

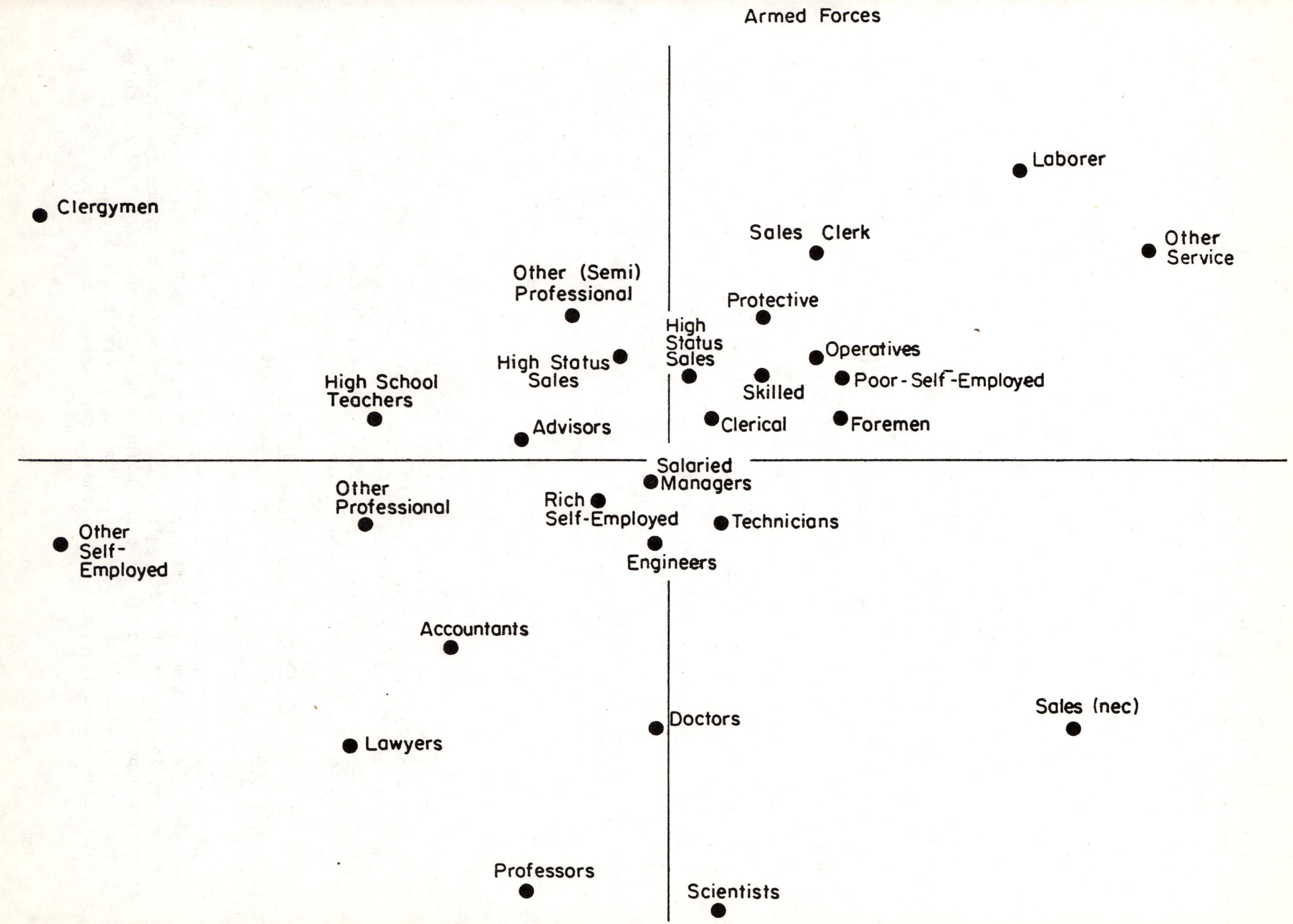

FIGURE 2: SMALLEST SPACE ANALYSIS PLOT OF SIMILARITIES OF WORK ATTITUDES AND ACTIVITIES FOR RESPONDENTS IN VARIOUS OCCUPATIONS. DATA ARE FOR BOTH MEN AND WOMEN (Converse and Robinson 1967)

is somewhat the flavor of a self-employed vs. salaried distinction in the dimension as well. The third dimension (not shown) clearly distinguishes the more masculine occupations (the self-employed, skilled and productive workers) from the more feminine ones (nurse, school teacher, secretary, public advisor).

In all, Figure 2 shows the general wisdom of the eight broad census classifications. But there are important distinctions within the categories that should be kept in mind. Within the professional category, as we have been arguing, it is best to separate the data-oriented from the people-oriented professions. Within the data-oriented, technicians should be considered separately (while Figure 2 places them closest to other clerical workers, we would not recommend lumping these groups together either). The managerial distinctions between salaried, self-employed (large firm) and self-employed (other) are quite important as well; within the self-employed category, a more appropriate distinction might be between retail trade and repair vs. other (mainly manufacturing and construction). While it seems safe to lump the high-status sales workers, they are obviously to be kept separate from sales clerks and lower-status sales workers, such as newsboys. Likewise, bookkeepers and secretaries should be kept separate from other clerical workers.

The lower-status sales and clerical workers are seen as much more similar to blue-collar workers than to other white-collar groups in the occupational similarity space of Figure 2. Yet it is probably the fact that they are in closer day-to-day contact with the higher status personnel that leads to the sense of relative deprivation which apparently characterizes them as it does not blue-collar workers. Figure 2 shows far less difference (also seen in the Minnesota Triple Audit data of England and Stein, 1961) within the major segments of the blue-collar domain than we would be led to expect from our earlier references or from the data presented in the next section. Foremen are the major exception; their attitudes and behavior put them closer to the professional-managerial part of the space. The same is true for protective workers, who are definitely different from household and other service workers. Other service workers seem as appropriately grouped with sales clerks as with household workers.

We have performed smallest space analyses on other bodies of occupational data at other places in this report. The reader may be interested in comparing Figure 2 with the results for further "life style" data from the Converse-Robinson study which appears in the occupational status section, or with the results for various vocational interest inventories. Both are given in the final chapter of this volume.

6. Some Further Data on Related Issues

a. The Blue-Collar World

Far more attention needs to be paid to the world of the less-educated working classes, where cognitive processes hypothesized by (usually middle-class) social scientists often simply do not apply. Common misunderstandings persist about the structure of blue-collar work. The most oft-cited assembly-line worker, as Blauner pointed out, comprises less than 5 percent of all automotive blue-collar workers. Although the data we have reviewed are somewhat unclear as to where the skilled worker fits in the total job satisfaction or status hierarchy, a clear hierarchy within the blue-collar domain is suggested by the available literature.

Argyris (1958) in his study of the "healthy" plant noted that non-skilled employees seldom mentioned intrinsic needs exhibited by the skilled: creativity, pride in work, variety, direction of others, and learning all aspects of their job. Unskilled workers were far more likely to describe non-involvement, routine, and isolation as <u>extremely important</u> features of their job. For such workers, Argyris argues, wages were increasingly being perceived "not as rewards for production, but as management's moral obligation for placing the employees in the kind of working world where frustration, failure and conflict are continuously being experienced." Such data led Argyris to predict that in the future increased wages would have to be paid to compensate for the greater dissatisfaction inherent in the duties of these occupations.

A most comprehensive study of 407 Detroit factory workers by Kornhauser (1965) revealed similar increases in intrinsic satisfactions among the skilled and higher level semi-skilled workers. In addition, correlated increments in overall job satisfaction (see Table 9) and several carefully validated indices of positive mental health were found as one progressed up the various skill levels (lowest mental health scores were found for that subgroup of workers in the largest manufacturing concerns as well as in others, regardless of size, among the repetitive semi-skilled who were machine paced). Job satisfaction was found to be a key mediating factor in mental health: in those relatively fewer instances where the lesser skilled mentioned greater satisfaction with the job, mental health scores were equivalent to the satisfied in the more skilled occupations. The reverse also obtained for the dissatisfied workers at each occupational level. These differences, as well as others we shall mention, held up when controlled for various personal and social background characteristics and were considered free of the contaminants of response sets.

Results shown in Table 9 are consistent with those given in Table 1 and Table 5, but not satisfactorily compatible with Figure 2. In addition to the two questions examined previously (job satisfaction and the willingness to re-enter current occupation if one were to start anew), we have included these same two questions which proved to be the outstanding predictors of both mental health and job satisfaction in the Kornhauser sample. These intrinsic features (corresponding closely to the questions Converse and Robinson used to tap achievement and curiosity), and to a much lesser extent wages, showed strongest and most consistent relations with more positive work feelings among the many job characteristics examined (pace and repetitiveness of work, supervision, opportunities for advancement, job security and work conditions). Nevertheless, Kornhauser challenges Herzberg's distinction between "motivators" (mainly intrinsic) and "satisfiers," since many workers in the sample did in fact explicitly mention extrinsic job features which they found personally motivating. Furthermore, Kornhauser sees, for example, workers' economic goals as having intense personal concern; hence he would dismiss the distinction between ego and non-ego motives. While his empirical contention is borne out by other data we have examined so far, and although there is admittedly certain conceptual overlap between extrinsic and intrinsic factors, the significant

60

Table 9

DIFFERENCES BETWEEN VARIOUS WORKING-CLASS OCCUPATIONS ON FOUR QUESTIONS
RELATED TO JOB SATISFACTION (from Kornhauser, 1965)

	Basic N*	A) Overall satisfaction Satisfied	Neither	Dissatisfied	B) Choose same job again	C) Job is interesting	D) Job uses abilities
Detroit Factories							
Skilled and high semi-skilled	176	77%	15%	8%	39%	82%	79%
Ordinary semi-skilled	128	71	18	11	23	69	64
Repetitive semi-skilled	103	56	24	20	16	29	22
Small Town Factory							
High and ordinary semi-skilled	40	77	15	8	52	81	63
Repetitive semi-skilled	38	47	22	31	22	26	18
Detroit Non-factory							
High semi-skilled	28	79	10	11	52	92	84
Ordinary semi-skilled	63	67	6	17	25	61	53
Detroit white collar	68	67%	19%	15%	54%	79%	76%

*Certain percentages are based on slightly smaller sample sizes because of non-response.

and consistent findings we have come up with thus far testify that Kornhauser's remarks are somewhat premature, especially since he has concentrated on the wage earning class and did not compare his results with other data that would be obtained from managerial and professional people. To be sure, abundant literature is available which seems to refute the Herzberg proposition, but there is also much evidence to support it (Burke, 1966, reviewed in Athanasiou's chapter). One of the major factors which influences findings on the Herzberg hypothesis is the occupational composition of the sample investigated. There has been recently a plethora of studies in this area and, considering the diversity and limited scope of the samples used, together with the polemical disposition of researchers, a definitive answer to Herzberg's proposition seems a long way off.

The final group covered in Table 9 contains factory clerical workers whose pay rates nearly approximated the average of the total blue-collar sample. Our finding of indeterminacy of this group regarding its "real" position vis-a-vis the blue-collar world remains unchanged. Clerical workers were the most interested in returning to their job, given the chance, yet their other job attitudes put them somewhat below the most skilled blue-collar workers. Incidentally, Table 9 conceals certain age differences reported by Kornhauser; older workers, as before, seem somewhat more satisfied, but the results are far from consistent. The interested reader is referred to Kornhauser's publication for more details on this and other important findings, as well as for a number of possibly useful attitude scales and their correlates.

Blauner (1964) has studied also the effects of work alienation among four groups of skilled blue-collar workers. Following upon his emphasis on the variable of control over work processes, Blauner found that the most satisfied workers, printers (as shown in Table 1), were very like medieval craftsmen in terms of the freedom they enjoyed to plan and finalize their own work. Less committed workers (e.g., skilled textile and auto workers), Blauner found to have far less discretion in their work schedule.

The largely negative attitudinal and mental health correlates shown for machine operators and lower semi-skilled workers evidently have little deterrent effect on their predilection for more of the same. In a recent nationwide survey, Morgan, et al. (1966) asked:

Some people would like to work more hours a week if they could be paid for it. Others would prefer to work fewer hours a week even if they earned less. How do you feel about this?

Of the total sample, only 16 percent preferred less work; a full 41 percent preferred more--despite the fact that the condition of overtime pay was not involved. And although the movement for a shorter work-week is being advocated by certain labor unions, the very occupations represented by these unions are among the most favorably disposed toward longer work hours: operatives, laborers, and craftsmen.[20] In fact, operative workers headed the list, with over half wanting more work; only a tenth wanted less.

---

[20]Service and clerical workers also had high interest in more work. The only groups not interested in more work hours turned out to be the ones who have control over their work hours and already put in the longest work week: managers, the self-employed, and farmers.

Tempting as it might be to attribute this to a simple desire for more money, it should be kept in mind that such a choice reflects negative feelings also. There are, however, definite ambiguities in the Morgan, et al. question that limit the above interpretation. For, significantly, when the question was posed differently as: "If you had two extra hours a day, what would you like to do with the extra time?" Wilensky (1964) found one in twenty of the "middle mass" chose work vs. two-thirds of the professors and 20-23 percent of lawyers and engineers.

b) <u>Work Values of Professionals and Other College-Trained People</u>

A more adequate look into the value structures of the (mainly scientific) professions comes from a huge NORC study of the professional labor force. Marsh and Stafford (1966) analyzed their responses to 13 value items, mostly replicates of those asked by Rosenberg (1957, see the scale section on occupational values). While all items intercorrelated positively, as was also found in this Converse and Robinson study, two distinct clusters of items in the NORC study suggested themselves--one mainly intrinsic (work with ideas, be creative, etc.), the other extrinsic (money, social standing and pleasant people to work with[21]). Some expected but interesting differences emerged when the scores on these two classes of factors were summed for professionals with graduate degrees. Academically employed professionals in each of eleven fields showed higher interest than non-academics in intrinsic values and lower interest in extrinsic values for eight of the eleven fields.

The results for the various professions are given in the table below:

INTRINSIC

		High	Medium	Low
E X T R I N S I C	High	Economics	Forestry Chemical Engineer Civil Engineer Electrical Engineer Mechanical Engineer	Business Physician
	Low	Physics Biochemistry Literature	Chemistry Mathematics Psychology	

The most interesting "bedfellows" turn out to be doctors and businessmen. These values of doctors are contrary to the Strong Vocational Interest Inventory results (see the section on vocational interest scales in the final chapter), collected in 1949, which indicated doctors to be more similar to scientists. Note here how similar are the patterns of the various engineering fields, although it should be mentioned that chemical engineers, whose earnings

---

[21]Among professionals, "working with people" judging from the correlation matrix, seems to have more of a leadership or manipulative connotation than an altruistic or affiliation one.

are a good deal higher than the other engineering categories, are close to qualifying for the upper right hand cell of the table.

Rosenberg's (1957) original study also uncovered some interesting value differences between college students whose studies were apparently heading them into different professional and managerial professions. Replies to value questions seemed to fall into three clusters: compliant (anxious to be well-liked, liking to take orders but not to give them, and expressing a positive view of human nature), aggressive (concerned about being successful, not bothered by giving orders, and suspicious), and detached (concerned about independence, preferred to make their own decisions, and bothered by having to take orders). As expected, compliance predominated among those in the social sciences and teaching; aggressiveness in business, management and law; and detachment among artists and scientists. The differentiations were present as well on a "faith-in-people" scale, with the compliant groups at the top of the scale, the detached in the middle, and the aggressive types mainly at the bottom. Medical students, to follow up the March-Stafford finding, showed a low to medium degree of "faith-in-people."

c) Child-rearing Determinants

Studies of intergenerational mobility have shown that children show a strong tendency to end up in occupations similar to those of their fathers. The passage from blue-collar to white-collar level seems the hardest to cross; there are interesting modified "easiest paths." For example, a semi-skilled worker in a manufacturing industry more likely will have a son in skilled work in manufacturing than in a semi-skilled position in some non-manufacturing concern (see the chapter on Occupational Mobility). Obviously, some transmittal of values, interests and attitudes must be occurring which makes certain job movements more likely than others.

A number of studies demonstrate that working-class parents foster attitudes in their children which make them dependent, indifferent, and apathetic (Bakke, 1940; Chinoy, 1952). More recently a study by Pearlin and Kohn (1966) isolates more crucial differences in child-rearing values and relates them to some of the occupational characteristics which have been discussed here. From samples of parents in Washington, D. C., and Turin, Italy, the authors obtained ratings of the importance of 17 characteristics in respondents' children. In only two of these seventeen indices--obedience and self-control--were significant differences shown between working- and middle-class parents, both mothers and fathers, in both Italy and the United States. The authors then investigated how much emphasis on these two values (in the Italian sample only) varied by (a) whether the father's work dealt mainly with people, data, or things; (b) how self-reliant the father was in his work, and (c) how closely he was supervised on his job. It was found that within both middle- and working-class occupations, emphasis on the value of self-control was far more prevalent in idea-oriented, most self-reliant and looser-controlled occupations. Conversely, importance of obedience was found in greater proportion among the thing-oriented, least self-reliant and closely-supervised occupations. Although (a), (b), and (c) are clearly related, each factor adds independent contributions in differentiating between parents who value self-control vs. obedience.

These results are clearly linked to results of our studies showing greater mention of intrinsic values among the middle-class occupations, where idea-oriented and self-reliant professions are far more prevalent. The Pearlin and Kohn results may also explain the zone of indeterminacy between lower white-collar and upper blue-collar occupations, wherein those in more self-reliant, idea-oriented work in the working-class occupations would foster the development of self and ego drives necessary for seeking more intrinsic values in one's work.

d) Cross-Cultural Differences.

That people as differentiated otherwise in Italy and the United States stress the same class-related child rearing values is hardly news to sociologists. Inkeles (1960) has shown that definite class values existed across nine European countries, Japan, and Australia. The most outstanding value distinguishing class levels was one used in the Pearlin and Kohn study, namely obedience. Only in Germany and Denmark did the relation between class and obedience fail to appear.

Inkeles, as stated in the beginning of this chapter, also had shown that increasing job satisfaction accompanied higher status positions in six nations for which surveys had been conducted. More recently, Hodge, et al. (1965) have shown that people in 23 diverse countries (developed or developing) essentially agree on the status ranking of various occupations. However, there exist interesting deviations from this consensus, as Hodge, et al. point out. Wilensky (1964) discovered an especially interesting deviation in Poland. There, where free enterprise is frowned upon and manual labor upgraded, skilled craftsmen fare slightly better and smaller entrepreneurs slightly worse in both prestige and satisfaction.

However, even government approval and status-elevation seem incapable of eliminating the dissatisfaction, drudgery, and dullness from routine blue-collar work, judging from a sample of Russian blue-collar workers (Zdravomyslov and Iadov, 1964). If we take the liberty to compare a job satisfaction question in the following way,

USSR			USA (skilled, semi-skilled, unskilled)	
Entirely satisfied	16%		Completely satisfied	27%
Satisfied	25	} 68%	Pretty satisfied	57%
Indefinite	43			
Dissatisfied	11		Not very satisfied	13%
Entirely dissatisfied	5		Not at all satisfied	3%

the results are quite similar. A number of caveats preclude further commentary on the interpretation of differences:

a) The Russian sample was composed of a random sample of Leningrad workers under age 30. By excluding older workers, whom we have found to be more satisfied, the U.S. sample thus has one built-in bias for more favorable attitudes.

b) The proportions of skilled to semi-skilled to unskilled in the Leningrad sample is unknown. In the U.S. samples we have found degree of skills to bear crucially on job satisfaction. This applies to the limited occupational scope of the Russian sample as well, with most favorable attitudes being expressed by skilled tradesmen, overall negative feelings by the unskilled workers, and the other groups falling about in the middle.

When the workers' evaluation of 10 components of their jobs were correlated with job satisfaction, some familiar findings occur. The major differentiators between all satisfied and dissatisfied workers turn out to be in the order: initiative, earnings, and chance for advancement. Two of the three are intrinsic (achievement-influence related) and the third is the "cultural universal" of money, which assumes far greater importance as work content becomes more repetitious. Even in the relatively high paid unskilled work, the most prevalent relation was between dissatisfaction and concern with earnings.

SUMMARY AND CONCLUSIONS

This chapter has exceeded its intended length, mainly because this review was begun with some intention to carefully document the "major" determinants of job satisfaction. Certainly this aim has been frustrated. Some studies show achievement factors to be most important for satisfaction, but they are mainly confined to (usually higher levels of) the white-collar world. Blue-collar workers seem to be more interested in pay rates; but this is not to say that better educated persons are not influenced by money. Their jobs, however, have built-in economic and security safeguards to begin with. Social relations on the job also appear as important work concerns, especially for women. Relations with one's supervisors and pressures at work are prominent sources of work discontent. In general, the findings reviewed here offer an array of concerns to be kept in mind when assessing job satisfaction. No one factor can be singled out as "the" determinant of job satisfaction; in fact, the evidence examined to date shows little convergence on the separation between "first order" and "second order" determinants. Nor is there any reason to doubt that these factors show subtle changes with variations in the job market and economic conditions. A newspaper article which came to attention recently reported that worker absenteeism in one factory had been cut dramatically by rewarding attendance with trading stamps--after other maneuvers had failed!

It would seem helpful to the reader who wants a capsule of what this chapter presents in a more positive vein, to recapitulate the main conclusions and offer some suggestions. These points are re-covered in increasing order of complexity.

1) All studies, both in the U.S. and other industrialized nations, show a clear connection between overall job satisfaction and social status, using gross indices of occupational status. On closer examination, important exceptions and indeterminacies appear in the overall relation--most notably between upper blue-collar and lower white-collar occupations. The Converse-

Robinson study revealed important variations within the broad census classifications as well. For example, technicians, engineers, and male school
teachers in the usual professional-technical category appear to have satisfaction levels comparable to those of lower white-collar and skilled blue-
collar occupations. Such findings are seldom acknowledged in studies of
this sort and need to be investigated further. Some of these variations are
reviewed more fully under the next point; for now we will point out that the
market is saturated with studies showing the overall trend--holding regardless
whether the question is open-ended or closed-ended, poorly or well worded,
free of or subject to response set, or taking into account or disregarding
the respondent's level of aspiration. Moreover, this status-satisfaction
relation holds no matter what aspect of the job one talks about (see Table 7);
so, even though we have argued that lower-status workers rate their jobs
primarily in extrinsic terms and higher-status in intrinsic terms, it makes
no difference. Higher-status workers have "the best of both worlds" anyway.

Nevertheless, lower-status workers are hardly on the verge of Marxian
revolt. To many of them, just having a job (which provides, besides more
money, a certain feeling of membership in society as well as constructive
use of time that otherwise would be wasted) makes them highly satisfied.
This hardly means that they are ecstatically attached to their jobs; rather
their general mood has been well-described as one of "fatalistic contentment."

Other background factors were found to consistently relate to job satisfaction as well. Women, older people, those free of close supervision (no
matter what the occupational level) and those having an orderly work history
were among those showing greatest satisfaction from their work. Men in
occupations mainly filled by women (i.e., teachers, sales clerks) are less
satisfied with their job than other men. Form and Geschwender (1962) have
shown that one's reference group can seriously affect level of job satisfaction as well. Manual workers whose occupational level was lower than that
of their father's, brother's or peer's had higher rates of job dissatisfaction.
These authors also point out that age may spuriously affect the relations
found between satisfaction and age-related background variables (e.g.,
marital status, number of children, wages and tenure).

With these underlying trends already firmly established, it is time for
occupational research to turn away from the search for universal determinants
of job satisfaction from samples of single departments, single industries,
or single occupations, and to realize the need for amalgamating more intensive
investigation within single occupations. Such a program is exemplified by
Porter's (see the 1963 issues of the Journal of Applied Psychology for a
number of these articles) studies of salaried managers. Certainly no one
would immediately generalize his results to cover either machine operators or
professors. The major problem then becomes one of isolating the major dimensions on which work varies and locating the largest homogeneous occupational
groups in society on these dimensions in a more meaningful search for the
crucial determinants and consequences of job satisfaction.

2) Most of the attitudinal and some of the behavioral data we have
examined lead us to suggest a number of important separations within the
eight broad census categories usually used in social surveys. Further
suggestions based on other sources and types of data will be examined in the

final chapter of this volume. For now, we suggest the arrangement of occupations by satisfaction given in Table 10. While based on a somewhat restricted range of occupations (we simply did not have at our disposal enough satisfaction data on lawyers, doctors, etc.) and representing some arbitrary classifications, this arrangement is presented to summarize simply the vast amount of evidence reviewed. Differentiations within the nine occupational categories are probably more trustworthy than those between categories.

3) The greatest distinction in attitudes made in this chapter was between intrinsic and extrinsic satisfactions, differentiated in Appendix A. As noted independently by Herzberg, et al. (1958) and Gurin, et al. (1960), extrinsic factors were found to be more often mentioned as dissatisfying features of one's job while intrinsic factors were more often noted as satisfying features (Table 2, first column). There is a strong occupational status differential in the Gurin, et al. data, however, which mitigates this overall trend (see the replies to Question 6 in Table 2). Those in higher white-collar jobs more often named intrinsic satisfactions and dissatisfactions, while those in lower blue-collar jobs voiced more concern about extrinsic satisfactions and dissatisfactions. Thus, persons in occupations requiring more educational background are seen to be more aware of the intrinsic, or ego-involving aspects of work, and less concerned with the extrinsic or external circumstances. This result is scattered throughout previous job attitude literature. It can be found in Weiss and Kahn's (1960) investigation into the meaning of work, and appears more recently in an article by Friedlander (1965).

It may be that this class-related phenomenon explains as much or more variance in extrinsic-intrinsic satisfactions across studies than the Herzberg hypothesis which relates these factors to job satisfaction. This relation with status is evident in responses to closed-ended value statements (Appendix D) and open-ended questions regarding desirable or undesirable elements in an ideal job (Appendix C, left side), and things liked or disliked about one's present job (Appendix C, right side). Moreover, Centers and Bugental (1966) found that higher status workers cited intrinsic features of jobs as most important in keeping them on their present jobs and lower status workers noted extrinsic factors (Appendix E). Nevertheless, the better educated are more satisfied with both the intrinsic and extrinsic features of their job (Table 7).

Although these findings do not bear directly on confirmation or refutation of the Herzberg hypothesis, they do, as do a number of other recent studies (e.g., Burke, 1966), cast some doubt on its generalizeability and predictive power. Dunnette, Campbell and Hakel (1965) have compiled the clearest arguments against the Herzberg hypothesis, namely, 1) it is usually found with only one technique, the critical incidents method; 2) it can be explained in terms of people describing good events in terms of things they themselves had done and bad things in terms of external factors; 3) it is clearly meant as a causal model, yet there is little evidence available to support the notion that making job content more attractive will lead to increased job satisfaction. To circumvent the single method shortcoming, Dunnette, et al. devised more controlled Q-methodology techniques, whereby some of the objections of point (2) could be overcome (however, a large social desirability component still appeared in the data). While some trace of the Herzberg

Table 10

HYPOTHESIZED DIFFERENCES BETWEEN OCCUPATIONS IN JOB SATISFACTION

	SATISFACTION					
OCCUPATION	Most Satisfied	Very Satisfied	Satisfied	Ambivalent	Slightly Dissatisfied	Somewhat Dissatisfied
Professional-Technical	Professors Librarians School teachers (female)	Public Advisors Other people-oriented Nurses Artists	Scientists Accountants	Engineers School teachers (male)	Technicians	
Managerial	Salaried (upper mgmt)	Salaried (other)	Self-employed (large firm)		Self-employed (other)	
Sales			High-status	Sales clerks (women)		Sales clerks (men)
Clerical			Secretaries Bookkeepers	Misc. clerical		Repetitive clerical
Skilled			Foremen	Craftsmen	Skilled	
Semi-skilled				Higher	Middle	Repetitive
Unskilled						Laborers
Service		Protective	Armed	Household Other (women)		Other (men)
Farmer		Owner (large)	Owner (small)			Laborer

proposition did appear in their results, more detailed analysis made it clear that it is a "grossly oversimplified portrayal of the mechanism by which job satisfaction or dissatisfaction comes about." The intrinsic factors of achievement, responsibility, and recognition proved to be more important sources of both satisfaction and dissatisfaction than certain extrinsic factors (e.g., working conditions, security, company policies and practices).

If these results bear some resemblance to our class-related contention, the composition of the Dunnette, et al. sample may explain why. Although these authors laudibly tested their instrument on six different occupational groups, they failed to include any blue-collar groups (although lower white-collar employees were included). Thus, their results may merely boil down to the central observation that intrinsic factors are more important to white-collar workers; and, in fact, a good deal of the literature supporting the Herzberg two-factor theory may reduce to this class-related phenomenon. It will be recalled that just the opposite stance was taken in reviewing Kornhauser's objections; i.e., Kornhauser found extrinsic factors to be more satisfying within the routine and repetitive occupations in the blue-collar world.

The Dunnette, et al. controlled methods do allow some ordering of the separate types of factors (it is interesting to see the achievement related factor coming out highest) which is not feasible with the arbitrary codes used in the representative samples we have examined to date. Moreover, there is much merit in having respondents look at a single incident at a time. The twelve sets of factors (six intrinsic, six extrinsic) which they isolated are important contributions to defining a proper universe of content for job satisfaction, and the entire set of items used is included in the scales dealing with general job satisfaction.

The primary purpose of this chapter, however, has been not so much to offer definitive contributions to theories about job satisfaction as it has been to pull together the variety of questions and instruments that have been used on representative cross-section samples. Replies to open-ended questions (as given in Appendices A and C) from representative samples, we think, are especially valuable in delineating the range of topics that ought to be covered when constructing closed-ended instruments; and we will be rating job satisfaction scales on such considerations in our scale evaluation section.

It is hoped that future researchers will avail themselves of the data in this chapter, both in comparing results from non-representative samples with those contained here, and in using these figures as benchmark data for future studies using representative samples. The dramatic differences between middle-class and working-class attitudes should underscore our opening comment: merely making the wording of an attitude question constant does not ensure that it will mean the same thing to all people. The working-class mentality represents perhaps the greatest frontier area in attitudinal research.

REFERENCES

Argyris, C. The organization: what makes it healthy. _Harvard Business Review_, November 1958, 107-116.

Bakke, E. _Citizens without work_. New Haven: Yale University Press, 1940.

Blauner, R. Work satisfaction and industrial trends in modern society. In Galenson, W. and Lipset, S. (Eds.), _Labor and trade unionism_. New York: Wiley, 1960.

Blauner, R. _Alienation and freedom: the factory worker and his industry_. Chicago: University of Chicago Press, 1964.

Burke, R. Are Herzberg's motivators and hygienes unidimensional? _Journal of Applied Psychology_, 1966, _50_, 317-321.

Cantril, H. _The pattern of human concerns_. New Brunswick, N.J.: Rutgers University Press, 1965.

Centers, R. and Bugental, Daphne. Intrinsic and extrinsic job motivations among different segments of the working population. _Journal of Applied Psychology_, June 1966, 193-197.

Chinoy, Ely. The tradition of opportunity and aspiration of American automobile workers. _American Journal of Sociology_, March 1952, 454.

Clelland, D. The impact of changing occupational distribution on community attitudes and patterns of participation. Paper read at 61st Annual Meeting of the American Sociological Association, 1966.

Converse, P. Attitudes and non-attitudes: continuation of a dialogue. Ann Arbor, Michigan: Survey Research Center, 1963.

Converse, P. and Robinson, J. _The structure and meaning of time use_, in press.

Dunnette, M., Campbell, J. and Hakel, M. Factors contributing to job satisfaction and job dissatisfaction in six occupational groups. Minneapolis: University of Minnesota, Department of Psychology (mimeo), 1965.

England G. and Stein, C. The occupational reference group--a neglected concept in employee attitude studies. _Personnel Psychology_, 1961, _14_, 299-304.

Form, W. and Geschwender, J. Social reference basis of job satisfaction: the case of manual workers. _American Sociological Review_, April 1962, _27_, 228-237.

Friedlander, F. Comparative work value systems. _Personnel Psychology_, 1965, _18_, 1-20.

Gross, N., Mason, W. and McEachern, A. Explorations in role analysis.
        New York: Wiley, 1958.

Gurin, G., Veroff J. and Feld, Sheila. Americans view their mental health.
        New York: Basic Books, 1960.

Guttman, L. A general nonmetric technique for finding the smallest Euclidian
        space for a configuration of points. Psychometrika, 1966 (in press).

Herzberg, F. Work and the nature of man. Cleveland: World Publishing Company,
        1966.

Herzberg, F., Mausner, B., Peterson, R. and Capwell, Dora. Job attitudes:
        review of research and opinions. Pittsburgh: Psychological Services,
        1957.

Hodge, R., Treiman, D. and Rossi, P. A comparative study of occupational
        prestige. In Bendix and Lipset (eds.), Class, status, and power.
        New York: Free Press, 1966.

Inkeles, A. Industrial man: the relation of status to experience, perception
        and value. American Journal of Sociology, July 1960, 1-31.

Kahn, R., Wolfe, D., Quinn, R. and Snoek, J. Organizational stress. New York:
        Wiley, 1964.

Kilpatrick, F., Cummings, M. and Jennings, M. The image of the federal service.
        Washington, D.C.: The Brookings Institution, 1964.

Kornhauser, A. Mental health of the industrial worker. New York: Wiley, 1965.

Marsh, J. and Stafford, F. Income foregone: the effects of values on pecuniary
        behavior. Chicago: National Opinion Research Corporation, 1966.

Morse, Nancy. Satisfactions in the white-collar job. Ann Arbor, Michigan:
        Survey Research Center, 1953.

Pearlin, L. and Kohn, M. Social class, occupation and parental values: a
        coss-national study. American Sociological Review, August 1966, 466-
        479.

Rosenberg, M. Occupations and values. Glencoe, Illinois: Free Press, 1957.

Schaffer, R. Job satisfaction as related to need satisfaction in work.
        Psychological Monographs, 1953, 67, Whole Number 364.

Schletzer, Vera. SVIB as a predictor of job satisfaction. Journal of Applied
        Psychology, February 1966, 5-8.

Veroff, J. and Feld, Sheila. Motives and Roles. In press.

Wattenberg, B. and Scammon, R. This U.S.A. Garden City, New York: Doubleday, 1965.

Weiss, R. and Kahn, R. Definitions of work and occupation. Social Problems, Fall 1960, 142-151.

Wilensky, H. Varieties of work experience. In Borow (Ed.), Man in a world at work. Boston, Mass.: Houghton Miflin, 1964.

Zdravomyslov, A. and Iadov, V. An attempt at a concrete study of attitude toward work. Soviet Sociology, 1964, Vol. III, No. 4, 3-15.

Appendix A

GURIN, et al. CODE CATEGORIES FOR RESPONSES TO QUESTIONS CONCERNING THINGS
LIKED AND DISLIKED ABOUT JOB
1958 Data: Gurin, et al. 1960; 1966 Data: Converse and Robinson, in press

	1958		1966		1966 Leave job because of
	Likes	Dislikes	Likes	Dislikes	
EXTRINSIC					
Economic					
11. Wages, salary, money	12%	12%	13%	5%	38%
12. Job security, retirement benefits, pension	3	3	4	1	9
19. Other economic	1	1	1	0	0
Non-economic					
21. Company, work conditions (general)	2	0	1	0	1
22. Work pressure, ease of work	6	6	2	4	3
23. Physical work	-	4	1	2	2
24. Convenience: place of work, hours of work	7	11	4	8	5
25. Employee benefits: free lunches; medical care	1	0	1	0	1
26. Physical working conditions	6	7	5	6	2
27. Work hours, amount of work	-	5	1	6	5
29. Other non-economic extrinsic	5	10	3	3	2
INTRINSIC					
Achievement related					
31. Responsibility, chance to make decisions	3	1	2	0	1
33. Complexity: figuring out things, problems	2	1	4	0	2
35. Use of abilities and talents	2	1	3	0	4
36. Competence and accomplishment	5	1	4	0	2
37. Reward and recognition from others	1	2	1	1	7
39. Other achievement related	2	1	4	1	2
Affiliation related					
41. Contact with people; being with people	20	0	29	0	2
43. Particular people on the job (except friends or boss)	13	5	3	4	1
44. Friendships	1	0	0	0	0
45. Superiors, boss, foreman	7	4	2	2	1
46. Helping people	5	1	4	0	0
49. Other affiliation related	1	2	1	2	1
Influence related					
51. Independence, influence, being own boss	7	2	5	2	1
52. Restraint by others, being pushed around, pressured	4	2	2	0	1
53. Leadership, supervising	1	0	1	0	0
54. Prestige, status	1	0	0	0	1
55. Teaching	1	0	1	0	0
59. Other influence related	0	1	0	0	1
Curiosity related					
61. Novelty, new things	8	2	12	0	2
62. Chance to learn things	2	0	2	0	1
63. Interesting work	7	1	6	4	5
69. Other curiosity related	1	0	1	0	3

Appendix B

DIFFERENCES BETWEEN PAST, PRESENT AND FUTURE RATINGS OF OCCUPATION
ON SELF-ANCHORING SCALE (Kilpatrick, et al. 1964)

Occupation	Employed Public		Federal Employees		College Teachers	
	Past[a]	Future[b]	Past	Future	Past	Future
All employees	0.7	1.0	0.9	1.1	1.0	0.5
Farmers	0.4	0.4				
Unskilled/semiskilled	0.5	1.0	0.5	1.4		
Skilled	1.0	0.7	0.8	1.0		
Clerical	1.1	1.3	0.9	1.2		
Professional/managerial	1.0	0.9	1.0	0.8		
Executives	1.3	0.8	1.0	0.9		
Natural scientists	1.0	0.9	1.4	0.8	1.1	0.5
Social scientists	1.8	1.1	1.2	1.1	1.1	0.6
Engineers	1.2	0.9	1.2	0.8	0.9	0.7
High school teachers	1.0	0.6				
Vocational counselors	0.9	0.7				

[a]Past = differences between present rating of job (Table 3) and job 5 years ago. All differences are positive since present ratings are all higher than past ratings.

[b]Future = differences between rating of job 5 years hence and present job (Table 3). All differences are positive since future ratings are all higher than past ratings.

Appendix C

PROPORTIONS OF NATIONAL SAMPLE MENTIONING FEATURES OF HYPOTHETICALLY IDEAL AND ACTUAL JOBS, WITH RELATION TO EDUCATION (Kilpatrick, et al. 1964)

	Feature of ideal/worst job	As	Relation to education Posi-tive (Job Factor)	Nega-tive	Feature of present job positive/negative	As	Relation to education Posi-tive (Job Factor)	Nega-tive
EXTRINSIC								
Economic								
11. Wages, salary	45/27	} 60/36	0	-	33/32	} 45/40	-	-
12. Security	15/9		0	--	12/8		--	-
Non-economic								
21. Fringe benefits								
22. Working conditions	41/48		-	--	22/23		-	--
23. Equipment	6/3		0	0	2/5		-	0
24. Pressure/work load	0/21	} 67/100		--	0/7	} 28/35		--
25. Physical work	0/10			+	--			
26. Leisure, vacations	10/4		+	0	4/0		0	
27. Desirable location	6/4		-	+	--			
INTRINSIC								
Achievement								
31. Responsibility	5/1		+	+	4/2		++	+
32. Sense of challenge	7/2		++	+	4/0		++	
33. Self-development	4/1		+	+	3/2		0	0
34. Self-expression	6/2		++	++	2/0		++	
35. Uses talents, training	14/7	} 55/24	-	+	14/2	} 37/15	+	+
36. Self-advancement	8/6		+	+	6/9		+	-
37. Sense of accomplishment	8/3		+	++	4/0		+	
38. Recognition for work	3/2		++	+	--			
Affiliation								
41. Personal relations (passive)	12/11		0	+	11/2		0	0
42. Personal relations (active)	19/3	} 43/39	++	+	11/2	} 34/9	++	+
43. Personal relations (other)	1/7		0	+	--		+	
44. Superiors, boss	11/18		-	0	12/5		--	-
Influence								
51. Self-determination	29/15	} 31/15	+	+	15/7	} 15/7	++	+
52. Prestige	2/0		+		--			
Curiosity								
61. Variety in work	10/21	10/21	+	++	7/4	7/4	+	+
GENERAL								
71. Interest, enjoyment	72/55		-	-	37/12		+	-
76. Useful, worthwhile work	14/1	} 86/60	++	++	6/0	} 59/12	++	
78. General fulfillment	--				16/0		0	
79. Religious, ethical	0/4		+		--			
Average number of responses	3.5/2.9							

Appendix D

OCCUPATIONAL VALUE ITEMS, AVERAGE SCALE VALUES (NATIONAL SAMPLE) AND RELATION TO EDUCATION (Kilpatrick, et al. 1964)

	Average Scale Rating	Relation to Education
EXTRINSIC		
Economic		
5. To be really successful in life, you have to care about making money	5.8	--
7. After you are making enough money to get along, then making more money in an occupation isn't very important	4.9	+
24. I would like my family to be able to have most of the things my friends and neighbors have	7.4	-
26. To me, work is nothing more than a way of making a living	4.2	--
Non-economic		
12. Success in an occupation is mainly a matter of luck	3.6	--
35. Success in an occupation is mainly a matter of knowing the right people	5.0	--
53. I like the kind of work you can forget about after the work day is over	6.7	--
INTRINSIC		
Achievement		
6. Work is most satisfying when there are hard problems to solve	6.5	++
8. To me, it's important in an occupation to have the chance to get to the top	7.8	0
9. It's important to do a better job than the next person	6.9	0
11. Success in an occupation is mainly a matter of hard work	7.3	0
25. It is more important for a job to offer opportunity than security	5.9	++
30. It would be hard to live with the feeling that others are passing you up in your occupation	6.1	0
32. To me, it's important in an occupation that a person be able to see the results of his own work	8.4	+
33. Getting recognition for my own work is important to me	7.6	0
36. To me, it's important to have the kind of work that gives me a chance to develop my own special abilities	8.1	++
48. Sometimes it may be right for a person to lose friends in order to get ahead in his work	4.1	-
52. A person should constantly try to succeed at work, even if it interferes with other things in life	6.0	-
Affiliation		
21. To me, a very important part of work is the opportunity to make friends	7.4	0
22. The main satisfaction a person can get out of work is helping other people	6.9	+
Influence		
19. It is satisfying to direct the work of others	6.6	+
29. To me, it's important in an occupation for a person to be able to carry out his own ideas without interference	6.7	+
54. To me, gaining the increased respect of family and friends is one of the most important rewards of getting ahead in an occupation	7.6	0
GENERAL VALUES		
1. A person has a right to expect his work to be fun	6.2	0
16. Even if you dislike your work, you should do your best	8.3	0
17. If a person doesn't want to work hard, it's his own business	5.4	0
18. Work is a good builder of character	8.2	0
20. Work is a way of being of service to God	7.7	0
31. Work helps you forget about your personal problems	7.2	0
50. To me, almost the only thing that matters about a job is the chance to do work that is worthwhile to society	5.6	+

Appendix E

PERCENTAGE OF EACH OCCUPATION CHOOSING EACH FACTOR AS ONE OF THE <u>THREE</u>
MOST IMPORTANT IN KEEPING THEM IN THEIR PRESENT JOB: MEN AND WOMEN
(Centers and Bugental, 1966)

Factors	Professional Managerial	Clerical Sales	Skilled	Semi-skilled Unskilled
INTRINSIC				
Work is interesting	68%	62%	61%	50%
Use of skill or talent	64	48	51	35
Feeling of satisfaction	68	46	46	39
EXTRINSIC				
The pay	59	66	70	74
Good co-workers*	25	46	40	52
Always sure of having job	16	31	33	49
N =	217	183	98	135

*Coded as intrinsic factor in previous tables in this chapter.

Appendix F

JOB SATISFACTION AND THOUGHTS OF LEAVING JOB: MEN ONLY
(Converse and Robinson, in press)

		Job Satisfaction			
				Not at all	Think about
	N	Completely	Pretty	Not very	changing job
Professional					
Artist	4	75%	25%	0%	25%
Professors	3	33	67	0	33
Advising profession	25	52	40	8	28
School teacher	16	19	75	6	56
Scientist, physician	15	36	57	7	43
Accountant	10	10	90	0	60
Engineer	43	23	70	7	56
Technician	27	26	67	7	67
Managerial					
Self-employed (large firm)	20	40	55	5	25
Self-employed (other)	32	25	75	0	41
Salaries	53	49	45	6	40
Clerical					
Other clerical	62	19	66	15	45
Sales					
High status (goods)	10	0	90	10	70
High status (services)	9	22	57	22	67
Sales clerks	7	14	43	43	86
Other sales	4	0	100	0	75
Skilled					
Self-employed	8	50	25	25	50
Foremen	38	40	55	5	29
Other skilled	147	27	59	14	39
Semiskilled					
Operatives	171	23	60	17	49
Service					
Protective	21	48	48	4	19
Armed forces	8	50	38	12	63
Other	24	8	83	8	46
Unskilled					
Laborer	<u>32</u>	<u>25</u>	<u>56</u>	<u>19</u>	<u>32</u>
Total Sample	789	28	60	12	44

4. JOB ATTITUDES AND OCCUPATIONAL PERFORMANCE:
A REVIEW OF SOME IMPORTANT LITERATURE

by Robert Athanasiou

With the decline of Frederick Taylor's (1911) "scientific management," a more humanistic approach (in some respects at least) to the effective utilization of manpower arose. Taylor's pragmatic and essentially pessimistic approach was based on the assumptions that workers were motivated primarily by money and that they were essentially "stupid and phlegmatic." He was little concerned with what the worker thought or whether he enjoyed his work. Taylor's ideas would surely be anachronistic if applied in today's world of high employment, highly mobile workforces, labor unions, and enlightened management.

We have shifted from Taylor's pessimism to a more hedonic reference frame, from solely monetarily induced motivation to psychological motivation of workers. While wages and fringe benefits still represent valid rewards, management is frequently concerned also with providing work experience satisfying in other respects as well. However, such concern is seldom altruistic.

Relation between Attitudes and Performance

It has long been the hope of those associated with the fields of management and industrial psychology that a firm relationship might be established between workers' attitudes and the various aspects of job performance. Unfortunately for the exponents of attitude psychology, the evidence for such a relationship is equivocal at best. Herzberg, et al. (1957, p. 99) cite fourteen studies showing a positive relation between morale and productivity, nine studies showing no relation, and three studies showing an inverse relation. While such a state of affairs seems paradoxical, a simple explanation may be available.

Methodological considerations are of prime importance in resolving this apparent paradox. There are many problems associated with the adequacy and validity of the measures of both productivity and attitudes in this area. Prior to the mid-1950's it is somewhat a rare event to discover a study in which the predictive value of instruments has been cross validated. The question of the validity and reliability of the criterion measure (i.e., productivity) in many of the studies remains moot. Even the basic assumptions concerning the nature and definition of the "morale" factors differ from author to author. It is the feeling of many investigators that "morale" is a term too loosely applied to independent aspects of job attitudes. The relatively simple dichotomy of morale factors into satisfaction and motivation components is a very useful distinction. Motivation implies the willingness to work or produce; satisfaction implies a positive emotional state which may be totally unrelated to productivity. As Katz and Kahn (1965) point out, many workers like their jobs merely because they are "a nice place to be." Most attitude studies to date have not attempted to separate motivational from emotional factors and have considered "morale" to be some undifferentiated combination of both or either one alone.

Several work related attitude scales have been derived on a strictly empirical basis with a minimum of theorizing. A number of such scales are presented in the latter portion of this review. These instruments typically begin as a large pool of assorted attitude and/or personality items. Through more or less standard item analysis techniques a portion of the pooled items is selected for use in a scale. The selection technique varies considerably in its rationale, efficiency, and validity from one study to the next, as do the type and quality of samples on which they are based. There is a general paucity of cross-validation efforts which tends to cause one to take most validity claims for these scales with the proverbial grain of salt.

Another major drawback with such scales is the lack of sound theoretical deduction prior to analyzing the results. In many studies the rationale for relating a group of items to some criterion is arrived at after data analysis. This is analogous to gauging the accuracy of a shotgun by analyzing only those pellets which hit the target. While such an approach can yield some results, it is frequently as important to know why and how many of the other pellets did not reach the target.

The shotgun approach to scale building may provide us with numerous valuable instruments for predicting behavior. And the pragmatic psychologist will maintain that in this case the means are irrelevant as long as the end is accomplished. It is rare, however, that such an approach will serve to significantly advance a science or explain in meaningful terms why we are able to measure and predict certain traits.

Even an unloaded shotgun may go off accidentally--that is, the empirical method of scale construction is not foolproof and may yield results which are quite misleading. Of the many that may be cited, one clear example of poor marksmanship and inept handling is found in the scale entitled "A Work Attitude Key for MMPI" (Tydlaska and Mengel, p.331). This study compares employees of a civilian chemical company with a sample of air force personnel (largely AWOL cases) and ignores common sense and APA standards[1] regarding comparison groups. Not only are the statistical techniques inadequately described (though a nonparametric measure was used) but derived scores were used for prediction purposes on the original population instead of an attempt at cross validation.[2] In short, even this instrument, which on the face of

---

[1]"If the validity of a test is demonstrated by comparing groups that differ on the criterion, the manual should report whether and by how much the groups differ on other available variables that are relevant. VERY DESIRABLE (Comment: Since groups which differ on a criterion may also differ in other respects, the test may be discriminating on a quality other than that intended. Types of mental disorder, for instance, are associated with age, education, and length of time in hospital. Confounding of this sort should be taken into account when appraising the usefulness of the test for diagnosis.)" (American Psychological Association, "Technical Recommendations," Washington, D. C., 1954)

[2]"When a scoring key or the selection of items is based on a tryout sample, the manual should report validity coefficients based on one or more separate cross-validation samples, rather than on the tryout sample or on a larger group of which the tryout sample is a part. ESSENTIAL" (APA, op. cit.)

things seems to follow a rather thorough empirical method of test construction, violates some of the most essential rules of scale building.

The confusion of methodology, hypotheses, samples, analysis systems, etc., makes it very difficult to compare studies or to ascertain whether one study supports or denies the findings of another. Even reviews of the literature show considerable deviation from one another with regard to the criteria for selecting studies and the variables of interest.

This report avoids taking a stand on just which variables should or should not be considered, or how they should be weighted, etc. There is, however, a growing consensus regarding the construction of useful indexes (e.g., absence rate, turnover rate, etc.) for research in the field of job attitudes. These indexes are discussed at length by Vroom (1964) whose book is commented on below.

The remainder of this chapter includes summaries of several reviews of the literature on job attitudes, a short discussion of the role of occupational choice, and some brief remarks on miscellaneous job attitude scales and their potential value.

Previous Literature Reviews

A number of valuable reviews of the literature have been written in the area of job attitudes. Brayfield and Crockett (1955) in their review hold to a fairly strict empirical approach and raise many questions which are still relevant to present investigations. In critically reviewing many studies, they emphasize the necessity for adequate consideration of procedural problems, analysis and design, and selection of criterion measures. Related to the methodological issue is the problem of whether to use the individual or the group as the unit of analysis in relating performance to satisfaction. Individual-level analysis requires a knowledge of each individual's performance and attitude scores, while group-level analysis is concerned with relating a group average opinion score with a measure of group productivity. There are, of course, distinct advantages to the individual-level approach especially with regard to meaningfully relating the psychological variable of attitudes to other variables such as absenteeism, tardiness, and accidents. A problem may arise, however, if an individual does not feel his psychological anonymity will be guaranteed. Writing about the Science Research Associates' Attitude Survey, Zardis (personal communication) favors the group approach, saying "...Because their /the employees/ anonymity is guaranteed comments are frank and sincere, yielding further important insights to management." Implicit in both the individual and group approaches is the assumption that biasing factors in production machinery, shift work, etc., will be adequately controlled.

After an extensive review of the literature, Brayfield and Crockett (op. cit.) conclude "...it appears that there is little evidence in the available literature that employee attitudes of the type usually measured in a morale survey bear any simple--or, for that matter, appreciable-- relationship to performance on the job."

Herzberg, Mausner, Peterson and Capwell (1957) in their review display
a more catholic viewpoint than do Brayfield and Crockett. Listing well over
1,000 references, Herzberg, et al. examine job attitude studies under the
various headings of job dissatisfaction, effects of attitudes, factors related to job attitudes, supervision of job attitudes, vocational selection
and job attitudes, and mental health in industry. The authors frequently
pull together, in a reasonably concise manner, the results of several
studies and state what would appear to be an elemental piece of knowledge.
This is not an easy thing to do in view of the problems mentioned above.
Nevertheless, an attempt at a synthesis of theory and empirical findings is
essential to the growth of knowledge in any area.

They conclude after thorough review "...that positive job attitudes are
a tremendous asset to industry is /a contention/ supported by much of the experimental evidence now available." In support of this statement they point
to "unequivocal" evidence of the relation of attitudes to turnover, absenteeism
and accidents (see pages 104-107 of their work for references).

The major differences between the Brayfield and Crockett article and the
one by Herzberg, et al. is succinctly summed up by Katzell writing in the
Annual Review of Psychology (1957, p. 243-244). He points out that the two
studies do not cover exactly the same literature, that their respective
definitions of "performance" differ and that Brayfield and Crockett are more
exacting in their criteria for including studies in their review. Katzell
further states "...perhaps the main disparity is that Brayfield and Crockett
state their generalization prior to their consideration of the parameters
involved in the relationships between attitudes and performance, whereas
Herzberg, et al. more appropriately take such influence into account in
arriving at their overall judgment." (Emphasis ours.)

An issue considered by both sets of authors is the nature of the
relationships among satisfaction, motivation, production, etc., for which
investigators might search. Brayfield and Crockett suggest that the assumption of a monotonic relation between production and satisfaction be re-examined
Fisher (1956) has also suggested questioning this assumption in his fruitful
discussion of the "twisted pear." Many of the predictions in the job satisfactions and performance area are based on the use of a linear homoscedastic
(equal variance) model which is assumed to be applicable to most psychological
data. Fisher points out that this model may be one of the least common and
suggests that the nonlinear heteroscedastic model be examined. While the
latter model may not explain a great deal more it is certainly more accurate
in the description of many observed relationships. For example, the linear
homoscedastic model assumes that if high job satisfaction is associated with
high production then low satisfaction should be associated with low production
That is, in an m by n matrix our predictions along the diagonal should be
equally accurate from cell to cell. The reality of the situation, however,
is such that we may accurately predict high production given high satisfaction but cannot as accurately predict low production given low satisfaction.
Correlational statistics measuring the magnitude of the relationship between
predictor (e.g., satisfaction) and criterion (e.g., production) give an
average statement of the predictive power without adequate consideration of
possible non-linearity or heteroscedasticity. The result is a coefficient
which may be considered to be somewhat attenuated. This condition is

illustrated below in a scattergram of a non-linear heteroscedastic function adapted from Fisher (ibid.).

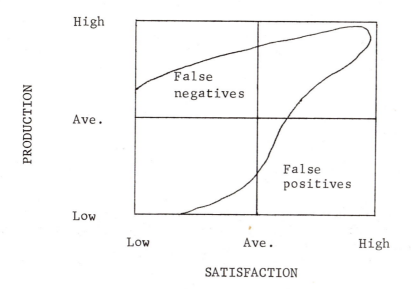

In the hypothetical case represented above, it is clear that high satisfaction is a good predictor of high production. On the other hand, low satisfaction tells us very little about production. Due to the wide variation evident on the left side of the figure, the Pearson r characterizing this relationship would be quite low. It is also evident that the false positive and false negative rates are highly sensitive to this configuration.

There are at least two ways in which the prediction problem may be attacked. One alternative is to simply disregard low scores, consider them unreliable, and give greater weight to high scores. A second approach would be to use multiple predictors, some of which functioned well at the low and others at the high end. Combining such scores on a multiple cut-off basis should, theoretically at least, greatly reduce prediction problems.

Herzberg, Mausner, and Snyderman (1959) have attacked the problem by advancing the hypothesis that there are some factors which are job satisfiers and others which are job dissatisfiers. Job content factors (e.g., achievement, recognition, responsibility) seem to contribute to satisfaction while a deficiency of context factors ("extrinsic" factors such as pay, hours, supervisory practices) in a job seems to contribute to dissatisfaction. Thus the two factors are supposed to function relatively independently of each other. Supporting data for this hypothesis was provided by Gurin, Veroff, and Feld's study (1960) of a nationwide probability sample.

A deficit of intrinsic or content factors, according to the theory of Herzberg, et al. can reduce satisfaction but a surplus of extrinsic factors will <u>not</u> increase satisfaction. Gordon (1965) and Halpern (1965) have reported testing these hypotheses with varying success. In particular, Halpern reported that the mean level of satisfaction was the same for both intrinsic and extrinsic factors although the intrinsic factors accounted for significantly more variance in the measure of overall satisfaction than did the extrinsic.

Burke (1966), in a review of the literature relevant to the Herzberg thesis, has suggested that the two factors (variously called intrinsic-extrinsic, content-context, and motivator-hygiene) may not be either independent or unidimensional. Table 1, adopted in its entirety from Burke's article, shows the varied and ambiguous findings which researchers have come up with in this area.

Some authors have not been gracious in their evaluation of the Herzberg, et al. hypotheses. A "theory-gelding" paper by Dunnette, Campbell and Hakel (1966) contends:

> ...that the two factor theory is shackled to the storytelling method and that the theory's proponents are now more concerned with the game....of protecting and nurturing this pet theory than in advancing knowledge about job motivation and job satisfaction. This is a serious charge; it probably stems as much as anything from our own feeling of disenchantment with the theory-guilding (sic) turn of events.

These authors further state "...that the two factor theory should be laid to rest so as to reduce the danger of further research or administrative decisions being dictated by its seductive simplicity."

Evidence for and against the Herzberg hypothesis is still accumulating and in this regard Vroom's (1964) comment is still relevant:

> Herzberg's conclusion that the variance in job satisfaction below some hypothetical level can be explained in terms of one set of variables can neither be accepted nor rejected... at this time. Corroboration of his position will require... experimental evidence of nonlinearity in relationships, a problem that is worthy of much more attention than it has received. Regardless of the outcome, Herzberg and his associates deserve credit for directing attention toward the psychological effects of job content, a problem of great importance in a world of rapidly changing technology.

Vroom (ibid.) has provided an excellent review of the literature regarding the determinants of job satisfaction and the relation of satisfaction to production. Vroom points out that much of the research in the past twenty five years has been concerned with providing "...a general picture of a 'satisfying work role.'" He further comments that while knowledge of work roles is valuable, it does not sufficiently explain the etiology of satisfaction or dissatisfaction. Personality factors (other than pathologies or maladjustment) in interaction with environmental factors might reasonably be expected to account for significantly more variance in the prediction of job satisfaction than either one alone. As Vroom suggests, "...A greater exchange between psychologists interested in occupational choice and job satisfaction would expedite the discovery of interactions between personality and work role variables. Conceivably, the psychological conditions which make a work role

TABLE 1

SUMMARY OF INVESTIGATIONS ATTEMPTING TO REPLICATE OR EXTEND HERZBERG'S THEORY (From Burke 1966)

Investigator	Subjects	Procedure	Findings
Friedlander (1963)	Engineers, supervisors, and salaried employees of a large manufacturing firm (200 of each)	Factor analysis of a 17-item questionnaire measuring the importance of various job characteristics to employee satisfaction	Three meaningful factors emerged. Two corresponded, in part, with motivators and hygienes, while the third seemed to draw from both motivators and hygienes.
Rosen (1963)	94 research and development personnel of varying specialties, educational levels, and organizational levels	Respondents rated the importance of the absence of 118 items to their desiring to leave their present position	Many of the most important items which if not present would cause the individual to seek other employment were similar to Herzberg's motivators.
Schwartz, Jenusaitis, & Stark (1963)	111 male supervisors employed by 21 public utility companies	Content analysis of written stories describing pleasant and unpleasant job experiences	Motivators were generally associated with pleasant experiences and hygienes with unpleasant experiences. One Herzberg motivator acted like a hygiene in this sample.
Ewen (1964)	1,021 full-time life in insurance agents divided into an experimental sample (541) and a cross-validation sample (480)	Factor analysis of a 58-item attitude scale completed by the experimental sample	Six interpretable factors emerged, of which three were hygienes and two motivators. Two of the three hygienes acted like motivators in both samples; the other hygiene acted like a motivator in the cross-validation sample, and like both a motivator and a hygiene in the experimental sample. One motivator acted both as a motivator and a hygiene.
Friedlander (1964)	80 students in an evening course in industrial or child psychology (part were full-time employees in various occupations and part were members of a cooperative work-study program)	Respondents rated the importance of 18 variables to job satisfaction and job dissatisfaction	The results indicated that motivators and hygienes are not opposite ends of a common set of dimensions. The majority of these job characteristics seemed to be significant contributors to both satisfaction and dissatisfaction on the job.
Friedlander & Walton (1964)	82 scientists and engineers in various specialties	Semistructured interviews in which respondents were asked for the most important factors keeping them in the organization and factors that might cause them to leave the organization	Reasons for remaining in an organization (primarily motivators) were different from, and not merely opposite to, the reason for which one might leave an organization (primarily hygienes).
Lodahl (1964)	50 male auto-assembly workers, and 29 female electronics-assembly workers	Factor analysis of data obtained from a content analysis of interviews	Two technological and three attitude factors emerged. The technological factors were different for the two samples, but the attitude factors corresponded rather well. Two of the three attitude factors resembled motivators and hygienes.
Myers (1964)	282 male scientists, engineers, manufacturing supervisors, and hourly technicians, and 52 female hourly assemblers	Content analysis of Herzberg-like interviews	Job characteristics grouped naturally into motivator-hygiene dichotomies. However one Herzberg motivator acted like a hygiene and other Herzberg motivators acted both as motivators and hygienes. Different job levels had different job characteristic configurations. The female configuration was different from the four male configurations, suggesting a sex factor. Common Herzberg motivators were absent from the hourly technician and hourly female assembler configurations suggesting a job-level factor.
Saleh (1964)	85 male employees at managerial levels in 12 companies	Herzberg-like interview, and a 16-item job-attitude scale (6 motivators and 10 hygienes) presented in a paired-comparison format	Preretirees looking backward in their careers indicated motivators as sources of satisfaction and hygienes as sources of dissatisfaction; preretiree looking at the time left before retirement indicated hygienes as sources of satisfaction.
Dunnette (1965)	114 store executives, 74 sales clerks, 43 secretaries, 128 engineers and research scientists, 46 salesmen, 91 army reserve personnel and employed adults enrolled in a supervision course	Factor analysis of Q sorts of two sets of 36 statements (equated for social desirability) for highly satisfying and highly dissatisfying job situations	Some Herzberg motivators were related to satisfying job situations but Herzberg hygienes were not related to dissatisfying job situations. One Herzberg motivator acted like a hygiene. There was also a positive relationship expected under Herzberg's theory. Thus the same factors were contributors to both satisfaction and dissatisfaction.
Friendlander (1965)	1,468 civil service workers from three status levels (Low, Middle, and High GS rankings) and two occupational levels (blue collar and white collar)	Factor analysis of a 14-item questionnaire measuring the importance of various job characteristics to satisfaction and dissatisfaction	White-collar workers derived greatest satisfaction from motivators while blue-collar workers derived greatest satisfaction from hygienes suggesting that subgroups may have different work-value systems.
Gordon (1965)	683 full-time agents of a large national, life insurance company	Respondents rated their degree of satisfaction and dissatisfaction with 54 items comprising 4 scales (motivators, hygienes, both, hygienes minus both). A measure of overall job satisfaction, self-reported production figures, and survival data were also available	Contrary to expectations, individuals highly satisfied with motivators did not have greater overall job satisfaction than individuals highly satisfied with hygienes; and individuals highly dissatisfied with hygienes were not less satisfied than individuals dissatisfied with motivators. A positive relationship was found between satisfaction with motivators and self-reported production, but no relationship between hygienes and production. This study offered no support to the theory that specific job factors effect attitudes in only one direction. Support is offered that primarily the motivators bring about superior performance.
Halpern (1965)	93 male college graduates working in various occupations	Rating of satisfaction with 4 motivators, 4 hygienes, and overall job satisfaction on respondent's best-liked job	Although the respondents were equally satisfied with both the motivator and hygiene aspects of their jobs, the motivators contributed significantly more to overall job satisfaction than did the hygienes.
Wernimont (1966)	50 accountants and 82 engineers	Self-description of past satisfying and dissatisfying job situations using both forced-choice and free-choice items	More motivators than hygienes were used to describe both job situations. Concludes that both motivators and hygienes can be sources of job satisfaction and job dissatisfaction.

attractive to a person just about to enter the labor market are analogous or identical to those who (sic) make it attractive to its occupant."

Effects of Specific Factors on Satisfaction as a Dependent Variable

Wages. In his review, Vroom discusses the effects on job satisfaction of supervision, work group, job content, promotional opportunities, hours of work, and wages. Experimental (as opposed to survey) data on the extrinsic factor of wages is of special interest since several recent findings are not in accordance with "common sense." For example, under certain work and commitment conditions, dissonance theory (Festinger, 1957, and Brehm and Cohen, 1962) predictions indicate greater satisfaction and/or performance to be associated with inequitable levels of pay. Adams (1964) and Athanasiou (1965) have investigated such hypotheses and found evidence supporting a dissonance theory interpretation. Much of the evidence attempting to relate wage levels to satisfaction is conflicting and confusing. Higher wage levels are frequently associated with factors such as experience, job level, productivity, etc., which may also have an effect on satisfaction.

The most cautious statement one may make is that many executives and economists may overestimate the significance of wages and that many social scientists may underestimate their importance. The contribution made by wages to satisfaction (or lack of dissatisfaction) may depend on such factors as their level in relation to living standards, their level compared with the level for other similar jobs and persons, and their level in relation to other needs such as security, etc. The data available on wages and satisfaction do not permit an analysis encompassing all the factors mentioned above. One frequent finding which may shed a ray of light on the problem is the observation that wages are frequently rated low on a list of job satisfiers but high on a list of dissatisfiers. One can only speculate as to the effect which something such as a guaranteed minimum income might have on satisfaction or dissatisfaction.

Supervisory Style. The search for a simple unitary relationship between styles of supervision and job satisfaction seems unlikely to be ended in the near future. There is really no reason to assume that such a relationship should exist, albeit in our culture implicit value judgments are made regarding the value of participative democratic supervision. It seems reasonable to suppose that different modes of supervision should be required for different jobs. Scientists in a research organization might be most satisfied under a laissez-faire system while construction workers might not. Vroom cites a study by Baumgartel (Vroom, 1964, p. 115) which indicated that scientists under directive leadership had less positive attitudes toward their director than those operating under laissez-faire or participative styles. The attitudes of the latter two groups were mixed.

Without attempting to duplicate Vroom's extensive review of the literature regarding supervision and satisfaction, it is probably reasonable to say that the type of supervision which will produce the most satisfaction in a given group of workers is one which is keyed to the nature of the job, the needs and personalities of the workers, and the personalities of the managers. To say that participative management or high consideration management or democratic supervision is always best extends conclusions far beyond available data.

Group Effects. Work group effects involving degree of interaction, group cohesion, and goal interdependence have long been recognized as important variables in production as well as in satisfaction studies. Regardless of the level of morale or satisfaction, a cohesive group will be productive only if the group's goals include a high production level. The interaction effect is dependent in part on group size, and several studies have indicated that large work groups frequently have lower morale and cohesiveness than smaller groups. Vroom covers many of the studies in this area and the interested reader is referred to his excellent text for further information.

Job Content. Job content factors have been the source of considerable interest for an extended period of time. The essentially visceral reaction most industrial psychologists display toward the dehumanizing effect of the assembly line is echoed in the many polls and studies investigating workers' attitudes toward "the line." Chase (1962) summarizes the results of a survey in a Connecticut automobile assembly plant:

> The survey showed, too, that the men hated being paced by a machine rather than by their own working rhythm....Many said that they were bored to the limit of endurance. "The job is so sickening, day in and day out plugging in ignition wires. I get through one motor, turn around, and there's another motor staring me in the face." ...The men said they had no chance to develop personal skills, and this made them feel stupid and inferior.

The men interviewed in this study cited by Chase had few grievances against the equipment, plant, supervision or working conditions--but many hated their job! Findings such as these tend to support the Herzberg theory that job context factors cannot create satisfaction if there is a deficit of job content factors.[3]

The relation between satisfaction and job content is, of course, more easily described in the non-technical manual job. There is considerable evidence, however, suggesting that the same relation exists in higher level and managerial jobs. The issue of self-actualization is one which crosses hierarchical divisions and social classes. Furthermore, the capacity for self-actualization is a function of both the job and the worker. In an economy such as our at present, in which satisfaction of the great majority of our physiological and safety needs are met, the importance of higher order needs such as self esteem, autonomy, and self-actualization becomes greater. It is certainly greater now than it was in either the Depression or Recovery periods of the 1930's and 40's.

---

[3]It may be that the nature of the job should not be emphasized to the exclusion of the consideration of personality factors. Fournet, et al. (1966) point out that while "...repetitiveness provides the opportunity for boredom..../whether/ the individual worker becomes bored with a repetitive job, however, depends on his resources for counteracting monotony within himself."

Organizational Structure Variables

Porter and Lawler (1965) have emphasized several new dimensions to the study of attitudes in industrial settings. Almost without exception the studies and review articles cited previously have largely ignored structural variables in the employing firm and their relations to employee attitudes. In their discussion of these variables, Porter and Lawler (p. 24) define structure "...to mean the positions and parts of organizations and their systematic and relatively enduring relationships to each other." They refer "...to the formal structure or organizations as might be indicated...in the formal 'organization chart.'" Seven structural properties are discussed as "independent variables," namely:

Sub-organization properties

1) Organizational levels
2) Line and staff hierarchies
3) Span of control
4) Size: subunits

Total-organization properties

5) Size: total organizations
6) Shape: tall or flat
7) Shape: centralized or decentralized

The first four are intra-organizational while the last three are inter-organizational variables. The seven variables are not necessarily independent though they have typically been investigated separately.

Porter and Lawler note that there is sufficient evidence to suggest that organizational level has a recognizable effect on morale. "Recent studies...seem to be nearly unanimous in concluding that job satisfaction or morale does increase monotonically with increasing levels of management, and that therefore middle managers are more satisfied than those below them in the organization but less satisfied than those above." Porter's own work (1962, 1963) tends to confirm this statement and shows that the pattern of needs and motives which comprise the potential for job satisfaction varies with management level. A fourteen country study of managerial attitudes by Haire, Ghiselli and Porter (cited in Porter and Lawler, 1965) gives an indication that the general pattern of greater satisfaction with increasing organization level holds true on an international basis as well.

Other attitudes showing changes with organizational level are inner-directedness (Porter and Henry, 1964) and Fleishman's (1953) consideration-structure factors. As one progresses higher in the organization greater emphasis seems to be put on inner-directedness and the initiation of structure.

With regard to line-staff hierarchies, Porter and Lawler report that available data confirm the reasonable expectations that people in line positions experience greater satisfaction and that persons in staff positions report a greater emphasis on other-directed traits. A finding by Dalton (cited by Porter and Lawler) supports the relation mentioned earlier between turnover and satisfaction. "...Dalton found that staff managers in three plants had a turnover rate between two and four times that of line managers."

•

With some reservations concerning methodology and subject selection, Porter and Lawler contend "...that subunit size is significantly related to differences in job attitudes. The evidence is strong that workers in small departments and work groups are better satisfied than workers in large departments and work groups...." It is interesting to note that the preponderance of studies cited by the authors show a positive relation between subunit size and accidents, absences, and turnover while at the same time showing a negative relation between subunit size and job satisfaction. It is not possible, however, to determine from these data the relation between satisfaction and the latter three variables.

The data available on the effect of total organization size do not demonstrate a very clear relationship between attitudes and gross size. Major factors in this lack of clarity are the contaminating effects of subunit size and changing patterns of attitudes between management levels--factors which none of the studies controlled. Nevertheless, Porter and Lawler cite a few studies which show some indications that satisfaction is negatively related to size and that, contrary to popular stereotype, "large companies place no more emphasis, perhaps even less, on conforming, organization-man type behavior than do small companies."

The tall-flat shape variable is distinguished relative to the size of the organization. An organization having a large number of levels in relation to its size is regarded as "tall." One having few management levels relative to its size is considered "flat." Here again, Porter and Lawler point out that there is a paucity of information but a wealth of potential hypotheses. They cite some evidence which indicates that managers in small flat companies show greater satisfaction than those in tall small companies. In larger companies (over 5000 employees) the relation between tallness, flatness, and satisfaction is equivocal, though possibly the reverse of the small companies. It seems that flat structures are more able to provide satisfaction in the area of self-actualization and tall ones in the area of security and social needs.

The last variable discussed by Porter and Lawler is that of shape on the basis of centralization-decentralization. As with some of the other variables, the relation with attitudes is far from being clear cut. It is the present writer's opinion that satisfaction with one's job in either a centralized or decentralized organization is more a function of personality than anything else. Other authors have noted that it would not be unreasonable to expect authoritarians to enter bureaucratic (centralized) organizations and be quite happy there, whereas individuals lower in authoritarianism would seek employment in other types of firms.

Fleishman (1963) has commented on a study by Litzinger (1963) in which bank managers employed by decentralized banks had higher consideration scores on the Leadership Opinion Questionnaire than their counterparts in centralized banks. However, there was no difference in their respective structure scores. Fleishman closes his report with the statement, "Whether this...is a result of the organizational situation, or whether managers possessing these traits tend to be selected for such decentralized operations is not yet known."

90

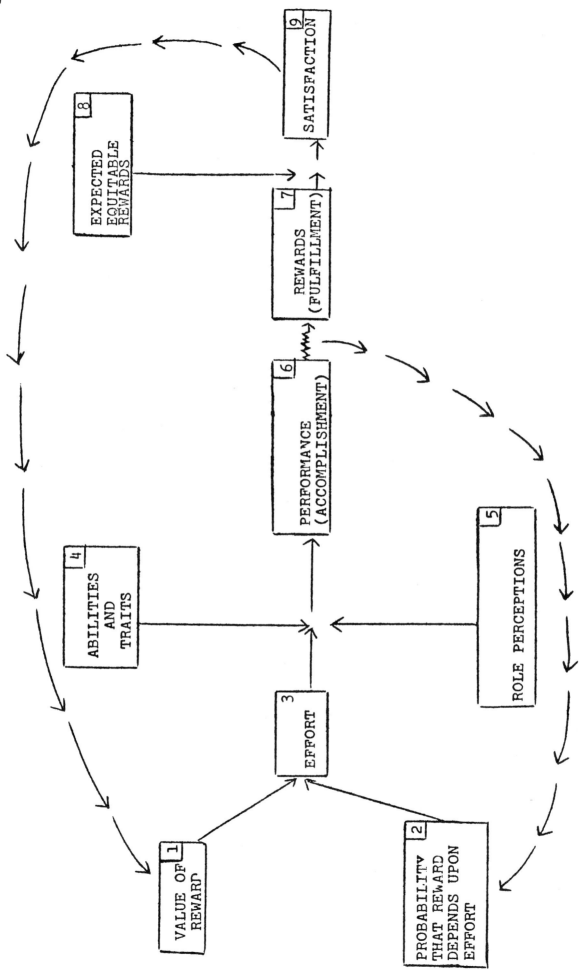

Figure 1: Tentative Theoretical Model Proposed by Porter and Lawler

The boxes in the model are:

1. VALUE OF REWARD
2. PROBABILITY THAT REWARD DEPENDS UPON EFFORT
3. EFFORT
4. ABILITIES AND TRAITS
5. ROLE PERCEPTIONS
6. PERFORMANCE (ACCOMPLISHMENT)
7. REWARDS (FULFILLMENT)
8. EXPECTED EQUITABLE REWARDS
9. SATISFACTION

At the 1966 meetings of the American Psychological Association, Porter and Lawler offered the tentative scheme in Figure 1 as a model summarizing the psychological factors likely to affect job satisfaction. The worker's job effort is seen as dependent on both the value of rewards (intrinsic or extrinsic) that are important to him and the probability that his efforts will gain him satisfactory rewards. Individual performance is then determined by the resulting effort the individual puts in on the job along with the worker's latent abilities and his perception of his role in the work process. Performance then leads to intrinsic or extrinsic rewards (or lack of them) which when matched with the rewards the worker expects from his efforts determines his degree of satisfaction. This last step, of course, involves the individual's perception of his environment and the possibility that workers can be dissatisfied for the sole reason that they are not doing as well as other people they regard as their equals (called "relative deprivation" by the social psychologists). Previous research relating job satisfaction to expectation levels is comprehensively summarized by Katzell (1963). While the Porter and Lawler model is admittedly still in the exploratory stage, it offers a creative synthesis of the factors affecting satisfaction that will undoubtedly advance future research.

Satisfaction as an Independent Variable

So long as the question of what gives rise to job satisfaction is not completely answered, one might well ask what evidence exists of the effects of job satisfaction or dissatisfaction. Vroom (op. cit.) discusses the relation of job satisfaction to absences, performance, turnover and accidents. As is frequently noted, the weakest relation is found between performance and satisfaction. Being mindful of the sometimes forgotten caveat that correlations do not infer cause and effect relationships, Vroom notes that accidents may cause dissatisfaction rather than the other way around. One might also consider that both accidents and dissatisfaction are caused by still another factor (such as working conditions) and so in reality are causally independent of each other.

The strongest relationships have been found between job satisfaction and absences and turnover. The most uniform finding has been that of a negative correlation between satisfaction and frequency of incidental absence. Some findings in this area have been clouded by the use of the group approach, i.e., correlating average group morale with average group absence. A preferable (and probably more meaningful) approach from the psychological point of view is to correlate individual satisfaction scores with individual absence rates. However, as noted earlier, the problem of anonymity and the possible consequences of its violation may mitigate the value of this approach.

Various studies have used different breakdowns of the population under scrutiny, and it is therefore difficult to make accurate comparisons of studies apparently dealing with the same variables. Metzner and Mann (1953) found sex, nature of job, status of job, and skill level to be factors in determining the relation between attitudes and absence. Specifically, no relation was found among white collar women between absences and attitudes. This may be due to the interim nature of many women's employment or the possibility that unique propensities cause women's absence rates. One might hypothesize that older women and career women would tend to react in essentially the same manner as men. In the above mentioned study, low level white collar and blue collar men demonstrated an inverse relation between frequency of absences and job attitudes. The duration of absence did not account for as much variance as did the frequency.

In recent years the hiring of new college graduates--especially engineers--has reached a level and stage of competition requiring large expenditures of time and money by contending firms. In consequence, at the time of hiring many firms have built up an investment of thousands of dollars in each new employee. Frequently, however, these new employees will stay on the job less than three years. Lopez (1965) reports a one-third turnover of management trainees and adds the comment, "Trainees were most likely to resign in their third year of employment and were far less likely to leave before or after that time." Meyer (1962), in a study of engineering hiring, reports that 47 percent had left within a seven year period. In another firm, nearly two-fifths of management trainees were reported to have left within three years (Athanasiou, 1965).

While it is not unreasonable to expect high turnover during periods of high employment, nonetheless this circumstance is expensive to both the firm and the employee. This is especially true when one considers the characteristics of those who leave. Compared with those who stay, the "leavers" are frequently described as more aggressive, independent, extraverted, intellectual (as opposed to pragmatic), original, and artistic. The stayers, on the other hand, are described as acquiescent, conforming, realistic, sincere and married (see Meyer, 1962 and Lopez, 1965 for a more complete description). The reason for leaving seems more often than not to be job dissatisfaction--particularly in the areas of self-actualization and autonomy. Porter (1962) has reported that lower and lower-middle managers rank the satisfaction of these two needs as the most deficient--though he does not relate these deficiencies to turnover or dissatisfaction. Both Lopez and Meyer conclude their reports with the suggestion that improved utilization of manpower talent should be achieved through the provision of satisfying job experiences.

Hulin (1966) has published a study in which the Job Description Index (see Chapter 5) was administered to 350 female clerical employees. After a lapse of five months the JDI scores of those girls in the original sample who had quit were compared with those who remained. Job satisfaction scores showed a significant relationship to turnover even after an extended period of seven more months. The results of this study demonstrate the value of the individual (versus group) approach and indicate that turnover can be predicted from knowledge of job satisfaction--at least among female clerical employees in a short labor market. The previous chapter by Robinson also presents some data relating to the use of satisfaction measures in predicting turnover.

Future studies of the relation between satisfaction and turnover probably should consider such factors as sex, job level, condition of the labor market and other extraneous factors on which information is easily obtained (cf. Hulin, ibid.). Satisfaction scores and re-enlistment rates in the armed forces, Peace Corps, etc., should also provide useful data.

Common sense suggests that there should be a positive relation between job satisfaction and job performance. Yet, in fact, there is no simple relation. It may be that workers show high satisfaction because their performance is high, or they may be more satisfied with low production if the group norm favors such a level. Vroom (1964, p. 184-185) cites the results of twenty studies which show correlations between satisfaction and production varying from -.31 to +.86. More than three-fourths of the coefficients are less than +.21. Since no one has seen fit to publish a journal of nonsignificant results, it is quite possible that there are innumerable studies reporting no relation between satisfaction and performance which will never see the light of day.

In summary, Vroom (p. 187) notes that,

The absence of a marked or consistent correlation between job satisfaction and performance casts some doubt on the generality or intensity of either effects of satisfaction on performance or performance on satisfaction. It also suggests that the conditions which determine a person's level of job satisfaction and his level of job performance are not identical. Some conditions may produce high satisfaction and low performance, others low satisfaction and high performance, and still others high satisfaction and high performance or low satisfaction and low performance.

The Use of Occupational Interest Inventories

A seldom surveyed corner of the job satisfaction-morale structure contains the idea of occupational choice and such instruments as the Strong Vocational Interest Blank and the Kuder Preference Record. "A score on an occupational scale of the (Strong) Vocational Interest Blank expresses the extent to which a person possesses likes and dislikes which distinguish members of that occupational group from men and women in general." (Strong, 1959.) It follows that the more "likes" and fewer "dislikes" a person actually encounters in his job the more satisfied he will be.

Cronbach (1960) has noted that "Strong's keys are not confined to vocational interests....In principle, the test could also be keyed to give an indirect measure of scholastic aptitude, of neurotic tendency, or even of soundness of financial credit." A simple extension of this principle would allow scoring the SVIB for selection, assignment, or an index of job satisfaction. Most of the present Strong keys, and therefore the items, are related to professional, semi-professional, or highly skilled occupations. A few exceptions are the low skill level keys for farmer, carpenter, etc. Due to this generally middle and upper class characteristic of the test, it may not be directly applicable across all occupational groupings. The Kuder Preference Record is thought to be somewhat better in this respect.

For selection purposes, a firm might devise a scoring key based on the likes and dislikes of its happier and/or more productive employees. For internal purposes, a content and factor analysis of scores of contrasted groups of satisfied and non-satisfied employees could yield valuable insights to management regarding the conditions, wants, etc., associated with satisfaction.

However, one problem (or advantage) in using occupational interest inventories for selection or satisfaction measurement instruments is their lack of face validity. While such a condition increases the difficulty of "faking good" it simultaneously tends to reduce the layman's confidence in the instrument. One can easily imagine the reaction of an applicant for an engineering sales job upon being asked to indicate his liking or disliking for "fashionably dressed people; carelessly dressed people; people who don't believe in evolution; socialists; Bolshevists." While psychologists recognize that responses to these items are only part of a larger pattern and do not in themselves yield any information, it is difficult to explain the use of such questions to the layman taking the test. The ethicality of such an approach to selection, etc., is a topic of considerable continuing debate as is the use of "direction of perception" type scales.

The Kuder Preference Record is an inventory somewhat different from the SVIB but it may be used in a similar manner. "Despite...differences in initial conception,..the inventories have converged on much the same sort of measurement. Through factor analysis of Strong keys and through case studies, it /is/...possible to translate SVIB occupational scores into trait description. Through use of regression equations and profiles of occupational groups, Kuder /trait/ scores can identify occupational categories into which people fit." (Cronbach, 1962.)

The potential user should investigate the utility of each of these inventories. The validity and reliability studies on the SVIB are phenomenal and unequaled in the field. The Kuder, on the other hand, has somewhat greater face validity and may prove easier to use in a counseling context.

The Job Analysis and Interest Measurement (see Chapter 13) is an instrument whose aim is similar to the Strong and Kuder but whose approach is different. This inventory attempts to derive a set of concepts, scales, scores, etc., which describe both the job and the individual who fits the job.

In our society nearly every job carries with it a certain set of behavioral and personality requirements which are not always in obvious association with the performance of the job itself. "Individuals bring to the job basic orientations and strategies and behavioral styles which are ways of organizing action into typical or preferred ways of responding to or applying power, ways of obtaining satisfactions or avoiding dangers, and ways of using mental, physical, and energy resources over a period of time." (JAIM manual supplement.) When the job's requirements and the individual's style are in phase it is likely that, other things being equal, he stands a better chance of doing well or succeeding at the job than the person whose behavioral style is antagonistic to the job requirements.

This idea is not unknown in the popular concept of assigning certain personalities to certain occupations. For example, the popular conception of the type of personality required of a truck driver is quite different from that thought to be typical of a poet. The industrial application of psychometric instruments which touch on personality characteristics has not, however, met with wide acceptance or approval. The JAIM, on the other hand, is not a personality instrument of the same genre as the MMPI. It has greater face validity than the MMPI and would probably not appear threatening to a normal person.   The JAIM is an experimental instrument which may prove useful in occupational counseling, improving job satisfaction, personnel selection, and assignment, if carefully and professionally used.

The Gordon Personal Inventory (GPI) is an instrument which is somewhat similar in character to the JAIM.   That is, it is an instrument which taps personality characteristics supposedly related to job content.   The GPI, however, seems to this reviewer to hold less promise than the JAIM.   The GPI's four scales--Cautiousness, Original thinking, Personal relations, and Vigor--show moderate intercorrelations which are frequently as high or higher than the instrument's claimed validity coefficients, and the repetitive scoring of a single item for the four scales tends to reduce the value of analysis of one person's scores across the four areas.   The GPI's use of a forced choice format is commendable but the number of items (20 tetrads) may be too small for the type of empirical item analysis needed for discrimination within (or between) occupations.

The items themselves are non-offensive, the test manual is of high quality, and if further predictive validity studies are accomplished the GPI may prove to be a useful instrument.   In its present form, however, it should be regarded as an experimental instrument and used with more than the usual amount of caution in a non-research setting.

Conclusions

After a consideration of the problems, inadequacies and generally low predictive capacity of attitude measurement devices, one might legitimately question why psychologists persist in attempting to "measure" attitudes.   One answer is "...because they are there."   Another answer involves the belief that what people "say" has (or should have) some relation to what they do. Still another answer is couched in the terms, "To understand behavior we have to start somewhere and this is as good a place as any."

Actually, we attempt to study attitudes in order to verify the hypotheses that 1) they are really there, 2) that they have some relation to what people do, and 3) that knowledge of attitudes will help us to understand behavior.   Certainly the data accumulated to date are disappointing in their failure to demonstrate expected level of support for any of these three hypotheses.

In sum, then, on the subject of job satisfaction and other job attitudes, there seems to be sufficient evidence to support the following conclusions:

1.   Job satisfaction in its various forms shows a negative relation to absences, turnover and accidents.   Cause and effect relations have yet to be clearly established.

2.   There is no clear relation of any sort between satisfaction and actual job performance.

3. A general concept of satisfaction as either a motivator or end state of need fulfillment has not been adequately developed; furthermore, the components of satisfaction need to be more clearly delineated.

4. Personality factors and organizational variables may affect the distribution and type of attitudes available for study.

5. Methodological variations with regard to survey versus empirical studies, validity of the criteria and measurement devices, etc., makes comparison of studies extremely difficult.

REFERENCES

Adams, J. Stacy. Wage inequities, productivity and work quality. Berkeley, California: Institute of Industrial Relations, 1964. Pp. 9-16. Reprint #220.

Athanasiou, Robert B. Opinion formation through dissonance reduction. Unpublished Master's thesis, Rensselaer Polytechnic Institute, Troy, New York, 1965.

Brayfield, A. H. and Crockett, W. H. "Employee attitudes and employee performance," Psychological Bulletin, 1955 (52), 396-424.

Brehm, J. W. and Cohen, A. R. Explorations in cognitive dissonance. New York: John Wiley & Sons, 1962.

Burke, Ronald J. "Are Herzberg's motivators and hygienes unidimensional?" Journal of Applied Psychology, 1966 (50), 317-321.

Cronbach, Lee J. Essentials of psychological testing. 2nd edition. New York: Harper and Row, 1960. P. 424.

Dunnette, M., et al. "Factors contributing to job satisfaction and job dissatisfaction in six occupational groups." Mimeo, University of Minnesota, 1966.

Festinger, Leon. A theory of cognitive dissonance. Evanston, Illinois: Row, Peterson, 1957.

Fisher, Jerome. "The twisted pear and the prediction of behavior," J. Consult. Psychol., 1959 (23), 400-405.

Fleishman, Edwin A. Manual for Leadership Opinion Questionnaire. Chicago: Science Research Association, 1960.

Fleishman, Edwin A. Recent results on the validity of the Leadership Opinion Questionnaire (Manual supplement). Chicago: Science Research Association, 1963.

Fournet, Glenn P., et al. "Job satisfaction: Issues and problems," Personnel Psychology, 1966 (19), 165-183.

Gordon, George G. "The relationships of 'satisfiers' and 'dissatisfiers' to productivity, turnover, and morale." APA convention paper, 1965, mimeo.

Gordon, Leonard V. (Manual for) Gordon Personal Profile. New York: Harcourt, 1963.

Gurin, G., et al. Americans view their mental health. New York: Basic Books, 1960.

98

Halpern, Gerald. "Relative contributions of motivator and hygiene factors to overall job satisfaction," APA convention paper, 1965, mimeo.

Herzberg, F., Mausner, F, Peterson, R. O. and Capwell, Dora F. Job attitudes: Review of research and opinion. Pittsburgh: Psychological Service of Pittsburgh, 1957.

Herzberg, F., Mausner, B. and Snyderman, Barbara B. The motivation to work. 2nd edition. New York: John Wiley & Sons, 1959.

Hulin, Charles L. "Job satisfaction and turnover in a female clerical population," Journal of Applied Psychology, 1966 (50), 280-285.

Katzell, R. "Personal values, job satisfaction and job behavior," in H. Borow (Ed.), Man in a world at work. Boston: Houghton Mifflin, 1964.

Litzinger, W. D. "Entrepreneurial prototype in bank management," Academy of Management Journal, 1963 (6), 36-45.

Lopez, Felix M. "Multiple approaches to the evaluation of an early identification program," APA convention paper, 1965, mimeo.

Metzner, Helen and Mann, F. "Employee attitudes and absences", Personnel Psychology, 1953, 6, pp. 457-485.

Perry, Dallis K., "Validities of three interest keys for U. S. Navy yeomen", Journal of Applied Psychology, 1955, 39, pp. 134-138.

Porter, Lyman W., "Job attitudes in management", Journal of Applied Psychology, 1962, 46, pp. 375-384; 1963, 47, pp. 141-148, 267-275, 386-397.

Porter, L. W. and Lawler, E. E. III, "Properties of organization structure in relation to job attitudes and job behavior", Psychological Bulletin, 1965, 64, pp. 23-31.

Strong, E. K., Jr., Manual for Strong Vocational Interest Blanks for Men and Women, Palo Alto, California, Consulting Psychologists Press, 1959.

Strong, E. K., Jr., Vocational Interests of Men and Women, Stanford, California, Stanford University Press, 1943 (especially p. 143).

Vroom, V., Work and Motivation, New York: Wiley, 1964.

Walther, Regis, Manual for Job Analysis and Interest Measure, Princeton, N. J. Educational Testing Service, 1964.

5.   GENERAL JOB SATISFACTION SCALES

It was somewhat of an arbitrary task to decide whether a particular instrument belonged in this section or whether it would be better covered in the subsequent chapters entitled "Job Satisfaction for Particular Occupations", or "Satisfaction with Specific Job Features", or "Concepts Related to Job Satisfaction". Nevertheless, we have attempted to distinguish those particular instruments which clearly fall into the latter categories, since we feel it would be less accurate to classify them with the instruments covered in this chapter than simply to cover them in separate chapters. However, not all of the purported job satisfaction scales reviewed in this chapter are really comprehensive general job satisfaction scales as they are based on limited occupational groups or job content coverage.

Because of the wide variety of situations in which job satisfaction data may be collected, many reputable occupational research and consulting firms do not publish overall satisfaction scales, but rather draw from an accumulating pool of items tested in previous studies. From this item file, they can construct unique instruments relevant to the particular workgroup or work problem with which they are dealing. Included among organizations keeping such a file are the Industrial Relations Center of the University of Minnesota and Psychological Services of Pittsburgh.   The Organizational Behavior section of the Institute for Social Research has used hundreds of relevant questions over the years, but has attempted only sporadically to compile a centralized listing of items.   Science Research Associates in Chicago, while keeping a large pool of items, also publishes the general SRA Attitude Survey, a worthwhile instrument which is now being revised. As a supplementary service, SRA adds optional sections dealing with particular aspects in which a company may be interested.

It seems that the measurement of job satisfaction is attempted either with one or two items on large samples or else with rather complex instruments which attempt to examine all possible underlying determinants of satisfaction for smaller groups of people. The decision of whether to use a single question or a battery of items should depend on what one hopes to learn from his study. There are numerous instances in the literature of studies in which the author offers as validational evidence for his ten to 30 item scale the fact that scale scores correlate highly with some single item index of the characteristic purportedly tapped by the scale. If the examination of total scores is as far as the researcher wishes to pursue analysis of his data, he might be better advised to use the single item index instead of wasting respondents' time and his own effort to compile scores on a lengthier instrument. If, on the other hand, he wants to examine various facets of job satisfaction, he should use a longer instrument. Considerations about the optimal amount of information, type of information, etc., are best handled within the Cronbach and Gleser framework, referenced in Chapter 1 of this volume.

The different types of single items, together with some of their advantages and drawbacks, are discussed in Chapter 3 (by Robinson). The reader may also want to check over the responses to open-ended questions contained in the Robinson chapter to judge the adequacy with which the longer research instruments exhaust the potential sources of satisfaction or dissatisfaction with work. We recommend the use of one or two open-ended questions in case a particular scale chosen from this section does not tap the aspect of the job in which the respondent is most interested. A respondent's choice of valued job features can be surprisingly idiosyncratic.

The following 13 instruments are reviewed in detail below:

1. Job Description Index (Smith, et al. 1965)

2. Index of Job Satisfaction (Kornhauser 1965)

3. Factors for Job Satisfaction and Job Dissatisfaction (Dunnette, et al. 1966)

4. SRA (Employee) Attitude Survey (1951 and 196?)

5. IRC Employee Attitude Scales (Carlson, et al. 1962)

6. Index of Employee Satisfaction (Morse 1953)

7. Job Satisfaction Scale (Johnson 1955)

8. Job Dimensions Blank (Schletzer 1965)

9. Job Satisfaction Index (Brayfield and Rothe 1951)

10. Job Satisfaction (Hoppock 1935)

11. Tear Ballot (Kerr 1948)

12. Employee Morale Scale (Woods 1944)

13. Work Satisfaction and Personal Happiness (Noll and Bradburn 1968)
Except for the last scale, these instruments are listed in rough order of merit.
We will now highlight some of the considerations used in this appraisal, and
offer some brief descriptive comments.

Some scales contained in this section manage an adequate coverage of the
field without requiring an excessive amount of the respondent's time. Of these
few, the instrument which appears to us to have the best credentials is the
Job Description Index. Lengthy, extensive and competent research went
into the construction of this instrument, which has been administered to workers
at all organization levels on a nationwide basis. In reservation, it must be
noted that the scale may be subject to minor response set problems and that
only one of the five job factors covered is "intrinsic" (see Chapter 3). While
very impressive reliability and validity data are given for the instrument, normative data (scale means and standard deviations) are available only from the authors.
Correspondence with the authors is recommended before use of the Index, as
they are interested in extending their library of normative data.

Kornhauser's Index of Job Satisfaction is another short instrument which
in its present form was used in survey situations but which may be modified to
self-administered format. The Index has more than adequate variety in item format,
a feature seldom found in job satisfaction instruments. Although the questions
were designed for a blue-collar sample, they are sufficiently representative and
universal to be used with white-collar workers as well. The major problem with
the instrument is that it was based on a priori judgments and that no empirical
item analyses or tests for homogeneity or reliability were reported to have been
employed in its construction. Some of the research findings suggest that it has
desirable validational qualities.

The psychometric report card for an instrument devised by Dunnette, et al.
is called, for the sake of labelling, Factors for Job Satisfaction and Job
Dissatisfaction. The instrument is not really a job satisfaction scale at all
but a series of descriptive statements designed for experimental use with Q-sort
procedures. The items are well-written, however, and an impressive amount of
solid methodological research went into their development (including admirable
attempts to control for social desirability). The instrument includes 12
general areas of job satisfaction and seems to cover this aspect of attitude
measurement more satisfactorily than any other instrument we have reviewed.

Norms are available for six diverse white-collar occupational groups but only
in attitudes toward single satisfying or dissatisfying incidents and not in
overall job attitudes. It would seem worthwhile for some researcher to develop
a forced-choice or rating scale format for these items to measure overall job
satisfaction, and to collect norms from blue-collar workers as well.

The SRA Attitude Survey, as mentioned above, is now (1967) being revised.
Previous manuals indicated that researchers or firms using the instrument would
be furnished with great detail regarding the psychometric and normative data
on each question used, an extremely valuable feature. Researchers may look
forward to the release of the new version of this instrument.

The I.R.C. Employee Attitude Scale, a descendant of the Triple Audit, has
the benefit of years of competent cumulative research at the Industrial Research
Center at the University of Monnesota. The monograph which describes the
scale reviewed here contains an impressive amount of normative and comparative
data, as well as analytic procedures of high quality. However, there are
little, if any, data bearing directly on the validity of the instrument.
Furthermore, the scale is not made available for general use by the Industrial
Relations Center, as mentioned in our opening remarks in this section.

Morse's Index of Employee Satisfaction seems to be reflecting two factors
of satisfaction rather than the four suggested in the form of subscales. The
major job satisfaction dimension encompasses three of these subscales, which do
have rather high internal consistency within themselves. The fourth scale
measures pride in one's work group, an apparently important variable according
to the correlates Morse presents. A major limitation of the instrument is
that it was devised for a long interview situation and hence is not directly
adaptable to shorter self-administered situations.

The value of Johnson's Job Satisfaction Scale is considerably diminished
by the restricted, if large, sample on which it was developed and some questionable claims for validation that are advanced. However, the scale possesses
adequate item coverage, item wording, reliability and homogeneity and contains
a number of interesting items that the researcher may want to examine.

Schletzer's Job Dimensions Blank appears to cover a sufficiently wide
sample of job factors. While good normative data are available, the Blank has
been applied only to those in professional occupations. One interesting feature
of the Blank is that the respondent is told to disregard irrelevant items so

that his final score will not be contaminated by them. Time restrictions preclude a more detailed review of this instrument, which is described in the author's dissertation.

The major advantage of Brayfield and Rothe's Job Satisfaction Index is that it has been around longer, and perhaps used more, than most measures. The items are very general and content-free, but do not allow the researcher to determine with which aspects of the job the employee is satisfied or dissatisfied. Hence, one or two general items may be as sufficient as the whole Index. A number of useful single items appear in the original Hoppock Job Satisfaction Blank devised in 1935. The four major items, surprisingly, are not as dated as one might expect and reflect not only the person's expressed satisfaction but also how he feels about his job compared to other jobs available to him or compared to jobs held by other people. However, evidence for reliability, homogeneity and validity is either sketchily presented or not presented at all.

Another old scale, the Kerr Tear Ballot, does tap a number of job factors, although it only uses ten items. The respondent procedure of tearing ballots from the form seems obsolescent today, but there may still be occasions when this more active form of response may be more appealing to employees. Older still is the Job Segment Evaluation Scale, and here some of the items do appear dated. They also require a fairly high level of verbal comprehension on the part of respondents. Advocates of Thurstone scaling methods may want to consider this one.

The final short scale, by Noll and Bradburn, is noteworthy less for its merits as a scale than because it sheds light on the interesting relation between job satisfaction and personal happiness.

In the following table, informal ratings are given on the characteristics of the first twelve instruments. The reader should read again the caveats regarding these ratings that are given at the beginning of this book. The ratings reflect the biases of one person's judgment and are meant to summarize considerations for use rather than to provide final judgments.

Feature of the Scale	Wood	Kerr	Hoppock	Brayfield and Rothe	Schletzer	Johnson	Morse	IRC	SRA*	Dunnette, et al.	Kornhauser	Smith, et al.
Items:												
Sampling of content	+	+	+	0	+	+	+	+	+	++	+	+
Item wording and simplicity	-	-	+	+	0	+	+	+	+	++	++	++
Item analysis	+	0	0	++	0	++	+	++	++	++	0	++
Freedom from Response set:												
Acquiescence	0	0	0	+	0	0	0	0	0	+	0	+
Social desirability	0	0	+	0	0	0	0	0	0	++	0	0
Statistical Procedures:												
Sample	-	+	0	+	+	-	+	++	+	++	+	++
Norms presented	+	++	+	+	++	+	+	++	+++	+	0	0
Reliability: test-retest	0	0	0	0	0	+	0	0	+	0	0	++
Homogeneity	0	+	+	+	0	+	+	+	0	++	0	+
Discrimination of known groups	0	+	+	+	0	0	+	0	0	+	++	++
Cross validation	0	0	0	0	0	0	0	0	0	0	0	++
Other procedures	0	+	0	+	0	0	+	+	+	++	+	++
Scale itself: Overall Rating	0	0	+	+	+	+	+	++	++	++	++	++

The above are scored according to the following scheme:

+++	Excellent and exemplary
++	Competent
+	Adequate
-	Inadequate
--	Incompetent
0	No information or not enough information (or too conflicting) to make a final judgment

* Being revised

THE JOB DESCRIPTION INDEX (Smith, et al. 1965)

Variable
The JDI attempts to measure job satisfaction in the areas of pay, promotion, supervision, type of work and the people on the job.

Description
The instrument consists of 72 items--18 in each of work, supervision, and people subscales and nine each in pay and promotions. Each grouping consists of a list of adjectives or descriptive phrases. The respondent is asked to write "yes" next to each item which describes his pay (promotion, etc.) and "no" for each item which does not. A question ("?") response is reserved for items on which the respondent cannot decide. "Y" answers are scored 3, "N" answers 0, and "?" answers as 1 point.

Sample
Various samples have been used in constructing and validating this scale. The interested reader may acquire further information through the references listed below. Responses of 952 people in seven different organizations were used in developing the JDI.

Reliability/ Homogeneity
Corrected split-half internal consistency coefficients are reported to exceed .80 for each of the scales. Some evidence for stability over time is reported by Hulin (1966).

Validity
Hulin (1966) reports a correlation of -.27 between satisfaction and turnover (over a 12 month period) for female clerical employees. Other studies involving convergent and discriminant validity have been carried out by the Cornell group (see reference).

Location
Locke, Edwin A., Smith, Patricia C., and Hulin, Charles L. Cornell Studies of Job Satisfaction: V. Scale Characteristics of the Job Descriptive Index. Mimeo, Cornell University, circa 1965.

Results and Comments
In addition to the extensive high quality research done on the JDI by the Cornell group there are several factors intrinsic to the scale which recommend its use. The verbal level of the items is quite low and does not require the respondent to understand complicated or vague abstractions.

While the JDI is neither a projective nor a direction of perception type instrument, it does approach "job satisfaction" somewhat indirectly. The instrument asks the respondent to describe his job rather than his feelings about it. It seems quite evident from the numerous studies with the JDI that one's perception of his job is highly colored by his satisfaction with it. The JDI is a face valid instrument which can be easily administered and scored in a short time.

There are a few characteristics of the JDI which do not add to its value, although they are not serious defects. The first of these is the problem of social desirability. While there is some relation between JDI scores and social desirability, the correlation is not high.

Results and Comments (continued)

The potential user, however, should keep in mind the possibility that scores may be affected in some way by this factor. The possibility of "faking good" also exists regarding the JDI and potential users would be wise to take all necessary measures to assure employees that their responses will remain anonymous.

The five subscales do not appear to be statistically independent, judging from the magnitude of the correlations at the bottom of this page. This may mean that JDI is tapping a general job satisfaction syndrome. The theoretical implications, however, suggest a general satisfaction factor rather than specific areas of satisfaction. It will be noted that only the "work" items (and perhaps the "people" items) deal with intrinsic job features. A more balanced set of intrinsic and extrinsic items appears in the Dunnette, et al., study reviewed below. With the impressive background of research and the valuable scale characteristics which the instrument possesses, it is quite likely to expect that the JDI will become a widely used and valuable instrument. Professor Smith currently teaches at Bowling Green University (in Ohio) and should be contacted for those interested for fuller scoring instructions for the instrument.

The reader may be interested in the following sample of the voluminous correlational data for each set of items which indicate the quality of the instrument:

	Work	Supervision	People	Pay	Promotion
Median item intercorrelation	.25	.29	.45	.29	.30
Median item validity	.44	.40	.52	.50	.35
Split half correlation (Uncorr.)	.73	.67	.75	.77	.78
Correlation with alternative method	.75	.72	.64	.78	.57
Work	X	.40	.53	.46	.43
Supervision		X	.30	.10	.20
People			X	.55	.37
Pay				X	.36

References

Smith, Patricia C., et al., Cornell Studies of Job Satisfaction: I, II, III, IV, V, VI. Mimeo, Cornell University, circa 1965.

Hulin, Charles L. "Job satisfaction and turnover in female clerical population," J. Appl. Psychol. 1966, 50, 280-285.

JOB DESCRIPTION INDEX

Items in Final Version of JDI

Each of the five scales was presented on a separate page.

The instructions for each scale asked the subject to put "Y" beside an

item if the item described the particular aspect of his job (e.g., work, pay,

etc.),   "N" if the item did not describe that aspect, or "?" if he could not decide.

The response shown beside each item is the one scored in the "satisfied"

direction for each scale.

Work		Supervision		People	
Y	Fascinating	Y	Asks my advice	Y	Stimulating
N	Routine	N	Hard to please	N	Boring
Y	Satisfying	N	Impolite	N	Slow
N	Boring	Y	Praises good work	Y	Ambitious
Y	Good	Y	Tactful	N	Stupid
Y	Creative	Y	Influential	Y	Responsible
Y	Respected	Y	Up-to-date	Y	Fast
N	Hot	N	Doesn't supervise enough	Y	Intelligent
Y	Pleasant	N	Quick-tempered	N	Easy to make enemies
Y	Useful	Y	Tells me where I stand	N	Talk too much
N	Tiresome	N	Annoying	Y	Smart
Y	Healthful	N	Stubborn	N	Lazy
Y	Challenging	Y	Knows job well	N	Unpleasant
N	On your feet	N	Bad	N	No privacy
N	Frustrating	Y	Intelligent	Y	Active
N	Simple	Y	Leaves me on my own	N	Narrow interests
N	Endless	Y	Around when needed	Y	Loyal
Y	Gives sense of accomplishment	N	Lazy	N	Hard to meet

Pay		Promotions	
Y	Income adequate for normal expenses	Y	Good opportunity for advancement
Y	Satisfactory profit sharing	N	Opportunity somewhat limited
N	Barely live on income	Y	Promotion on ability
N	Bad	N	Dead-end job
Y	Income provides luxuries	Y	Good chance for promotion
N	Insecure	N	Unfair promotion policy
N	Less than I deserve	N	Infrequent promotions
Y	Highly paid	Y	Regular promotions
N	Underpaid	Y	Fairly good chance for promotion

INDEX OF JOB SATISFACTION (Kornhauser 1965)

Variable	This index attempts to measure the amount of overall job satisfaction and dissatisfaction associated with occupational level.
Description	The job-satisfaction index combines 11 separate indicators including responses to nine direct questions and volunteered favorable and unfavorable comments about the job.
Sample	The sample population of 407 Detroit factory workers was drawn from 13 large and medium-sized automotive manufacturing plants. Only hourly paid workers actually engaged in factory jobs were included. Respondents were white native born men on the payroll at least three years, age either 20 to 29 or 40 to 49; all but two percent were members of the UAW-CIO. Supplementary samples were drawn from the following populations: manual workers from six Detroit manufacturing companies, factory workers from eight plants in small towns outside metropolitan Detroit; office workers (salaries comparable to manual workers') from six Detroit automotive companies and from three manufacturing companies. Interviews were taken during 1953-4.
Reliability/ Homogeneity	No measures of reliability, including "coder reliability", are reported.
Validity	The prediction was made that job-level factors produce measurable differences in job satisfaction -- under the assumption that all other determinants (such as personal background) are sufficiently similar from one occupational group to another so that they do not exert serious differential effects that distort or obliterate the job-level effects. One test of the accuracy of this view is that satisfaction should be more frequently reported at succeeding levels on the occupational scale, and this proved to be the case.
Administration	Scores were obtained by adding together arbitrarily assigned weights (see items) for coded responses judged to be indicative of the disignated characteristic. The total raw score was then grouped into nine intervals to form the final index score. A trained interviewer and coder are required.
Location	Kornhauser, A., Mental Health of the Industrial Worker, New York: John Wiley & Sons, Inc. 1965, pp. 84 and 156-185.
Results and Comments	This Index is really an exploratory instrument. Measures of reliability and validity should be more fully presented. The author's predicted pattern -- that the more skilled jobs had higher proportions of satisfied workers -- corresponded to the occupational gradient he described in respect to mental health. In tests for item discrimination-ability, the author found that the

intrinsic appeals of work were more closely interrelated with total job feelings than were any other of the job characteristics studied.

The Index of Job Satisfaction was also found to be related to feelings of job importance, feelings toward boss, and attitude toward company.

The Index was mainly devised for survey uses with an interviewer and would have to be altered for self-administration. Alternative sources of potential interview survey questions are those given in Robinson's chapter as well as in Kahn, et al. (1964).

In some of the research on open-ended questions described in Robinson's chapter, it was found that people who mention positive features of their job also tend to mention more negative features. In the absence of inter-item correlation data, this finding should be considered in coding items B3 through B6.

Reference   Kahn, R., et al. Organizational Stress New York: Wiley, 1964.

INDEX OF JOB SATISFACTION

Score

0-2	B82	When you start off for work, do you usually feel that you want to go to work or that you don't want to? (Why is that? How do you mean?)

0-2 B9a   On the whole would you say that your job is (show card)
1) really interesting and enjoyable _____
2) or would you say that it is all right but not very interesting _____
3) or would you say that it is dull and monotonous? _____

0-2 B10   Would you say your job gives you a chance to use your abilities or is the job too simple to let you use your abilities (How is that? How do you mean?)

0-2 B16a How do you feel about your present wages? Would you say you are (show card)
_____ completely satisfied
_____ well satisfied
_____ neither satisfied nor dissatisfied
_____ a little dissatisfied
_____ very dissatisfied

0-2 B19   a. On the whole, what do you think of the company where you work?
b. What do you think of the way they treat their employees?
(Would you tell me a little about your feelings on the way they treat employees?)

0-2 B23a Are there times when you think about leaving the kind of work you are doing now?
Yes _____   No _____   Other comment:

0-2 F21a In which one of these general parts of your life would you most like to have things different than they are? (show card and read)
_____ Your spare-time activities
_____ Your friendships
_____ Your home and family
_____ Your job
_____ Your religious life

0-2 F21c Which one of these on the cards above are you best satisfied with in your life?

0-6 B4   Would you look at this card (show card) and say which of these statements tells best how you feel about your job? Would you say you are
_____ Completely satisfied
_____ Well satisfied
_____ Neither satisfied nor dissatisfied
_____ A little dissatisfied
_____ Very dissatisfied

-9   (Favorable versus unfavorable comments re job)

A2a   On the whole how do you feel about your life and the way it has been
          working out? (How do you mean? In what ways? I'm interested in
          any thing else you can tell me on how your life has been working
          out)

   b   Well, I think I understand that all right. Let's switch to some
          other things about how your life has been working out. How have things
          gone for you?

   3   Now which of these statement here (show card) comes nearest to saying
          how you feel about your life in general? Would you say you are
          (responses as in Q B4)
          Comments: _____

   4a   Do you feel that you have had good breaks in life or bad breaks?
          (If answer to a is "good breaks" or "both good and bad", ask b, then
          c. If answer to a is "bad breaks", have things gone well for you?)

   b   In what ways have you had good breaks?
          (If say no "breaks", say: I mean in what ways have things gone well
          you?)

   c   In what ways have you had bad breaks (as in b)

   5a   What things give you a lot of satisfaction in your life as it is now?
   b   What other kinds of things do you get a lot of satisfaction from?

   6a   Almost everybody feels sometimes that his life isn't going along just
          the way he wants it to. In what ways do you feel your life isn't
          just they way you'd want it to be?

   b   What other kinds of things would you say you aren't well satisfied
          with in your life?

   c   What things get you down most?

   d   Do you feel that you can do much to make your future what you want
          it to be?
          (How do you mean? In what way? What kinds of things do you feel
          you can do?)

(Favorable versus unfavorable responses re jobs)

B3a   What do you think of your job (In what way, etc.)
   b   What other feelings do you have about your job?

B4-   See above

B5a   What things do you particularly like about the job?
   b   What other things about your job do you get satisfaction from?

B6a   What things don't you like about the job?
   b   What (other) things are there about the job that are not just the way
          you would like them?

FACTORS FOR JOB SATISFACTION AND JOB DISSATISFACTION (Dunnette, et al. 1966)

Variable	This study was designed to test the Herzberg theory of job satisfaction which states that a set of intrinsic factors -- Achievement, Responsibility, Work itself, Recognition, and Advancement -- are mainly responsible for job satisfaction; and a set of extrinsic factors -- Co-workers, Supervision-technical, Supervision-human relation, Salary, Security, Company policies and practices, and Working conditions -- are mainly responsible for job dissatisfaction.
Description	The authors utilized the Herzberg factors (listed above) but sought to avoid both the subjectivity inherent in interpreting interviews and the possible biasing effects of social desirability. Their aim was to measure job satisfaction and dissatisfaction using a Q-sort deck technique based on 12 of Herzberg's factors. The initial pool of 286 items (144 positively worded and 144 negatively worded) was rated by 25 graduate students and faculty on content and social desirability; 144 items remained after the authors eliminated those items with social desirability ratings at the extremes and those whose content was not agreed upon by at least 20 judges.

A sample of 112 employees was asked to rate separately the 72 positively and 72 negatively worded statements on a nine-point scale according to how well each statement described previous unusually satisfying and dissatisfying job situations. These two sets of items were factor analyzed separately. The final Q-sort deck of 36 positively and 36 negatively worded items were composed of those statements with the highest loadings on factors that corresponded to Herzberg's 12 factors. |
| Sample | The preliminary 144 statements were rated by 112 night school students in supervisory training courses who were also employed in local firms. Subjects receiving the final set of items included 133 store managers of a large nationwide chain, 89 sales clerks, 44 secretaries, 129 engineers and research scientists employed by a manufacturing firm, 49 machine equipment salesmen and 92 male army reservists (a total of 536 subjects). |
| Reliability/ Homogeneity | No test-retest reliabilities are reported.
The 72 positive and 72 negative Q-sort deck items were factor analyzed separately. Those items describing satisfying situations yielded 17 factors of which 11 were interpretable. Those describing dissatisfying situations yielded 19 factors of which ten were interpretable. (The precise factors found are not given; see items on the following pages for loadings of final 72 statements on appropriate factors.)

Q-type factor analysis was done for each of the six occupational groups in the sample of 536 for both the positive and negative statements (a total of twelve matrices). Clusters of five or more persons within the six occupational groups were then defined by factor loadings (only loadings of .40 or better were used). |

Validity   No validity data were given.

Location   Dunnette, M. D., Campbell, J. P. and Hakel, M. D., "Factors
                  contributing to job satisfaction and job dissatisfaction in six
                  occupational groups", The University of Minnesota, mimeo, 1966.

Administration   The subjects were asked to rate the statements on how they con-
                  tributed to the satisfying or dissatisfying situations previously
                  described by the subject. Each set of 36 statements was presented
                  in Q-sort deck form. The subjects were required to sort these
                  statements in a forced choice manner into seven categories approxi-
                  mating a normal distribution -- 2, 5, 7, 8, 5, 5, 2. Each statement
                  was scored by assigning it the number of the category in which the
                  subject had placed it.

Results and   The Q analyses show a great diversity of the groups of factors perceived
   Comments   as producing satisfaction or dissatisfaction. The factors of
                  achievement, responsibility, and recognition were perceived by many
                  subgroups as contributing to both satisfaction and dissatisfaction.
                  However, the factor of work itself usually was mentioned only in
                  describing satisfaction.

                  The authors conclude from the study that the Herzberg two factor
                  theory is much too simplistic to account for the complex patterns
                  of results obtained.

                  The Q-sort decks developed in this study were meant to be reviewed
                  as a technique for assessing Herzberg's categorization of factors
                  producing satisfaction and dissatisfaction rather than a new valid
                  and reliable instrument to measure overall job satisfaction.
                  However, since the comprehensiveness and competence of the research
                  is generally superior to that underlying most job satisfaction measures,
                  the items and factors warrant inspection by researchers.

36 Statements Comprising Different Job Dimensions for

Satisfying Job Situations, with

Loadings on Relevant Factors and Mean Social

Desirability* Scores (SD) for Each Dimension

Factor Loading	Achievement (SD = 6.08)
.50	I felt a great deal of satisfaction because of doing a job well.
.75	I successfully completed a difficult assignment (or solved a difficult problem).
.69	I had a sense of achievement in my job.
.73	I gained a feeling of worthwhile accomplishment from my job.

Responsibility (SD = 6.14)
.45	I was responsible for my own efforts.
.47	I had a great deal of responsibility on my job.
.68	I enjoyed the feeling of responsibility my job gave me.
.73	I had considerable decision making power.

Work Itself (SD = 5.79)
.81	My job was very interesting.
.85	I enjoyed the kind of work I did.
.67	The actual duties on my job were challenging.

Recognition (SD = 5.92)
.61	I received plenty of recognition.
.69	I was told that I had done a good job.
.71	I received praise for the work I did.

Advancement (SD = 5.59)
.64	My progress toward a promotion was satisfactory.
.78	There were many opportunities for advancement.
.53	I felt I was getting ahead in the company.

Co-workers (SD = 5.68)
.62	I got considerable cooperation from the people I worked with.
.82	I liked the people with whom I worked.

Factor Loading	Supervision-Technical (SD = 5.21)
.91	I had a top notch supervisor.
.73	My supervisor was a good manager.
.73	My boss showed himself to be very competent.

Supervision-Human Relations (SD=5.36)
.82	My supervisor was willing to listen to suggestions.
.64	My boss backed me up.
.72	I felt my supervisor and I understood each other.

Salary (SD = 5.59)
.77	I felt satisfied with my salary.
.49	My pay was better than that for similar jobs in other firms.
.66	My salary was a good one.

Security (SD = 5.14)
.83	I always felt secure in my job.
.65	The company did a good job of providing steady employment.

Company Policies and Practices (SD = 4.75)
.58	Company policies were well communicated.
.53	Company personnel policies were well defined.
.66	Personnel policies and practices in the company were good ones.

Working Conditions (SD = 4.90)
.80	I felt satisfied with the working conditions (heating, lighting, ventilation, etc.) on the job.
.60	Compared with most other jobs the working conditions were very satisfactory.
.83	My physical surroundings were very pleasant.

*Social Desirability was rated on a scale from 1 (low desirability) to 7 (high desirability).

Statements Comprising Different Job Dimensions for

Dissatsifying Job Situations with Loadings

on Relevant Factors and Mean Social Desirability*

Scores (SD) for Each Dimension

Factor Loading	Achievement (SD = 2.40)
57	I felt a great deal of dissatisfaction because of doing a job poorly.
73	I failed to complete a difficult assignment (or solve a difficult problem).
45	I didn't have a sense of achievement in my job.
55	I never gained a feeling of worthwhile accomplishment from my job.

Responsibility (SD = 2.98)

66   I had no responsibility for any of my own efforts.

76   I had very little responsibility on my job.

67   I was dissatisfied because my job gave me very little responsibility.

48   I had hardly any decision making power.

Work Itself (SD = 3.23)

85   My job was not very interesting.

81   I disliked the kind of work I did.

59   The actual duties on my job were not challenging.

Recognition (SD = 2.93)

56   I received very little recognition.

63   No one told me I had done a good job.

65   I didn't receive any praise for the work I did.

Advancement (SD = 3.50)

63   My progress toward a promotion was unsatisfactory.

53   There were few opportunities for advancement.

78   I felt I wasn't getting ahead in the company.

Co-workers (SD = 2.38)

80   I got very little cooperation from the people I worked with.

67   I disliked the people with whom I worked.

Factor Loading

Supervision-Technical (SD = 3.75)

.83   I didn't have a top notch supervisor.

.82   My supervisor was not a good manager.

.79   My boss showed himself to be pretty incompetent.

Supervision-Human Relations (SD=3.27)

.73   My supervisor was not willing to listen to suggestions.

.74   My boss didn't back me up.

.74   I felt my supervisor and I misunderstood each other.

Salary (SD = 3.07)

.84   I felt dissatisfied with my salary.

.67   My pay was not as good as that for similar jobs in other firms.

.76   My salary was a poor one.

Security (SD = 3.08)

.73   I never felt secure in my job.

.73   The company didn't do a good job of providing steady employment.

Company Policies and Practices (SD=3.87)

.74   Company policies were poorly communicated.

.73   Company personnel policies were poorly defined.

.74   Personnel policies and practices in the company were not very good.

Working Conditions (SD = 3.65)

.71   I felt dissatisfied with the working conditions (heating, lighting, ventilation, etc.) on the job.

.71   Compared with most other jobs the working conditions were very unsatisfactory.

.57   My physical surroundings were very unpleasant.

*Social desirability was rated on a scale from 1 (low desirability) to 7 (high desirability).

SRA (EMPLOYEE) ATTITUDE SURVEY (1951 and 196?)

Variable | The inventory attempts to measure employees' attitudes toward their job, company, working conditions, etc. It is a global instrument which includes a multitude of factors in attitude assessment.

Description | Formerly called the Employee Inventory, this instrument has been widely used since 1952. Its purpose is to provide an accurate measurement of employee attitudes toward the work environment. Tens of thousands of persons in hundreds of organizations throughout the country have been surveyed. The result is an accumulation of data covering a vast variety of business situations. From this pool of information, standards have been developed against which a firm's results can be compared.

The heart of the Attitude Survey is a series of 78 standardized items. In addition to the basic survey there are two optional sections. One consists of twenty-one items designed specifically for the company surveyed, covering questions that management wants answered. The other section of 31 items is tailored to tap opinions of supervisors, field salesmen and retail salesmen.

NOTE: As of March 1966, SRA advises that the manual for the survey is being revised and updated and new reliability data is being developed. The following discussion is based on the previous form of the Survey the manual for which is copyrighted 1951.

Reliability/ Homogeneity | Test-retest reliability estimates over a one week period are reported as exceeding .85.

Validity | The inventory is reported to have yielded results which compared favorably with extensive non-directive interviews.

Location | SRA Attitude Survey, Science Research Associates, Business and Industrial Division, Chicago, Illinois 60611.

Results and Comments | The value of this instrument has been augmented by the superb form of reporting of results. The organization being surveyed is given normative data on each question in clear concise form. The score for the total organization is shown in relation to other organizations and department scores are also shown as well as the spread of scores. Percent favorable and percent ? are shown for each question.

Such reporting based on adequate norms may be of great benefit to a firm interested in surveying its employees attitudes.

Information on cost, etc. may be obtained from SRA.

The following are sample items from the Survey:

	Agree	?	Disagree
1. The hours of work here are O. K.	▱	▱	▱

	Strongly Agree	Agree	Disagree	Strongly Disagree
2. My counterparts in other companies seem to have a much better deal than I.	▱	▱	▱	▱

IRC EMPLOYEE ATTITUDE SCALES (Carlson, et al. 1962)

Variable	The instrument attempts to measure employee attitudes toward seven aspects of work, viz, General morale, Co-workers, Hours and pay, Working conditions, Type of work, Supervision and Communication.
Description	The scale consists of 76 Likert type items (22 were experimental) and is ontologically related to earlier studies by the Minnesota group (see Results and Comments). The item content is straightforward and the verbal level of the items would not seem to restrict the scales use to any particular class of employees. The seven subscales mentioned above should be separately interpreted.
Sample	The sample consisted of handicapped workers (N=638), selected from lists of such persons in the Minneapolis area, and a set of normal "controls" (N=530) selected from the same companies. Each person was classified into one of four groups: skilled blue-collar, skilled whit collar, unskilled blue-collar and unskilled white-collar.
Reliability/ Homogeneity	Reliability information was completed by the analysis of variance method (Hoyt 1941). The coefficients range from .65 to .94 with an apparent mode in the .80's. Detailed item analyses and factor analyses are presented for each of the eight groups.
Validity	Little, if any, data bearing on the validity of the instrument are presented by the authors. The main interest in the study apparently was the construction of homogeneous scales. Differences in the manner in which each subscale correlated with general job satisfaction for each group is presented but this seems to deal only peripherally with validity.
Location	Carlson, Robert, et al. Minnesota Studies in Vocational Rehabilitation XIII. The Measurement of Employment Satisfaction. Minneapolis: Industrial Relations Center, The University of Minnesota, 1962 Bulletin 35.
Results and Comments	The Industrial Relations Center at the University of Minnesota, Minneapolis has carried out a series of studies involving job attitudes in which instruments have been continually revised and reformulated since 1951. The scope of all these studies is far too great to summarize in the analytic paradigm employed regarding other scales in this volume. The normative data, methods of analysis, methods of scale construction, etc., for all the studies listed below tend to be of high quality and the interested reader is advised to contact the Industrial Relations Center for further information regarding the availability and use of the Triple Audit, the Minnesota Employee Attitude Scale, and the Importance Questionnaire.

119

The following are some sample items from the instrument:

I feel that the work I do is very important.

I need a promotion if I am to stay happy here.

My boss is where he is because he knows the work.

(Respondents check one of five ordered boxes from: strongly agree, agree, undecided, disagree or strongly disagree.)

INDEX OF EMPLOYEE SATISFACTION (Morse 1953)

Variable	This instrument measures job satisfaction on four factors -- intrinsic satisfactions, pride in one's work group, company involvement, and pay or status --derived from a previous factor analysis.
Description	Four items comprise each subscale which contain two to four Likert type items and two to zero open-ended codings. Scale items were selected from a larger series of items on the basis of item content and inter-item correlations. Scores on each item vary from one to five, so that scores each subscale vary between 4 (high) and 20 (low).
Sample	The sample consisted of 580 white-collar employees, at various organizational levels.
Reliability/ Homogeneity	No test-retest reliability data were reported. Adequately high internal consistency is evidenced by the fact that average inter-item correlations were in the .40's and .50's for each subscale.
Validity	Of the four subscales, only pride-in-group-performance produced correlations as predicted. Group pride was found to relate to the amount of voluntary help members gave each other, friendships in the group, supervisor identification with employees and the absence of antiproductivity group norms.
	The other three scales correlated substantially with each other leading one to suspect that they were tapping the same basic dimension. All three scales predicted an individual's desire to stay in the company, but not his productivity.
Location	Morse, N. Satisfactions in the White Collar Job Ann Arbor: Institute for Social Research, 1953.
Administration	Five of the 20 items were originally coded from extensive interview materials so that overall administration time cannot be estimated. The respondents were placed in high, medium and low groups (approximately an equal number of employees fell in each group) on the basis of the following score boundaries:

	High	Medium	Low
Intrinsic	4-7	8-11	12-20
Group pride	4-8	9-12	13-20
Company involvement	4-8	9-12	13-20
Pay and status	4-8	9-10	11-20

Results and Comments	It would appear that it would be more accurate to refer to this instrument as a two factor rather than a four factor measure. The second factor, pride in the group, does not seem directly to reflect job satisfaction in the pure sense of the term.

Intrinsic Job Satisfaction Index

1. "How well do you like the sort of work you are doing?"
   code: Five-point scale varying from strong like to strong dislike.
2. "Does your job give you a chance to do the things you feel you do best?"
   code: Five-point scale varying from yes (strong) to no (strong).
3. "Do you get any feeling of accomplishment from the work you are doing?"
   code: Five-point scale varying from strong sense of task completion to no sense of task completion.
4. "How do you feel about your work, does it rate as an important job with you?"
   code: Five-point scale varying from very important to of no importance.

Pride-in-Group-Performance Index

1. "How well do you think your section compares with other sections in the Company in getting a job done?"
   code: Five-point scale ranging from very good, one of best in company, to very poor, one of worst in company.
2. Answers to the section comparison question were also coded on the degree of emotional identification with the section that employee showed. (The use of "we" as opposed to "it" or "they" was one of the indications to the coder of identification.)
   code: Three-point scale: strong identification, mild identification, indifference or lack of identification.
3. "How well do you think your division compares with other divisions in the Company in getting a job done?"
   code: Five-point scale ranging from very good, one of best in company, to very poor, one of worst in company.
4. Answers to the division comparison question were also coded on degree of emotional identification with the division the employee showed.
   code: Three-point scale: strong identification, mild identification, indifference or lack of identification.

Company Involvement Index

1. "How do you like working here?"
   code: Five-point scale ranging from strong like, complete satisfaction to strong dislike.
2. "Would you advise a friend to come to work for the Company?"
   code: Three-point scale including: yes, pro-con, and no.
3. An overall coder rating of the employee's feelings about the fairness of the company, based on answers to questions throughout the interview.
   code: Three-point scale including: feels company fair and generous, feels company fair but very exacting, feels company unfair.
4. An overall coder rating of the employee's degree of identification with the company based on answers to questions throughout the interview.
   code: Three-point scale including: strong identification, some identification, and no identification.

Financial and Job Status Index

1. "How well satisfied are you with your salary?"
   code: Five-point scale ranging from very well satisfied to very dissatisfied.
2. "How satisfied are you with your chances of getting more pay?"
   code: Five-point scale ranging from very satisfied to very dissatisfied.
3. "How about your own case, how satisfied are you with the way things have been working out for you?" (This question was preceded by two questions on "getting ahead here at the Company" and was answered in that context.)
   code: Five-point scale ranging from very satisfied to very dissatisfied.
4. Coder overall rating of degree of frustration evidenced by respondent in advancing in his job or in his main vocational objectives. Answers to questions throughout the interview were used to measure the degree to which employee felt his vocational desires were blocked.
   code: Five-point scale ranging from strong frustration to high adjustment, no frustration.

JOB SATISFACTION SCALE (Johnson 1955)

Variable   This instrument claims to measure opinions in a large number of work areas which are apparently related to job satisfaction.

Description   The questionnaire consists of 99 items to be answered on the basis of a yes-no dichotomy with the "?" category reserved for items which do not apply to the individual. The following work areas are covered in the questionnaire: physical and mental exertion; physical surrounding and working conditions; relations with employers; relations with other employees; advancement, security, and finances; interest in, liking for, and emotional involvement in the job; job status and job information; future, goals, and progress toward goals; and evaluation in retrospect.

Items covering the various aspects of the work areas "...were collected through reference to existing scales and literature, and supplemented through logical analysis..."

Sample   Various collections of "teachers" were used in the study. Unfortunate the author does not specify grade level, age, location, etc.

Reliability/
  Homogeneity   Test-retest reliability over a three week period is reported as .90 using a sample of 98 teachers. The average biserial correlation between total score and work category (sic) is reported as .45.

Validity   Face validity of a sort is claimed by the author in the following manner: "Since use was made of the findings of previous studies concerned with job satisfaction and its measurement in constructing the questionnaire, the latter should be expected to have some validity if these other studies were themselves valid." Such claims for validation are hardly compelling.

The author also reports that no item of the questionnaire was scored unless 8 out of 10 graduate students in psychology and education (serving as judges) were in agreement as to the item's relevance to job satisfaction. A population of 1,184 teachers rated each item on importance and are reported to have "upheld previous judgments that th work categories...were important to job satisfaction."

Furthermore, the 98 teachers in the reliability study completed single item self-ratings of job satisfaction using an 11 point scale with "1" representing complete dissatisfaction, "6" average satisfaction, and "11", complete satisfaction. This "criterion" is reported to have a retest reliability of .89 and to correlate .64 with scores on the questionnaire.

Finally, pair comparison ratings of 18 teachers by each other on the dimension of job satisfaction yielded a correlation of .61 with scores from the questionnaire.

Location	Johnson, George H., "An instrument for the measurement of job satis-faction", Personnel Psychology, 1955, 8, pp. 27-37.
Administration	Self administered in 45 minutes to one hour. Scoring direction is apparent from item content and the use of a template should permit a quick summation of items for area or total scores. Directions are as follows:

> The following questions concern your feelings and attitudes regarding your work and your plans. They are specific and require that you circle the "Yes" or the "No" --whichever is the answer appropriate for you. If you are doubtful, make the best answer you can, but answer either "Yes" or "No". You should circle the "?" only if the question does apply to you. Some of the questions are very similar but have somewhat different meanings, so answer every question even though you may feel that it has already appeared in the list.

Results and Comments	Several points may be raised with regard to the possible value of this instrument. First, the population on which it was developed is not sufficiently described to allow a potential user to make com-parisons with other populations. There are aspects of teacher's jobs which are unique to that profession such as tenure, vacation, etc., which may greatly affect responses to certain items on the questionnaire.

Second, the attempts to establish validity of the instrument seem to fall short of an adequate demonstration of validity. To claim validity by association with other tests on the basis of interest item similarity may be very misleading. Graduate students in psychology and education may or may not be qualified to judge whether an item is relevant to job satisfaction. And relevance is not quite the same thing as discriminating power or validity. With regard to the single item self-rating of satisfaction one may question why a 99 item questionnaire is required if total score correlates .64 with the self rating. The author contends that "...the specifics contributing to satisfaction...rather than the job satisfaction level itself is (sic) of considerable importance, and can be obtained from the questionnaire, but not from the ratings." If this is true, then it would be desirable to know the relative contribution to validity made by each section of the questionnaire. The author's use of "a paired-comparison technique" is perhaps the most compelling evidence of validity to be offered. The limited size (N=18) and apparent homogeneity of the sample in this case, however, restricts the application of the findings.

Third, no attempt was made to cross-validate the item selection process or to select items on any basis other than internal consistency.

The verbal level of the questionnaire sections varies widely indicating that some modification might be necessary if the scale were to be used across occupational groupings and not limited to college graduates.

Nevertheless, on the whole, the psychometric data for the instrument are far more extensive than most measures in the literature. It is unfortunate that such a variety of data are not available for many other scales.

Adjustment Items, Grouped by Area of Coverage, with Reliability and Internal Consistency Indexes for Each

Area and Item	% Agreement on Test-Retest	r bis. Females	r bis. Males
Physical and Mental Exertion			
1. Does your present job tire you too much physically?	94.7	.57	.65
2. Does your present job force you to maintain too fast a pace?	94.8	.48	.38
3. Does your work have a bad effect on your health?	97.9	.49	.65
4. Does your present job require you to work too long hours?	89.6	.39	.31
5. Do you get restless during working hours, and feel that the day is dragging endlessly?	93.8	.50	.65
6. Do you think your job gets more difficult for you each year?	91.2	.46	.47
7. Do you feel your work suffers because you have too much to do?	79.6	.47	.49
Relations with Associates			
8. In general, do you get along well with the persons with whom you work on your present job?	98.9	.05	.08
9. Does your present position force you to work with certain individuals whom you dislike?	79.2	.39	.36
10. Have you made real and lasting friends among your working associates?	96.8	.32	.38
11. Do you feel that your general interests and attitudes are about the same as those of your fellow workers who have similar jobs?	81.5	.38	.44
12. Do you feel that others could make your work easier if they cared to do so?	78.0	.45	.32
13. Do those with whom you work sometimes seem unreasonable in their dealings with you?	83.9	.46	.29
14. Do you feel that your associates stimulate you to do better work?	84.8	.53	.57
Relations with Employer			
15. Do you feel that your employer unfairly takes the credit for work you have done?	95.7	.45	.27
16. Do you feel that you know where you stand with your present employer?	88.3	.59	.52
17. Are there too many people telling you what to do at present?	94.9	.48	.28
18. Do you feel at ease in the presence of the people under whom you work?	95.9	.36	.23
19. Is it necessary for you to do things you dislike in order to get promotions?	94.6	.48	.63
20. Do you sometimes wonder whether the people under whom you work approve of your work?	81.7	.38	.36
21. Do you feel that there should be more people to help with the work you are doing?	84.1	.42	.30
22. Do you believe other people advance ahead of you by unfair means such as special influence or politics?	92.4	.50	.61
23. Do you feel that you have been required to take more responsibilities in your work than you desire?	93.8	.48	.36
24. Do the people under whom you work make available the materials, information and assistance you need to do your best work?	88.9	.63	.57
25. Are the people under whom you work desirous of and			
26. Are the policies and problems of the people under whom you work adequately explained to you?	84.1	.59	.74
27. Do you get along satisfactorily with the people under whom you work?	100.0	.50	.60
28. Do you feel respect and regard for the people under whom you work?	96.8	.75	.62
29. Do you feel that the people under whom you work make unfair demands on your free time?	87.6	.40	.49
30. Do you feel that you can always trust the people under whom you work?	89.8	.59	.66
Security, Advancement, and Finances			
31. Do you feel you are paid a fair salary for the work you do?	91.3	.46	.55
32. Have you been able to get the promotions and pay increases which you feel you deserve?	81.8	.47	.62
33. Is your income sufficient to meet your financial obligations and support your family?	89.0	.39	.47
34. Are you kept from dressing as you would like because of insufficient income?	99.0	.46	.52
35. Are you kept from living as you would like because of insufficient income?	93.6	.50	.53
36. Are adequate and fair arrangements for absences due to illness made for your position?	87.5	.19	.16
37. Does the method of payment of your earnings frequently cause you inconvenience?	85.6	.25	.35
38. Are you afraid of losing your job?	99.0	.17	.14
39. Do you feel as efficient as the average person with whom you work?	100.0	.20	.08
40. Do you feel that there is any prejudice toward your age group in your occupation (e.g., that you are too young or too old)?	85.3	.40	.26
41. Do you have eventual retirement security in your job?	93.8	.23	.06
Interest in, Liking for, and Emotional Involvement in the Job			
42. Does your job give you more real personal satisfaction than the things you do in your spare time?	86.0	.47	.47
43. Do you feel that you must look outside your work for those things that make life worthwhile and interesting?	88.0	.61	.52
44. Do you find your work so interesting that it is on your mind a lot when you are not at work?	87.0	.36	.32
45. Are you so interested in your work that you talk about it a great deal even after working hours?	90.5	.30	.28
46. Would your life seem empty without your work to occupy you?	86.3	.29	.52
47. Would you continue to work if it were not financially necessary?	96.8	.44	.59
48. Do you feel that you are really interested in your present job?	94.9	.70	.75
49. Do you often feel that your work is monotonous and boring?	93.8	.51	.57
50. Would you like to secure a different job, either in the same or another occupation?	79.5	.68	.61

Area and Item	% Agreement on Test-Retest	r bis. Females	r bis. Males
52. Do you like your present job better than any other you have ever had?	89.0	.46	.60
53. Is your present job in the area of work (not necessarily the same job) you wish to remain in permanently?	86.8	.46	.46
54. Would you decline an opportunity to change your present job for one of equal pay, security and status?	77.3	.53	.45
55. If you had a choice, would you choose a job in your present line of work over one in any other line of work?	81.7	.50	.50
56. Did you really want to enter your present job yourself when you started it?	88.6	.33	.25
57. Are you sorry you took the particular job you have now?	97.9	.43	.65
58. Are you actively looking for another job at present?	96.9	.32	.57
59. Do you feel that you are "in a rut" vocationally?	95.9	.58	.61
60. Does your present job sometimes get you badly flustered and jittery?	90.5	.42	.36
61. Do you frequently come home upset, angry or irritable because of something that happened at work?	91.4	.57	.55
62. Do you often come home at night with a feeling of satisfaction over work well done?	100.0	.44	.78
63. Do you frequently get discouraged in your present job?	88.4	.56	.66
64. Are you generally happy and cheerful when at work?	96.9	.55	.60
65. Do you worry a lot about your daily work?	84.5	.38	.54
66. Are you glad to get back to your job after a vacation?	95.9	.48	.68
67. Do you think your job has "smothered" your personality?	93.8	.43	.85

Job Information, Training and Status

Area and Item	% Agreement on Test-Retest	r bis. Females	r bis. Males
68. Do you feel you have had adequate preparation for the job you now hold?	86.6	.32	-.08
69. Do you feel that you have an adequate understanding of what is expected of you in your present job?	98.9	.39	.35
70. Do you think your work is worthwhile and important?	98.9	.30	.50
71. Do you feel that your work utilizes your full abilities?	77.9	.37	.45
72. Are you proud of your job and the work you do?	99.0	.40	.32
73. Are you ashamed of your job?	99.0	.04	.26
74. Do you feel that your family and friends respect your job?	97.9	.40	.34
75. Do you feel that people in general respect your job?	95.8	.41	.55
76. Do you feel that your working associates regard you as an equal?	95.9	.32	.23
77. Do you feel that your job detracts from your status in the community where you live?	97.9	.27	.43
78. Are you embarrassed when people ask you what work you do?	94.8	.26	.45

Area and Item	% Agreement on Test-Retest	r bis. Females	r bis. Males
79. Do you feel competent and fully able to handle your job?	90.7	.43	.10

Physical Surroundings and Work Conditions

Area and Item	% Agreement on Test-Retest	r bis. Females	r bis. Males
80. Are you satisfied with the degree to which your present job gives you opportunity to express your own ideas?	88.6	.52	.51
81. Is your work too confining to suit you?	91.7	.29	-.10
82. Do you feel your place of work is too far from your home?	87.6	.46	.41
83. Do you consider your work surroundings to be as pleasant as they should be?	93.8	.45	.47
84. Does your occupation force you to live in home surroundings which are uncomfortable or inadequate according to your standards?	100.0	.33	.26
85. Do you feel that your work is too dirty or too noisy?	90.0	.27	.15
86. Is there adequate transportation available to you in going to and from work?	88.7	.51	.53
87. Does your job give you enough varied experiences?	95.9	.38	.18
88. Do you feel that your job requirements change too often for you to keep up adequately?	90.7	.47	.55
89. Do you feel your work ties you down or restricts your freedom too much?	88.9	.63	.57

Future, Goals and Progress Toward Goals

Area and Item	% Agreement on Test-Retest	r bis. Females	r bis. Males
90. Does your present job help you toward the financial goals you have set yourself?	89.4	.44	.59
91. Does your present job help you toward the occupational goals you have set yourself?	95.8	.62	.63
92. Do you think it is possible to attain your vocational goals in that portion of your life that is still ahead of you?	96.9	.35	.34
93. Do you regard your present position as a lifetime career?	80.9	.32	.33
94. Does your vocational future look promising to you?	96.9	.56	.52
95. Do you expect your job to give you more satisfaction the longer you have it?	92.6	.58	.56
96. Do you feel that you will become more proficient at your work the longer you have it?	98.9	.45	.39

Evaluation in Retrospect

Area and Item	% Agreement on Test-Retest	r bis. Females	r bis. Males
97. Do you feel you have made a success of your job thus far in your career?	98.9	.42	.28
98. If you could start over again, at 18, would you choose a different line of work?	92.1	.61	.62
99. Do you feel less satisfied with your work as time goes on?	85.6	.43	.48

JOB DIMENSIONS BLANK (Schletzer 1965)

Variable	This instrument attempts to measure general job satisfaction by tapping a number of job components, not all of which are applicable to each person's job. Inapplicable items are then disregarded in the person's final score.
Description	In all, the respondent is asked to rate 62 aspects of his job as to whether he is satisfied, not satisfied, not sure about an aspect, or whether he feels the aspect is not applicable. The final score is determined by taking the percentage of satisfied responses, subtracting the number of disatisfied responses, dividing this total by the number of relevant items, and then adding 100 to each score (to prevent negative scores).
Sample	One hundred professional people constituted the sample. The average score for the group was 162 with a standard deviation of 29.
Reliability/ Homogeneity	No information of this kind is reported in the materials available to us, although it may appear in the original dissertation.
Validity	The instrument **correlates moderately** with Brayfield and Rothe's measure and Hoppock's index.
Location	Schletzer, V. "A study of the predictive effectiveness of the Strong Vocational Interest Blank for Job Satisfaction" (Unpublished doctoral dissertation, University of Minnesota, 1965)
Remarks	This scale was brought to our attention rather late in our search procedure, so we did not have time to review it adequately. We refer the interested reader to the original dissertation.

JOB DIMENSIONS

After each of the following items:
Draw a circle around the S if you are satisfied with that item. Draw a circle around
the D if you are dissatisfied with that item.
Draw a circle around the ? if you are not sure.
Draw a circle around the NA if the item is not present in or appropriate to your job.
Mark each item with your present job in mind.

		S	?	D	NA
1.	Your earnings				
2.	Financial security				
3.	Prospects for a comfortable retirement				
4.	Prospects for future earnings				
5.	Time for recreation and/or family activities				
6.	Opportunities for travel				
7.	Time for travel				
8.	Community in which you live				
9.	Your prestige in the community				
10.	Your prestige on the job				
11.	Opportunities for promotion				
12.	Prestige in your profession				
13.	Administrative details of job				
14.	Committee work required				
15.	Written reports necessary				
16.	Non-professional aspects of the job				
17.	Routine activities of the job				
18.	Time for study in your field				
19.	Opportunity to advance professionally				
20.	Opportunity to talk-shop				
21.	Opportunity to direct work of others				
22.	Opportunity to help in policy-making				
23.	Opportunity to be your own boss				
24.	Interesting co-workers				
25.	Intelligent, competent co-workers				
26.	Fun and relaxation with co-workers				
27.	Competition				
28.	Demands of clients or patients				
30.	Demands of supervisors				
31.	Intellectual challenge				
32.	Variety of activities required				
33.	Chance to improve skills				
34.	Chance to do research				
35.	Experience				
36.	Physical fatigue				
37.	Pressure on job				
38.	Hours				
39.	Opportunity to use learned skills				
40.	Opportunity to use aptitudes and abilities				
41.	Opportunity to use education				
42.	Fulfillment of personal needs				
43.	Feeling of achievement				
44.	Feeling of being needed				

Job Dimensions (continued)

		S	?	D	NA
45.	Feeling of accomplishment				
46.	Full credit for work done				
47.	Thanks from those you benefit				
48.	Recognition from your supervisors				
49.	Recognition from your peers				
50.	Personal satisfaction of job well done				
51.	Chance to see results of work				
52.	Chance to follow job through to its conclusion				
53.	Chance to evaluate own work				
54.	Evaluation of work by others				
55.	Opportunity to use initiative				
56.	Freedom to make decisions				
57.	Personal autonomy				
58.	Freedom to use own judgment				
59.	Opportunity to do socially significant tasks				
60.	Opportunity to improve health of others				
61.	Opportunity to improve appearance or comfort of others				
62.	Opportunity to help others find success or happiness				

Job Satisfaction Index (Brayfield and Rothe 1951)

Variable   This scale seems to be a general index of job satisfaction inferred from attitude toward work.

Description   In constructing the scale it was the authors' intent to provide an overall index of job satisfaction applicable across occupational categories. Seventy-seven men in a Personnel Psychology class at the University of Minnesota for members of an Army Specialized Training Program served as judges in a Thurstone scaling paradigm. The average age of the judges was 30 years and the majority had had several years occupational experience ranging from unskilled labor to professional occupations.

Items were selected for the index on the basis of Q value (less than 2.00), lack of reference to a specific aspect of a job, and lack of social desirability. Eighteen items covering almost the entire attitude range in 1/2 step intervals and which met the above criteria were selected for the final scale from an original pool of 255. Likert scoring was then applied to the items using the Thurstone scale value to indicate scoring direction. That is, items at the satisfied end of the scale received 5 points for Strongly Agree, 4 for Agree, 3 for Undecided, etc. Items at the dissatisfied end received 5 points for Strongly Disagree, 4 for Disagree, 3 for Undecided, etc. The possible range of scores is therefore 18 to 90 points with a high score representing satisfaction. The "neutral" point is at 54.

Sample   Several samples were used in various phases of the study and are described below.

Reliability/ Homogeneity   A split half coefficient of .87 (corrected) is reported for a sample of 231 clerical female employees.

Validity   The index is able to discriminate between groups who were assumed to be differentially satisfied with their jobs. The mean scores of 40 people in an adult night school course in Personnel Psychology who were also employed in a personnel position were contrasted with 51 people in the same course but who were not employed in personnel positions. The authors make this dichotomy based on the following assumption: "Those persons in the class employed in occupations appropriate to their expressed interest should, on the average, be more satisfied with their jobs than those members of the class employed in occupations inappropriate to their expressed interest in personnel work." The Personnel group's mean score was 76.9 (SD = 8.6) and the Non-Personnel group's was 65.4 (SD = 14.02). The difference in means is reported as being significantly different at the 1% level (presumably by a one tailed test, ed.).

The Job Satisfaction Index was also reported to correlate .92 with the Hoppock blank on the same night school population.

Location   Brayfield, A. H. and H. F. Rothe, "An Index of Job Satisfaction,"
              J. Appl. Psychol. (35), 1951, pp. 307-311.

Administration   Self administered in about 10 minutes. Scoring is readily ac-
              complished by summing the response category values.

Results &   The Job Satisfaction Index (JSI) is a simple, straightforward,
Comments   transparent instrument which might be useful for a superficial survey
              of general job satisfaction. Since it does not provide area scores
              or give information about specific items of discontent it would be
              difficult to use for counseling and would not enable management to
              modify particular practices, etc.

                   Brayfield, Wells and Strate (1957) discovered that the JSI cor-
              related + .40 (for men) with the Science Research Associates Inven-
              tory and + .32 with the Weitz Test of General Satisfaction. A cor-
              relation of + .49 is reported with the Rundquist-Sletto Morale Scale
              for the same group of 41 male city government employees. The scores
              of female employees showed a lower split half reliability and no sig-
              nificant correlations between JSI and the instruments mentioned above.
              The authors hypothesize that the correlation between job satisfaction
              and general life satisfaction for men results because the job plays
              a more significant role in the lives of men than of women. They sug-
              gest, in fact, "...that, when the job is perceived as important in
              the life scheme as may be the case for...males..., general satisfac-
              tion becomes a function, in part at least, of job satisfaction."

References   Brayfield, A. H., R. V. Wells, and M. W. Strate, "Interrelationships
              Among Measures of Job Satisfaction and General Satisfaction," *J. Appl.
              Psychol.* (41), 1957, pp. 201-205.

Instrument

The plus (+) and minus (-) signs below indicate the apparent scoring direction for the item and do not, of course, appear on the original scale. Items marked (+) are scored 5 points for Strongly Agree, etc. Items marked (-) are scored 5 for Strongly Disagree, etc.

JOB QUESTIONNAIRE

Some jobs are more interesting and satisfying than others. We want to know how people feel about different jobs. This blank contains eighteen statements about jobs. You are to cross out the phrase below each statement which best describes how you feel about your present job. There are no right or wrong answers. We should like your honest opinion on each one of the statem<ents. Work out the sample item numbered (0).

0. There are some conditions concerning my job that could be improved.
STRONGLY AGREE   AGREE   UNDECIDED   DISAGREE   STRONGLY DISAGREE

+ 9. I am satisfied with my job for the time being.
STRONGLY AGREE   AGREE   UNDECIDED   DISAGREE   STRONGLY DISAGREE

-10. I feel that my job is no more interesting than others I could get.
STRONGLY AGREE   AGREE   UNDECIDED   DISAGREE   STRONGLY DISAGREE

-11. I definitely dislike my work.
STRONGLY AGREE   AGREE   UNDECIDED   DISAGREE   STRONGLY DISAGREE

+12. I feel that I am happier in my work than most other people.
STRONGLY AGREE   AGREE   UNDECIDED   DISAGREE   STRONGLY DISAGREE

+13. Most days I am enthusiastic about my work.
STRONGLY AGREE   AGREE   UNDECIDED   DISAGREE   STRONGLY DISAGREE

-14. Each day of work seems like it will never end.
STRONGLY AGREE   AGREE   UNDECIDED   DISAGREE   STRONGLY DISAGREE

+15. I like my job better than the average worker does.
STRONGLY AGREE   AGREE   UNDECIDED   DISAGREE   STRONGLY DISAGREE

-16. My job is pretty uninteresting.
STRONGLY AGREE   AGREE   UNDECIDED   DISAGREE   STRONGLY DISAGREE

+17. I find real enjoyment in my work.
STRONGLY AGREE   AGREE   UNDECIDED   DISAGREE   STRONGLY DISAGREE

-18. I am disappointed that I ever took this job.
STRONGLY AGREE   AGREE   UNDECIDED   DISAGREE   STRONGLY DISAGREE

Revised job satisfaction blank.

+ 1. My job is like a hobby to me.
STRONGLY AGREE   AGREE   UNDECIDED   DISAGREE   STRONGLY DISAGREE

+,2. My job is usually interesting enough to keep me from getting bored
STRONGLY AGREE   AGREE   UNDECIDED   DISAGREE   STRONGLY DISAGREE

- 3. It seems that my friends are more interested in their jobs.
STRONGLY AGREE   AGREE   UNDECIDED   DISAGREE   STRONGLY DISAGREE

- 4. I consider my job rather unpleasant.
STRONGLY AGREE   AGREE   UNDECIDED   DISAGREE   STRONGLY DISAGREE

+ 5. I enjoy my work more than my leisure time.
STRONGLY AGREE   -AGREE   UNDECIDED   DISAGREE   STRONGLY DISAGREE

- 6. I am often bored with my job.
STRONGLY AGREE   AGREE   UNDECIDED   DISAGREE   STRONGLY DISAGREE

+ 7. I feel fairly well satisfied with my present job.
STRONGLY AGREE   AGREE   UNDECIDED   DISAGREE   STRONGLY DISAGREE

- 8. Most of the time I have to force myself to go to work.
STRONGLY AGREE   AGREE   UNDECIDED   DISAGREE   STRONGLY DISAGREE

JOB SATISFACTION (Hoppock 1935)

Variable	Most of these job satisfaction questions are straightforward ratings but there are some questions concluded in a comparative framework, e.g., how well the person's job compares with those of other people, how well it compares with spare time activities.
Description	Hoppock tried many different questions in this landmark publication. The nine listed here are the ones asked of residents of New Hope, Pennsylvania, which constitute the ones most valuable for normative purposes and for the assessment of social changes.
	A total job satisfaction index is composed of items I, II, III and V and apparently based on the average score for each item. That is, if the person chooses the "least satisfied" of the seven alternatives for each of the four items, he gets a score of 100 and 700 if he chooses the "most satisfied" alternatives for each item.
Sample	The total population of New Hope, Pennsylvania was surveyed in 1933. Only 12 percent of the employed refused to participate, giving a total sample of 309 employed respondents across the entire occupational hierarchy.
Reliability/ Homogeneity	No test-retest data were apparently collected. A split-half correlation between items I and III vs. II and V was .93.
Validity	The author does present some data indicating attitudinal differences between satisfied and dissatisfied teachers but these and the other validational data presented by the author appear to bear only peripherally on validity as it is considered today.
Location	Hoppock, R. Job Satisfaction New York: Harper, 1935.
Administration	The questions are self-administrable in less than ten minutes. The score ranges from 100 (extreme satisfaction) to 700 (extreme dissatisfaction) resulted in the following distribution for the New Hope respondents:

100 - 199	6%
200 - 299	6
300 - 399	10
400 - 499	12
500 - 599	40
600 - 700	26
	100%

Results and Comments	The mean score was 494. Hoppock was perhaps the first to note the relation between satisfaction and occupational status. Unskilled manual workers scored 401, semi-skilled 483, skilled and white-collar 510, sub-professional and lower management 548 and professional and upper-management 560.

Despite its age and the occasionally obscure topics covered in this book, this research still deserves examination. The questions continue to be used to this day. For example, research into the IRC and Schletzer scales (presented previously) employed the major four items of this scale.

I. Choose the ONE of the following statements which best tells how well you like
your job.   Place a check mark (√) in front of that statement:

1.	I hate it	2%
2.	I dislike it	2
3.	I don't like it	11
4.	I am indifferent to it	9
5.	I like it	63
6.	I am enthusiastic about it	9
7.	I love it	5
	Total	101%

II. Check one of the following to show HOW MUCH OF THE TIME you feel satisfied with
your job:

8.	All of the time	41%
9.	Most of the time	27
10.	A good deal of the time	8
11.	About half of the time	9
12.	Occasionally	5
13.	Seldom	5
14.	Never	5
	Total	100%

III. Check the ONE of the following which best tells how you feel about changing your jo

15.	I would quit this job at once if I could get anything else to do	13%
16.	I would take almost any other job in which I could earn as much as I am earning now	4
17.	I would like to change both my job and my occupation	7
18.	I would like to exchange my present job for another job in the same line of work	4
19.	I am not eager to change my job, but I would do so if I could get a better job	43
20.	I cannot think of any jobs for which I would exchange mine	18
21.	I would not exchange my job for any other	12
	Total	101%

IV. If you could have your choice of all the jobs in the world, which would you choose?
(Check one):

22.	Your present job	48%
23.	Another job in the same occupation	16
24.	A job in another occupation	36
	Total	100%

V. Check one of the following to show how you think you compare with other people:

25.	No one likes his job better than I like mine	19%
26.	I like my job much better than most people like theirs	16
27.	I like my job better than most people like theirs	11
28.	I like my job about as well as most people like theirs	37
29.	I dislike my job more than most people dislike theirs	8
30.	I dislike my job much more than most people dislike theirs	2
31.	No one dislikes his job more than I dislike mine	6
	Total	99%

VI.   Which gives you more satisfaction? (Check one):

32.	Your job	66%
33.	The things you do in your spare time	34
	Total	100%

VII.   34.   Have you ever thought seriously about changing your present job?

Yes	39%
No	51
Omitted	9
Total	99%

VIII.   35.   Have you ever declined an opportunity to change your present job?

Yes	26%
No	63
Omitted	10
Total	99%

IX.   36.   Are your feelings today a true sample of the way you usually feel about your job?

Yes	86%
No	6
Omitted	7
Total	99%

TEAR BALLOT (Kerr 1948)

Variable	The <u>Tear Ballot</u> appears to be a measure of general job satisfaction or morale.
Description	The <u>Tear Ballot</u> represents an early attempt to measure job satisfaction in a probably unique fashion. Responses to the 10 item scale are recorded by having the subject tear the edge of the page at designated spots rather than having him record his responses in pencil or ink. The manual maintains that this method of recording responses assures anonymity and "...not only accomplishes its technical purpose but also it wins the employees' respect for the investigators."

Items were chosen for the scale which seemed to represent the prominent themes in psychological and personnel literature in the mid-1940's. The item were appraised and revised by a panel of five industrial psychologists and the vocabulary level was checked against the Thorndike word list.

Sample	A large number of studies utilizing various populations have been accomplished with this scale. The relevant data on sample characteristics are presented below where applicable.
Reliability/ Homogeneity	Corrected split half coefficients are reported to range from .65 to .88 for unspecified populations. The manual does not report a test-retest reliability coefficient.
Validity	The manual reports numerous validity studies in which the variable correlated with job satisfaction ranges from percent hearing loss to empathic ability.

The following correlations between the Tear Ballot and specific variables are presented in the manual:

Variable	Correlation
1) job tenure rate	.25
2) percent hearing loss (age held constant)	-.42
3) average popularity rating	.82
4) satisfaction with collective bargaining organization	.74
5) empathic ability	.44
6) frequency of grievance and catharsis sessions with management	-.76
7) unexcused absenteeism	-.44
8) percent of unexcused absenteeism due to illness only	.79 (sic)

Further data are presented in the manual.

Location	Kerr, W. A., "On the validity and reliability of the job satisfaction Tear Ballot," <u>J. Appl. Psychol.</u>, 1948, <u>32</u>, 275-281.

Location (continued)

Psychometric Affiliates, <u>The Tear Ballot for Industry</u>. Chicago: no date given on manual.

Administration   The scale is self administered and "an average employee can answer all questions and cast his anonymous ballot within two or three minutes." Assuming that in "tearing" his ballot the average employee is not overly zealous, scoring may be accomplished quite rapidly.

Results and Comments   It is unusual that so short a test should show both such high apparent reliability and validity. If use of this test is contemplated the establishment of local norms and validity indexes is strongly recommended.

The orientation of workers toward tests is probably quite different today than it was twenty years ago. It is doubtful that a significant advantage is to be obtained through the use of a "tear ballot" over a more common pencil and paper test.

Normative data are presented for various groupings of employees (N=8 to N=554) in various occupations. The data are grouped by age, sex, occupation and geographic location. There is no indication of the relation of education level to <u>Tear Ballot</u> scores and no indication as to the age of the normative data.

The following items are a sample of the <u>Tear Ballot</u> questions:

1) Does the company make you feel that your job is reasonably secure as long as you do good work?

5) Are most of the workers around you the kind who still remember you when you pass them on the street?

9) Do you have confidence in the good sense of management?

EMPLOYEE MORALE SCALE (Woods 1944)

Variable

This scale represents an attempt to measure attitude dimensions which may be associated with job satisfaction or morale.

Description

134 Thurstone scaled items are arranged in 17 groups with an average of about eight items per group. A respondent is instructed to choose the one statement in a group which most accurately represents his attitude. Based on item content the groups may be labeled as follows: Instructions, Responsibilities, Suggestions, Supervisors, Plans, Nature of Work, Favors, Courtesy, Public Relations, Interests, Advancement, Career Opportunity, Pay and Ability, Working Conditions, Recognition, Promotion, Outside Influences.

Item content appears to be of a relatively high verbal level which may greatly restrict the application of this scale across occupational groupings.

Sample

The original item pool of 427 statements was mailed to 200 people of which "most were the general run of employee" and an unreported percentage were supervisors of various levels. Only one-third of the raters returned usable data.

Reliability/ Homogeneity

No estimate of reliability is reported.

Validity

Items for the scale were selected from the original pool on the basis of scale position and semi-interquartile range in standard Thurstone manner. The resulting scale was then administered to another sample of 42 federal employees, all employed by the same agency in various field offices, doing the same kind of work at approximately the same rate of pay. Analysis of the results of one third of the group does not seem to reveal any significant pattern and it is difficult to say what claim the scale makes for validity.

Location

Woods, A. "Employee attitudes and their relation to morale", J. Appl. Psychol., 1944, 28, pp. 285-301.

Administration

Self administered in about three quarters of an hour. Scoring is relatively easy, and consists of noting the scale value for the item checked in each section.

Results and Comments

This scale represents an early attempt to isolate and measure variable in an area which is highly relevant for today's researchers. Users of this scale in its present form may encounter some difficulties. The verbal level of the individual items is probably too difficult to allow for testing a wide range of occupational groupings. Some employees may also find it difficult to choose, out of a block of ten or twelve statements, one statement which adequately represents their attitude.

Results and Comments (continued)

It is possible that this scale could be improved by choosing three or four items from each group and using Likert format.   This might serve to ease response effort and increase the score variance.   The interested reader is referred to Edward's (1957, pp. 201-219) discussion of the Scale-Discrimination technique.   In any case the value of this scale may best be assessed by comparing responses of groups judged to exhibit differential levels of morale or satisfaction.

References   Edwards, Allen L.   <u>Techniques of Attitude Scale Construction</u>, New York: Appleton-Century-Crofts, 1957.

Job Segment Evaluation Scale

This scale is designed to analyze the attitudes of employees in various jobs. Each of the following statements represents a numerical value indicative of a degree of attitude. We are not interested in individual attitude measurement in this case; therefore you are asked not to write your name on this form.

You are asked to check the one statement in each of the following groups which most closely represents your opinion on the subject.

Scale Value

I

1. I feel that I receive too many instructions that are meaningless. — 2.7
2. There is no use following all instructions too carefully for some supervisors do not understand the details of the job. — 2.3
3. Our supervisors always appreciate the employee's point of view regarding instructions. — 7.9
4. One should call the supervisor's attention to points which the instructions do not cover. — 8.0
5. There are many times when one needs to do what is best at his own risk when instructions are inadequate. — 7.6
6. If instructions conflict the employee should seek the advice of his immediate superior at once. — 8.3
7. If instructions are not carried out one should promptly explain to the supervisor. — 7.7
8. If instructions conflict the employee is justified in ignoring them and continuing as he has always done. — 2.5
9. Instructions are often unimportant and should not be taken too seriously. — 1.3
10. Instructions don't mean a thing for the supervisors do not know the job. — 0.3

II

1. It will benefit an employee to assume responsibilities whenever possible. — 8.4
2. It is always a pleasure to assume responsibilities here. — 8.9
3. In the best interest of the organization an employee should always assume any responsibility that is necessary. — 8.8
4. The supervisors rather than the employee get paid for taking on responsibilities. — 3.2
5. It is to the employee's best interest always to assume responsibilities when necessary. — 7.7
6. The officials do not expect employees to assume responsibilities so they shouldn't assume any unnecessary risks. — 2.6
7. It makes little difference to the supervisor whether or not an employee takes over additional responsibilities. — 2.7
8. An employee will gain nothing by assuming unnecessary responsibility. — 1.3
9. It is always best to let others assume responsibilities for nothing is gained by taking unnecessary risks. — 1.3
10. It would be to the employee's advantage, not only to make decisions, but to assume responsibility for his decisions in the absence of a superior. — 8.3

III

1. Employees here are always anxious to make constructive suggestions about their work. — 8.4
2. It is generally to the employee's advantage to offer suggestions for improvement of the organization and its work. — 8.3
3. There are times when constructive suggestions are appreciated here. — 7.9
4. Constructive suggestions would not be appreciated here. — 2.1
5. It is not worth while to offer suggestions on how to improve the work — 1.3

IV

1. Our supervisors are capable men. — 8.7
2. If the supervisors were more capable they wouldn't be criticized so much. — 2.1
3. Our officers are the very best men for the job. — 8.6
4. The officers have earned their positions by being good administrators. — 8.5
5. Most of the officers are good men but there are a few who aren't. — 6.9
6. Officers are just like anyone else; some are good and some are bad. — 6.5
7. There are a few good fellows among the officers. — 4.7
8. The officers would be better liked if they didn't act like they were so much better than anyone else. — 1.0
9. The officers are a bunch of politicians. — 1.0
10. The officers would be better liked if they weren't a bunch of capitalists. — 0.7

V

1. It will help the organization if the employees try to keep acquainted with the plans of the management. — 8.0
2. It makes very little difference whether the employee shows interest in the plans of the management. — 2.3
3. It is to the employee's interest to keep acquainted with the plans of the management. — 7.1
4. I can't be bothered with so-called plans of the management. — 0.8

VI

1. The work we are doing is really a great service to mankind — 8.8
2. Our work is really a racket. — 0.6
3. Out work is not so important but somebody has to do it. — 2.7
4. The public should be encouraged to support the work we are doing. — 7.4
5. The work we are doing is one of those necessary evils. — 1.8
6. It is only fair to advise the public that there are better ways of investing their money than here. — 0.8
7. The work we are doing is not very essential. — 1.6

VII

1. It is a pleasure to do favors for fellow workers here. — 8.7
2. An employee should, if necessary, go out of his way to help fellow employees. — 7.6
3. Employees should do favors for each other. — 7.3
4. It is all right to do favors for fellow employees if they have done one for you. — 4.9
5. It is best to let fellow employees know that they cannot expect favors from you. — 1.9
6. If you start doing favors for fellow workers you will soon be imposed upon. — 1.3
7. It is all right to do a favor for a fellow employee now and then. — 4.3
8. Nothing is gained by doing a fellow employee a favor. — 0.6

VIII

1. It is a pleasure to be courteous to the kind of employees we have here. — 9.0
2. It is wise to treat fellow employees courteously. — 8.0
3. There is no need to be particularly courteous to fellow employees. — 2.3
4. It doesn't do any harm to speak to fellow employees but it isn't necessary. — 2.6
5. Fellow employees here deserve to be snubbed. — 0.3
6. It is wise to treat fellow employees courteously when the officers are around, but otherwise it isn't necessary. — 0.4
7. It is best to avoid speaking to fellow employees as much as possible. — 1.2
8. It helps bring fellow workers around to snub them now and then. — 0.6
9. In the long run it is best to ignore fellow workers as much as possible. — 0.4
10. It is generally a good practice to be courteous to fellow workers. — 7.3
11. It is against the best interests of the organization to be rude to fellow employees. — 8.0
12. It is very rude to ever snub a fellow worker. — 7.8

IX

1. Employees must always be courteous to the public when dealing with the public for the organization's reputation and good name largely depend on these contacts. 9.0
2. Employees should be courteous to the public whenever possible. 8.1
3. Some of the folks who come into this office are pests and you can't waste too much time on them. 2.5
4. It really saves time and trouble to explain things fully to everyone who has dealings with the organization. 7.8
5. We are all proud of our organization and its work and are anxious to have the public think well of us. 9.1
6. In dealing with the public you just have to make it snappy or you will never get your work done. 4.1
7. There is no "quitting time" on an employee's duties to make the public understand and like the organization and its work. 8.8

X

1. I like the work here because it is so interesting. 8.9
2. There is absolutely nothing interesting about the work here. 0.6
3. The work is so monotonous I'm glad to forget about it after quitting time. 0.7
4. This work is so trying I am really glad when it is time to quit. 1.2
5. I wish something could be done to make this work a little more interesting. 1.3
6. I really hate this job but what can one do about it. 0.5
7. I wouldn't change jobs with anyone. 9.1
8. I would like my job better if there were any future in it. 4.4
9. An employee here cannot be blamed for looking for a better job elsewhere. 3.0
10. There is no reason to object to a job in this organization. 7.6
11. The future possibilities of this job are unlimited. 9.0
12. This is a good chance for a career. 8.7

XI

1. Political pull rather than training makes for advancement here. 1.5
2. The management makes it worthwhile for an employee to improve his training. 8.0
3. The management offers the employee unlimited opportunity for training to improve his work and service. 8.9
4. There is little use in bothering with outside training for the management has most of us pegged where it wants us. 1.1

XII

1. This organization offers ideal opportunities for a career. 8.9
2. As a career this job has absolutely nothing to offer. 1.3
3. The career boys here are the ones with a drag. 1.0
4. If one were interested in a career he would not stay here too long. 2.4
5. There is no use in my thinking of a career; things are set against me. 0.1
6. This work has many features which makes it worthwhile as a career. 7.7

XIII

1. Employees here are well paid in proportion to their ability. 8.3
2. The best way to get a raise is to tend to business. 7.8
3. You never get a raise here until you ask for it. 3.3
4. Some employees here are paid according to their ability but others are not. 3.3
5. The employees would be better satisfied if they were paid on the basis of ability. 3.3
6. If an employee feels he isn't getting what he is worth it would be to his advantage to discuss the matter with the management. 8.6

The most able employees are not always the best paid. 4.2

8. Working overtime without pay is all right once in a while, but that happens too often here. 3.4
9. We are always glad to work overtime for extra effort is always recognized in some way here. 8.4

XIV

1. Our working conditions here are ideal. 9.4
2. Working conditions here aren't so bad. 6.6
3. There are many things that can be done to improve our working conditions. 4.8
4. How can the management expect us to get anything done under the present working conditions? 2.5
5. Working conditions here couldn't be much worse. 0.6
6. Working conditions here are about the same as anywhere else. 4.5

XV

1. The employees here appreciate the credit that is gladly given by the management for good work. 8.9
2. Sometimes credit is given for good work here and sometimes not. 4.3
3. You may as well take advantage of the other fellows good ideas to get credit for yourself, that's what everyone else does. 1.0
4. You don't get any extra consideration here anyway, so you may as well take credit for all you can whether you deserve it or not. 0.9
5. The management is fairly good about recognition of work well done. 7.1

XVI

1. The best qualified people always get the promotions here. 7.7
2. More employees would stick with the organization if the chances for promotion were better. 4.4
3. The chances for promotion are ideal here. 9.1
4. Employees are always given plenty of opportunity for promotion. 8.5
5. The best qualified people do not always get the promotion. 4.1
6. It doesn't pay to work hard for promotion here for there aren't any opportunities anyway. 2.3
7. So many young fellows get the promotions when they should go to those who have been here longest. 4.1
8. It doesn't do a young fellow any good to work hard for the older men get the promotions anyway. 1.7
9. There are a few opportunities for promotion, but generally they aren't so good. 3.2
10. It seems to make little difference whether an employee works hard to earn a promotion. 1.9
11. Promotions are a matter of luck and political pull. 0.9
12. Anyone is foolish to refuse a promotion even if he knows he isn't fitted for the job. 2.7
13. If a fellow isn't fitted for the job he should refuse a promotion. 6.1

XVII

1. An employee should always try to keep outside influence from affecting his work. 8.3
2. An employee has outside problems, too, and the management should expect them to influence his work occasionally. 3.9
3. The management has been very considerate on occasions when I was having problems and worries outside the line of duty. 8.5
4. The management doesn't care what happens to the employees outside their line of duty. 1.6
5. There is nothing the matter with the job here, I am just worried by some conditions outside the line of work. 5.3
6. I haven't been able to do my best because so many other matters were troubling me. 3.9

WORK SATISFACTION AND PERSONAL HAPPINESS
(Noll and Bradburn 1968)

Variable

This short work satisfaction scale was used as an independent variable in a study of sources of personal happiness.

Description

There are three open-ended questions which make up the scale. Responses indicating that the respondent was "very satisfied" in his reply to a particular question scored as 1; otherwise responses scored as 0. Scale scores run therefore from 0 (no "very satisfied" replies) to 3 (three "very satisfied" replies).

Sample

The questions were asked in two waves of a cross-section panel sample in the mid-1960's. The number of employed people in these samples was 2428 for the first interview and 1925 for the second interview. Most of the results that follow, however, are based on samples of size 1451 and 1062 for the two waves.

Reliability

The following correlations (gamma) were obtained between the items. First figures are for the first interview; those in parentheses for the second interview.

		Earnings	Kind of Work
	Earnings	X	
Satisfaction with	Kind of work	.41 (.58)	X
	Work as a whole	.70 (.72)	.85 (.84)

Validity

No data bearing directly on validity are reported.

Location

Noll, D. and Bradburn, N. "Work and Happiness." Paper presented at the 1968 meetings of the American Sociological Association in Boston. These data will also be reported in Norman Bradburn, The Structure of Pyschological Well-Being, Chicago: Aldine Press (in press).

Administration

The items should take less than three minutes to complete in an interview situation, perhaps a little longer in a questionnaire.

Results and Comments

As hypothesized, work satisfaction and happiness were significantly correlated--gamma = .43 in the first interview and .41 in the second interview for men, and at .28 in the first interview and .44 in the second interview for women. There were no systematic differences in the size of these correlations for groups varying in occupational prestige.

Work satisfaction was related to both general feelings of high "positive affect" and low "negative affect," but relations were higher with positive affect than with negative affect. No differences were found, however, between changes in work satisfaction and the two facets of affect. Adequacy in doing one's job was related to low feelings of negative affect, but not to positive affect.

Greatest feelings of unhappiness and negative affect and lowest feelings of positive affect were reported by people who were un-employed. A job advancement index (reproduced below) was found to be related to positive affect but not negative affect.

Reference   Bradburn, N. and Caplovitz, O. <u>Reports on Happiness</u>. Chicago: Aldine Press, 1965.

ITEMS

Work <u>satisfaction</u> index:

  1) How satisfied are you with your earnings?

  2) How satisfied are you with the kind of work that you do?

  3) Taking all things together, how do you feel about your work (business) as a whole?

Personal happiness:

  1) Taking all things together, how would you say things are these days--would you say you're <u>very</u> happy, <u>pretty</u> happy, or <u>not too</u> happy?

  2) Positive affect

  3) Negative affect   Indices described in Bradburn and Caplovitz (1965)

Job <u>advancement</u> index (Score one for each asterisk; scores run from 0 to 5)

  1) Is this the best job you have ever held?   Yes*   No

  2) Did you receive a raise in the last year?   Yes*   No

  3) Did you receive a promotion in the last year?   Yes*   No

  4) Do you think your chances for advancement
     are good, fair, or poor?   Good** Fair* Poor

6. JOB SATISFACTION FOR PARTICULAR OCCUPATIONS

These scales were developed for particular occupational groups and, of course, can be used on other groups, but usually only after careful rewording and/or reanalysis. They would probably be most useful to anyone looking for a scale that can be applied directly to the same (or highly similar) type of occupations. Two of the scales were developed for managers, two for scientists and the final one for mechanics. The five scales in order of presentation are:

1. Need Fulfillment Questionnaire for Management (Porter 1962)

2. Managerial Job Attitudes (Harrison 1960)

3. Job Attitudes and Job Satisfaction of Scientists (Hinrichs 1962)

4. Attitudes of Scientists in Organizations (Pelz and Andrews 1966)

5. Job Satisfactory Inventory (Twery, et al. 1958)

Porter's Need Fulfillment Questionnaire is one of the few job attitude instruments based on an elegant psychological theory --the Maslow hierarchy of needs. The Maslow paradigm postulates that security needs are the most basic human wants and that until these are satisfied, there is little desire for satisfaction for less basic needs (in order: social, esteem, autonomy and self-actualization). That is, one does not strive for self-actualization needs until the previous four needs have been essentially guaranteed. Since results to date are not perfectly consistent with the theory, the instrument ought to be tried out on rank and file personnel to see if the theory holds adequately for those for whom security and social needs should be paramount. (For some research which is throws doubt on this point, attention is drawn to a referenced monograph by Beers.) The item format is strictly on a frame-of-reference basis, a too-seldom-used variation in the manner of asking job attitude questions. Almost no psychometric data are presented on the instrument; however, it was Porter's intention to investigate a theory of job satisfaction rather than to create an instrument for its measurement. The reader is referred to previous attempts to measure job satisfaction as a function of need satisfaction, including Schaffer's inventory, which is presented in Chapter 7.

Harrison's factors from his multidimensional analysis of managerial job

attitudes were those that survived an empirical cut from 78 items and contain
a number of valuable items which load on relatively pure factors of managerial
attitudes. Normative, reliability and validity data are lacking, which limits the
applicability of this instrument.

Hinrich's questionnaire also covers a broad range of occupational topics and
includes items dealing not only with work content but with attitudes toward
society, feelings about the type of organization in which one is employed, and
attitudes toward one's professional obligations. It was developed for use with
chemists, and while there are shortcomings with the original sample, it is better
than most industrial attitude studies in this respect. On the whole, the questionnaire probes into enough interesting areas to warrant review by those intending
future studies with workers in this profession.

The same evaluation can be made of the eight indices constructed by Pelz
and Andrews in their investigation into the orientations of scientists. One
great advantage of these indices is that they have been correlated with various
measures of job performance. Furthermore, organization structural variables are
taken into account, as are differences between intrinsic and extrinsic job factors.
For normative data on job attitudes of representative samples of scientists,
however, the reader is better advised to refer to the Kilpatrick, et al. study,
reviewed in Robinson's chapter.

The Job Satisfaction Inventory, as devised by Twery, et al., has an interesting
methodological background. It was used on a blue-collar sample and the hypothetical factor structure on which it was constructed held up extremely well
empirically. Some of these factors are quite specific to Air Force mechanics,
however, and a richer source of factors can be found in the Dunnette, et al.
study (Chapter 5) and the Gurin, et al. code categories reviewed in Robinson's
chapter.

Four other scales for special groups have come to our attention which do not
seem to be worth more detailed review than given here below. There are undoubtedly
dozens of such scales available that we have not run across. As a representative offering, then, we will reference the four available to us.

1. Military Base Morale consists of 21 rather general items dealing with
   four areas (the Air Force, the Air Site, personal commitment and
   satisfaction with the job). Internal consistency of the scales does not
   appear to be particularly high although correlation of a combined score
   with outside ratings was .52. The scales are published in Miller, D.
   and Medalia, N. "Efficiency, leadership and morale in small military
   organizations" The Sociological Review, 1953, 3, 93-107.

2. <u>Job Attitude Inventory</u> is a set of 40 Likert items which were asked
of a random sample of the members of the National Association of
Life Underwriters four times in the last seven years. Response rates
have only been about 30 percent,.however. Scores are available for six
areas: overall job satisfaction, income-security, home office
support, job prestige, job demands, managerial support. Interesting
longitudinal data (but no reliability and validity information)
is contained in <u>1964 Survey of Agency Opinion</u>, File 1440 of Life
Insurance Agency of Management Association.

3. <u>Job Satisfaction for Salesmen</u> is a short five item scale which claims
a reproducibility coefficient of .95. Three items deal with supervisor
relations, one with the probability that the salesmen would work for
the company if he had it to do all over again, and one with chances
for advancement. Cause and effect relations seem obscure in the data
presentation. The items are presented in Pearson, J., et al. "Sales
Success and Job Satisfaction", <u>American Sociological Review</u> 1957, <u>22</u>,
424-7.

4. <u>The Faculty Morale Scale</u> covers 34 aspects of academic life that may
be sources of satisfaction or dissatisfaction. The instrument lacks
face validity and even the scale publishers caution that the instrument has yet to advance beyond the experimental stage. Further
information is available from Psychometric Affiliates, Box 1625,
Chicago 90, Illinois.

NEED FULFILLMENT QUESTIONNAIRE FOR MANAGEMENT (Porter 1962)

Variable   The scale purports to measure the magnitude, importance and degree of need satisfaction of managers in relation to Maslow's (1954) hierarchy of needs.

Description   Five need categories, chosen to represent a hierarchy of pre-potency of needs, were studied--security, social, esteem, autonomy, and self actualization. Each of the thirteen items on the scale attempted to measure not only the existing degree of need fulfillment but also the discrepancy between achieved and expected levels in addition to the relative importance of the category. Each scale item, therefore, required three separate responses on 7 point subscales. The data derived from these responses are of two types. The first is a deficiency measure obtained by subtracting the response to "How much of the characteristic is <u>now</u> connected with your position" from the response to "How much of the same characteristic <u>should there be</u>". Referring to the sample item below (see "Instrument"), the deficiency score represents the difference between ratings on subscales a and b. The second type of data is simply a ranking of needs based on the response to the "How important is this?" subscale. Refer to the Results & Comments section of this report for an evaluation of this method of scaling.

This scale requires that the respondents display a greater than average level of verbal facility. It is unlikely that it could be successfully used if respondents showed a very wide range of educational attainment.

Sample   The questionnaire was sent by mail to approximately 6000 managers and executives, half of whom were members of the American Management Association. About 1/3 were returned in usable condition. Levels of management were represented as follows:

President and chairmen of Boards	6%
Vice President or equivalent	32%
Upper middle, division managers	35%
Lower middle, department managers	22%
Lower, first and second level	5%

Forty-two percent of the sample fell in the modal age range of 35-44 years and approximately 75% of each of the above groups held college degrees. The distribution of respondents by company was: 66% from manufacturing, 7% from transportation and public utilities, 7% from finance and insurance, 5% from wholesale and retail trades, and 15% from other types. The author stresses that a nationwide sample was obtained and that, "except by chance, any particular company would not be represented more than a few times in the total sample."

Reliability/ Homogeneity	No reliability estimate is presented by the author.
Validity	The nature of the study in which this questionnaire was used was more heuristic than validity-oriented. The author, therefore, chooses to rely on the face validity of the instrument.
Location	Porter, Lyman W., "Job Attitudes in Management: Parts I, II, III, IV," <u>J.Appl.Psychol</u>., 1962 (46) 375-384; 1963 (47) 141-148, 267-275, 386-397.

See also:

Porter, Lyman W., "Job Attitudes in Management: <u>Perceived Satisfaction and Importance of Needs</u>," Berkeley: Institute of Industrial Relations, University of California, Reprint No. 229, 1964.

Administration	Self administered in less than ½ hour. Scoring may be accomplished in a number of ways. Each of the five subcategory scores should remain distinct for most analyses.
Results & Comments	Since the respondent is not asked about satisfaction, <u>per se</u>, the author contends that the method of scaling used in this questionnaire reduces the probability that any simple response set determines the expression of satisfaction. An <u>a priori</u> assumption was made that the <u>less</u> the difference between "How much x is there," and "How much x there should be," the <u>greater</u> the satisfaction with the characteristic in question. This method takes into consideration the idea of "expectation" which may reasonably be supposed to vary among management levels. The question really asked of the respondents is, "How satisfied are you in terms of what you expected from this particular management position?"

While such findings should most likely not be considered as evidence for the validity of a questionnaire it should be noted that the results presented by the author do square well with theoretical expectations. For example, Presidents rank autonomy quite low when considering deficiency of need satisfaction. Virtually all other levels of management indicate that their second greatest deficiency is in the area of autonomy. The ranking of deficiencies in need satisfaction categories shows the expected vertical trend from lower to upper management--for example:

Management Level	Need Category				Self Actualization
	Security	Social	Esteem	Autonomy	
Lower	4	5	3	2	1
V P	3	5	4	2	1
President	4	2	3	5	1

Porter's intention was not so much to construct a valid reliable scale as it was to collect data to test hypotheses about need hierarchies However, through careful use, test-retest studies, etc. this instrument may be able to provide valuable information for management within a singl« company.

For previous studies measuring job satisfaction from a "need satis« faction" perspective, see Gordon (1953) and Schaffer (1963). Beers (1965 has most recently cast doubt on the empirical adequacy of the Maslow need paradigm.

References

Beers, M., Leadership, Employee Needs and Motivation, Columbus, Ohio: Bureau of Business Research, Ohio State University, 1965.

Gordon, O. J., "Human needs and industrial morale" Personnel Psychology 1953, 8, 1-18.

Maslow, A. H., Motivation and Personality, New York: Harper, 1954.

Porter, W., "A study of perceived need satisfaction in bottom and middle management jobs", J. Appl. Psychol., 1961 (45) 1-10.

Schaffer, R. H. "Job satisfaction as related to need satisfaction in work« Psychological Monographs 1953, 67, (whole No. 364).

Following will be listed several characteristics or qualities connected with your management position. For each such characteristic, you will be asked to give three ratings:

a. How much of the characteristic is there now connected with your management position?
b. How much of the characteristic do you think should be connected with your management position?
c. How important is this position characteristic to you?

For each of the 13 items, the respondents were instructed to answer the above three questions by circling a number on a rating scale extending from 1 to 7, where "low numbers represent low or minimum amounts, and high numbers represent high or maximum amounts." A typical item appeared as follows on the questionnaire:

The opportunity for independent thought and action in my management position:

(a) How much is there now?
    (min) 1 2 3 4 5 6 7 (max)
(b) How much should there be?
    (min) 1 2 3 4 5 6 7 (max)
(c) How important is this to me?
    (min) 1 2 3 4 5 6 7 (max)

Categories of Needs and Specific Items

Listed below are the categories of needs studied in the investigation, along with the specific items used to elicit information on each category. The items were randomly presented in the questionnaire, but are here listed systematically according to their respective need categories. The rationale behind the categorization system has been presented in the previous article (Porter, 1961b) and will not be repeated here. It can be pointed out, though, that the system is designed to be in general agreement with Maslow's hierarchical classification scheme based on the supposed "prepotency" (or priority) of various types of needs (Maslow, 1954). The categories, arranged from lowest-order (most prepotent) to highest-order (least prepotent), and their specific items follow:

I. Security needs

1. The feeling of security in my management position

II. Social needs

1. The opportunity, in my management position, to give help to other people

2. The opportunity to develop close friendships in my management position

III. Esteem needs

1. The feeling of self-esteem a person gets from being in my management position

2. The prestige of my management position inside the company (that is, the regard received from others in the company)

3. The prestige of my management position outside the company (that is, the regard received from others not in the company)

IV. Autonomy needs

1. The authority connected with my management position

2. The opportunity for independent thought and action in my management position

3. The opportunity, in my management position, for participation in the setting of goals

4. The opportunity, in my management position, for participation in the determination of methods and procedures

V. Self-actualization needs

1. The opportunity for personal growth and development in my management position

2. The feeling of self-fulfillment a person gets from being in my management position (that is, the feeling of being able to use one's own unique capabilities, realizing one's potentialities)

3. The feeling of worthwhile accomplishment in my management position

MANAGERIAL JOB ATTITUDES (Harrison 1960)

Variable	There are actually eight attitude domains (described below) which were uncovered from a multidimensional analysis of a large battery of 78 items.
Description	Eight empirical clusters emerged from Likert responses to the initial items. In all, the eight clusters comprised a total of 28 items, as follows:

    1) Opportunity to advance and accomplish (6 items)
    2) Working conditions (2 items)
    3) Non-economic stability and security (4 items)
    4) Personal relations with one's supervisor (4 items).
    5) Compensation (4 items)
    6) Communications from the top (3 items)
    7) Working relations (2 items)
    8) Operating standards (3 items)

Sample	In all, 186 first-level and second-level supervisors in one section of a Proctor and Gamble manufacturing plant. No further information is reported.
Reliability/ Homogeneity	No estimate is reported outside of the factor analytic information itself.
Validity	'Domain validities' (sic) ranged from .83 to .96. The more standard type of validity coefficients are not reported.
Location	Harrison, R., "Sources of variation in manager's job attitudes", Personnel Psychology 1960, 13, 425-34.
Administration	Regular Likert format with respondents rating each item on a five-point scale of favorableness.
Comments	The areas covered include both intrinsic and extrinsic factors.

Items in the Eight Major Clusters

Cluster 1. Opportunity to Advance and Accomplish

How do you feel about your chances of having a job in the Company which will give you a real feeling of satisfaction and accomplishment?

How do you feel about the opportunities a man on your level in line work has in the Company to rise to a position which fully utilizes his abilities?

How do you feel about the progress you've made in the Company up to now?

How do you feel about the amount of freedom you have to run your own job in the way that seems best to you?

What do you think of the attitude of higher management toward the importance of your job?

How do you feel about the confidence a management person can have that his ability and effort will be adequately rewarded by the Company?

Cluster 2. Working Conditions

How are the working conditions for hourly people in the plant?

How are your working conditions generally?

Cluster 3. Non-Economic Stability and Security

How do you feel about the support you get from higher management in your efforts to enforce rules and maintain discipline?

What do you think of the consideration given your views when changes are contemplated which will affect your department or your operation?

In general, how do you feel about the changes in management practices that have been taking place at this plant in the last five years?

How do you feel about the amount of job rotation which has been taking place in management recently?

Cluster 4. Personal Relations With Own Immediate Supervisor

How is your supervisor at getting people to work well together?

Rate the job your superior does in letting you know how you stand with him.

How is your superior at letting you know how you are doing on different parts of your job?

How is your superior at giving recognition for good work?

Cluster 5. Compensation: Pay and Benefits

How do you feel about your earnings, compared to those of nonmanagement people in the plant?

How do you feel about your earnings, when you take into account the difficulty and responsibility of your job?

How do Company retirement benefits for management compare with what other companies have to offer?

Over-all, how do Company benefits for management (Disability Benefit Plan, Hospital Plan, Group Life Insurance, Profit Sharing, etc.) compare with what other companies offer?

Cluster 6. Communications from Top Management

How good a job does top management do in telling people at your level what they ought to know about the Company?

How good a job does top management do in telling people at your level what they ought to know about what's going on in the plant?

Rate the job top management does in telling people at your level what they ought to know about how salary increases are decided upon.

Cluster 7. Working Relations with Other In-Plant Groups

How do you feel about the way different departments cooperate in this plant?

What do you think of how clearly your responsibilities to other departments are defined?

Cluster 8. In-Plant Standards of Operation

In general, how is the quality of new hourly employees who have been hired in the plant recently?

What do you think of the quality standards in use in the plant?

What do you think of the quality of the ideas and suggestions which the hourly people have?

JOB ATTITUDES AND JOB SATISFACTION OF SCIENTISTS (Hinrichs 1962)

Variable   This scale purports to measure several attitudinal factors related to a scientist's job and his job satisfaction.

Description   Seventy-nine Likert type items are grouped under two major categories: "The World of Work in General" and "The Individual as a Scientist." The former category includes items dealing "with the broad area of attitudes toward society as a whole, plus more restricted attitudes related to the economic sphere of society (business, government, the academic world)." The latter category mentioned above deals with professional attitudes.

                  Within each of the major categories there are three different fields of emphasis, viz., factors affecting productivity, satisfaction, and norms or standards of behavior. (See Results and Comments section for item numbers for these categories.)

                  This scale was originally designed to study the attitudes and opinions of Ph.D. level chemists.

Sample   Somewhat less than one third of the nation's Ph.D. graduates in chemistry (N = 385) for the year February, 1960 to February, 1961, selected from about half the schools which grant the Ph.D. in chemistry were included in the "New Graduates" sample.

                  Three industrial organizations (petroleum research, pharmacentical research lab, and a general chemical company) provided 286 Ph.D.'s for the "industrial" sample. Years of full time experience in chemistry for this sample ranged from less than 1 to more than 25 years in a distribution which was very nearly rectangular.

Reliability   No estimate of reliability is reported by the author.

Validity   The author reports a significant negative relation of unspecified magnitude between evaluated industrial performance and attitudes valuing freedom and support in research. A positive relation is shown between the choice of industrial over academic employment and materialist expedient attitudes as well as the belief that science and industrial values are not incompatible. Such evidence bears only indirectly on valid

Location   Hinrichs, John R., "The Impact of Industrial Organization on the Attitude of Research Chemists," Ph.D. thesis, Cornell University, 1962; University Microfilms, Ann Arbor, Michigan, Pub.No. #62-5828.

Administration   Self administered in about 1/2 hour. Scoring is accomplished by summing the responses to the whole questionnaire or those components which are of interest.

The questionnaire items may be classified by content in the following categories:

CLASSIFICATION OF QUESTIONNAIRE ITEMS BY CONTENT
(Data are item numbers)

Scope Classification	Evaluative Classification		
	Actual Conditions	Ideal Conditions	Comparative
The World of Work In General			
a. Productivity	14, 17, 18, 31, 44, 45, 60, 64	6, 11, 20, 58, 64, 67, 66	5, 26, 62
b. Satisfaction	3, 7, 19, 28, 30, 35, 38, 41, 48, 50, 52, 53	4, 43, 49	10
c. Norms	9, 36, 42, 46, 47, 56, 2-9	16, 23, 51, 68, 2-4	
The Individual			
a. Productivity	21, 37, 39, 70, 2-2, 2-5, 2-6, 2-8	2, 8, 22, 29, 34, 54, 55	
b. Satisfaction	1, 13, 15, 24, 25, 33, 57, 2-7	27, 40, 61, 2-3	
c. Norms	69, 2-1	12, 32, 59, 63	

155

A factorial analysis of the questionnaire items yields the following main components:

Component I - Attitudes valuing freedom and support in research; a belief that industry raises barriers to worth-while scientific activity.

Component II - Materialistic, expedient attitudes reflecting acceptance of business values, possibly at the expense of science values.

Component III - Attitudes indicating acceptance of industrial research with the belief that science and indus-trial values are not incompatible. Applied re-search is valued. (Hinrichs, 1962, p. 72)

Items Comprising Component I:

```
 2    3   17   18   35
38   41   42   44   45
46   48   52(-) 53   58
64
```

Items Comprising Component II:

```
 2(-)  4    6   15   17
19    20   27   30   33(-)
38    39   40   44   51(-)
55(-) 57(-) 58(-)

2-1   2-7   2-9
```

Items Comprising Component III:

```
 6    8   18   27   38
33   41(-) 49   50   51
52   55   60   65   68

2-4   2-7(-)  2-9
```

The (-) sign following some item numbers indicates a negative loading on the factor and the scoring of the item should be reversed if it is included in the factor score.

Results &
Comments

The following table shows the interrelationships among variables. Only significant correlations are shown.

INTERRELATIONSHIPS AMONG THE VARIABLES IN THE STUDY

VARIABLE	Variable 1	2	3	4	5	6	7	8
1. Component I (Agree)	-							
2. Component II (Agree)	X	-						
3. Component III (Agree)	X	X	-					
4. Choice of industry over academic employment	Neg.	Pos.	Pos.	-				
5. No. of years experience in chemistry		Pos.	Pos.	X	-			
6. General job satisfaction in industry	Neg.	Neg.	Pos.	X		-		
7. Satisfaction with salary in industry	Neg.			X		X	-	
8. Evaluated performance	Neg.			X	Pos.	Pos.	Pos.	-

This study could have been greatly improved through the use of a follow up of the new graduates, a reliability study and item analysis based on discriminating between groups, e.g., industrial vs. academic or high productive vs. low productive.

The author's conclusions may serve to stimulate further research on the relationship of job attitudes and satisfaction as well as the relation between satisfaction and production for professional personnel.

Although factors (components) I and III may seem to be useful for selection purposes, this instrument is still in the experimental phase and any such use should be approached with great caution. If use is intended for groups other than chemists, some items will have to be modified and new norms, etc., derived.

A number of statements dealing with various aspects of science and the chemistry profession are listed below. In the columns on the right side of the page, please indicate whether you agree or disagree with each statement. Circle only one of the five alternatives for each item:

1. Strongly Agree, 2. Agree, 3. Neutral, 4. Disagree, or 5. Strongly Disagree.

Please be sure to answer all items.

How much do you agree or disagree with each of these statements?	SA	A	N	D	SD
	1	2	3	4	5

1. Scientists are usually not very well known in their communities.

2. A chemist must have freedom to formulate and develop his own research ideas to produce significant research results.

3. Too many industrial jobs require a man to move to a different location every so often.

4. If a man's salary is high enough, he "feels" recognized.

5. Scientific research by government agencies is less efficient than research by private industry.

6. A scientist is bound to have a somewhat limited perspective unless he works on field problems and applications at least once in a while.

7. In general, there is not enough differential between the earnings of scientists and those of people in the highly skilled trades.

8. The research man who has a practical outlook on problems gets the best results.

9. Too many universities today are mass-producing degrees without enough concern for the quality of their graduates.

10. There is as much satisfaction in teaching science as in doing research.

11. It's a good idea for a chemist to specialize in one particular area.

12. A scientist owes it to his profession to have a private study at home for after hours work.

13. Scientists are not any more dedicated to their work than most professional people.

14. Poor utilization of available talent has caused the present so-called "shortage of scientists and engineers."

15. Women think it is more glamorous for a husband to be an industrial executive than a research chemist.

16. There is so much marginal stuff coming out in the technical journals now that a limitation on publications should be set.

17. Many good scientific ideas have "died on the vine" because they have not received adequate support from people in authority.

18. The only thing holding back a surge of creative research is insufficient financial backing.

19. Everyone wants a chance to gain a certain amount of power over other people.

20. Supervisors of industrial research don't necessarily have to be top-notch technical men.

21. The quality of a chemist's work is not dependent on the calibre of his associates.

22. For a scientist, the only kind of pressure for results which is effective is self-imposed pressure.

23. Strict professional standards are more necessary in medicine than in chemical research.

24. A good research man doesn't really have to worry about security of employment; he can easily get another job if need be.

25. A good researcher quickly withers away in routine work.

26. There is more "red tape" in the government than in big industry.

27. Scientific research is more meaningful if the researcher has a chance to see how well his findings work in an applied situation.

28. Getting ahead in any technical job depends primarily on a man's technical competence.

29. A research chemist should be free from administrative details.

30. In a university setting there is a considerable amount of pressure to conform to established methods of solving problems.

31. Chemists who were in the upper half of their college graduating class do significantly better work on the job in applied research and development than do those in the lower half.

32. A man's commitment to his profession should never come before his responsibility to his family.

33. To any chemist "worth his salt," the most important thing in a job is the opportunity to do sound scientific work.

34. A good research chemist approaches problems with a theoretical outlook.

35. Most recognition for industrial research goes to management or the company rather than to the individuals who did the work.

36. It's pretty appropriate to describe our society as the "era of crass commercialism."

37. Many scientists do their best work under pressure for results.

38. In any organization, the people in power get there by manipulating other people.

39. Many chemists waste time trying to investigate every possible angle before making a decision.

40. Adequate financial rewards are of major importance in getting scientists to do the best possible job.

41. Getting ahead in industry is based more on politics than it is on knowledge.

42. There are too many low-grade "hacks" doing chemical research today.

43. It's important to work for an organization which is concerned about your personal welfare.

44. A lot of times in industry a good research chemist is stifled by being put under a supervisor who is not technically qualified.

45. Social conformity and scientific creativity are incompatible.

46. Most companies look on scientific research solely as a means of protecting profits by keeping ahead of competition.

47. A lot of industrial research is taken to the pilot plant stage without enough basic laboratory work.

48. In industry, scientists' talents are channeled too closely to what is proven and profitable.

49. It's important to belong to an organization that is well thought of in the community.

50. Most chemists are interested in pursuing knowledge for its own sake.

51. Scientists who let an organization force them to do a slip-shod research job are really dishonest to the profession.

52. In general, chemists going into industry don't have any trouble making their scientific goals jibe with the company's objectives.

53. Company security regulations keep a lot of good industrial research results out of the literature.

54. Chemists do their best work when they work alone.

55. A chemist must have freedom in applying his own ideas to solve technical problems if he is to produce significant research results.

56. A lot of times the controls built into research experiments are really "frosting on the cake."

57. Most scientists are more interested in their profession than in an opportunity to move up in the organization for which they work.

58. To encourage effective research, industrial laboratories should try to create an atmosphere similar to a university setting.

59. It's a sign of a pretty limited perspective if a scientist gets so immersed in his data that he doesn't give a damn for anything else.

60. As a rule, research chemists in industry are able to work on projects which make full use of their individual training and skills.

61. Most scientists would rather be recognized for an outstanding achievement by an honorary award than by a money award.

62. A research team of 5 chemists is more productive than 5 chemists working alone.

63. A scientist should not be held personally responsible for the validity of his research findings.

64. It's a waste of talent to use chemists who were in the upper half of their college graduating class in administrative jobs.

65. Most significant basic chemical research is done in universities.

66. Industrial management has been defined as "a process of making decisions based on a limited amount of information." This definition could be applied to chemical research just as well.

67. Good organization and administration are essential to effective scientific research.

68. High professional standards of chemical research must be maintained at all costs.

69. If a research chemist is inquisitive and curious in purposeless ways he's probably wasting time.

70. Most truly productive research people try to "get away from it" when they are on vacation so that they can really dig in when they get back.

2-1. A lot of research people elaborate and add more detail to a job than is needed.

2-2. A research chemist can do a good job even if he doesn't have many supporting personnel.

2-3. It doesn't matter too much what kind of work a scientist does as long as it gives him a general sense of satisfaction and accomplishment.

2-4. A scientist going into industry owes his first loyalty to his company.

2-5. Sometimes researchers hide their laziness under the guise of freedom to pursue individual research goals.

2-6. A research chemist can produce good results even if his superiors don't fully understand what he is trying to accomplish.

2-7. A chemist can put up with monotonous work if the pay is OK.

2-8. Technical knowledge is much more important to a chemist than his ability to deal with other people.

2-9. The primary goal of scientific research is to raise the standard of living in this country.

If you are presently employed full time, please answer the following six questions.

2-10. How satisfied are you with the latitude you have to attack problems in your own way?

____ Very satisfied
____ Fairly satisfied
____ So-so
____ Rather dissatisfied
____ Very dissatisfied

2-11. How satisfied are you with the opportunities you have to do creative work?

____ Very satisfied
____ Fairly satisfied
____ So-so
____ Rather dissatisfied
____ Very dissatisfied

2-12. How well do you feel your salary reflects your professional education and experience?

____ Very well
____ Fairly well
____ So-so
____ Rather poorly
____ Very poorly

2-13. How satisfied are you with the consideration given to your ideas?

____ Very satisfied
____ Fairly satisfied
____ So-so
____ Rather dissatisfied
____ Very dissatisfied

2-14. How satisfied are you with the information you get about the use made of your work?

____ Very satisfied
____ Fairly satisfied
____ So-so
____ Rather dissatisfied
____ Very dissatisfied

2-14. Is there any part of your work that could be handled by a person having less experience or training?

____ A great deal
____ Quite a bit
____ Some
____ Little
____ Very little

Please rank the following ten job factors in the order in which they are important to you in a job. The most important item should be ranked as "1" down to the least important with a rank of "10".

Your Ranking	Job Factor
____	Chance to use your training and skills
____	Encouragement of initiative
____	Chance for professional recognition
____	Take home pay
____	"Interest potential" of the work
____	Congeniality of associates
____	Opportunity to do creative work
____	Social value of work (i.e. to human society)
____	Opportunity to move up in the organization
____	Chance to contribute to fundamental scientific knowledge

Assume that these five magazines arrived in the mail on the same day. Number them in the order in which you would first glance through them (not necessarily a detailed reading).

____	U. S. News and World Report
____	Chemical and Engineering News
____	Scientific American
____	Journal of the American Chemical Society
____	Atlantic Monthly

ATTITUDES OF SCIENTISTS IN ORGANIZATIONS (Pelz and Andrews 1966)

Variable

In all, eight indices of the work orientation of scientists were constructed. A major job satisfaction theme is contained in the indices as is a professional vs. status orientation.

Description

These indices were built from a general pool of items planned so that most of the general relations within the pool could be summarized as easily as possible. The indices are formed from the items as numbered below:

a) Stimulation from own ideas (13E, 13J, 62L)
b) Desire for self-actualization (62A, 62B, 62J, 62L)
c) Professional orientation (62A, B, I, J, L, M)
d) Science orientation (62A, L, M)
e) Provision for self-actualization (63A, B, J, L)
f) Desire for advancement in status (62C, D, H)
g) Status orientation (19B, 19C, 62C, 62D, 62H)
h) Provision for status (63C, D, H)

Sample

The data came from 1311 scientists and engineers located in eleven different laboratories. This total is comprised of 641 professional in five industrial locations, 144 university professors, and 526 scientists and engineers from five government laboratories. This sample was not intended to be representative, as the authors took their measurements in any organization which would cooperate. Both research and development laboratories and Ph.D. and non-Ph.D. level employees were included.

Reliability/
Homogeneity

The median test-retest reliability for individual items was .62. Intensive inter-item analysis was performed before the indices were constructed. Average inter-item correlation was the neighborhood of .40, a respectable level. The item correlations seemed to hold up across differences in occupation.

Validity

No validity data per se is given, although the text is concerned with all sorts of relations which bear on validity. These are too complex too attempt to summarize here.

Location

Pelz, D. and Andrews, F., Scientists in Organizations New York: Wiley, 1966.

Administration

Self-administered as part of questionnaires ranging from one to three hours to complete.

Results and
comments

Differences between (b) and (e) and between (f) and (h) were used as indices of job satisfaction; these were found to be moderately relate to actual provision (indices e and h), but highly related to performance. Both intrinsic and extrinsic factors were found to be important in job satisfaction.

Instrument   Question 13. Listed below are several sources from which projects
can originate...Regardless of the actual origins of your projects, what
sources (in general) offer you the most stimulus to perform well?

    (Ten sources were listed, and for each the respondent rated
    "amount of stimulus" on a five-point scale from "none" to
    "very strong." Some of the sources were:)

    E. My own previous work or plans
    J. My own curiosity

    Question 19. Scientists and engineers may differ widely in their
characteristic approach to their work -- both the kinds of problems that
attract them, and the way they go about the task. How closely does
each statement describe the approach you typically prefer to use?

    (Nineteen statements followed. Respondent rated "how closely
    statement describes me" on a seven-point scale from "not at all"
    to "completely." Selected items were:)

    B. I mainly prefer problems that will help to build my professional
        reputation.

    C. I mainly prefer problems that will lead to advancement in organi-
        zational status.

    Question 62. Listed below are different kinds of opportunities
which a job might afford. If you were to seek a job, how much importance
would you presonally attach to each of these (disregarding whether
or not your present job provides them)?

    (Thirteen factors were listed, which respondent rated on "importance
    I would attach" using a five-point scale from "slight or none" to
    "utmost." For example:)

    A. To make full use of my present knowledge and skills
    B. To grow and learn new knowledge and skills
    C. To earn a good salary
    D. To advance in administrative authority and status
    H. To associate with top executives in the organization
    I. To build my professional reputation
    J. To work on difficult and challenging problems
    L. To have freedom to carry out my own ideas
    M. To contribute to broad technical knowledge in my field

    Question 63. Now to what extent does your present job actually
provide an opportunity for each of these factors?

    (The same factors is in Question 62 were rated on a five-point
    scale from "slight or none" to "complete".

JOB SATISFACTION INVENTORY (Twery et al. 1958)

Variable	This instrument is devised to measure seven dimensions of job satis faction. One is a general factor and the remainder deal specifical with supervision, co-workers, job duties etc.
Description	The seven dimensions of job satisfaction were hypothesized beforeha and these a priori groupings were then checked empirically. Three were chosen to represent each dimension. Of the seven hypothesized dimensions, five came out as expected with two supervisory factors combining to make a sixth dimension.
Sample	The sample consisted of 467 aircraft and engine mechanics at the journeyman level of proficiency from two SAC base and one Training Command base.
Reliability/ Homogeneity	No test-retest reliability data are reported. Scale homogeneity wa determined by factor analytic procedures.
Validity	No validity data are reported.
Location	Twery, R., Schmid, J. and Wrigley, C. "Some factors in job satisfa tion" Educational and Psychological Measurement, 1958, 18, 189-202
Administration	The 21 statements were rated on a five point scale, but there is no mention of the exact type of format that was used.
Results and comments	Methodologically this is an interesting study, as there are few instances in the literature where hypothetical and empirical factor match up so closely. Some of the factors are so job-specific, howe that the applicability to other types of workers is limited.

The relation between the items and the hypothetical and empirical dimensions is given in the following table

Hypothesized dimension of job satisfaction	Items defining hypothetical dimension			Items defining empirical dimension
General Attitude to the Job	4+,	11+,	18+	4, 11, 18, 13, 20
Supervisor as a Technician	1-,	8-,	15-	1, 8, 15, 12, 19
Supervisor in a Social Role	5-,	12-,	19+	
Co-workers	7+,	14+,	21+	7, 14, 21
Higher Echelon	2-,	9-,	16-	2, 9, 16
Job Duties	6-,	13+,	20-	6, 20
Living Conditions	3-,	10+,	17-	3, 10, 17

JOB SATISFACTION INVENTORY

1. My supervisor can't even do the job duties his men do.

2. My squadron could do a much better job if there were less interference from above.

3. I wish very much that I could get away from this base.

4. In all ways my present job is the best job I ever had.

5. My supervisor should mix with his men a lot more.

6. I am kept too long on the same job.

7. Compared with other men that I have worked with, I think that my present coworkers are excellent.

8. My supervisor should have a lot more technical knowledge about his job.

9. Air Force red tape makes it impossible for me to do a good job.

10. This is a good place to be at.

11. I am entirely satisfied with my job.

12. My supervisor doesn't understand his men at all.

13. I prefer my present job duties to all other types of military assignment.

14. I like very much the men I work with.

15. My supervisor could use a lot more training as a technician.

16. Air Force rules and regulations prevent me from doing my best.

17. I don't like the living conditions here.

18. I am enthusiastic about my job.

19. My supervisor gets excellent cooperation from his men.

20. My job duties are boring and monotonous.

21. When I need help I can always count on my fellow workers.

7.   SATISFACTION WITH SPECIFIC JOB FEATURES

Some of the general scales reviewed in previous chapters have subscales which deal with particular job features, but the eight instruments reviewed here are intentionally limited to certain aspects of the job.   The instruments are as follows:

1.   Supervisory Behavior Description (Fleishman 1957)
2.   Attitude toward the Supervisor (Nagle 1953)
3.   Satisfaction with Supervision (Draper 1955)
4.   Attitudes toward the Supervisor (Schmid, et al. 1957)
5.   Employee Opinion Survey (Bolda 1958)
6.   Need-Satisfaction in Work (Schaffer 1953)
7.   About Your Company (King 1960)
8.   Group Morale Scale (Goldman 1958)

Four of the eight scales deal with supervision.   Of these four, Fleishman's Supervisory Behavior Description has the most impressive psychometric record regarding norms, reliability and internal structure.   A few reservations should be noted: the evidence for validity for this scale could be more compelling, although relations with certain important criteria have appeared consistently. In addition, the Likert format is subject to the usual response set liability. The instrument does appear to have been used in a variety of settings, however, and has the valuable supplementary feature of an analogous form (the Leadership Opinion Questionnaire reviewed under "Leadership Styles", Chapter 11) available for supervisors' self-perceptions.

Nagle's Attitudes toward the Supervisor seems the most satisfactory of the remaining three scales dealing with supervision, mainly because some attempt has been made toward validation.   Like the other two scales --Draper's Attitude toward Supervision and Schmid,et al.'s Attitude toward the Supervisor--it was built following proper item analytic procedures.   The Nagle and Draper scales seem to cover the content area better than the Schmid, et al. scale.

Most of the methodological efforts behind Schaffer's Need-Satisfaction in

Work scale are impressive, as are his general research findings. Unlike other instruments in this section, this one deals strictly with internal psychological constructs (affection, dependence, etc.). Unfortunately, norms are available only for the twelve need areas individually since the author did not report on the analysis of the inter-item structure of his need-satisfaction items. The sample on which the instrument is devised is small and atypical, which may further limit generalizations about its potential.

The Employee Opinion Survey is a competently constructed scale which covers three aspects of job satisfaction: two extrinsic (working conditions and financial benefits) and one primarily intrinsic (job activities). King finds three dimensions underlying the single set of attitudes About Your Company, a discovery which suggests that all sorts of Pandora's boxes may await occupational attitude research in this component (or perhaps in other single components) of job satisfaction. The instrument has a general factor which includes all items in its major dimension, however, and the scale appears to be of reasonable quality. The same overall impression is gained from Goldman's Group Morale Scale which apparently was constructed by careful item analytic procedures. We do not find the author's validational evidence compelling but we feel that other statistical and normative data appear more than adequate. The major problem with the scale in our opinion is that it has yet to be applied to many work groups of sufficient size.

SUPERVISORY BEHAVIOR DESCRIPTION (Fleishman 1957)

Variable | This instrument elicits information from subordinates about supervisor's behavior on two factors (consideration and initiating structure).

Description | Consideration, indicating how considerate the supervisor is of employee feelings, and initiating structure, indicating the extent to which the supervisor facilitates group interaction toward goals attainment, emerged from factor analytic studies as the major factors predicting leadership performance. The instrument consists of 28 items measuring consideration and 20 reflecting initiating structure. Items are usually rated on a five-point scale: always, often, occasionally, seldom and never. Since these are assigned weights of 0 (never) to 4 (always), or the reverse, highest possible scores are 112 for consideration and 80 for initiation.

Sample | A number of survey sites were utilized, although most research was done in one machine manufacturing concern. Data are available on the ratings of officers by ROTC students and on ratings of civil service supervisors by their employees. Average scores for foremen appear to run about 75 on consideration, and about 40 on initiating structure, with standard deviations of about 14 and 8 respectively. For variations in norms and more complete sample descriptions, consult the original source.

Reliability/ Homogeneity | Test-retest reliabilities over 11 months of .58 and .87 for consideration and .46 and .75 for initiating structure were reported. Split-half reliabilities for various samples varied between .68 and .98. The dimensions were found to be independent in two samples but in one industrial sample a correlation of -.33 was found between the dimensions.

Validity | High scores on consideration appear to be related to low absentee rates of subordinates and low accident rates, but also to low proficiency ratings. High scores on initiating structure appear to have the opposite effects -- high proficiency ratings were accompanied by high absenteeism, turnover and labor grievance.

Location | Fleishman, E., "A leader behavior description for industry" in Stogdill and Coons (eds.), Leader Behavior: Its Description and Measurement Columbus, Ohio: Ohio State University Bureau of Business Research 1957.

Administration | Self-administered (usually in a group setting) in 10 to 15 minutes.

Results and Comments | The main dimensions are also used in the Leadership Opinion Questionnaire (reviewed under "Leadership Styles" in this volume). The Leadership form is filled out by supervisors relevant to their own behavior while the present instrument is filled out by subordinates. The two forms may be used simultaneously to measure agreement between the perceptions of supervisors and subordinates on leadership behavior.

Consideration:

1. He refuses to give in when people disagree with him.
2. He does personal favors for the foremen under him.
3. He expresses appreciation when one of us does a good job.
4. He is easy to understand.
5. He demands more than we can do.
6. He helps his foremen with their personal problems.
7. He criticizes his foremen in front of others.
8. He stands up for his foremen even though it makes him unpopular.
9. He insists that everything be done his way.
10. He sees that a foreman is rewarded for a job well done.
11. He rejects suggestions for changes.
12. He changes the duties of people under him without first talking it over with them.
13. He treats people under him without considering their feelings.
14. He tries to keep the foremen under him in good standing with those in higher authority.
15. He resists changes in ways of doing things.
16. He "rides" the foreman who makes a mistake.
17. He refuses to explain his actions.
18. He acts without consulting his foreman first.
19. He stresses the importance of high morale among those under him.
20. He backs up his foremen in their actions.
21. He is slow to accept new ideas.
22. He treats all his foremen as his equal.
23. He criticizes a specific act rather than a particular individual.
24. He is willing to make changes.
25. He makes those under him feel at ease when talking with him.
26. He is friendly and can be easily approached.
27. He puts suggestions that are made by foremen under him into operation.
28. He gets the approval of his foremen on important matters before going ahead.

Initiating Structure.

1. He encourages overtime work.
2. He tries out his new ideas.
3. He rules with an iron hand.
4. He criticizes poor work.
5. He talks about how much should be done.
6. He encourages slow-working foremen to greater effort.
7. He waits for his foremen to push new ideas before he does.
8. He assigns people under him to particular tasks.
9. He asks for sacrifices from his foremen for the good of the entire department.
10. He insists that his foremen follow standard ways of doing things in every detail.
11. He sees to it that people under him are working up to their limits.
12. He offers new approaches to problems.
13. He insists that he be informed on decisions made by foremen under him.
14. He lets others do their work the way they think best.
15. He stresses being ahead of competing work groups.
16. He "needles" foremen under him for greater effort.
17. He decides in detail what shall be done and how it shall be done.
18. He emphasizes meeting of deadlines.
19. He asks foremen who have slow groups to get more out of their groups.
20. He emphasizes the quantity of work.

168

ATTITUDE TOWARD THE SUPERVISOR (Nagle 1953)

Variable	This questionnaire covers worker's perceptions of the supervisor's style of behavior as well as the worker's personal relations with the supervisor.
Description	There are 22 items in the scale, to which there are two (yes-no), three (usually, occasionally, never) or four alternatives. The 22 items were reduced from an original pool of 56 items according to item analytic procedures.
Sample	A total of 208 (out of 223) office staff employees in 14 departments of a Louisville, Kentucky plant of a large manufacturing concern comprised the sample.
Reliability/ Homogeneity	No test-retest data are reported. Split-half reliability of .87 was calculated.
Validity	Scale scores correlated -.90 with an index of supervisor sensitivity, -.71 with a company sensitivity scale and .67 with a cooperation scale. The first correlation seems high in the light of the scale's reliability
Location	Nagle, B., "Productivity, employee attitude, and supervisor sensitivity." M.A. Thesis, Purdue University, 1953. Permission to use the scale must be obtained from Purdue University, Lafayette, Indiana.
Administration	The scale is self-administered in about 10 minutes. Item alternatives starred below are scored 1 with the other scored 0. Scores range from a highest positive value of 22 to a low of 0.
Results and Comments	Attitude scores were lower for supervisors of large departments (r=-.40). Further experience with the scale can be found in Guion and Robins, "A note on the Nagle attitude scale", Journal of Applied Psychology, 1964, 48, 29-30.

Answer each question by checking the alternative which best represents your feeling about your immediate supervisor.

1   Does your immediate supervisor give you an opportunity to prove you, ability?
*a. _____ Frequently
b. _____ Yes, but not as often as he could
c. _____ Rarely

2   In your opinion, does your immediate supervisor spend sufficient time planning the work of your department?
*a. _____ Yes
b. _____ No

3   Does your immediate supervisor criticize you in front of others?
a. _____ Criticizes in front of others
*b. _____ Saves criticism for private occasions

4   Does your immediate supervisor 'follow through' on his promises?
a. _____ No
*b. _____ Yes

5   Do you feel that you have proper opportunity to present a problem, complaint, or suggestion?
*a. _____ Yes
b. _____ No

6   Does your immediate supervisor avoid you when he knows you want to see him about a problem?
a. _____ Usually avoids me
b. _____ Occasionally avoids me
*c. _____ Never avoids me

7   Does your immediate supervisor take an interest in you as a person as well as in how well you do your job?
a. _____ Yes
*b. _____ No

8   In your opinion, does your immediate supervisor spend sufficient time directing the work of your department?
*a. _____ Yes
b. _____ No

9   Are you criticized by your immediate supervisor for happenings over which you have no control?
a. _____ Often
b. _____ Occasionally
*c. _____ Never

10 Does your immediate supervisor explain to you the 'why' of an error to prevent recurrence of the error?
*a. _____ Usually
b. _____ Occasionally
c. _____ Never

11 When a change is ordered in your work procedure, are you usually given sufficient explanation of why the change is necessary?
*a. _____ Yes
b. _____ No

12 Does your immediate supervisor give you 'straight answers' when you ask something?
*a. _____ Usually
b. _____ Occasionally
c. _____ Never

13 On the job does your immediate supervisor take a reasonably democratic attitude toward you?
*a. _____ Yes
b. _____ No

14 Does your immediate supervisor delay in taking care of your complaints?
a. _____ Usually delays
b. _____ Occasionally delays
*c. _____ Never delays

15 Do you feel that your immediate supervisor is interested in getting your ideas and suggestions?
a. _____ No
*b. _____ Yes

16 Does your immediate supervisor give you recognition for work well done?
*a. _____ Usually
b. _____ Occasionally
c. _____ Never

17 Do you know how you stand with your immediate supervisor?
a. _____ No
*b. _____ Yes

18 If something happens which puts your immediate supervisor 'on the spot' what is he most likely to do?
*a. _____ Almost always takes the responsibility himself
*b. _____ Usually takes the responsibility himself
c. _____ Usually puts the responsibility on the employee
d. _____ Almost always puts the responsibility on the employee

19 Is your immediate supervisor courteous and friendly to you?
*a. _____ Always
b. _____ Usually
c. _____ Seldom

20 Do you feel promotions in your department are usually based more ability than on 'personality'?
*a. _____ Yes
b. _____ No

21 How well does your immediate supervisor keep you informed about what going on around the plant?
*a. _____ He usually keeps me well informed
b. _____ He rarely keeps me well informed

22 Do you feel at ease around your immediate supervisor?
*a. _____ Yes
b. _____ No

* Starred responses are scored 1; nonstarred responses are scored 0.

SATISFACTION WITH SUPERVISION (Draper 1955)

Variable	The scale attempts to measure worker's satisfaction with immediate supervisors, primarily in terms of personal rather than formal work relationships.
Description	The scale was developed in conjunction with a survey of plant non-managerial employees of a midwestern farm tractor manufacturer. The original scale contained 15 items though the form presented here has only fourteen. One item has been dropped since its discriminating power was relatively low and its content seemed to be out of line with the other scale items. While the verbal level of the items is not low they seem fairly straightforward and direct. The items were selected from a questionnaire previously used at the same company, and through consultation with management personnel.
Sample	The author does not clearly describe his sample. Apparently, it includes 1345 non-management employees from various departments.
Reliability	A split half coefficient of .91 (corrected) is reported for a random sample of 250 employees.
Validity	Item analysis of a random sample of 500 questionnaires indicated that all the items can discriminate at the .01 level or better (sic). Further comment related to validity will be found in the Results and Comments section.
Location	Draper, Richard D., "Higher levels of management and employee attitude toward the foreman," Ph.D. dissertation, Purdue University, 1955. Ann Arbor: University Microfilms, Inc., Pub. No. 11, 622.
Administration	The scale may be completed in less than 15 minutes. Scoring may be accomplished by summing the number of answer categories marked with (*) which are chosen.
Results and Comments	The study for which this scale was developed revealed that higher levels of management influence employee attitudes through the foremen and that attitudes toward the foremen will vary depending on the foreman's supervisor. No relation was found between pay method and attitude and only a slight relation between work pacing (i.e., "...The amount of freedom which an employee has to work at his own rate of speed.") and attitude toward the foreman. Although the sample is larger than most encountered in this sort of work it represents workers in one company who were members of one union. Local norms should be established for the proper use of this scale.

1. Does your immediate supervisor take an interest in you as a person as well as in how well you do your job? No. Yes (*).

2. Does your immediate supervisor give you "straight answers" when you ask him something? Usually (*). Occasionally. Never.

3. Generally speaking, does your immediate supervisor criticize you in front of others? Yes. No (*).

4. Does your immediate supervisor usually follow through on his promises? No. Yes (*).

5. Do you feel that you have proper opportunity to present a problem, complaint, or suggestion to your immediate supervisor? Yes (*). No.

6. Are you criticized by your immediate supervisor for happenings over which you have no control? Often. Occasionally. Never (*).

7. Is your immediate supervisor usually prompt in taking care of your complaints? Yes (*). No.

8. Do you feel that your immediate supervisor is interested in getting your ideas and suggestions? No. Yes (*).

9. Does your immediate supervisor usually give you recognition for work well done? Yes (*). No.

10. Is your immediate supervisor usually courteous to you? Yes (*). No.

11. Is your immediate supervisor concerned about your safety on the job? Yes (*). No.

12. When you are given a new job, do you feel you are reasonably well trained for that job? Yes (*). No.

13. Does your immediate supervisor try to see that you have the things you need to do your job? Yes (*). No.

14. Generally speaking, is your immediate supervisor a good supervisor? Yes (*). No.

ATTITUDES TOWARD THE SUPERVISOR (Schmid, et al. 1957)

Variable	This is a short scale covering workers' perceptions of their supervisors' style of behavior.
Description	There are 14 items in the scale, with five alternative Likert-type responses to each format. The items emerged from factor analysis of 60 items dealing with various aspects of job satisfaction.
Sample	A total of 238 supply, clerical and personnel specialists at one Air Force Base were given the 60-item questionnaire.
Reliability/ Homogeneity	No test-retest data are reported. A Kuder-Richardson internal consistency coefficient of .90 was reported for 17 items from which the final set of 14 is given below. Factor loadings of .31 to .57 for the items were reported as additional evidence of homogeneity.
Validity	No validity data are reported.
Location	Schmid, J., Morsh, J., and Detter, H. Analysis of Job Satisfaction Research Report AFPTRC-TN-57-30, March 1957, ASTIA Document #098935.
Results and Comments	The other two factors to emerge were "Sense of personal achievement" and "Stress". Readers may wish to examine the items comprising these scales in the original reference.

ATTITUDE TOWARD THE SUPERVISOR
(AS) SCALE

Answer each item by entering the appropriate letter in the space provided according to the following scale:

A. Strongly agree
B. Agree
C. Undecided
D. Disagree
E. Strongly Disagree

_____	60	My supervisor is admired and respected by all of his men.
_____	6	My supervisor praises his men for a job well done.
_____	*27	My supervisor ignores opinions of those who disagree with him.
_____	30	My supervisor confidently handles emergency situations.
_____	*9	My supervisor takes all the credit when others do good work.
_____	*3	My supervisor ignores the feelings of his men.
_____	12	My supervisor always backs up his men.
_____	24	My supervisor treats his men unusually well.
_____	15	My supervisor considers the safety of his men above all else.
_____	*45	My supervisor gives instructions that are hard to understand.
_____	*33	My supervisor has the wrong opinion of some of his men.
_____	39	My supervisor has genuine interest in his work.
_____	57	My supervisor works hard and welcomes additional responsibilities.
_____	*51	My supervisor is not always fair in judging our work.

*Items marked with an asterisk indicate negative attitudes.

EMPLOYEE OPINION SURVEY (Bolda 1958)

Variable

Three subscales contained in a questionnaire purport to measure employee's attitudes toward working conditions, job activity and financial benefits.

Description

The Working Conditions and Job Activities scales each have ten and the Financial Benefits scale nine items scored on the basis of a yes-no dichotomy. Items for the three subscales were selected from a large pool on the basis of tetrachoric correlation between item score and subscale total score as well as item popularity (difficulty) indexes.

Item content is simple and direct, indicating that the scales may have a wide range of applicability with regard to occupational groupings.

Sample

Seven hundred and one production and maintenance employees, of the Post Division, General Foods Corporation, both men and women, participated in the study. All subjects had been employed for one or more months. 350 subjects formed the primary item analysis group and a similar number formed a hold-out group.

Reliability/
  Homogeneity

Split half reliabilities (corrected), computed from hold-out group data, were reported as follows: Working Conditions, .82; Job Activity, .86; Financial Benefits, .65.

Validity

Concurrent validity is shown by the correlations between mean departmental attitude scores and pair comparison ratings of departmental effectiveness by upper management. The reliabilities of the ratings are reported as .79 for production departments and .87 for maintenance departments. Foremen and foreladies for each of the production and maintenance departments were rated by their bosses using the checklist of Supervisory Performance (Harding, 1953). The total checklist score is represented as an index of Supervisor Quality and correlations with mean departmental attitudes are shown in Results & Comments below.

Item selection procedures apparently did not include cross validation against either internal or external criteria.

Location

Bolda, R. A. "A study of employee attitudes and supervisor sensitivity to attitudes as related to supervisory and departmental effectiveness." Ph.D. thesis, Purdue University, 1958. Ann Arbor, Michigan: University Microfilms, Inc., L. C. Card No. MIC 58-7961.

Administration

Self administered in less than five minutes for all three scales. The asterisks below indicate apparent scoring direction and were not included on the original questionnaire. Scoring may be accomplished in less than one minute per person.

Results &
Comments
    While total score or subscale totals might be useful for some
purposes, the value of this instrument will probably lie in providing
a key for internal improvement. For such a purpose, item responses
and profiles will be of greatest use to management.

<u>Correlations</u> <u>between</u> <u>Employee</u> <u>Attitude</u> <u>Means</u>
<u>and</u> <u>Supervisory</u> <u>and</u> <u>Departmental</u> <u>Criteria</u>

Attitude toward:

Group	Working Condition	Job Activity	Financial Benefits
Production men	.31	--	--
	.48*	--	--
Production women	.49	--	.46
	.84*	.49	.57
Maintenance men	--	--	--
	--	--	--

NOTES: The upper coefficient represents the correlation between at-
        titude means and supervisor quality while the lower coefficient
        is the correlation with departmental effectiveness.

* Indicates p $<$ .01 by one tailed test; all other p $<$ .05.

References
    Harding, Francis D. "Development and analysis of a foremen check-
list." Unpublished doctoral dissertation, Purdue University, Lafayette,
Indiana, 1953.

JOB ACTIVITY SCALE

1. Do they expect too much work from you on your job?
   Yes ( )   No (*)

2. Is your present job the kind of work you would like to keep doing for a living?
   Yes (*)   No ( )

3. Have you ever felt that you are not learning anything on your job?
   Yes ( )   No (*)

4. Do you sometimes feel that your job counts for very little in the plant?
   No (*)   Yes ( )

5. Does your job allow you to use your abilities as much as you would like?
   No ( )   Yes (*)

6. If you were going to work for another company, would you like to do the same kind of work which you are now doing?
   No ( )   Yes (*)

7. Do you usually feel that you are doing something worthwhile on your job?
   No ( )   Yes (*)

8. Would you take a different job at the same rate of pay in your department if it were offered to you?
   No (*)   Yes ( )

9. Is your job often dull and monotonous?
   Yes ( )   No (*)

10. Would you say that you worked at an interesting kind of job?
    No ( )   Yes (*)

WORKING CONDITIONS SCALE

1. Considering the type of work you do, would you say the working conditions are as good as they could be?
   Yes (*)   No ( )

2. Would you say that working conditions are above average as compared with other plants?
   Yes (*)   No ( )

3. Does poor lighting in your department keep you from doing a good job?
   No (*)   Yes ( )

4. Is your department kept as clean as it could be?
   No ( )   Yes (*)

5. Does the temperature in your department ever get too high or too low?
   Yes ( )   No (*)

6. Considering your work, are your working conditions comfortable and healthful?
   No ( )   Yes (*)

7. Is it ever so noisy in your department that you cannot do your work?
   No (*)   Yes ( )

8. Is enough attention paid to the safety and comfort of employees in the plant?
   Yes (*)   No ( )

9. Do most of the people in your department think the working conditions are O.K.?
   No ( )   Yes (*)

10. Are you often in danger of physical injury because of poor working conditions in your department?
    Yes ( )   No (*)

FINANCIAL BENEFITS SCALE

1. If you try to collect on your hospitalization insurance would you probably run into a lot of red tape?

    No (*)   Yes ( )

2. Do you think that a better job could be done in handling pay matters here?

    Yes ( )   No (*)

3. Do you think that a better job could be done in handling benefit matters?

    No (*)   Yes ( )

4. Do you think that the life insurance which you carry through the company amounts to enough to provide for your family?

    No ( )   Yes (*)

5. Have you ever felt that you are underpaid for the work that you do?

    Yes ( )   No (*)

6. Should employees be getting better health and accident insurance for the amount of money they contribute in the employee plan here?

    No (*)   Yes ( )

7. As compared with other companies, do you think the hospitalization insurance plan offered here is a good one?

    No ( )   Yes (*)

8. Do you feel satisfied with the life insurance plan which employees of this company participate in?

    Yes (*)   No ( )

9. Do employees in other companies have more insurance protection than you have in the company's plan?

    No (*)   Yes ( )

NEED - SATISFACTION IN WORK (Schaffer 1953)

Variable

This instrument is based on the theory that the mechanisms which operate to make people satisfied or dissatisfied in general also make them satisfied or dissatisfied at work.

Description

Over 125 items (not reproduced here) were devised to measure the strength of 12 human needs. The 24 items reproduced here consisted of two items to measure the degree to which each of the 12 needs were satisfied in the person's job. These items were rated on a five-point Likert scale from "completely" satisfied to "not at all" satisfied.

Sample

The author used an "opportunity" sample of 72 persons (out of 113) who mailed back their replies. These were mainly professionals and managers (37) and clerical and sales workers (20); respondents were usually under 40 and apparently from the New York City area.

Reliability/ Homogeneity

No test-retest data are reported. The correlations between the two items for each of the 12 need areas are as follows:

A)	Recognition and approbation	.66
B)	Affection and interpersonal relationship	.20
C)	Mastery and achievement	.29
D)	Dominance	.61
E)	Social welfare	.49
F)	Self-expression	.06
G)	Socioeconomic status	.63
H)	Moral value scheme	.48
I)	Dependence	.71
J)	Creativity and challenge	.72
K)	Economic security	.78
L)	Independence	.53

Validity

The best prediction of job satisfaction was obtained on the need seen as most important to the individual (r=.54). The second most important need correlated .47; the third, .36; the fourth, .18; etc. There were some reversals in this trend for less important needs.

Location

Schaffer, R., "Job satisfaction as related to need satisfaction in work" Psychological Monographs, 1953, 67, Whole Number 364.

Administration

Self-administered in about 15 minutes. The letter preceding the items below identify the need area as specified under Reliability/Homogeneity above.

Results and Comments

The correlation between "creativity and challenge" need satisfaction with job satisfaction was .51 and for "social welfare" .47, which are practically as high as the correlation between the respondents' most important need and satisfaction.

Results and Comments (continued)

The multiple correlation was .54 for the first need, .58 for the first two needs, but then decreased with the addition of more needs e.g., .57 for three, .45 for ten.

Correlational data on the need-strength items indicated two clusters: passive or hostility-restraining (affective, social welfare, moral value and dependence) and aggressive or assertive (recognition, dominance, status and independence). No such data are available for the need-satisfaction items presented here.

Item homogeneities for areas B, C and F are, of course, quite low.

DIRECTIONS. In this section you are asked to rate your satisfactions with spe-cific aspects of your work. DO NOT consider your attitude toward your job as a whole (you have already done that in another part of the questionnaire). As you read each statement, think about how well you are satisfied with the specific item. Let your feelings be your guide in rating these items.

Use this scale:

>   5) completely satisfied
>   4) very well satisfied
>   3) well satisfied
>   2) slightly satisfied
>   1) not at all satisfied

You can use any of the numbers as often as you like. Rate every item.

A) 1. On my job when I do a piece of work I know that I'll get enough praise for it.

B) 2. Where I work I get all the opportunity I want for making friends and enjoying the company of my fellow-workers.

C) 3. When I've finished a day's work I can really be satisfied with the know-ledge that I've used all my skills and abilities.

D) 4. In the course of my work I have all the opportunity I might want to direct others.

E) 5. My work results in benefits to many people.

F) 6. My work offers me a real opportunity for self-expression.

G) 7. The income I receive from my job enables me to live in a manner which I con-sider adequate.

H) 8. I do not have to do anything on my job which is not in accordance with my ideas of right and wrong.

I) 9. In my work I get all the help and supervision I need.

J) 10. There is ample opportunity in my work to use my ingenuity and inventiveness.

K) 11. I feel that my job is a secure one.

L) 12. I have as much freedom as I want on my job.

A) 13. In my work I always get the credit I deserve for any work I do.

C) 14. I have to concentrate and put forth some effort to do my work, but it is not too hard for me.

J) 15. I often have to think up some new ways of doing things and solving problems in the course of my work.

B) 16. My job gives me plenty of opportunity to enjoy time with my family and friends.

L) 17. On my job I am free from too much supervision.

D) 18. I have as much responsibility as I want with respect to supervising the work of others.

E) 19. My work is as worthwhile as most others I would want to be in with respect to helping other people.

H) 20. In my job I am completely free of any worry about violating my religious or ethical values.

F) 21. On my job I can always act just the way I picture myself--I don't have to act like somebody else.

I) 22. I get all the help and advice that I need from my supervisors.

K) 23. My job is quite permanent. It will be there as long as I might want it. If not, I at least know that I'll always have some sort of adequate income.

G) 24. My present job enables me to have a good social standing.

ABOUT YOUR COMPANY (King 1960)

Variable	This instrument purports to measure various employee perceptions of the organization.
Description	There are 20 Yes-No items in the scale. Factor analysis of the item generated three factors, one general and two specific: respect for personal rights, and opportunity for self-improvement.
Sample	A total of 735 respondents from ten plants took part in the study.
Reliability/ Homogeneity	No test-retest results were reported. Internal structure was determined by combining items on factors which had loadings over .3 on that factor. A split-half reliability of .92 was secured.
Validity	No data on validity were reported.
Location	King, D. C., "A multiplant factor analysis of employees' attitudes toward their company," J. Applied Psych. 1960, 40, 241-3.
Administration	Self-administered in less than 15 minutes.

All items loaded over .6 on the general factor and should be used to compute the overall score of satisfaction with company. "Respect for Personal Rights" consists of items 4,6,7,9,11 and 15, while "Opportunity for Self-improvement" uses items 7,9,11,13,14,16,17,18 and 19.

1. Would you say that the company is usually hardboiled and tough with its employees?

2. Do you like to have your friends know where you work?

3. Considering everything about the company, are you fairly well satisfied with it?

4. Does the company sometimes interfere with your personal rights?

5. Do you think your company has more dissatisfied employees than most companies?

6. Do the top people respect your rights as a person?

7. If you were in real trouble would you probably get a square deal from the people at the top?

8. Is there any other company around here where you would rather work?

9. Do you feel that the top men in the company are trying to do the right thing?

10. If you were starting over again, would you probably go to work here?

11. Do you have confidence in the business judgment of top management?

12. Is there a friendly feeling in your company between the employees and management?

13. Do you think the company is really trying to improve relations with its employees?

14. Does management usually keep you informed about the things you want to know?

15. Does the company ever take advantage of the employees?

16. Is your company a good one for a person trying to get ahead?

17. Does your company offer enough chance for self-improvement and learning?

18. Do employees usually have to fight for what they get in your company?

19. Do the people at the top pay enough attention to ambition and effort?

20. Would you say that your company is a better place to work than most around here?

GROUP MORALE STUDY (Goldman 1958)

Variable	This scale examines work group morale from four angles: individual motives, homogeneity of attitude, interpersonal relations and leadership.
Description	The scale consists of 20 positive and negative statements rated on standard Likert five-point agree-disagree scales. These items were culled from a larger universe of 156 items by item analytic procedures.
Sample	The scale was originally developed from judgments of 124 students and 184 student nurses. Subsequent data were obtained from five Great Books groups (N=46) three campus groups (N=103), three classroom groups (N=57) and three labor union groups (N=65).
Reliability/ Homogeneity	No test-retest data are reported. Split half reliability for 209 subjects is reported as .88.
Validity	The author's validational evidence is difficult to ascertain. Analysis of variance methods were used to discover significant between-group variance, but this would not seem to bear on validity, since other group cohesiveness measures or correlates were not employed.
Location	Goldman, B., A Study of Group Morale Psychometric Affiliates, 221 North Lasalle St., Chicago, Illinois, 1958.
Administration	The 20 items take 10-15 minutes to complete. The item division into subscales is as follows: Individual motives: 1,8,13,18 Homogeneity of attitude: 2,7,11,15,16 Interpersonal relations: 3,6,9,12,14,19,20 Leadership: 4,5,10,17
Results and Comments	Fairly complete normative data are given for the scale. Mean scores appear to run in the high 50's (out of a possible 80) for groups high in cohesiveness and under 50 for less cohesive groups. The fact that all subscales intercorrelate significantly indicates that the computation of overall scores is a reasonable procedure.

Sample items

1. I feel that what I am doing here gives me a chance to make friends.

2. I believe that all my associates in this group hold beliefs that are unreasonable.

3. Most of my associates here would help me if I needed help.

4. The leader of this group is out for his own advancement; he doesn't care about me.

8. FACTORS FROM SOME MULTIDIMENSIONAL ANALYSES OF JOB SATISFACTION

Edward Peay
Marilyn Wernander
University of Michigan

Much of the recent work in the area of job satisfaction has stemmed from the theories of Herzberg as first proposed in Herzberg, Mausner and Snyderman (1959). These authors attempted to examine job satisfaction and dissatisfaction, using an interview technique as the source of both their data and their analytic tools. The subjects, drawn at random from nine major companies in the Pittsburgh area, fell into one of two occupational categories, engineers and accountants. The authors planned to obtain about 200 interviews with a maximum of about fifty per company. During the interview, the subject was asked to describe a time when he felt "exceptionally good" and another time when he felt "exceptionally bad" about his job. The subject was then asked to describe several aspects of these situations such as what elements of the situation produced the good or bad feelings, and how the situation affected the subject's attitude toward his job.

The coding categories and specific factors used to analyze the interview were derived from the interview data itself. These data were divided into three categories: first-level factors, second-level factors, and effects. Only the first-level factors, which are the objective elements of the job situations which the subject reports as causing good or bad feelings, are relevant for this report. The specific first-level factors used to analyze the interview were: Recognition, Achievement, Possibility of growth, Advancement, Salary, Interpersonal relations, Supervision-technical, Responsibility, Company policy and administration, Working conditions, Work itself, Factors in personal life, Status, and Job security. In addition to the above specific factors, the sequences from the interviews were divided into four groups obtained by varying the direction and duration of feeling (good or bad, short or long). Table 1 summarizes the results of the interview coding. From this analysis, the authors found that when the subjects reported feeling "exceptionally good" about their jobs, they most often mentioned in description intrinsic factors concerned with the job itself: the "motivators". Further, when the subjects described situations that made them feel "exceptionally bad" about their jobs, they most often mentioned extrinsic factors concerned with the work environment: the "hygienes". "Motivators" and "hygienes", then, would comprise the basic two dimensions underlying job satisfaction and dissatisfaction.

Herzberg, et al.'s provocative work has provided the stimulation for many subsequent studies attempting to assess the validity of the two-dimensional theory of job satisfaction and dissatisfaction. Numerous studies have tested various implications of the theory itself in multiple settings, while many others have applied the interview technique to related problems.

In the first category is a study by Friedlander (1965) in which the Herzberg distinction between growth (intrinsic) and environment (extrinsic) aspects of the job situation was tested across occupational levels with samples of white collar (engineers and scientists) and blue collar (support workers) employees in the same government research installation. Fourteen characteristics of the job situation taken from Herzberg, et al. were rated on their importance in producing job satisfaction and dissatisfaction. It was found that while intrinsic factors were important elements in satisfaction and dissatisfaction for white-collar workers, extrinsic factors were the most important determinants of blue collar workers' satisfaction and dissatisfaction.

Friedlander (1964) also directly tested the non-bipolarity of job satisfaction and dissatisfaction hypothesized by Herzberg, using a sample of 80 workers in a variety of occupations who were enrolled in a psychology course. In this study, two questionnaires were administered one week apart: one asking the respondent to rate each of 18 aspects of the job situation on its importance as a source of satisfaction, and the other asking him to rate the same 18 variables as sources of dissatisfaction. The results confirmed Herzberg's implication that the variables are not bipolar, but found that intrinsic factors are much more important than extrinsic ones for both satisfaction and dissatisfaction.

Using the same interview technique, Schwartz, et al. (1963) tested the theory with exclusively supervisory personnel. The authors used a variation of the critical incidents technique developed by Herzberg on a sample of 111 scale supervisors from the utility industry. Written protocols referring to periods of high and low job satisfaction were analyzed and scored for Herzberg's 16 first-level factors of job attitude. The results were similar to those found by Herzberg and were taken as confirming his findings. Job-related factors were found to be related to high satisfaction situations, and context-related factors to low satisfaction.

When Wernimont (1966) tested the two factor theory using a different instrument, however, the results were less encouraging. In this study, a forced choice questionnaire of 50 negatively-worded and 50 positively-worded items derived from Herzberg's intrinsic and extrinsic factors was administered to a sample of 50 accountants and 82 engineers from a variety of midwestern companies. The subjects described a satisfying experience and then checked on each item one statement that had contributed on their satisfaction; they then followed the same procedures for a dissatisfying situation and the negatively worded items. They also selected the ten each of the positive and negative statements that best described, respectively, the satisfying and dissatisfying experience. It was found that the data did not support the Herzberg theory, for the subjects endorsed about the same proportion of intrinsic and extrinsic factors in both satisfying and dissatisfying situations. Intrinsic factors were checked more often in both satisfying and dissatisfying situations.

Myers (1964) used the interview technique in a large and exhaustive study of a single electronics firm, using both white and blue collar workers. Protocols from each subject, involving periods of high and low job satisfaction, were scored for the Herzberg's 14 "first level" and 12 "second level" factors. Extensive analyses were made by job category, but, in general, Herzberg's contention of the non-bipolarity of "satisfiers" and "dissatisfiers" was supported.

TABLE 1

Percentage of Each First-Level Factor Appearing in High and Low Job-Attitude Sequences

	Duration of Feelings					
	High			Low		
	Long *	Short	Total	Long *	Short	Total
1. Achievement	38	54	41 †	6	10	7
2. Recognition	27	64	33 †	11	38	18
3. Work itself	31	3	26 †	18	4	14
4. Responsibility	28	0	23 †	6	4	6
5. Advancement	23	3	20 †	14	6	11
6. Salary	15	13	15	21	8	17
7. Possibility of growth	7	0	6	11	3	8
8. Interpersonal relations—subordinate	6	3	6	1	8	3
9. Status	5	3	4	6	1	4
10. Interpersonal relations—superior	4	5	4	18	10	15 †
11. Interpersonal relations—peers	4	0	3	7	10	8 †
12. Supervision-technical	3	0	3	23	13	20 †
13. Company policy and administration	3	0	3	37	18	31 †
14. Working conditions	1	0	1	12	8	11 †
15. Personal life	1	0	1	8	7	6 †
16. Job security	1	0	1	2	0	1

* The Long column includes the frequency of lasting attitudes resulting from both long-range and short-range sequences.

† Differences of totals between high and low statistically significant at .01 level of confidence.

Turning now to studies in related aspects of job satisfaction which utilize Herzberg's interview technique or follow implications of his theory, we find an effort by Friendlander and Walton (1964) in which the Herzberg interview technique was used to analyze one's reasons for leaving or remaining with an organization. The authors employed a sample of 82 "productive" scientists and engineers at a large government research facility. The open-end responses were coded as work process- and work content- related by two independent judges. The results confirmed Herzberg's theory in that work-process reasons were found to be significantly related to "staying" and work-content reasons to "leaving" the organization.

Saleh (1964) extended the application of the theory to later stages of the worker's career in his study of 85 male managerial "pre-retirees" (age 60-65) in 12 Cleveland companies with compulsory retirement at 65. Saleh assessed job satisfaction and dissatisfaction with Herzberg's semi-structured interview technique, adding a scale of forced choice items in which each of ten "hygiene" statements and six "motivator" statements were paired with all others. Two hypotheses derived from Herzberg's theory were supported by the results: when looking back over their middle years, the "pre-retirees" saw motivation factors as having produced satisfaction, and hygiene factors as having produced dissatisfaction; in pre-retirement years, by contrast, the subjects saw hygiene rather than motivation factors as producing satisfaction.

A third rough category of studies inspired by Herzberg, et al.'s two-factor theory of job satisfaction is comprised of those studies employing factor or cluster analysis in an attempt either to test or to extend the theory. A factor analytic approach to testing the theory was adopted by Ewen (1964) who used two samples of full-time life-insurance agents (the second sample only for cross validation). The study employed a 58 item four-choice attitude questionnaire and subjected inter-item correlations to factor analysis from which six factors were obtained: 1) Manager interest in agents; 2) Company training policies; 3) Salary; 4) Work itself; 5) Prestige or recognition; 6) General morale and satisfaction. The author examined the original data to determine whether the six factors, which corresponded roughly with Herzberg's "intrinsic" and "extrinsic" factors, were sources of job satisfaction in line with the hypothesized pattern. Herzberg's theory was not supported by the results.

A factor analytic study by Friedlander (1963) was indirectly based on the two-factor theory. Two hundred workers from each of three employment levels, engineering, supervisory, and salaried, responded to a questionnaire of 39 items of which 17 dealing with the employee's sources of satisfaction were factor analyzed. Three factors emerged, which were labeled 1) Social and technical environment, 2) Intrinsic self-actualizing work aspects, and 3) Recognition through advancement.

In a study by King (1960), data on attitudes toward the company were gathered from replies to a questionnaire given to 735 employees of ten industrial companies in Indiana. The questionnaire consisted of 20 dichotomously scored items derived from various item analyses for internal consistency and validity over eight plants. Inter-item tetrachoric correlations were factor analyzed, and three factors obtained: 1) General factor of overall bias toward company; 2) Respect for personal rights; and 3) Opportunity for self-improvement.

Harrison (1960) focused on the job attitudes of higher-level employees, using a sample of 186 supervisors at a single plant of a large manufacturing company. A questionnaire was developed by selection, on the basis of their relevance to managers, of 78 items from a previously developed questionnaire. The five-point response scale of "favorability" was dichotomized on responses, and inter-item correlations were obtained. Factor analysis yielded eight factors: 1) Advancement opportunity; 2) Working conditions; 3) Non-economic security; 4) Personal relations with supervisor; 5) Pay and benefits; 6) Communications from top management; 7) Working relations with other important groups; 8) In-plant standards of operation.

Somewhat different factors were found by Twery, et al. (1958) in a study of military personnel. In this study, the sample consisted of 467 aircraft analysis mechanics from three air force bases. A instrument comprised of 21 job satisfaction items with responses on a five point scale was administered and inter-item correlations obtained. Three analyses were performed: factor analysis with commonalities, factor analysis with unities, and an item clustering technique. All three analyses produced the same five factors or clusters: 1) General attitude toward the job; 2) Satisfaction with supervisor; 3) Satisfaction with higher echelon; 4) Satisfaction with living conditions; 5) Satisfaction with co-workers.

Employees of an insurance company were studied by Roach (1958). The resulting factors were more particularly oriented toward the specific job setting than was the case in other studies. A 62-item, five-choice "employee opinion survey" was used on a sample of 2070 employees (75 percent female) of a large insurance company. The items were sorted a priori by judges into ten tentative categories, and scores for categories (summed item scores) were correlated. These and item-category correlations were subjected to a factor analysis from which 12 factors emerged: 1) Overall evaluation of company; 2) General attitude toward supervisor; 3) Pride in company; 4) Intrinsic job satisfaction; 5) Enforcing of job standards; 6) Supervisory consideration; 7) Work load and pressure; 8) Treatment of the individual; 9) Development and progress; 10) Administration of salaries; 11) Communications; 12) Co-workers.

Similarly, a study by Clarke and Grant (1960) indicate that the purpose of the research, in this case the preparation of an attitude questionnaire for the use of a single company, can affect the kinds of factors uncovered. In this study, factor analysis was used in both the construction and analysis of results of an attitude questionnaire administered to two samples, each of 550 management personnel of a large public utility. A preliminary questionnaire of 93 items was factor analyzed on a trial sample of 640, and the final questionnaire was constructed on the basis of loadings on 12 factors of this first analysis. (The number of items on the final questionnaire is not reported.) The final questionnaire results were factor analyzed and 15 factors were obtained, most of them of specialized relevance to the company involved.

A different method was used by Harrison (1961) in studying hourly employees, but the results were comparable to those obtained in several factor analytic studies. Two samples of 350 and 650 hourly paid men from two similar medium-sized manufacturing plants were each given a separate questionnaire of 80 items chosen for "general interest" from a common pool of 100 items. Sixty-eight items were common to both questionnaires. Item responses were in terms of five degrees of satisfaction, but were dichotomized for analysis. Inter-item correlations for each sample were subjected to a "cluster analysis" by Tryon's method, yielding 12 clusters for one sample and nine for the other. The important clusters common to both samples included: 1) Consideration of foreman; 2) Foreman's technical competence; 3) Working conditions; 4) Advancement opportunities; 5) Employee benefits; 6) Earnings; 7) Friendliness and fairness of management.

Gordon (1966) took a slightly different approach in considering employee morale from the standpoint of individual needs. In this study, a sample of several hundred civilian workers at an Air Force base was administered a test consisting of items constructed on the basis of eight tentative need categories. Four factors were obtained from a factor analysis, of which three were interpretable: 1) General satisfaction; 2) Recognition of status; and 3) Self-respect.

Finally, Astin (1958) considered the factors affecting prospective employees in his study of college students. He examined the kinds of anticipated job rewards important to college freshmen, using a sample of 200 freshmen from various colleges, who were administered a questionnaire 21 items selected according to categories of anticipated job rewards. Responses were in terms of a seven-point "desirability" score. Inter-item correlations were subjected to a cluster analysis, with four clusters emerging: 1) Managerial aggressive--independence and dominance; 2) Status need--monetary and prestige awards; 3) Organization need--need for structure; 4) Physical activities, large city environment--no interpretation. The relationship of the clusters to the "majors" of respondents was subjected to statistical analysis.

While the Herzberg two-factor theory was the center of attention in the area of job satisfaction, the controversy surrounding it as well as the confusion created by the wide variety of complementary and contradictory findings led to an attempt at classification by Dunnette, et al. (1966). In their extensive study, the authors reviewed and compared a wide range of studies, and employed new methods in an effort to avoid some of the possibly confounding effects of previous approaches. The authors criticized the proponents of the two factor theory for being shackled to the critical incidents methodology, and for assuming causative linkages between variables from mere description while failing to explicate the nature of the relationship between certain job features and job satisfaction-dissatisfaction. In brief summary of Dunnette, et al.'s careful and thorough research methodology--described earlier in this volume (see Chapter 5, "General Job Satisfaction")--the authors developed two sets of standardized statements to be used as Q sort decks by respondents for describing previously satisfying and dissatisfying job events. All statements were rigorously pre-tested to make sure that they were equated on social desirability and that they tapped the following 12 Herzberg dimensions: (Intrinsic) Achievement, Responsibility, Work itself, Recognition and Advancement; (Extrinsic) Co-workers, Supervision-technical, Supervision-human relations, Salary, Security, Company policies and practices, and Working conditions. Q-type factor analyses carried out on two (for satisfying and dissatisfying situations) person-person correlation matrices for each of six occupational groups revealed that the job dimensions Achievement, Responsibility and Recognition were cited by many respondents as being more important for both satisfaction and dissatisfaction than certain other job dimensions such as Working conditions, Company policies and practices, and Security.

Having reviewed the wide range of studies of job satisfaction stemming from Herzberg's seminal theories, we find it helpful to compare the various factors and dimensions found in these studies with those aspects of job satisfaction found to be important by Dunnette, et al. For this purpose, we present a chart indicating, for each factor (or cluster) analytic study discussed, the emergent factors which correspond to those of Dunnette, as well as any others.

Authors' Note:

In the time period between the writing of this chapter and the publication of the volume, the amount of research centering around the Herzberg hypotheses has expanded even more rapidly than in the time period preceding this article. We regret that we are unable to update this literature review. However, we would refer the interested reader to a more thorough review of the arguments for and against the Herzberg hypotheses which appear in two articles in the Winter, 1967 issue of Personnel Psychology, one by House and Wignor and the other by Whitsett and Winslow.

	General	Achievement	Responsibility	Work Itself	Recognition	Advancement	Co-workers	Supervision-Tech. Comp.	Supervision-Superv. Hum. Rel.	Salary	Security	Company Policy	Working Conditions	Other
Astin, 1958	X													Managerial-Aggressive, Status-Need, Organization-Need, City Environment
Ewen, 1964				X	X					X				Training Policies
Friedlander, 1963				X		X								Social and Technical Environment
Gordon, 1955	X	X			X									
Harrison, 1960						X	X		X	X	X	X	X	Standards of Operation
Harrison, 1961		X				X		X	X	X			X	Employee Benefits (Higher Management Factors)
King, 1960	X					X								Respect for Personal Rights
Roach, 1958	X	X		X		X	X		X	X		X		Communications, General Attitude toward Supervisor
Twery, et al., 1958	X					X	X		X		X		X	Higher Echelon Growth
Herzberg, et al., 1959		X	X	X	X	X		X		X	X	X	X	International Relations, Personal Life, Status

References:

Astin, A. W. "Dimensions of Work Satisfaction in the Occupational Choices of College Freshmen" J. Appl. Psych. 1958, 42, 187-190.

Clarke, A. V., Grant, D. C. "Application of a Factorial Method in Selecting Questions for an Employee Attitude Survey" Personnel Psych., 1961, 14, 131-139.

Dunnette, M. M., Campbell, J. P., Hakel, M. D. "Factors Contributing to Job Satisfaction and Job Dissatisfaction: Mimeographed Report".

Ewen, R. B. "Some Determinants of Job Satisfaction: A Study of the Generality of Herzberg's Theory" J. Appl. Psych., 1964, 48, 161-163.

Friedlander, F. "Underlying Sources of Job Satisfaction". J. Appl. Psych. 1964, 48, 388-392.

Friedlander, F. "Job Characteristics as Satisfiers and Dissatisfiers." J. Appl. Psych., 1964, 48, 388-392.

Friedlander, F. "Comparative Work-Value Systems" Personnel Psych., 1965, 18, 1-20.

Friedlander, F., Walton, E. "Positive and Negative Motivations toward Work" Admin. Sci. Quart., 1964, 9, 194-207.

Gordon, O. J. "A Factor Analysis of Human Needs and Industrial Morale." Personnel Psych.,8, 1-18.

Harrison, R. "Sources of Variation in Managers' Job Attitudes." Personnel Psych., 1960, 13, 425-434.

Herzberg, F. The Motivation to Work, New York: Wiley, 1959.

Herzberg, F., Mausner, B., Peterson, R. O., and Capwell, D. F. Job Attitudes: Review of Research and Opinion, Pittsburgh, Pa.: Psychological Service of Pittsburgh, 1957.

King, D. C. "A Multiplant Factor Analysis of Employees' Attitudes toward Their Company" J. Appl. Psych, 1964, 44, 241-243.

Meyers, M. S. "Who Are Your Motivated Workers?" Harvard Bus. Rev., 1964, 42, 73-88.

Roach, D. E. "Dimensions of Employee Morale" Personnel Psych.,1958, 11, 419-431.

Saleh, S. D. "A Study of Attitude Change in the Preretirement Period." J. Appl. Psych..1964, 48, p.310.

Schwartz, M. M , Janusaites, E., Stark, H. "Motivational Factors Among Supervisors in the Utility Industry." Personnel Psych., 1963, 16, 45-53.

196

Twery, R., Schmid, J., Wrigley, C. "Some Factors in Job Satisfaction: A Comparison of Three Methods of Analysis" Educ. & Psych. Meas., 1958, 18, 189-202.

Wernimont, P. F. "Intrinsic and Extrinsic Factors in Job Satisfaction." J. Appl. Psych., 1966, 30, p.41.

9. CONCEPTS RELATED TO JOB SATISFACTION

The scales in this category tap aspects of job satisfaction from a particular theoretical or substantive orientation. For the collection of measures in this chapter, the labels to be covered include alienation, tension, motivation, identification with the organization, closeness of supervision and the meaning of work. The scales and their order of presentation are as follows:

1. Indices of Alienation (Aitkin and Hage 1966)

2. Alienation from Work (Pearlin 1962)

3. Job-related Tension (Kahn, et al. 1964)

4. Job Motivation Index (Patchen 1965)

5. Identification with the Work Organization (Patchen 1965)

6. Defining Dimensions of Occupation (Pearlin and Kohn 1966)

7. Meaning of Work Scales (Guion 1965)

8. Meaning of Work (Tausky 1968)

The sociological concept of alienation was adapted to the work situation by Aitkin and Hage in their study of the effects of a centralized and formalized organization on its employees. Since the sample consisted of social workers, the items need to be modified for use on more general populations. Although the six indices of alienation appear to cover the topic from a number of different angles, the items are fairly transparent and are subject to response set. The items were factor analyzed to ensure homogeneity of item content, as were items measuring the separate concepts of formalization and centralization; some researchers may find these latter two indices useful as well.

Pearlin's alienation items seem to represent a purer measure of the sociological concept than the Aitkin and Hage index, in which a job satisfaction theme is dominant. The four items are, and have been, easily adapted to work environments other than the one on which the scale was developed (a mental hospital). Since the main purpose of Pearlin's study was to find which conditions foster alienation, the author presents little direct evidence bearing on the validity of the scale. Internal homogeneity seemed satisfactory. An additional scale of "obeisance," a variable which was found to have a suppressive effect on alienation, is included for the reader's interest.

A number of useful indices (constructed this time, however, within a role theoretic framework) are contained in Kahn, et al.'s study of organizational stress. One of these measures, a Job Tension Index, is reviewed in detail here because it was applied to a national probability sample of the work force. The items cover a variety of job problem areas and intercorrelate at an acceptable level, although they are subject to response set. The index as a whole was associated with a host of interesting role-related variables such as ambiguity and conflict. An outline of other interesting measures used in Kahn, et al.'s study is appended to this section.

Patchen has recently proposed a series of five measures of employee morale and motivation of which two are reviewed here -- a Job Motivation Index and an Identification with the Work Organization Index. The author is to be commended for his overriding concern with validating his items against a variety of criterion variables. His measures do not always stand up impressively on the matters of validition and reliability, but the items appear well-written and make one wonder how other instruments would fare when put to the stringent tests which Patchen attempts. In several studies, only between two and four items could be found on which to build the Job Motivation Index, and although eight items are proposed for the Identification scale, only three or four appear adequately justified on the basis of Patchen's data.

Somewhat related to identification with the organization measures are those instruments which attempt to assess whether the professional employee's main orientation is toward the organization in which he is employed or whether his general frame of reference is his membership in his profession. These measures are considered in Chapter 10, dealing with "Occupational Values".

Self-reliance and closeness of supervision have been found to relate to job satisfaction, with opposite effects -- employees in highly self-reliant jobs were more satisfied, while those closely supervised were less satisfied. Pearlin and Kohn's measures of these two variables are quite short but the results obtained with them are highly provocative. Both appear to have satisfactory internal homogeneity as indicated by Guttman coefficients.

The final instruments covered in this section are concerned with the "meaning of work." Guion uses semantic differential ratings. Semantic differential ratings have been used empirically to survey and chart the dimensional structure of a number of psychological domains; Guion's work appears to be the latest concentrated study of this nature in the area of work. Researchers who feel comfortable with the semantic differential methodology may want to examine the scales used and the factors extracted from Guion's analysis. The reader is also referred to two additional current investigations into the meaning of work listed at the end of this scale review.

Tausky's scale makes use of Guttman scale analysis to generate four types of orientations toward work among blue collar workers. While Tausky's scoring procedure is not entirely clear and data on scale validity are lacking, his findings are based on a national cross-section. Tausky finds evidence of fairly well-rooted orientations toward work in this group.

There are two other empirical measures that should be mentioned in the present context: the first is Dubin's (1956) forty-item measure of Central Life Interests. Dubin's attempt to assess work attitudes within the framework of similar attitudes toward other activities in a person's life is a praise-worthy effort, but the underlying assumptions and resulting conclusions of the measure have been duly criticized by Wilensky (1964) and Kornhauser (1965). The criticism is not entirely consistent, however, for Wilensky essentially agrees with Dubin's contention that work is not a central life interest of workers, while Kornhauser maintains just the opposite. Dubin has recently claimed parallel results for a German industrial sample.

Balma, et al. (1957) developed an error choice measure (see the Union-Management section under Chapter 12, "Other Work Attitudes") of Management Identification which demonstrated adequate reliability and validity properties. Because of ethical considerations, however, they did not publish the instrument.

References:

Balma, M., Maloney, J. and Lawshe, C. "The role of foremen in modern industry: the development of a measure of management identification," Personnel Psychology 1957, 11, 195-205.

Dubin, R. "Industrial workers' worlds: A study of the central life interests of industrial workers," Social Problems, 1965, 3, 131-142.

Kornahuser, A. Mental Health of the Industrial Worker, New York: Wiley, 1965.

Wilensky, H. "Varieties of work experience" in Henry Borow (ed.), Man in a World at Work, Boston: Houghton-Mifflin Co., 1964, pp. 125-154.

INDICES OF ALIENATION (Aitkin and Hage 1966)

Variable   This study attempts to examine the relationship between two types of alienation --alienation from work, and alienation from expressive relations-- and two structural properties of organizations -- centralization and formalization. In all, there are indices for six aspects:

1. Work alienation
2. Alienation from expressive relations
3. Hierarchy of authority
4. Participation in decision-making
5. Job codification
6. Rule observation

Description   "Alienation from work" reflects a feeling of disappointment with career and professional development, as well as disappointment over the inability to fulfill professional norms. This index was composed of six questions. "Alienation from expressive relations" reflects dissatisfaction in social relation with supervisors and fellow workers. This index was composed of two questions. Scoring information on these alienation indices was not given.

The authors define "hierarchy of authority" as the extent of reliance upon supervisors in making decisions about individually assigned tasks, and "participation in decision-making" as the degree to which staff members participate in setting the goals and policies of the entire organization. The hierarchy index is composed of five statements, to which the responses could vary from 1 (definitely false) to 4 (definitely true). Individual scores were computed from the average of the replies of each respondent; they were then combined into an organizational score determined by computing the average of all social position means in the agency. Organizational scores varied from 1.50 to 2.10. The participation index is based on four questions, to which the responses could vary from 1 to 5, or "never", "seldom", "sometimes", "often" or "always". This index was scored as above; the agencies' scores ranged from 1.68 to 3.69.

The index of job codification reflects the degree to which members must consult rules in fulfilling professional responsibilities. It is based on five questions, scored, like the hierarchy index, from 1 (low) to 4(high). Agencies' scores were between 2.22 and 2.70. The index of rule observation reflects the degree to which employee are observed for rule violations. Composed of two statements, it was scored as above, with the actual scores ranging from 1.11 to 1.90.

Multivariate analysis was introduced to determine the relative importance of the relationships between measures of centralization and formalization and alienation.

Sample   The sample population was drawn from 16 social welfare agencies
                  located in a large midwest metropolis in 1964. Ten agencies were
                  private; six were either public or branches of public agencies; the
                  agencies varied in size from 12 employees to several hundred.

                  Data were collected on 314 supervisory and non-supervisory personnel
                  excluding non-supervisory administrative and maintenance personnel.
                  Sampling included professionals, such as psychiatrists, social workers,
                  and rehabilitation counselors. Information obtained from respondents
                  was pooled to reflect properties of the 16 organizations which were
                  the units of analysis in the study.

Reliability/   Test-retest reliability was not estimated. The items in the
  Homogeneity   alienation indices were selected on the basis of a principal
                  components solution factor analysis of 13 items concerning the
                  degree of satisfaction with various aspects of the respondents'
                  work situation. The original battery of 13 items was taken from
                  Gross, et al. (1958). Correlation between the two indices was .75.

Validity   In attempting to determine the net effect of independent variables,
                  the authors employed partial and multiple regression analysis.

Location   Aiken, M. and Hage, J., "Organizational alienation: a comparative
                  analysis", Am. Soc. Rev., 1966, 31, pp. 497-507.

Administration   The indices were formed from an interview schedule.

Results and   The authors found that lack of participation in agency decision-
  Comments   making was strongly related to alienation from work (r=.59). Since
                  the agencies performed non-uniform tasks, they tended toward
                  decentralization as measured by the index of hierarchy of authority.
                  Even so, correlation with the alienation indices was .49 (work) and
                  .45 (expressive relations). When the effect of the other variables
                  was removed, the degree of participation in decision-making was
                  revealed to have a strong and independent effect on alienation from
                  work.

                  The agencies were found to have relatively little formalization,
                  as measured by the indices. But the author found a direct relationship
                  between the degree of job codification and alienation from work
                  (r=.51), and a fairly strong relationship between the index of rule
                  observation and both alienation indices: r=.55 (work), r=.65
                  (expressive relations). The authors add that in a forthcoming paper
                  they examine the above relationships while controlling for
                  environmental factors such as age, size, and major function of the
                  organization.

                  The utility of most of these indices may be limited by their content
                  to professional or semi-professional agencies.

                  Items for the centralism and formalism indices were determined from
                  factor analysis of "hirarchy of authority" items and roles" items
                  (Hall, 1961, 1963).

202

References:

Gross, N., Mason, W. and McEachern, A. <u>Explanations in Role Analysis</u> New York: Wiley, 1958, Appendix B.

Hall, R. H., "An emperical study of bureaucratic dimensions and their relation to other organizational characteristics", unpublished Ph.D. dissertation, Ohio State University, 1961.

_____, "The concepts of bureaucracy: an empirical assessment", <u>Am. J. Sociol</u>, <u>69</u> (July, 1963), pp. 32-40.

Alienation from Work:

1. How satisfied are you that you have been given enough authority by your board of directors to do your job well?
2. How satisfied are you with your present job when you compare it to similar positions in the state?
3. How satisfied are you with the progress you are making towards the goals which you set for yourself in your present position?
4. On the whole, how satisfied are you that (your superior) accepts you as a professional expert to the degree to which you are entitled by reason of position, training and experience?
5. On the whole, how satisfied are you with your present job when you consider the expectations you had when you took this job?
6. How satisfied are you with your present job in light of career expectations?

Alienation from Expressive Relations:

1. How satisfied are you with your supervisor?
2. How satisfied are you with your fellow workers?

Index of Hierarchy of Authority:

1. There can be little action taken here until a supervisor approves a decision.
2. A person who wants to make his own decisions would be quickly discouraged here.
3. Even small matters have to be referred to someone higher up for a final answer.
4. I have to ask my boss before I do almost anything.
5. Any decision I make has to have my boss' approval.

Index of Participation in Decision-making:

1. How frequently do you usually participate in the decision to hire new staff?
2. How frequently do you usually participate in decisions on the promotion of any of the professional staff?
3. How frequently do you participate in decisions on the adoption of new policies?
4. How frequently do you participate in the decisions on the adoption of new programs?

Index of Job Codification:

1. I feel that I am my own boss in most matters.
2. A person can make his own decisions without checking with anybody else.
3. How things are done here is left up to the person doing the work.
4. People here are allowed to do almost as they please.
5. Most people here make their own rules on the job.

Index of Rule Observation:

1. The employees are constantly being checked on for rule violations.
2. People here feel as though they are constantly being watched, to see that they obey all the rules.

ALIENATION FROM WORK (Pearlin 1962)

Variable	This scale attempts to measure work alienation from the viewpoint of subjectively experienced powerlessness within the work organization.
Description	There are four items in the scale, with one point scored for any of the alienated responses. The purpose of the study was to find conditions fostering alienation rather than its consequences or the validity of the scale. Another aspect of the measure is "obeisance", which mitigates alienation. This four-item scale is presented as well.
Sample	Nursing personnel (1338 of 1315 contacted) at a large federal mental hospitals were administered the scale. Nursing assistants comprised 70 percent of the sample, charge personnel 16 percent and registered nurses 14 percent.
Reliability/ Homogeneity	No test-retest data are reported. A reproducibility coefficient of .91 was obtained for the four items.
Validity	No direct evidence bearing on validity was obtained although a number of theoretically interesting findings are presented under "Results and Comments" below.
Location	Pearlin, L., "Alienation from work: a study of nursing personnel" American Sociological Review 1962, 27, 314-326.
Results and Comments	Intense alienation was most likely to occur (a) where authority figures and their subjects stand in relations of great positional disparity, (b) where authority is communicated in such a way as to prevent or discourage exchange and where the superordinate exercises his authority in relative absentia. Findings (a) and (b) did not hold for people with an "obeisant" regard for status. Alienation was found among limited and high achievers who were not satisfied with extrinsic aspects of the job and among those who have few friends at work or who work alone.

Alienation Scale (Alienated response underlined)

1. How often do you do things in your work that you wouldn't do if it were up to you?

    Never   Once in a while   Fairly often   <u>Very often</u>

2. Around here it's not important how much you know, it's who you know that really counts.

    <u>Agree</u>   Disagree

3. How much say or influence do people like you have on the way the hospital is run?

    A lot   Some   <u>Very little</u>   <u>None</u>

4. How often do you tell (your superior) your own ideas about things you might do in your work?

    <u>Never</u>   <u>Once in a while</u>   Fairly often   Very often

Obeisance Scale (Obeisant response underlined)

1. Do you ever feel like disagreeing with what (your superior) wants you to do or how he (or she) wants you to do it?

    Often sometimes <u>rarely</u> or <u>never</u>?

2. I figure my supervisor knows better what's good for my ward or else she (or he) wouldn't be a supervisor.

    <u>Agree</u> or disagree?

3. The best way to get along on this job is to mind your own business and just do as you're told.

    <u>Agree</u> or disagree?

4. I like the idea of nurses and nursing assistants standing up when the doctor comes into the nursing station.

    <u>Agree</u> or disagree?

JOB-RELATED TENSION (Kahn, et al. 1964)

Variable	This index attempts to measure the amount of tension experienced in connection with work, specifically as a response to the job.
Description	The index consisted of 15 statements describing what the authors judged to be symptoms of conflict or ambiguity. Respondents were asked to estimate how often they were bothered by each type of symptom on a five-point Likert scale.
Sample	Data on this index were collected from a national sample of 725 employed adults. In addition an intensive survey of 53 supervisory employees were asked 11 of the same items plus three new ones; this intensive survey also utilized a number of the interesting empirical measures regarding conflict and ambiguity on the job (described below).
Reliability/ Homogeneity	No test-retest reliability figures are given but an intercorrelation analysis of the items was performed. For the national sample, only two inter-item correlations were negative and less than ten were positive but not significant at the .05 level. On the whole, the average inter-item correlation appears to be in the middle .20's. The intercorrelation matrix figures for the intensive sample were quite close to those found in the national sample.
Validity	The survey utilized an open-ended question to elicit information about the number, content and intensity of job-related worries. These were found to be closed related to the tension index. Some indirect relations between tension and satisfaction were found.
Location	Kahn, R., et al. Organizational Stress New York: Wiley, 1964.
Administration	Respondents choose one of five fixed alternatives: never, rarely, sometimes, rather often, and nearly all the time. Estimated administration time is less than 15 minutes. Total score is the average response for each item to which the respondent replies. For the national sample this score lies between "rarely" and "sometimes" -- in quantitative terms 1.7.
Results and Comments	In the national population, tension scores were found to be higher for the better-educated and the self-employed and to reach a peak for those between 25 and 35.
	In addition to the tension index, several measures of conflict and ambiguity within organizations were constructed within a role theory framework. Satisfaction was found to be related to both conflict and ambiguity.
	A Role Conflict Index was constructed by showing each "role sender" a list of job activities drawn up by each supervisory respondent and then asking the former 1) if he would like the supervisor to do the

activity in the same or different way or 2) if he would like him
to spend the same amount or more (or less) time on the activity.
Each role sender was asked how he would like the respondent to be
different. He was also asked to contrast the respondent with an
ideal supervisor on a 22-adjective checklist.

Ambiguity Indices dealt with how clearly the respondent felt the
role sender evinced his expectations and evaluations of the respondent
and with how clearly the respondent understood the limits of his own
authority.

Normative Expectations attempted to assess expectations of behavior
applicable to persons in all supervisory positions, regardless of
actual behavior. A factor analyses of the items in this index revealed
seven factors, of which the first five were labelled: Rules orientation, Nurturance of subordinates, Closeness of supervision,
Universalism-particularism, Promotion-achievement orientation.
Those interested in the measurement of role-related aspects should
also consult Gross, et al.'s (1958) pioneering ventures in this
aspect of work behavior.

In addition to the role-related measures, Kahn, et al. constructed a
Job Satisfaction Index and a Confidence in Organization Index which
could be useful to other researchers. Data on these instruments were
only collected for the intensive sample, but they were factor analyzed
along with a most comprehensive battery of personality scales.

eference   Gross, N., Mason, W. and McEachern, A.   Explorations in Role Analysis
New York: Wiley, 1958.

Interviewer introduced items by asking respondents:

All of us occasionally feel bothered by certain kinds of things in our work. I'm going to read a list of things that sometimes bother people, and I would like you to tell me how frequently you feel bothered by each of them.

In the national survey respondents were then presented the following items:

A. Feeling that you have too little authority to carry out the responsibilities assigned to you
B. Being unclear on just what the scope and responsibilities of your job are
C. Not knowing what opportunities for advancement or promotion exist for you
D. Feeling that you have too heavy a work load, one that you can't possibly finish during an ordinary workday
E. Thinking that you'll not be able to satisfy the conflicting demands of various people over you
F. Feeling that you're not fully qualified to handle your job
G. Not knowing what your supervisor thinks of you, how he evaluates your performance
H. The fact that you can't get information needed to carry out your job.
I. Having to decide things that affect the lives of individuals, people that you know
J. Feeling that you may not be liked and accepted by the people you work with
K. Feeling unable to influence your immediate supervisor's decisions and actions that affect you
L. Not knowing just what the people you work with expect of you
M. Thinking that the amount of work you have to do may interfere with how well it gets done
N. Feeling that you have to do things on the job that are against your better judgment
O. Feeling that your job tends to interfere with your family life

In the intensive study items L-O were omitted from the total <u>Tension</u> index and the following items were used instead:

P. Feeling that your progress on the job is not what it should be or could be
Q. Thinking that someone else may get the job above you, the one you are directly in line for
R. Feeling that you have too much responsibility and authority delegated to you by your superiors

JOB MOTIVATION INDEX (Patchen 1965)

Variable | This instrument is an attempt to measure the level of aroused motivation on the job, from the standpoint of devotion of energy to job tasks.

Description | The job motivation indices consist of four five-point Likert scales. From among 22 items tried as indicators of general job motivation, two questions (Q1 and 2) were selected from one study as showing evidence of validity; these were combined into Index A. From another study, two new items (Q3 and 4) showed evidence of validity and were added to the shorter index to form the four item Index B. Index C is composed of Q 1, 2 and 3 (which are relevant for inter-group comparisons), used in a third study.

Sample | The sample population was 834 non-supervisory personnel from dispersed plants of the Tennessee Valley Authority and 233 from a private electronics firm. The two engineering divisions of TVA employ mostly civil, mechanical and electrical engineers; the three steam plants employ monitor technicans, skilled craftsmen and laboratory technicians. At the electronics firm, electrical engineers, craftsmen, semi-skilled production workers, salesmen and electrical workers were interviewed.

Reliability/ Homogeneity | Test-retest data was secured from a sub-sample of 49 employees of the electronics firm. Reliability for Index A was .80 at the individual level. Scale homogeneity was sought through inter-item correlations, which were positive but low.

Validity | Motivation scores correlated moderately (median $r=.35$) with supervisors' ratings of "concern for doing a good job" in one plant, but only slightly (median $r=.15$) in another. The relations between motivation and absence rates were more substantial (ranging from .20 to .53). Relations between motivation and work efficiency were again mixed, although one correlation of .54 was obtained between motivation and production volume.

Differences in motivation expected on the basis of occupational status were confirmed. A correlation of .50 was found between motivation and job satisfaction over 90 work groups.

Location | Patchen, M., Some Questionnaire Measures of Employee Motivation and Morale Monograph No. 41, Ann Arbor, Michigan: Institute for Social Research, 1965.

Administration | Less than 10 minutes. Scoring requires simple summation.

Results and Comments | Group motivation scores followed a number of theoretical predictions on aspects of the work situation, such as perceived achievement opportunities, control work methods and identification with one own occupation. The author concedes that this index may not be too

Results and Comments (continued)

useful in detecting fine differences within units where job motivation
is relatively homogeneous. He also noted special circumstances when
it would be most useful to use Index A, Index B or Index C. Index
B (all four items) is recommended for intensive study of a single
work group. Of the five indices that the author constructed (see
the following scale write-up), this one posed greatest difficulty
in terms of finding items that demonstrated consistent reliability
and validity.

1. On most days on your job, how often does time seem to drag for you?

    (1) _____ About half the day or more

    (2) _____ About one-third of the day

    (3) _____ About one-quarter of the day

    (4) _____ About one-eighth of the day

    (5) _____ Time never seems to drag

2. Some people are completely involved in their job --they are absorbed in it night and day. For other people, their job is simply one of several interests. How involved do you feel in your job?

    (1) _____ Very little involved; my other interests are more absorbing

    (2) _____ Slightly involved

    (3) _____ Moderately involved; my job and my other interests are equally absorbing to me

    (4) _____ Strongly involved

    (5) _____ Very strongly involved; my work is the most absorbing interest in my life.

3. How often do you do some extra work for your job which isn't really required of you?

    (5) _____ Almost every day

    (4) _____ Several times a week

    (3) _____ About once a week

    (2) _____ Once every few weeks

    (1) _____ About once a month or less

4. Would you say you work harder, less hard, or about the same as other people doing your type of work at (name of organization)?

    (5) _____ Much harder than most others

    (4) _____ A little harder than most others

    (3) _____ About the same as most others

    (2) _____ A little less hard than most others

    (1) _____ Much less hard than most others.

IDENTIFICATION WITH THE WORK ORGANIZATION (Patchen 1965)

Variable	This instrument attempts to measure employee organizational identification, that is, the sense of solidarity with other memebers of the organization, especially with the top leaders.
Description	The instrument consists of **eight modified** Likert-type items. Scores assigned to each response are indicated by numbers in parentheses before the items as given below. From the eight items, three indices were computed: Index B, based on the sum of scores on Q 1, 2, and 3, used both at TVA and at the electronics company; Index C, composed of Q1, 2, and 3, and also Q5, which was used only at the electronics company; and Index D, a seven item index including all items used at TVA which showed evidence of validity (five other questions were discarded).
Sample	The sample population was the same as that described for the previous motivation measure.
Reliability/ Homogeneity	Reliability sample was the same as that described for the motivation index, and also included one engineering division at TVA. Test-retest reliability coefficients for the different indices were as follows: Index B, .69 for individuals and .75 for work units; Index C, .75 for individuals and .79 for groups; Index D, .71 for individuals and .98 for a small number of work groups. The inter-item correlation matrix showed items 2, 3, and 4 moderately correlated but items 6,7,8 with almost no inter-correlation among themselves or with items 2, 3, and 4.
Validity	Following the same procedure of supervisory ranking described for the motivation index, judges ranked individual employees they knew personally on their "sense of belonging" to the organization. Ranking scores were then correlated (median $r=.24$) with index scores.
	The items were also related to a probable behavioral indicator of identification -- the use of a TVA sticker on one's car. Over five times as many "high" identifiers than "low" identifiers had a sticker.
	To evaluate the construct validity of the Index, scores were correlated with turnover data, with employees' expectation of remaining with the organization, length of service, attendance, and with the TVA cooperative program. Significant relations were found with length of service and expectation of remaining with the organization.
Location	Patchen, M., <u>Some Questionnaire Measures of Employee Motivation and Morale: A Report on Their Reliability and Validity</u>, monograph #41, Ann Arbor, Michigan, Institute for Social Research, 1965.
Administration	Estimated administration time: under ten minutes. Scoring is accomplished by simple summation.

Results and Comments

While the first five items showed adequate intercorrelations, questions 6, 7, and 8 used at TVA showed no correlations with other items and there is some question as to what they may be measuring. For the electronics firm data, question 4 showed negative and positive relations with other items, an indication that it was properly discarded from the total index for this group.

In addition to the two measures described here, Patchen presents data on three other indices too specialized to cover here. The three indices are:

1) Interest in Work Innovation (6 items)
2) Willingness to Disagree with Supervisors (4 items)
3) Acceptance of Job Changes Index (5 items)

Substantial item reliability and validity information is given for these indices as it was for the two indices reviewed here.

Identification with the work organization indices

1. If you could begin working over again, but in the same occupation as you're in now, how likely would you be to choose (TVA) as a place to work?

    (1) _____ Definitely would choose another place over (TVA)
    (2) _____ Probably would choose another place over   (TVA)
    (3) _____ Wouldn't care much whether it was (TVA) or some other place
    (4) _____ Probably would choose (TVA) over another place
    (5) _____ Definitely would choose (TVA) over another place for my occupation.

2a. Following are two somewhat different statements about the relations between management and employees at TVA:

    a. The relations between management and employees at (company name) are much different than in most other companies, because in (company name) both are working together toward the same goals.

    b. Relations between management and employees at (company name) are not really very different than in other companies; management is looking out for the organization's interests, and employees have to look out for their own interests.

    Which of the two statements above comes closer to your own opinion?

    (5) _____ Agree completely with A
    (4) _____ Agree more with A than with B
    (3) _____ Agree more with B than with A
    (1) _____ Agree completely with B

The following almost identical question was used at the electronics company:

2b. Following are two somewhat different statements about the relations between management and employees at (name of company):

    a. The relations between management and employees at (company name) are much different than in most other companies, because we (company name) both are working together toward the same goals.

    b. Relations between management and employees at (company) are not really much different than in other companies; management is looking out for the organization's interests, and employees have to look out for their own interests.

    Responses scored as in 2a, above.

3a. How do you feel when you hear (or read about) some one criticizing the TVA method of public power or comparing it unfavorably to private power?

    (1) _____ I mostly agree with the criticism
    (2) _____ It doesn't bother me

(4) _____ It gets me a little mad
(5) _____ It gets me quite mad
_____ I never hear or read such criticism

3b. The following similar question was used at the electronics company:

How do you feel when you hear (or read about) some one criticizing (company name) or (company name) products, or comparing (company names) unfavorably to other companies?

(2) _____ It doesn't really bother me; I don't care much what other people think of (company name)
(4) _____ It bothers me a little
(5) _____ It bothers me quite a bit; I'm anxious to have people think well of (company name)
_____ I never hear or read such criticism

4. If someone asked you to describe yourself, and you could tell only one thing about yourself, which of the following answers would you be most likely to give? (Put a number 1 next to that item.)

_____ I came from (my home state)
_____ I work for (TVA)
_____ I am a (my occupation or type of work)
_____ I am (my church membership or preference)
_____ I am a graduate of (my school)

If you could give two answers, which of the items above would you choose second? (Put a number 2 next to that item.) If you would give three answers, which one of the items would you choose third? (Put a number 3 next to that item.) (Scored 1 through 4, with those choosing (TVA) as first choice getting a 4 and those not choosing it at all getting a 1.)

5. If you have or were to have a son, how would you feel if someone suggested that he work for the same company that you work for? (If you are a woman, answer for a daughter.)

(5) _____ Would completely approve
(4) _____ Would generally approve, but with some reservations
(3) _____ Would neither approve nor disapprove
(2) _____ Would disapprove a little
(1) _____ Would strongly disapprove

6. In general, how often do you tell someone in your immediate family (wife, child, parent, brother, sister) about some project that TVA has done or is doing?

(5) _____ Once a week or more
(4) _____ Several times a month
(3) _____ About once a month
(2) _____ Once every few months
(1) _____ About once a year
_____ Don't have any immediate family to talk to

7. In general, how often do you tell someone <u>outside</u> your immediate family (friends, neighbor, store clerk, etc.) about some project that TVA has done or is doing?

    Responses same as in Q6.

8. During the past two years, how many times has your part of TVA had a dinner a picnic or other social event outside of office hours?

    (5) _____ Five or more times
    (4) _____ Four times
    (3) _____ Three times
    (1) _____ Once
    (0) _____ Never that I know of

    <u>If any social events held</u>:

    How many of these social events did you attend?

    (5) _____ Five or more
    (4) _____ Four
    (3) _____ Three
    (2) _____ Two
    (1) _____ Once
    (0) _____ None

    (Score on item 8 was proportion of events attended, recorded on a five point scale.)

DEFINING DIMENSIONS OF OCCUPATION (Pearlin and Kohn 1966)

Variable   This study produced two instruments to assess dimensions of occupation which help to define the job: (1) a scale of closeness of supervision (2) an index of job-required self-reliance. The scale purports to measure the degree of occupational supervision to which a man is subject as a limitation on the amount of self-direction a job permits, while the index is supposed to measure the degree to which a job requires self-reliance.

Description   The scale consists of three questions which, the authors report, together from a "reasonably satisfactory Guttman scale." The items are listed below in ascending order of "easiness". Responses to items are not reported in the original source.

The index consists of four items out of an unspecified "list of qualities" which respondents selected as being important to doing well at their work. The index was formed by the assignment of a weight of "four" if an item was ranked first in importance, "three" for second rank, "two" for third, and "one" if it was considered important even though unranked. Scores were summed for each respondent, with a high score indicating that work requires self-reliance.

Sample   The sample population consisted of 341 fathers drawn from approximately equal number of middle-and working-class parents of fifth-grade children in Turin, Italy, described as a "principal industrial center with a lively political climate".

Reliability/   The author report the scale's reproducibility to be .95, its
Homogeneity   scalability .83. On the unidimensionality of the index, the authors state that "...the four items, taken three at a time and dichotomized in the basis of whether or not the attribute is considered important, form quite satisfactory Guttman scales. But the cutting points are such that we cannot use all four items in one scale, and the requirement that we score each item dichotomously (for independence) unduly restricts the power of the index."

Validity   Though no direct tests of validation were performed, the main results of the study were in line with theoretical expectations. Parents in self-reliant occupations and parents without close supervision were more likely to stress self-control values in child-rearing, while more dependent and closely supervised employees stressed obedience. These results held up when controlled for education but not for occupation (see comments below).

Location   Pearlin, L. I., and Kohn, M. L., "Social Class, Occupation and Parental Values: A Cross-National Study", Am. Sociol. Rev., 1966, 4, pp. 466-479.

Administration   The scale and index formed part of an interview schedule and should take less than ten minutes to complete.

Results and
Comments

The authors report that by using Rosenberg's (1962) technique of test-factor standardization, they found that the differential occupational experiences of middle-and working-class men largely account for the difference in the extreme valuation of obedience, but that the working-class overall still is more likely to value obedience -- an effect which must be attributed to other aspects of class than occupational differences. The authors further report that among men of similar occupational circumstances, education is only weakly and inconsistently related to parental rules, and that occupation rather than education accounts for virtually all the variation in a fathers' values.

References

Kohn, M., "Social class and parental values", American Journal of Sociology, 1959, 64, 337-351.

Rosenberg, M., "Test factor standardization as a method of interpretation", Social Forces, 1962, 41, 53-61.

Closeness of Supervision Scale

1) How much control does your direct supervisor exercise over your work?

2) Do you feel that you are able to make decisions about the things that have true importance to your work?

3) Do you have much influence on the way things go at your work?

Index of Job-Required Self-Reliance

Rank the following as to their importance to doing well at your work (many items listed the four-reliant ones are shown below)

1) to understand one's self

2) to be intelligent

3) to have trust in one's self

4) to have a sense of responsibility

MEANING OF WORK SCALES (Guion 1965)

Variable
Research into the "meaning of work" was undertaken by use of the semantic differential and of subsequent dimensions appearing from factor analyses of these data.

Description
Following standard semantic differential tradition, the author had six work concepts rated on 64 semantic differential scales. The concepts used for a sample of employed persons and for a student sample were as follows:

Employed	Student
The Ideal Job	The Ideal Job
My Job	My Vocational Future
The Things I Do at Work	Vice President
The People I Work With	Clerk
Me -- at Work	Doctor
My Spare Time	Mechanic

Factor analysis of each group of scales suggested five dimensions common to all, with certain exceptions.

Sample
The following samples are mentioned: 1) 63 employees at various levels within a single company; 2) an unknown number of students in an industrial psychology class; 3) an unknown number of people from an extension class, and two people (one highly motivated, one not) that each of them knew.

Reliability/
Homogeneity
Test-retest reliability is not given. Scale homogeneity was determined by factor analysis.

Validity
The stimulation factor (perhaps "evaluative" in standard semantic differential terminology) for two content concepts correlated .76 and .78 with the Brayfield-Rothe Scale (see Chapter 5). Correlation for other concepts were in the low .36's.

Location
Guion, R., "Measurement of the meaning of work." Paper presented at the American Psychological Association September 4, 1965. The author is continuing to conduct research in this area at Bowling Green State University in Ohio.

Administration
Standard semantic differential instructions. See Osgood, et al. 1957.

Results and
Comments
Scales loading on:
Cluster 1 (evaluation): stimulating-deadening, interesting-boring, exciting-dull, promising-disappointing, challenging-monotonous gratifying-frustrating.
Cluster 2 (autonomy): governed-unrestricted, guided-free, dependent-independent
Cluster 3 (structure): certain-doubtful, precise-vague, material-abstract, detailed-general

220

Results and Comments (continued)

Cluster 4 (social aspects): verbal-silent, verbal-nonverbal, compari-
able-secluded, outward-inward
Cluster 5 (status): clean-dirty, office work-factory work, inside-
outside

The author maintains that his results partially support Herzberg's
theory. Satisfied workers were higher on each of five factor
scores than less satisfied workers, although the differences were
very small for extrinsic factors (pay, company policies). Some of
the factors have not been encountered before (e.g., structure) and
may be useful to add to the list of job factors to be considered.
Overall, however, the five factors seem rather pale compared to those
found by Dunnette, et al. and found in the answers to open-ended
questions (see Chapter 3). The author might have added
scales dealing with more specific aspects of work (such as pay or work
pressure), even though 64 scales were already employed. Some of
these 64 scales seem tangential to the work situation (e.g.,
nonpolitical-political, outspoken-reserved).

There is other research currently underway into the meaning of work
that deserves attention as well. Paul Kimmel and Lauren Wispe (1966)
at the Office of Manpower and Training are approaching the problem
using a variety of less structured analytic techniques. Robert
Smith (1965) of the Survey Research Center is studying the meaning
of work to children using a "Man from Mars" technique, whereby the
child is asked to describe what work is to a mythical Martian who
knows nothing about work. Both studies have much more to add about
the relation of intrinsic and extrinsic factors in the definition of
work.

References

Smith, R. Attitudes of Teenagers Toward Work and Play Ann Arbor,
Michigan: Institute for Social Research, 1965.

Kimmel, P. and Wispe, L. "A proposal for a pilot study of the
meaning of work" mimeo. Office of Manpower and Training, U. S.
Department of Labor, Washington, D.C., 1966.

Osgood, C., et al. The Measurement of Meaning Urbana, University
of Illinois Press, 1957.

Sample Item

THE IDEAL JOB

```
disappointing____:____:____:____:____:____:____:promising
   outspoken____:____:____:____:____:____:____:reserved
    irregular____:____:____:____:____:____:____:systematic
  challenging____:____:____:____:____:____:____:monotonous
      private____:____:____:____:____:____:____:public
             .                              .
             .                              .
             .                              .
  office work____:____:____:____:____:____:____:factory work
         easy____:____:____:____:____:____:____:difficult
```

MEANING OF WORK (Tausky 1968)

Variable: This scale taps four possible orientations toward work: instrumental, quasi-expressive, and two levels of expressive orientation.

Description: There are six items in the scale which deal with context such as whether the respondent would work if he had to and what types of job situations he would prefer. The following table shows the distribution of scale types in a national cross-section of men in blue-collar jobs:

		High school not completed	High school completed
Instrumental	11%	14%	7%
Quasi-expressive	22%	15%	27%
Expressive A	52%	57%	50%
Expressive B	15%	14%	16%
	100%	100%	100%

Sample: A total of 267 males in blue-collar occupations from a national sample, completed the questions. The sample was interviewed by National Opinion Research Center early in 1967. The occupational division of this sample was as follows: Craftsmen, Foremen 42%; Operatives 43%; and Laborers 15%.

Reliability: A Guttman coefficient of reproducibility of .91 was reported for the six-item scale.

Validity: No data bearing on validity are reported.

Location: Tausky, C. "Meanings of Work among Blue-Collar Men." Paper presented at the meetings of the American Sociological Association, August, 1968. The paper was written at the University of Massachusetts.

Administration: The following scoring pattern of responses into types was employed.

	Item 1	2	3	4	5	6
Instrumental	-	-	-	-	-	-
	+	-	-	-	-	-
Quasi-expressive	+	+	-	-	-	-
Expressive A	+	+	+	-	-	-
	+	+	+	+	-	-
Expressive B	+	+	+	+	+	+
	+	+	+	+	+	+

The author does not describe how other response patterns were coded, although there must have been many such "error response" patterns.

Results and Comments: Education (noted above) was the most important discriminator of work meanings. Job "desirability" and job learning time did not differentiate between respondents' outlooks on the meaning of work.

The author noted the following interesting difference between the blue-collar workers and a group of managers on an item not used in the scale. While 74% of the workers said they would not sacrifice nervous strain for more pay and prestige, only 26% of the managers gave this response.

MEANING OF WORK INSTRUMENT

1. If you were out of work, which would you rather do?

       - Go on welfare (9%)*
       + Take a job as a car washer that paid the same
         as welfare (91%)

2. If by some chance you had enough money to live comfortably without working, do you think that you would work anyway, or would you not work?

       - Would not work (18%)
       + Would work anyway (82%)

3. Which kind of work would you rather have?

       - Average pay from work that is looked down on by
         the people you know (33%)
       + Low pay from work that is respected by the people
         you know (67%)

4. Is the most important thing about getting a promotion . . .

       - Getting more pay? (67%)
       + Getting more respect from friends and neighbors (33%)

5. Which job would you choose if you could be sure of keeping either job?

       - Better than average pay as a truck driver (73%)
       + Less than average pay as a bank clerk (27%)

6. If you could be sure that your income would go up steadily without getting a promotion, would you care about being promoted?

       - No (74%)
       + Yes (26%)

---

* Percentages giving response in parentheses.

+ Response indicating higher level response to the meaning of work

10.   OCCUPATIONAL VALUES

For the most part, the literature on occupational values overlaps topics
treated in previous sections of this volume. The intrinsic vs. extrinsic and
people-oriented vs. idea-oriented distinctions discussed in Robinson's chapter
are of prime concern for the first five of the seven scales reviewed in this
section. The seven scales reviewed in this chapter are:

1. Occupational Value Scales (Kilpatrick, et al. 1964)

2. Occupational Values (Rosenberg 1957)

3. Faith-in-People Scale (Rosenberg 1957)

4. Scale of Inner-and Other-Directedness (Bowers 1966)

5. Inner-Other Social Preference Scale (Kassarjian 1962)

6. Career-Oriented Occupational Values (Marvick 1954)

7. Career Orientation in the Federal Service (Slesinger 1961)

Perhaps the most inclusive set of value statements about work is contained
in Kilpatrick, et al. These items, in common with other empirical measures
reviewed in the work, suffer from the lack of research into reliability, internal
structure and validity. Being in rating scale format, they are also subject to
response set limitations. However, few empirical measures have at their disposal
the rich fund of normative data which is available for this instrument. The
items seem well-written and cover a wide range of values, although, as noted in
Robinson's chapter, they may contain too many items concerned with achievement
and too few concerned with curiosity or affiliation needs.

Kilpatrick, et al.'s work benefitted a great deal from the pioneer efforts
of Rosenberg in this area. Although Rosenberg focused his studies solely on
the work values of college students, the value clusters he obtained still
exposed the importance of the basic distinction between intrinsic and extrinsic
factors. (In Robinson's chapter it was found that level of education was the
leading predictor of this distinction). Rosenberg's original instrument
consisted of only ten statements, of which six were used to define the three
major value orientations: people, self-expression and extrinsic rewards. As

a short form, the items may still be useful. They were employed recently in a large NORC study of the professional labor force and again generated some interesting differences among respondents in various occupational groups (see Marsh and Stafford 1966, also reviewed in Robinson's chapter). In the original study, Rosenberg found those people in commerce and law to be extrinsically-oriented, those in art and science more self-expressive, and those in social work and teaching more people-oriented.

Closely related to the people-oriented items in Rosenberg's value battery were scores on his <u>Faith-in-People</u> scale, (sometimes called Misanthropy, from the attitude found at the opposite end of the scale.) These five items have proved to be useful indices in a number of studies. In his original studies, Rosenberg found the expected relations between high faith-in-people and career choices such as social work, personnel work and teaching.

Riesman's distinction between inner-directed and other-directed social character could be viewed as an aspect of the self-expressive vs. people-oriented contrast which Rosenberg uncovered. Indeed, the contrast is directly evident in a number of items constructed to operationalize Riesman's observations. There exist two quite competent empirical sources of such items, which attest to the inspirational impact of his ideas. The most recent scale, devised by Bowers, may be somewhat the better of the two, but there is little to criticize in Kassarjian's earlier version.

Bowers' <u>Scale of Inner-and Other-Directedness</u> is a 17-item forced-choice measure in which the item pairs have been equated on social desirability. This latter refinement constitutes perhaps its major advantage over Kassarjian's instrument. Bowers' large sample seems restricted because it included only middle-management personnel, but this is actually the group to which Riesman's observations pertained in the first place. While test-retest reliability is not reported and the split-half correlation is not particularly high, an impressive amount of validity information is described.

Solid test-retest and internal consistency data are available for Kassarjian's <u>Inner-Other Social Preference Scale</u>. Most of the validity checks on his scale held up as well. Kassarjian also uses a forced-choice format, although scores range from 0 to 144 on his 36-item instrument, giving a larger range than Bower's instrument. A major advantage of this instrument is that normative data is available for 25 of the items for a cross-section sample of

Los Angeles adults. Small-town background, foreign birth, more education, higher occupational status and advancing age were all found to relate to inner-directedness in this sample.

As we mentioned above, we consider these two instruments to be extremely well constructed but we feel they have some other qualities which we should bring to the reader's attention. First of all, there seems too little evidence that the two orientations offer much in the way of describing personal syndromes or types. On both instruments, inner-other-directedness is normally distributed, with few people at the "inner" or "other" extreme. It would appear that for the attitudes and behaviors sampled, most people rely on criteria other than those hypothesized as the underlying dimension, or that they are employing a mixed strategy (i.e., applying an "inner" orientation to some items, an "other" orientation to other items, and completely independent orientations to the rest). Thus, Peterson (1964) uncovered eight dimensions by subjecting a Likertized form of Kassarjian (and other) items to a factor analysis. This finding should serve as a warning to those who search for single "basic" ideological dimensions on which most of people's attitudes and behaviors can be easily classified and predicted. If such single dimensions do exist, empirical research into attitudes and values has surely been unsuccessful in locating them. It is more likely, as the diversity of research findings does imply, that people apply some basic ideological dimensions on certain types of occasions. The problem then becomes one of isolating the major dimensions and ascertaining the frequency with which people use the dimensions on these certain occasions. The inner-other distinction may be quite useful within this context, but complexity of research findings to date surely indicates that the distinction does not exhaust the number of possibly salient ideological dimensions.

Readers interested in the large body of previous empirical research into Riesman's scheme should be sure to examine Lipset and Lowenthal's Culture and Social Character (1961) and the references contained in the short literature review in Center's (1962) article. One of the tests Centers proposed for the Riesman scheme was to see whether people in various occupations who on an a priori basis would be predicted to stress inner-directed or other-directed values would in fact do so. While Kassarjian had found college students in social sciences and education to be more other-directed and those in arts and sciences more inner-directed, Centers was not as successful in finding expected occupational differences in the public. Miller and Swanson (1958), on the other hand, were more fortunate in finding value differences (in child-rearing practices, however) using an a priori scheme similar but not identical to that of Riesman. These latter authors drew a distinction between "entrepreneurial" and "bureaucratic" family structure and employed a dichotomous classification. They classified a family as having an entrepreneurial structure if the husband met any of the following first three characteristics or if either the bushand or the wife met either of the last two: if he

(a) was self-employed

(b) gained at least half of his income in the form of fees, profits or commissions

(c) worked in a small-scale organization, i.e., one having only two levels of supervision

or if he or she

(d) was born on a farm

or (e) was born outside the United States

They classified all other respondents as bureaucratic. Miller and Swanson found that about half their sample qualified as entrepreneurial; by far the largest proportion of the entrepreneurial group --about a third-- qualified solely on the basis of farm birth of either the husband or wife. Some recent research has raised the issue of whether age factors (older people being more entrepreneurial) played a contaminating role in Miller and Swanson's analyses.

The final two value measures we shall consider are at least conceptually independent from those discussed thus far. They deal with whether the person's main work orientation is to his career within the present organization or to career opportunities within his profession. This "local vs. cosmopolitan" distinction has been used extensively in the sociological literature (see Kornhauser 1962 for one review). Some authors have treated the distinction as a dichotomy with a person being classed as either institution-oriented or profession-oriented. Other investigators, noting the considerable number of respondents not falling clearly into either extreme, have treated the distinction as a continuum, leaving room for a third or hybrid category. Finally, some research indicates that highly motivated scientists are strong in both professional and institutional orientation.

Marvick's Career Oriented Occupational Values scale consists of 16 items, half of which involve a task orientation and half a personal benefit orientation. On the basis of a single direct questions, Marvick classified his sample into "institutionalists", "specialists" or "hybrids". On the whole, "specialists" tended to place most emphasis on task-oriented factors, and institutionalists most emphasis on benefit-oriented factors, much as hypothesized. However, many of the differences were not large or significant, and for some items the hybrids did not fall in the middle as one would expect. Standard reliability and homogeneity data is lacking in this study and the validity data, represented by the results above, is not compelling.

Many of the same shortcomings are still present in Slesinger's extension of Marvick's work. Slesinger adds a new dimension (rule-oriented vs. program-oriented) to Marvick's scheme by inserting a single supplementary item to the 16 proposed by Marvick. Slesinger concludes that the four types, isolated by the two dimensions, lead to basic, if not always statistically significant, distinctions between managerial orientations.

This topic has been investigated most recently by Pelz and Andrews. The reader is referred to the relevant items in their scales presented in Chapter 6. Pelz and Andrews isolated a single component of "science orientation" in explaining high productivity --the component of freedom to follow one's own ideas. The researcher's interest in "broad mapping of new areas" was found to be of additional benefit to higher productivity.

228

References:

Centers, R. "An Examination of the Riesman Social Character Typology" *Sociometry* 1962, 25, 231-240.

Kornhauser, W. *Scientists in Industry: Conflict and Accomodation* Berkeley, California: University of California Press 1962 p. 118-130.

Lipset, S. and Lowenthal, L. *Culture and Social Character* Glencoe, Illinois: Free Press 1961.

Miller, D. and Swanson, G. *The Changing American Parent* New York: Wiley 1958

Peterson, R. "Dimensions of Social Character: An Empirical Exploration of the Riesman Typology" *Sociometry* 1964, 27, 194-207.

OCCUPATIONAL VALUE SCALES (Kilpatrick, et al. 1964)

riable
This instrument attempts to assess the pattern (or relative importance) of occupational values among various occupational groups. The domain of values covered includes both intrinsic, extrinsic and general work factors.

scription
The occupational value scale consists of 30 statements, each placed by a respondent on a non-verbal ten-point agree-disagree scale. The statements are concerned with financial reward, occupational movement, status and recognition, personal relations on the job, occupational competitiveness, self-development, opportunity vs. security, sense of duty, among many others. Respondents were also asked two free-response questions designed to elicit descriptions of attributes of an ideal occupation and of a least satisfying ("worst") occupation.

mple
The sample consisted of 5,078 respondents: 1,502 federal employees, a national sample of the general employed public of 1,142 respondents, a sample of high school, college, and graduate students of 1,146 respondents, 283 high school teachers and vocational counselors, 470 college teachers, and 503 respondents drawn from business. Respondents for each sample were chosen by careful probability sampling procedures.

liability/
Homogeneity
No quantitative data on test-retest reliability or internal homogeneity were reported. However, comparisons of results from the free-response questions and item scaling were quite consistent. (One exception is status ratings since in general people do not admit readily to status striving per se in response to open-ended questions.)

lidity
No attempts at validation per se were performed. Value differences were in line with previous results.

cation
Kilpatrick, Franklin P., Cummings, Milton C., Jr., Jennings, M. Kent, The Image of the Federal Service, Washington, D. C.: The Brookings Institution, 1964, pp. 58-85.

_____, Source Book, Washington, D. C., The Brookings Institution, 1964, pp. 133-174.

ministration
The items formed part of a long interview schedule in this study. If the scales are self-administered, estimated time of administration is about 30 minutes; administration by the card-sort method is much shorter.

sults and
Comments
It was found that the higher the education, income and occupation levels in the employee samples, and the higher the academic grades among students, the higher was the personal involvement with work,

Results and Comments (continued)

the more complex was the value structure, and the greater was the
emphasis on abstract, long-term, ego-rewarding and intrinsic values.
Conversely, the lower the attainment level, the more simple was the
structure of occupational concerns and the greater was the emphasis
on the physical, material, immediate and extrinsic values. Women
differed significantly from men over the different populations
by consistently stressing socially related values as opposed to
"breadwinner" and career-related values. Federal employees showed
a marked concern with supervision and with passive personal
relationships.

The authors remarked that the type of scaling procedure employed is
too rough to permit fine comparisons between the average amount of
agreement or disagreement with one statement and the average amount
with another.

		Average * Scale Rating
1.	A person has a right to expect his work to be fun	6.2
5.	To be really successful in life, you have to care about making money	5.8
6.	Work is most satisfying when there are hard problems to solve	6.5
7.	After you are making enough money to get along, then making more money in an occupation isn't very important	4.9
8.	To me, it's important in an occupation to have the chance to get to the top	7.8
9.	It's important to do a better job than the next person	6.9
11.	Success in an occupation is mainly a matter of hard work	7.3
12.	Success in an occupation is mainly a matter of luck	3.6
16.	Even if you dislike your work, you should do your best	8.3
17.	If a person doesn't want to work hard, it's his own business	5.4
18.	Work is a good builder of character	8.2
19.	It is satisfying to direct the work of others	6.6
20.	Work is a way of being of service to God	7.7
21.	To me, a very important part of work is the opportunity to make friends	7.4
22.	The main satisfaction a person can get out of work is helping other people	6.9
24.	I would like my family to be able to have most of the things my friends and neighbors have	7.4
25.	It is more important for a job to offer opportunity than security	5.9
26.	To me, work is nothing more than a way of making a living	4.2
29.	To me, it's important in an occupation for a person to be able to carry out his own ideas without interference	6.7
30.	It would be hard to live with the feeling that others are passing you up in your occupation	6.1
31.	Work helps you forget about your personal problems	7.2
32.	To me, it's important in an occupation that a person be able to see the results of his own work	8.4
33.	Getting recognition for my own work is important to me	7.6
35.	Success in any occupation is mainly a matter of knowing the right people	5.0
36.	To me, it's important to have the kind of work that gives me a chance to develop my own special abilities	8.1

48. Sometimes it may be right for a person to lose friends in order to get ahead in his work   4.1

50. To me, almost the only thing that matters about a job is the chance to do work that is worthwhile to society   5.6

52. A person should constantly try to succeed at work, even if it interferes with other things in life   6.0

53. I like the kind of work you can forget about after the work day is over   6.7

54. To me, gaining the increased respect of family and friends is one of the most important rewards of getting ahead in an occupation   7.6

*Scores may vary between 1 (strongly disagree) to 10 (strongly agree). Average scores are for a national cross-section sample. For a classification of these statements and the relation of scores to respondents' educational level see Appendix D to Robinson's chapter.

OCCUPATIONAL VALUES (Rosenberg 1957)

Variable   This instrument attempts to categorize people into occupational
            value complexes, described as "self-expression-oriented", "people-
            oriented", and "extrinsic-reward-oriented".

Description   The total instrument consists of a list of ten occupational values
            with accompanying directions for a respondent to "consider to what
            extent a job or career would have to satisfy each of these require-
            ments before (he) could consider it IDEAL". Values may be ranked
            high, medium or low in importance, with the top two values ranked
            as most important. Intercorrelation of the ten responses showed
            the three clusters of orientations noted above. The self-expressive
            cluster consisted of items 1 and 3, the people-oriented items 5 and
            10 and the extrinsic-reward items 2 and 4. Scores on each orienta-
            tion thus ranged from 0 (if the person rated both items "low") to
            7 (if the person rated both items "high" and then picked them as
            most important and next most important).

Sample   The sample used was a nationwide sample of 4,585 college students
            in 1952. The instrument was first administered to a sample of 2,758
            Cornell students in 1950, and to 1,571 Cornell students in 1952.

Reliability/   Estimates of test-retest reliability are not reported. The clusters
  Homogeneity   were obtained by noting the highest intercorrelations among the
            matrix of all ten items. A clear ordering of "self-expressive",
            "people-oriented" and "extrinsic-reward" values were found, with
            those at the expressive and extrinsic extremes placing the least
            value on each other's values.

Validity   No direct test of validity was performed. However, the value
            choices were in line with occupational choices. Each respondent's
            occupational choice was ranked by a weighted average according to
            emphasis placed on the three value complexes. Highest scores in the
            "self-expression" complex were students opting for architecture,
            art, and journalism, drama (average 5.6). The people-oriented
            complex was stressed by students planning to enter social work,
            medicine, teaching, social science, and personnel work (average
            4.2). Students planning to enter real estate or finance, sales-
            promotion, hotel management, law, advertising and business, placed
            greatest stress on the "extrinsic-reward" complex (average 3.4).

Location   Rosenberg, M., Occupations and Values, Glencoe, Illinois: The Free
            Press, 1957, pp. 10-24.

Administration   Estimated administration time is about ten minutes. Scoring by the
            weighted averages requires summation of response weights; first
            choice=4, second=3, high=2, medium=1, low=0.

Results and
Comments

It was found that students' occupational choices generally corresponded with their occupational values. Among 944 Cornell students who answered questionnaires both in 1950 and in 1952, there was a general trend toward increased consistency between occupational choice and values, with slightly more respondents changing occupations to fit values than the obverse.

It would seem that "status and prestige" could have been added to the extrinsic cluster.

Occupational Values

"Consider to what extent a job or career would have to satisfy each of these requirements before you could consider it IDEAL"

(Indicate H=high, M=medium, L=low)

The ideal job for me would have to ...

1. Provide an opportunity to use my special abilities or aptitudes

2. Provide me with a chance to earn a good deal of money

3. Permit me to be creative and original

4. Give me social status and prestige

5. Give me an opportunity to work with people rather than things

6. Enable me to look forward to a stable, secure future

7. Leave me relatively free of supervision by others

8. Give me a chance to exercise leadership

9. Provide me with adventure

10. Give me an opportunity to be helpful to others

Now go back and look at the requirements you rated high. Rank them in the order of importance to you by writing next to each it:

1. for the most important

2. for the next in importance

and so on for all the H's on your list. Do not rank the M's and L's.

FAITH-IN-PEOPLE SCALE (Rosenberg 1957)

Variable	This scale attempts to assess one's degree of confidence in the trustworthyness, honesty, goodness, generosity, and brotherliness of the mass of men.
Description	The instrument consists of a Guttman-type scale of two forced-choice and three agree-disagree-? statements, which was formed from nine related items culled by judges from an original group of 36 items. Positive responses are those indicating absence of faith in people. Range of scores is 1 to 6.
	The author intended the dimension covered by this scale to be relevant to occupational choice, under the assumption that inter-personal attitudes could influence the individual's perception of his career.
	Five sociologists at Cornell sorted out the faith-in-people items.
Sample	The sample used was a nationwide sample of 4,585 college students in 1952. The instrument was first administered to a sample of 2,758 Cornell students in 1950, and to 1,571 Cornell students in 1952.
Reliability/ Homogeneity	The author presents no test-retest reliability data.
	The coefficient of reproducibility for the five-item scale was .92. The author notes that while the fifth item did not meet the Guttman 80-20 positive-negative marginal standard, it was included because the other four items produced a Rep of over .90.
Validity	Evidence of validity may be found in the fact that the group of respondents whose occupational choices were social work, personnel work, and teaching had the largest proportion of high scores on the scale, while the group choosing sales-promotion, business-finance, and advertising had the greatest proportion of low scores. This relationship remained even when sex difference was controlled. Consistent with these findings, students with a high faith-in-people were more likely to select people-oriented occupational values while those with low faith-in-people were more likely to choose extrinsic values. (The value statements are presented in the previous scale write-up.)
Location	Rosenberg, M., Occupations and Values, Glencoe, Illinois: The Free Press, 1957, pp. 25-35.
Administration	Estimated administration time is about five minutes. Scoring requires simple summation of item codes.
Results and Comments	In correlating scores on the scale with single-question indices, it was found that high scorers were less willing to use unscrupulous means to get ahead, less likely to believe in the superior efficiency of "contacts" over ability, and less likely to believe it very important to get ahead in life.

Faith in People Scale

1. Some people say that most people can be trusted. Others say you can't be too careful in your dealings with people. How do you feel about it?

    _____ Most people can be trusted.

    _____ You can't be too careful.

2. Would you say that most people are more inclined to help others, or more inclined to look out for themselves?

    _____ To help others.

    _____ To look out for themselves.

3. If you don't watch yourself, people will take advantage of you.

    Agree   Disagree   ?

4. No one is going to care much what happens to you, when you get right down to it.

    Agree   Disagree   ?

5. Human nature is fundamentally cooperative.

    Agree   Disagree   ?

SCALE OF INNER-AND OTHER-DIRECTEDNESS (Bowers 1966)

Variable	This scale attempts to measure inner-and other-directedness among middle management executives, following David Riesman's definitions of inner-and other-directedness.
Description	The instrument consists of seventeen forced-choice item pairs, or thirty-four statements. Respondents were instructed to choose the statement of a pair which they personally agreed with more, or disliked less.
	Source of items is given as The Lonely Crowd by H. W. Gross (sic). Items were screened by two panels of experts (otherwise undescribed) as being representative of the two orientations. The item pairs themselves were constructed on the basis of social desirability scores and semantic relationships. In pretests, subjects answered the items on the basis of social desirability; and item pairs were equated again as they were tested to see if that factor had, in fact, been controlled.
Sample	The sample population was a group of 3,970 middle management personnel 1,119 from industry, 1,903 from the government, and 948 from the military, altogether representing twelve organizations. The sample populations were further divided into supervisory and non-supervisory samples.
Reliability/ Homogeneity	The split-half reliability was reported to be .72. The internal consistency of item pairings was tested by Chi-square tests.
Validity	Evidence for predictive validation was adduced by successful tests of hypotheses regarding relation of ID-OD scores to socialization practices in childhood: training in self-reliance, work, thought and ambition, and degree of parental strictness. There were further successful tests of hypotheses regarding relation of ID-OD scores to such career factors as types of work satisfaction, types of commitment to the organization, and ways of coping with change in the work situation.
Location	Information on the use of this scale may be obtained from: Raymond V. Bowers, Department of Sociology, The University of Arizona, Tuscon, Arizona.
Administration	Estimated administration time is about 15 minutes. Scoring requires simple summation of item scores. Thus, scores range from 0 (complete inner-directedness) to 17 (complete other-directedness).
Results and Comments	It was found that government executives, with a mean score of 8.5, were more other-directed than military executives (7.4) or industry executives (6.8). Contrary to Riesman's thesis, older employees were found to be more other-directed; this was thought to be due to their longer experience in a bureaucracy. This instrument seems to be well validated, and to be especially useful because of the opaqueness of the items.

Which of these statements do you agree with more? Circle its letter, either
A or B. If you agree with both, choose the one you like better. If you
disagree with both, choose the one you dislike less (the one you agree with
more). <u>Your choice should be a description of your own personal likes and
feelings</u>. You cannot be given a score unless you make a choice for each pair
so please do not skip any.

(Sample Items)

4. A. Wasting time shouldn't particularly bother a person.
    B. Anyone who doesn't take work seriously should be disliked.

5. A. Being "people-minded" is preferable to being "job-minded".
    B. A person should like to find out what great men have thought about
        various problems in which he is interested.

14. A. What matters is what people can accomplish.
    B. Its all right to be an individual but a person shouldn't want to be
        very different from those around him.

INNER-OTHER SOCIAL PREFERENCE SCALE (Kassarjian 1962)

Variable

This is a scale to measure Riesman's concepts of the inner-directed and other-directed social character structure.

Description

The scale consists of 36 forced-choice items, each of which has an inner-directed and an other-directed alternative. The items cover a wide variety of hypothetical activities and social behavior preference In addition to the forced-choice, the respondent indicates how strongl he agrees with each alternative. If a person cannot make a choice, he is given a score of 2. If he agrees with the other-directed choice he gets a score of 1, and 0 if he agrees strongly. Similarly, 3 or 4 are awarded for inner-directed choices. The totally other-directed person would score 0, the completely inner-directed 144.

Sample

Kassarjian's sample consisted of 150 college students in an introducto psychology course and 96 graduate students who filled out mail questionnaires (response rate was 50 percent). In a subsequent articl Centers (1962) used a subset of 25 items on a probability sample of 1,077 adults in Los Angeles.

Reliability/
Homogeneity

A test-retest reliability of .85 was obtained from 52 of the under-graduate sample. Item test-retest values varied from .32 to .94 and 24 of the 36 coefficients were over .70 (this may refer to item-test correlations). All items, except two, were found to be internally consistent at the .05 level.

Validity

A correlation of .69 was obtained between scale scores and a scale of actual participation in various types of behavior indicating inner- or other-directed values. In the graduate student sample there was a significant difference between scores of those students in the social sciences and education (mean=79) and those in natural science and philosophy (mean=94). Kassarjian found no difference between inner- and other-directed people on conformity in an Asch experiment; however, he notes that another survey showed that other-directed people were more influenced by the opinions of important figures. No relation was found between scale scores and other personality variables which could reflect the same trait, viz., the F-scale and SI scale of the MMPI.

Location

Kassarjian, W. "A study of Riesman's theory of social character", Sociometry 1962, 25, 213-230.

Administration

Self-administered or as part of an interview. Should take about half an hour.

Results and
Comments

Graduate students were more inner-directed than those in the under-graduate sample (mean score 87 vs. 72). Those from small towns were slightly more inner-directed.

Results and Comments (continued)

Small-town background, foreign birth, more education, higher-status occupation and advancing age were all found to relate significantly to inner-directedness when Centers (1962) applied 25 items in the scale to his cross-section sample. Men and Republicans were also more inner-directed. However, those in occupations requiring more self-reliance and those feeling more self-competent were no more inner-directed than the undergraduate sample; this could be due to age differences although it would be in line with Riesman's predictions.

Kassarjian interprets his data as supporting Riesman's contentions but Centers interprets his data as not supporting them.

Reference   Centers, R., "An examination of the Riesman social character typology: a metropolitan survey", <u>Sociometry</u> 1962, <u>25</u>, pp. 231-240 This article gives references to a number of earlier measures of inner-and other-directedness.

I-O SOCIAL PREFERENCE SCALE *

*First and fourth columns are scored as inner-directed; second and third columns are scored as other-directed.

Direction: A number of controversial statements or questions with two alternative answers are given below. Answer every item as it applies to you. Indicate your preference by writing appropriate figures in the boxes to the right of each question. Some of the alternatives may appear equally attractive or unattractive to you. Nevertheless, please make a real attempt to choose the alternative that is *relatively more* acceptable to you.

If you definitely agree with alternative (a) and disagree with (b), write 2 in the first box and leave the second blank:

a	b
(2)	( )

If you definitely agree with (b) and disagree with (a), write 2 in the second box leaving the first blank:

a	b
( )	(2)

If you have a slight preference for (a) over (b), write:

a	b
(1)	( )

If you have a slight preference for (b) over (a), write:

a	b
( )	(1)

Do not write any combination of numbers except one of the four given. Never write more than one figure in for any one question. There are no right or wrong answers to this questionnaire. Do not spend too much time on any one item. And please do not leave out any of the questions unless you find it really impossible to make a decision.

1. With regard to partying, I feel
   a. the more the merrier (25 or more people present);
   b. it is nicest to be in a small group of intimate friends (6 or 8 people at most).

2. If I had more time
   a. I would spend more evenings at home doing the things I'd like to do;
   b. I would more often go out with my friends.

3. If I were trained as an electrical engineer and liked my work very much and would be offered a promotion into an administrative position, I would
   a. accept it because it means an advancement in pay which I need quite badly;
   b. turn it down because it would no longer give me an opportunity to do the work I like and am trained for even though I desperately need more money.

4. I believe that
   a. it is difficult to draw a line between work and play and therefore one should not even try it;
   b. one is better off keeping work and social activities separated.

5. I would rather join
   a. a political or social club or organization;
   b. an organization dedicated to literary, scientific or other academic subject matter.

6. I would be more eager to accept a person as a group leader who
   a. is outstanding in those activities which are important to the group;
   b. is about average in the performance of the group activities but has an especially pleasing personality.

7. I like to read books about
   a. people like you and me;
   b. great people or adventurers.

8. For physical exercise or as a sport I would prefer
   a. softball, basketball, volleyball, or similar team sport;
   b. skiing, hiking, horsebackriding, bicycling, or similar individual sport.

9. With regard to a job, I would enjoy more
   a. one in which one can show his skill or knowledge;
   b. one in which one gets in contact with many different people.

10. I believe
    a. being able to make friends is a great accomplishment in and of itself;
    b. one should be concerned more about one's achievements rather than with making friends.

11. It is more desirable
    a. to be popular and well-liked by everybody;
    b. to become famous in the field of one's choice or for a particular deed.

12. With regard to clothing
    a. I would feel conspicuous if I were not dressed the way most of my friends are dressed;
    b. I like to wear clothes which stress my individuality and which not everybody else is wearing.

13. On the subject of social living
    a. a person should set up his own standards and then live up to them;
    b. one should be careful to live up to the prevailing standards of the culture.

14. I would consider it more embarrassing
    a. to be caught loafing on a job for which I get paid;
    b. losing my temper when a number of people are around of whom I think a lot.

15. I respect the person most who
    a. is considerate of others and concerned that they think well of him;

243

16. A child who has had intellectual difficulties in some grade in school
   a. should repeat the grade to be able to get more out of the next higher grade; a ( ) b ( )
   b. should be kept with his age group though he has some intellectual difficulties.

17. In my free time
   a. I'd like to read an interesting book at home; a ( ) b ( )
   b. I'd rather be with a group of my friends.

18. I have
   a. a great many friends who are, however, not very intimate friends; a ( ) b ( )
   b. few but rather intimate friends.

19. When doing something, I am most concerned with
   a. "what's in it for me" and how long it will last; a ( ) b ( )
   b. what impression others get of me for doing it.

20. As leisure-time activity I would rather choose
   a. woodcarving, painting, stamp collecting, photography, or similar activity; a ( ) b ( )
   b. bridge or other card game, or discussion groups.

21. I consider a person most successful when
   a. he can live up to his own standards and ideals; a ( ) b ( )
   b. he can get along with even the most difficult people.

22. One of the main things a child should be taught is
   a. cooperation; a ( ) b ( )
   b. self-discipline.

23. As far as I am concerned
   a. I am only happy when I have people around me; a ( ) b ( )
   b. I am perfectly happy when I am left alone.

24. On a free evening
   a. I like to go and see a nice movie; a ( ) b ( )
   b. I would try to have a television party at my (or a friend's) house.

25. The persons whom I admire most are those who
   a. are very outstanding in their achievements; a ( ) b ( )
   b. have a very pleasant personality.

26. I consider myself to be
   a. quite idealistic and to some extent a "dreamer"; a ( ) b ( )
   b. quite realistic and living for the present only.

27. In bringing up children, the parents should
   a. look more at what is done by other families with children; a ( ) b ( )
   b. stick to their own ideas on how they want their children brought up regardless of what others do.

28. To me it is very important
   a. what one is and does regardless of what others think; a ( ) b ( )
   b. what my friends think of me.

29. I prefer listening to a person who
   a. knows his subject matter real well but is not very skilled in presenting it interestingly; a ( ) b ( )
   b. knows his subject matter not as well but has an interesting way of discussing it.

30. As far as I am concerned
   a. I see real advantages to keeping a diary and would like to keep one myself; a ( ) b ( )
   b. I'd rather discuss my experiences with friends than keep a diary.

31. Schools should
   a. teach children to take their place in society; a ( ) b ( )
   b. be concerned more with teaching subject matter.

32. It is desirable
   a. that one shares the opinions others hold on a particular matter; a ( ) b ( )
   b. that one strongly holds onto his opinions even though they may be radically different from those of others.

33. For me it is more important to
   a. keep my dignity (not make a fool of myself) even though I may not always be considered a good sport; a ( ) b ( )
   b. be a good sport even though I would lose my dignity (make a fool of myself) by doing it.

34. When in a strange city or foreign country I should have no great difficulty because
   a. I am interested in new things and can live under almost any conditions; a ( ) b ( )
   b. people are the same everywhere and I can get along with them.

35. I believe in coffee breaks and social activities for employees because
   a. it gives people a chance to get to know each other and enjoy work more; a ( ) b ( )
   b. people work more efficiently when they do not work for too long a stretch at a time and can look forward to special events.

36. The greatest influence upon children should be
   a. from their own age group and from educational sources outside the family since they can be more objective in evaluating the child's needs; a ( ) b ( )
   b. from the immediate family who should know the child best.

CAREER-ORIENTED OCCUPATIONAL VALUES (Marvick 1954)

Variable   This instrument attempts to distinguish career types among higher-level bureaucrats in a federal agency by analysis of differing group attitudes toward specific job conditions.

Description   The instrument consists of a list of 16 "Factors Important in a Job", half of which involve a task orientation, and half a personal benefit orientation. A respondent was asked two three-point Likert type questions on each item: how important was the factor to him, and whether his present job provided this factor.

In this study, the author attempted to establish whether career perspectives were having differential effects on the interests of agency personnel, and further to establish what the stable content of these interests was. Paired responses to the two questions on each factor were coded in ratio form, and placed in three rating categories: deprivation (2:3, 1:2, or 1:3), detachment (2:2, 3:3, 3:1, 2:1, 3:2), and gratification (1:1).

Sample   The population sample was a group of 204 top-level professional and administrative personnel of a federal agency carrying on a research-co-ordinating and research-subsidizing program for the national defense establishment. Respondents were divided into three categories by self-rating: "institutionalists"--civil or military service career persons; "specialists"--scientists, lawyers, engineers, accountants; or "hybrids"--both government science and specialty-group persons.

Reliability/   No estimates of reliability were reported.
Homogeneity

Validity   Magnitudes of differences in emphasis were not often very significant statistically, but, as the author remarks, a marked polarization cannot be expected in the presence of agency pressures creating a common value hierarchy. He relies on the <u>direction</u> of frequency to confirm his hypotheses. The author predicted one of a pair of rank orders of career groups in each of the three categories of demand-expectation ratios with respect to each of 16 job considerations. Of these 48 rank order prediction pairs, 41 proved correct.

Location   Marvick, D., "Career perspectives in a bureaucratic setting", Ann Arbor, Michigan: University of Michigan Press, 1954 (Michigan Governmental Studies, No. 27).

Administration   Estimated administration time is about 16 minutes.

Results and   It was found that there were distinctive patterns of demands and
Comments   expectations for each career group, patterns which showed great stability over a range of eight skill considerations and two sets of four place considerations. Specialists were found to be preoccupied with place considerations (and tended to see themselves are relatively

Results and Comments (continued)

gratified or deprived by comparison with their co-workers). Hybrids were not preoccupied with either set of considerations, but rather with the personal development of their careers: they were concerned critically only with matters of salary, influence, and advancement.

These items were not purposely constructed to measure the variables in question. Rather they represent results obtained from a secondary analysis of data available from a previous study. These items therefore should be considered as suggestive of a scale area that needs further refinement and elaboration.

FACTORS IMPORTANT IN A JOB

	How important is this to you in most jobs?			Does your job in ONR actually provide this?		
	Very impor-tant	Fairly impor-tant	Not impor-tant	Quite a bit	In some ways	Not at all
1. Opportunity to learn (Acquiring new skills and knowledge)............	☐	☐	☐	☐	☐	☐
2. Influence (Being able to make important decisions—exercising authority —having help of important people)............................	☐	☐	☐	☐	☐	☐
3. Getting ahead in the organization (Having a chance to get a better job in the organization)..	☐	☐	☐	☐	☐	☐
4. Getting ahead professionally (Furthering professional career—being with people who can help one get ahead)............................	☐	☐	☐	☐	☐	☐
5. Full use of abilities (Having enough freedom, responsibility, and authority to do a job the way it should be done)............................	☐	☐	☐	☐	☐	☐
6. Salary (Earning enough money for a good living)....................	☐	☐	☐	☐	☐	☐
7. Prestige in organization (Having an important job in the organization— one with status and prestige).................................	☐	☐	☐	☐	☐	☐
8. Originality (Working with new ideas—being original—using initiative)..	☐	☐	☐	☐	☐	☐
9. Availability of support (Working with people who will stand behind a man —who can help out in a tough spot when needed)....................	☐	☐	☐	☐	☐	☐
10. Importance of task (Having a job that means something—that is neces-sary and valuable and essential)..............................	☐	☐	☐	☐	☐	☐
11. Competence (Knowing the job—being fully competent to do the work).	☐	☐	☐	☐	☐	☐
12. Prestige in community (Having a job seen by people outside the organiza-tion as being an important and meaningful job)....................	☐	☐	☐	☐	☐	☐
13. Respect for co-workers (Working with people who are competent and re-spected by others for their abilities)............................	☐	☐	☐	☐	☐	☐
14. Work enjoyment (Enjoying the work itself)........................	☐	☐	☐	☐	☐	☐
15. Security (Being reasonably sure that the job is fairly permanent).......	☐	☐	☐	☐	☐	☐
16. Good personal relations (Being with people who are congenial—easy to work with)..	☐	☐	☐	☐	☐	☐

CAREER ORIENTATION IN THE FEDERAL SERVICE (Slesinger 1961)

ciable

This instrument attempts to classify junior federal bureacrats along
two dimensions defining personnel adaptations in federal bureaucracy.
The first dimension is "career perspective", or career-oriented vs.
profession-oriented, and the second is "orientation to bureaucratic
structures", or rule-oriented vs. program-oriented. The four
"adaptations" located along the two dimensions are administrators
(career- and program-oriented), managers (career-and rule-oriented),
experts (profession- and program-oriented), and technicians
(Profession- and rule-oriented).

scription

Following Marvick (immediately preceeding), career perspective was
determined by a self-assignment question; bureaucratic structure
orientation was ascertained from responses to a question on whether,
or to what degree, the respondent found it more convenient sometimes
to overlook or break rules. Respondents were also given a list of
17 job values, 16 of which were the same as those used in the Marvick
study, and asked to indicate the importance to them of each item.
Item scores were based in the proportion checking the "very important"
category for each job value. Each "adaptation" type was then
characterized according to the degree and direction that its scores
differed from the mean score for the remainder of the sample.

mple

The sample population consisted of 368 present and former junior
management assistants, the majority of whom were drawn from 12
participanting federal agencies, and the rest of whom were drawn from
12 non-participating agencies, state and local government, and
non-government occupations. Two thirds of the sample were from middle-
class background.

liability/
Homogeneity

No test-retest reliability is reported.

lidity

An internal validity check on the assignments in the bureaucratic
structure orientation dimension was provided by a three-point
"initative" scale scored by coders of questions concerning the intra-
agency function of the job. Those classified as program-oriented
by the prior questions consistently scored higher on the initial
scale than did the "rule-oriented". Correlation of "adaptation"
types with choices of job values was another form of internal validity
check. It was found that the pattern of emphasis on job values
supported the characterization of each type. The author felt that
there were sufficient differences to justify the conclusion that
valid types had been identified, though differences were only
occasionally strongly significant. A behavioral validity check was
provided by an item on job mobility: it was found that administrators
and managers (both career-oriented by definition) were less likely
to leave government service.

ation

Slesinger, Jonathan A., "Personnel adaptations in the federal
junior management assistant program", Ann Arbor, Michigan: University

Location (continued)

of Michigan, Institute of Public Administration, 1961
(Michigan Governmental Studies, No. 41)

Administration   Estimated administration time for the 17-item job value list is
about 17 minutes. Scoring requires simple summation of response
codes.

Results and   The modal "adaptation" type, as predicted, was found to be that of
Comments   manager, with 141 respondents. The other "adaptation" types were
distributed as follows: there were 91 to 94 administrators, 43
technicians, and 32 experts in the sample.

In general, administrators and managers both displayed their predicted
organizational form of reference in choice of important job values,
but differed in greater emphasis on the importance of influence and
use of abilities for administrators, and the importance of security
managers. Experts and managers were both concerned with the skill-
bound values, but revealed their respective program-and rule-orienta-
tion by the experts' greater emphasis on the importance of a meaningful
task, and on the technicians' interest in upward mobility and
competence.

Instrument   <u>Item added to Marvick's list of 16 Factors Important in a Job</u> (above)
Nature of Organization (working in an agency with particular goals --
a special kind of mission or purpose).

11.   LEADERSHIP STYLES

We have already examined measures which tap employees' perceptions of supervisors in Chapter 7, and now we look at the other side of the coin -- the reactions of supervisory personnel to those under their charge as well as to the various other role requirements of their position.   The first seven instruments in this section may be used as measures of the adequacy of present supervisors or perhaps for selecting supervisory personnel.   The first four instruments in various ways place heavy emphasis on the human relations aspect of supervising; the measures are listed in judged order of merit.   The full list of nine scales described in this chapter is as follows:

1.   Leadership Opinion Questionnaire (Stogdill and Coons 1957)
2.   The SRA Supervisory Index (Schwartz 1956)
3.   Leadership Practices Inventory (Nelson 1955)
4.   How Supervise? (File and Remmers 1948)
5.   A Proverbs Test for Supervisor Selection (Reveal 1960)
6.   A Managerial Key for the CPI (Goodstein and Schrader 1963)
7.   Managerial Scale for Enterprise Improvement

Also

8.   Organizational Control Graph (Tannenbaum 1966)
9.   Profile of Organizational Characteristics (Likert 1967)

The Leadership Opinion Questionnaire has perhaps the most to recommend it, although it is not specifically designed as a selection device.   The scale seems to meet most of our evaluative criteria, although as noted in our scale write-up, it would benefit from more complete validational data.   The scale does appear to be free of an intelligence bias which often plagues leadership scales.   Overall, the validational and normative data are superior to those found on other instruments in this section.

Readers preferring a scale free of bias from response set may be more interested in the SRA Supervisory Index.   This is a short 24 item forced-choice scale, for which the reliability and validity data seem adequate although not unusually good. Human relations content constitutes only a quarter of the total score, with attitudes towards top management, supervisory responsibilities and subordinates being the other aspects tapped.

The Leadership Practices Inventory also is purportedly free of intelligence and educational biases. The items seem well written and are presented in a forced-choice format which, although somewhat transparent, should overcome major response set problems. However, reliability and validity information from the material we have is sketchy, although that which is given is impressive. Little normative data are reported since the major function of the Inventory thus far has been its use in conjunction with a management development program. The Inventory is probably well worth examination for not only is the theory of four stages of leadership behind the measure consistent with most other competent research in this field, but also research with the Inventory has uncovered some interesting empirical relations between the four stages.

The items in How Supervise? are similarily plagued by item transparency; there is also substantial research evidence that the instrument may be contaminated with an intelligence or educational bias. Reliability, validity and normative information tend to be somewhat vague, although item content and respondent sample seem adequately covered. How Supervise? does deserve consideration from those readers interested in this area, although we suspect that the instruments reviewed first are more appropriate for most purposes.

For those readers looking for indirect measures of supervisory attitude with no human relations overtones the Proverbs Test or a special Managerial Key for the California Psychological Inventory may be of interest. However, the Proverbs Test may be little more than a subtle IQ test. Supervisors are mainly distinguished from non-supervisors by the fact that the former are far less willing to agree with simple proverbs, much as the acquiescent response set has been found to be less prevalent in the better-educated segments of society. Although Managerial CPI Key suffers from the lack of cross-validation, the instrument on which it is based was carefully constructed and may hold promise for areas outside of personality assessment. Along this same line, Beers (1965) reports that three sub-scales of the Ghiselli Self-Description Inventory (initiative, self-assurance and aspiration level) have all been found to correlate with measures of managerial success.

We find the Managerial Scale for Enterprise Improvement repugnant on both psychometric and conceptual grounds. It is based on the assumption that better managers will be less critical of the organization.

There are three other leadership instruments which came to our attention too late for a more complete review -- the Leadership Evaluation and Development Scale (LEADS), a Forced-Choice Human Relations Scale, and the Leadership Q-Sort Test. In one small study, Mowry's LEADS (Los Angeles: Psychological Services Inc., 1964) was found a better predictor of salary and performance ratings than the Leadership Opinion Questionnaire. It is well to keep in mind, however, that the differences in predictive ability were not great and that the study was conducted by the test publishers. The ability-test nature of LEADS (eight human relations problems, followed by several multiple-choice questions) made it correlate much more highly with intelligence than did the LOQ. From other comments in the study, however, it does appear to be well-constructed.

We were unsuccessful in locating the scale items for the Forced-Choice Human Relations Scale. The instrument contains twenty-four tetrads which deal with four areas: top management, supervisor's role requirements, employees and human relations practices. Psychometric data on the scale are promising -- a split-half reliability coefficient of .91 and correlations of .33 to .61 with various internal and external criteria. The one reference we presently can give to the scale is Schwartz and Geroski's article in the Journal of Applied Psychology, 1960, 44, 233-236.

The manual for Cassel's Leadership Q-Sort Test (Chicago, Ill.: Psychometric Affiliates) contains an impressive amount of statistical data which serves to obscure rather than to illuminate the properties of the test. Scores are given for six subscales of the test, but there is no information on how to interpret them, much less on what the total score reflects. The research on the instrument was carried out on fairly restricted samples (Air Force officers, prisoners, and research psychologists). The sixty items do seem to cover a reasonable variety of leadership behavior, but no research is reported on the internal structure of the items. However, some readers may find more merit in this test.

Within the context of leadership styles, it may be relevant to mention Chapman and Campbell's Superior-Subordinate Scale (Journal of Social Psychology 1957, 46, 277-286) which is designed to measure whether a person identifies with a superior or his subordinate in conflict situations between the two. The scale consists of 20 Likert-type and 17 forced choice items. It appears to be well constructed and has been used with some success in experimental contexts.

Appended to this section are two research devices which hold high promise of measuring leadership variables at the organizational level. The first of these is Tannenbaum's Control Graph, which is based on simple Likert scale ratings of how much influence people at various levels in the organization have in determining the policies and actions of the total organization. The second instrument, the Profile of Organizational Characteristics, a **scale recently developed by Rensis Likert, can be used as an indicator of where the organization** stands in relation to what Likert feels are the ideal patterns of management. Although Likert and others have produced abundant evidence that considerate, participative, and non-restrictive supervision leads to more productive and effective work groups, more evidence is needed that supervisory styles directly influence the worker's motivational level. For some very skeptical remarks on this latter hypothesis, we recommend Beer's Leadership, Employee Needs and Motivation (Columbus, Ohio: Bureau of Business Research, Ohio State University, 1965).

Miller's Handbook of Research Design and Social Measurement (New York: David McKay 1965) lists five further instruments that can be of use in organizational research:

1. Stogdill and Shartle's Work Patterns Profile, in which supervisory personnel estimate the percentage of their work time devoted to 14 types of tasks (inspection, research, planning, preparing procedures, coordination, evaluation, interpretation, supervision, personnel functions, consultation, public relations, negotiating scheduling and technical operations).

2. Hemphill's Executive Position Description, which deals with an executive's awareness of activities, responsibilities, demands, restrictions and characteristics of his position.

3. Stogdill and Shartle's Responsibility, Authority and Delegation Scales which are designed to reflect administrative personnel's perceptions of these functions.

4. Tannenbaum, Weschler and Massarik's Multirelational Sociometric Survey, in which interpersonal variables regarding five aspects of work activities are tapped: the prescribed, the perceived, the actual, the desired and the rejected.

5. Weiss and Jacobson's Analysis of Structure of Complex Organizations, another sociometric device, which enables the researcher to depict the

organization coordination as established through the activities of
liason persons and the existence of inter-group contacts.

A far larger compendium of organizationally-relevant measures is currently
being put together by Bernard Indik at Rutgers University and we refer interested
readers to this work as well.

Finally a recent and very promising attempt to formulate a multi-factor
instrument to measure leadership is given by Bowers and Seashore in the September, 1966 issue of the Administrative Science Quarterly (pp. 238-263). From
a review of the major literature on leadership (much of this literature is covered
in the pages which follow in the present chapter), Bowers and Seashore postulate
that "four dimensions emerge, which appear to comprise the basic structure of what
one may call 'leadership':

1) Support. Behavior that enhances someone else's feeling of personal worth
   and importance.

2) Interaction facilitation. Behavior that encourages members of the group
   to develop close, mutually satisfying relationships.

3) Goal emphasis. Behavior that stimulates an enthusiasm for meeting the
   group's goal or achieving excellent performance.

4) Work facilitation. Behavior that helps achieve goal attainment by such
   activities as scheduling, coordinating, planning, and providing resources
   such as tools, materials, and technical knowledge."

At the present time, instruments to measure these characteristics are being
refined so that we are unable to review them in this volume. Bowers and Seashore
do, however, present empirical data on the usefulness of these four variables in
accounting for differences in organizational performance as part of a study of
40 agencies of a life insurance company.

LEADERSHIP OPINION QUESTIONNAIRE (Stogdill and Coons, 1957)

Variable
>This questionnaire yields scores on two apparently orthogonal dimensions labeled consideration and structure.

A high score on the structure dimension seems to be characteristic of individuals who prefer to direct and organize group activities, to schedule work and control the communication of information. It is probably unfair to characterize high scorers on this dimension as autocratic and authoritarian though one could easily expect them to lean this way.

Consideration is a dimension which is supposedly characterized by neutral respect, trust and concern for others, and empathy.

Description
>The forty item questionnaire contains 20 items on each of the dimensions of consideration and structure. The items are scaled in Likert fashion and scored on a five point basis from zero to four. The possible range of scores is from 0 to 80 with the usual range being from 30 to 70.

Sample
>A considerable number of populations have been tested with this instrument and the particular population will be identified with the relevant statistic below.

Reliability
>Test-retest reliabilities are reported as follows:

Structure: $r = .74$ (31 first line employees)
$r = .67$ (24 Air Force NCO's)

Consideration: $r = .80$ (31 first line employees)
$r = .77$ (24 Air Force NCO's)

Internal consistency measures range from .79 to .82 for Structure and .62 to .89 for Consideration.

Validity
>From data reported by the authors it would appear that LOQ scores are not dependent on intelligence as are some other measures. The correlations of intelligence with LOQ are either low or negative. Personality dimensions, however, may be reflected by LOQ scores since Consideration correlates low to moderately with empathy, benevolence and agreeableness. Structure correlates in the same range with ambition, meticulousness, and the F scale.

Most of the validity studies reported by the authors are of the present employee type and seem more like a series of job analyses than validity studies. In administering the LOQ to samples of pharmaceutical company foremen, petrochemical company supervisors, department managers and plant superintendents in a shoe manufacturing company, hospital supervisors, and bank managers, the correlations between performance and test factors vary from + .61 through zero to - .79. The LOQ has shown that it can discriminate, on the basis of attitudes, between various levels and types of supervisory performance depending on the organizational variables which are operating. The author urges that validity studies be carried out to determine the appropriate pattern of consideration and structure for a particular organization.

Location
Science Research Associates, Inc. The Leadership Opinion Questionnaire, Chicago: SRA, 1960.

Stodgill, R. M. and Coons, A. E., eds. Leader Behavior: Its Description and Measurement, Columbus: Ohio State University Bureau of Business Research, 1957.

Administration
Self administered--requiring about 1/4 hour. Scoring is accomplished through the use of a self scoring format similar to that employed by the Supervisory Index in less than 3 minutes per person.

Results and Comments
The LOQ may prove to be a useful instrument for highlighting successful management patterns within an organization for the purposes of improving internal operations. Since there is a large body of evidence which strongly suggests that various levels of management as well as different organizations may require different combinations of consideration and structure, it is not safe to assume, a priori, that "high" scores are good and low ones bad. Individual studies are necessary to determine the patterns associated with the most desirable outcome.

Once the nature of an optimal pattern has been determined, the LOQ may be used for counseling, evaluation of training programs and possibly for selection.

Caution should be exercised when using this test for selection purposes. A person's scores may reflect the form of supervision required for his present job and give no indication of his ability to change his methods of supervision. In fact, it may well be the man who is capable of applying different amounts of consideration and structure to different people at different times, who makes the best manager.

NORM TABLE (abstracted)

Group	Median Structure Score	Semi-Interquartile Range for Structure	Median Consideration Score	Semi-Interquartile Range for Consideration
GenSupvPers. N=780	48	10	54	10
1stLnAdmClerks N=100	54	8	58	11
Foremen N=200	50	9	53	11
Executives N=185	46	11	55	9
Eng.Supervisors N=64	49	10	52	8
Educ.Supervisors	42	11	62	8

256

References   Bass, B. M. "Leadership opinions as forecasts of supervisory success." J. Appl. Psychol., (40), 1956, pp. 345-46.

_____ . "Leadership opinions as forecasts of supervisory success: A replication." Personnel Psychol., (11), 1958, pp. 515-18.

Fleishman, E. A. "The description of supervisory behavior." J. Appl. Psychol., (36), 1953, pp.1-6.

_____ . "The measurement of leadership attitudes in industry." J. Appl. Psychol., (36), 1953, pp. 153-8.

Stroud, P. V. "Evaluating a human relations training program." Personnel, (36), 1959, pp. 52-60.

Instrument   The instructions and a sample of items from the <u>LOQ</u> are included below:

INSTRUCTIONS:

For each item, choose the alternative which most nearly expresses your opinion on how frequently you <u>should</u> do what is described by that item. Always indicate what you, as a supervisor, or manager, sincerely believe to be the desirable way to act. Please remember--there are no right or wrong answers to these questions. Different supervisors have different experiences and we are interested only in your opinions.

SAMPLE ITEMS:

Structure--

      Assign persons under you to particular tasks. (4) always (3) often (2) occasionally (1) seldom (0) never

      Stress importance of being ahead of other units. (4) a great deal (3) fairly much (2) to some degree (1) comparatively little (0) not at all

      Let the persons under you do their work the way they think is best. (0) always (1) often (2) occasionally (3) seldom (4) never

Consideration--

      Back up what persons under you do. (4) always (3) often (2) occasionally (1) seldom (0) never

      Speak in a manner not to be questioned. (0) always (1) often (2) occasionally (3) seldom (4) never

      Put suggestions made by persons in the unit into operation. (4) often (3) fairly often (2) occasionally (1) once in a while (0) very seldom

The numbers in parentheses indicate the scoring weights for the response categories and are not, of course, included on the actual questionnaire form.

THE SRA SUPERVISORY INDEX (Schwartz, 1956)

Variable
This scale yields a total score and sub-scores in four areas:

1) feeling toward top management, pay, company policy, etc.
2) attitudes toward the duties and responsibilities of a supervisor
3) attitudes toward the supervisor's subordinates
4) human relations, supervisory technique

Area score correlations with total score range from .71 to .83 and the average scale intercorrelation is .41, indicating that the scales are not independent. The high internal homogeneity coefficient (split-half reliability) is further indication of this.

Description
The instrument is a 24 item forced-choice scale on which the individual is asked to choose from each tetrad the item with which he most agrees and the one with which he least agrees. Items were collected on the basis of readability, broad range and pertinence to the aspects of industrial life. "Inspectional factor analysis" was used to group the pool of items into the four categories mentioned above and tetrads were formed on the basis of item preference and discrimination indices.

A positive score is attained on each tetrad by selecting as "most agree" the item attributed to "good" supervisors and/or as "least agree" the item attributed to "poor" supervisors. Selecting a discriminating item in the wrong direction yields a negative score. The item score range is thus from minus 2 to plus 2. Total scores have a possible range of from minus 48 to plus 48 and an actual range of from plus 2 to plus 38 is reported.

Sample
The original item pool was collected from a sample of white male supervisors in a steel plant in the Philadelphia area. The majority of supervisors were from production departments and fell in the 35 to 45 year age bracket. The average tenure was 8 1/2 years and a large proportion were front line managers. A second group of 73 supervisors was chosen from another plant producing machine parts. This "validation" sample was similar in composition to the first group.

Reliability
The odd-even split half coefficient is reported as .91 (corrected.)

Validity
A Pearson coefficient of .33 is reported between Total Score and ratings of administrative and production skills for the 73 supervisors.

Location
Science Research Associates, Inc. Supervisory Index, Chicago: SRA, 1960.

Schwartz, S. L. "The development of a forced choice scale for the evaluation of supervisory attitude and behavior in industry," Ph.D. thesis, Temple University, 1956. University Microfilms, Inc., Ann Arbor, Michigan, Pub. No. 24,853.

Administration   Self administered. No time limit is advised since most people
will finish in about 20 minutes. Scoring is accomplished through the
use of a "self-scoring" answer sheet. A carbon paper insert is sand-
wiched between the combined answer and score sheets yielding a pattern
of marks on the completed test score sheet. The pattern may be interpreted through the detailed instructions printed on the score sheet.
Area and total scores may be obtained for an individual in less than
five minutes.

Results and   The publisher presents percentile norms for production supervisors
Comments   and for middle managers. The median raw score for production supervisors is about 22 and for middle managers 19. The semi-interquartile
range for both groups is about 9 points.

References   Schwartz, S. L. and Geroski, N. "A forced choice measure of human
relations attitudes and techniques." J. Appl. Psychol., (44), pp. 233-6,
1960.

Information and inquiries regarding the use of this instrument
in research and validation studies should be addressed to:

Industrial Division
Science Research Assoc., Inc.
259 East Erie Street
Chicago 11, Illinois

Instrument   INSTRUCTIONS:

In this section are a number of statements about plants, supervisors, and workers. These statements are grouped in sets of four. Read each set of four to find the one statement that you AGREE WITH MOST. Then fill in the circle beside the statement you select in the column headed MOST.

Then review the other three statements in the set to find the one that you AGREE WITH LEAST; fill in the circle beside that statement in the column headed LEAST.

Here is a sample set:

	MOST	LEAST
When a worker starts to gripe, his supervisor shouldn't listen to him............................	0	0
Management tries to help supervisors solve whatever problems may arise................................	0	0
A supervisor should set an example for his men to follow...	0	0
Many employees are very lazy.........................	0	0

LEADERSHIP PRACTICES INVENTORY (Nelson 1955)

Variable

The Inventory purports to place an individual into one of four management orientation categories: bureaucratic-regulative, autocratic-directive, idiocratic-manipulative, and democratic-integrative. These styles are hypothesized as lying on a developmental continuum, with the democratic view being most desired.

Description

There are fifty forced choice pairs of items. Item pairs contrast the management styles in various possible combinations of bureaucratic-autocratic and idiocratic-democratic alternatives. The items themselves refer to hypothetical content-free decisions which supervisors are likely to face in the areas of formal authority, technology, individual personalities, group membership and the leader's own personal qualities. A Human Relations Index, which sums up the total percentage of idiocratic and democratic choices, defines the fundamental continuum. Thus, the score runs from 0 when the individual chooses the bureaucratic-autocratic alternative for each of the fifty items, to 100 when the individual always chooses the idiocratic or democratic response.

Sample

Reportedly, the inventory has been administered to many management groups, but these groups are not described in any materials we have. On the Human Relations Index, engineering students are said to have scored 66, administration students 72 and graduate students in the social sciences 82, although further identification information is not given.

Reliability/
  Homogeneity

Test-retest reliability on the Human Relations Index is over .80 and over .60 for categorizing individuals into one of the four leadership orientations. Split-half reliabilities are reported to be at the same level.

Validity

Clinical psychologists using projective materials were able to predict with significant accuracy a person's leadership attitudes on the scale. Leadership attitudes have also been found to correlate with management ratings.

It was found that supervisors who scored higher on the Human Relations Index were in charge of groups with lower accident records and better morale.

Location

Nelson, W., "Leadership practices inventory". Management Research Associates, 185 N. Wabash, Chicago, Illinois.

Administration

Self administered in about 20 minutes. An individual raw score should be obtainable in less than two minutes.

Results and Comments   The four leadership styles neatly meet one criterion of the "unfolding" model --a bureaucratic person sees himself least like the democratic person (and vice versa), while the idiocratic person sees himself closer to a technocrat than to a bureaucrat.

It seems to us that a person could fake this scale if he so desired, the author's comments on this point notwithstanding.

Sample Questions:

You will find several different leadership practices for the same problem situation, but each problem should be judged independently on its own merits. Sometimes you may not see much difference between the two suggested solutions or may not like either. ALWAYS MAKE BOTH IDEAL AND ACTUAL CHOICES EVEN IF YOU ARE FORCED TO GUESS.

3. A new employee will get along alright if he

   (a) follows the supervisor's instructions and develops the right work habits

   (b) works with the other men in his department in turning out the day's production

32. The supervisor can give out new orders and information most effectively by

   (a) discussing them with the employees and getting their questions and comments

   (b) explaining the orders or information to each employee concerned

50. To understand how employees really feel about things, the supervisor should

   (a) notice their reaction to the work, to him and to his orders

   (b) maintain a frank, informal, give-and-take relationship with them

HOW SUPERVISE? (File and Remmers 1948)

Variable   This test purports to measure an individual's knowledge and insight concerning human relations in industry. Item content indicates that this instrument is best used with supervisory personnel.

Description   Three forms (A, B, M) of this instrument are available. Forms A and B each contain a total of 70 items in three sections: Supervisory Practices, Company Policies and Supervisory Opinions. These two forms are equivalent. Form M contains 100 items in the same three categories. The items in form M are supposedly those form A and B items which discriminate best among upper level managers.

Each item is answered by circling one of three choices-- D desirable, ? uncertain, U undesirable; or, A agree, ? uncertain, DA disagree. Scoring is based on the number of "correct" answers minus the number of "wrong". Those marked "uncertain" are not scored. The possible range of scores is therefore from -70 to +70 on forms A and B and -100 to +100 on form M. When forms A and B are combined the actual range of scores, across lower, middle and upper management groups, is reported as +4 to +138. The items were selected from a pool of 204 items administered to the test construction sample which is reported to have consisted of approximately 750 supervisors. A theoretical key was obtained from the answers of eight unnamed experts and "37 members of the supervisory staff of the government's Training Within Industry program." The final item pool was selected on the basis of an item analysis using total score as the internal criterion.

Sample   The construction sample mentioned above included supervisors from 10 industries of various size, major product, internal organization, and geographic location. Other large samples were used for various studies and are described below where relevant.

Reliability   The split half coefficient for form M is reported as .87 for a sample of 594 office and higher level supervisors.

A sample of 828 unidentified people are reported to have yielded scores with single form reliabilities of .77 and a total score coefficient of .87. It is not clear from the authors' report what type of coefficient was used.

Validity   For the purposes of data analysis, managerial populations were divided in the following manner:

Level I - Top management including higher office supervision, major department heads and their advisors.

Level II - General foremen, office supervisors and production area supervisors.

Level III - <u>Operating supervisors</u>, persons in charge of blue collar workers, non office personnel.

<u>How Supervise</u>? is apparently able to distinguish between the three levels of management described above. Comparison of scores (form A and B combined) for 828 managers (approximately 1/4 at each of levels I and III and 1/2 at level II) reveals that level I supervisors score higher and show less variance than level II and III. Second level supervisors show the same relation to level III.

589 supervisors in the rubber industry showed a gain in mean score for all three managerial groups and a reduction in standard deviation when pretraining scores were compared with post-training scores. The author does not, however, make clear the nature of the training involved.

This instrument appears to have face validity which may make it useful for counseling purposes. No fakability studies are reported, however.

Location   File, Q.W. and Remmers, H.H., <u>How Supervise</u>? New York: The Psychological Corporation, 1948.

Administration   Self administered in about 20 minutes. Raw scores may be obtained in less than 4 minutes for form M.

Results and
Comments

The value of this instrument is mitigated by the obvious transparency of item content and by the fact that one may reasonably expect that brighter individuals will score better than those less bright regardless of their true opinions. In addition, for all three forms an average of four-fifths of the items in each section are keyed in the same direction, raising the question of response set. By consistently answering in one category for two of the sections and another category for the third section, a lower level manager could receive a score placing him at the 70th percentile. Such a response pattern should ideally yield a raw score of zero, i.e., number right = number wrong.

While early studies of <u>How Supervise</u>? seemed optimistic in their conclusions, other studies have cast some doubt on the usefulness of this test. Weitz and Nuckols (1953) were unable to report significant relationships between any of a variety of scoring methods and a combination of three objective criteria of successful supervision. They did show, however, a relation between educational level and <u>How Supervise</u> scores. Millard (1952) tends to support the supposition that <u>How Supervise</u>? is really an intelligence test. Maloney's (1952) report of reading ease scores of <u>How Supervise</u>? tends to confirm this suspicion.

Reliability, normative and validity data as presented in the latest (1948) revision of the test manual must be carefully interpreted by the potential user. Local validity studies should be carried out in any case. Item analysis using an external criterion is recommended.

References   File, Q.W., "The Measurement of Supervisory Quality in Industry,"
             J.Appl.Psychol., (29) 1945, pp. 323-337.

             File, Q.W. and Remmers, H.H., "Studies in Supervisory Evaluation,"
             J.Appl.Psychol., (30) 1946, pp. 421-425.

             Maloney, P.W., "Reading ease scores for File's How Supervise?" J.
             Appl.Psychol., (36) 1952, pp. 225-227.

             Millard, K.E., "Is How Supervise? an Intelligence Test?" J.Appl.Psychol.,
             (36) 1952, pp. 221-224.

             Rosen, N.A., Personnel Psychology (14) 1961, pp. 87-99. A review of
             the literature dealing with the How Supervise? test. A comparison
             of How Supervise? with measures of intelligence, personality, etc.
             is not covered.

             Weitz, J. and Nuckols, R.C. "A validation study of How Supervise?"
             J.Appl.Psychol., 1953, 37, pp. 7-8.

Sample Questions:

SUPERVISORY PRACTICES

The following is a list of practices followed by different supervisors. Some of these will seem desirable to you and some undesirable. If an item does not apply to your department, please answer as you would if you were in a position where such a problem could arise.

D desirable   ? uncertain   U undesirable

Draw a circle around the answer which best expresses your opinion.

1. Asking your workers for suggestions before setting up an important project...D ? U
2. Admitting it to your workers when you make a wrong decision......D ? U
3. Giving each worker a frank statement of whether or not he is improving; if so, how much.......................................D ? U

COMPANY POLICIES

The following is a list of the methods used by different companies in handling their relations with employees. Some of these methods will seem desirable to you and some undesirable. Please answer each item according to YOUR OPINION of its value in producing good employer-employee relations.

D desirable   ? uncertain   U undesirable

Draw a circle around the answer which best expresses your opinion.

21. Requiring supervisors to spend a part of their time handling the complaints of workers under them.............................D ? U
22. Asking the advice of labor leaders on certain worker problems....D ? U
23. Keeping employees well-informed on the business outlook and the company's plans for adjusting to it.............................D ? U

SUPERVISOR OPINIONS

The following opinions are held by various supervisors in positions similar to your own. You will probably agree with some of the statements and disagree with others. Please indicate how you feel about each item by marking the statements as follows:

A agree   ? uncertain   DA disagree

Draw a circle around the answer which best represents your opinion.

53. What the worker thinks is unimportant so long as he is doing his job well...A ? DA
54. So-called "mental fatigue" is actually nothing but laziness......A ? DA
55. Most employees do better work if they get a good bawling out every so often...A ? DA

A PROVERBS TEST FOR SUPERVISOR SELECTION (Reveal, 1960)

Variable   This is an empirically derived test which uses responses to folklore proverbs to distinguish between supervisors and non-supervisors.

Description   This test is an empirically derived selection of 75 proverbs with which agreement is scaled in 4 point Likert fashion. The subject is asked to indicate to what extent a good supervisor would agree with a given proverb. The original pool of 404 proverbs was trimmed to 75 through item analysis and cross validation procedures over several populations and separate administrations. Several scoring keys were developed and tested on hold-out populations. For the "right versus wrong" key discussed in this review the possible range of scores is from +59 to -60 with a range reported by the author of from +43 to -36. This key takes "into account the direction, positive or negative, that answers had in relation to the supervisory and non-supervisory groups. This key of 75 items had weights of plus one (+1) and minus one (-1). The individual scores equalled the algebraic sum of the weights from responses ..."

Sample   Two hundred fifteen male supervisors and 157 non-supervisors comprised the experimental and cross validation groups. The supervisors were all first line men in manufacturing firms and were solicited through membership in N. M. A.. The non-supervisory personnel came from the same firms and same departments as the supervisors.

The major differences between the two groups were average time in their particular business (S = 14.02 years, non-S = 9.4 years) and years of schooling (S = 12.62 years, non-S = 12.03). The average age of supervisors was 39.8 (SD = 7.6) and that of non-supervisors 38.8 (SD = 7.04). Both groups had nearly three dependents, almost all were married and owned automobiles. The managers had spent an average of 7.23 years (SD = 5.5) as supervisors and supervised an average of 16.62 persons (SD = 9.03).

Reliability   The reliability of the scale using the key presented below is estimated, by the author, as .80; with a standard error of 6.25. This reliability estimate is derived from analysis of variance of the scores of 57 non-supervisors and a random sample of 43 supervisors.

Validity   A biserial correlation of .57 is reported by the author when scale scores are compared with the criterion of supervisor versus non-supervisor classification in the hold-out group. For this same group the mean score of supervisors is 9.44 (SD = 9.47) and that of non-supervisors is 1.02 (SD = 8.26). Second order partialing out of the effects of education and years in the business has minimal effect on the validity coefficient.

Location   Reveal, Robert, Jr. "The Development and Validation of a Proverbs Test for the Selection of Supervisors." Ph.D. dissertation, University of Southern California, 1960. Ann Arbor, Michigan: University Microfilms, Inc., pub. no. MIC 60-2352.

Administration   Self administered in about one hour. Scoring may best be accomplished through the use of stencils. In the example below, an item score of plus 1 (+1) is given when the subject marks the answer shown in the +1 column. An item score of -1 is given when a subject marks the answer shown in the -1 column. The symbol (--) indicates that the item is not to be scored for the column in question. Some items may be scored either +1 or -1 depending on the answer given while other items may only be scored in one direction. Careful examination of an answer sheet must be made to insure that only one response is indicated for each proverb.

Results and
Comments   This scale--except for one major fault--is unusually well designed. The use of a cross validation paradigm considerably increases the confidence one may have in the validity of the scale. The items are not transparent and the set which is established (see Directions) may serve to reduce personal anxiety in the subject.

Two cautions should be noted. First, the validity demonstrated here is of the concurrent type and applies only to manufacturing personnel already on the job. Local norms for different industries should be established and predictive studies carried out before the instrument is used for selection purposes.

Second, the question of response set is something with which a potential user must deal. By consistently answering only in the "Nearly Always Disagree" category a candidate could achieve a score or 27 points placing him well within the supervisor category.

The following decile norms have been calculated from the author's data.

Supervisor's Raw Score N = 115	Decile	Non-supervisor's Raw Score N = 57
29 and up	9	20 and up
28-23	8	19-14
22-20	7	13-8
19-14	6	7-5
13-11	5	4-2
10-8	4	1-(-1)
7-5	3	-2-(-4)
4-2	2	-5-(-10)
1 or less	1	-11 or less

Instrument   DIRECTIONS: Proverbs and common sense sayings have been used by people for many years in their day-to-day dealings with other people. These expressions give an indication of people's feelings and attitudes toward other people and toward life in general.

Below and on the following pages is a list of common expressions. After each statement are boxes permitting a person to check the extent to which they might AGREE or DISAGREE with what is being said.

In this survey, please do not give your own opinion about each proverb, even though you might personally feel the same as the answer you give.

Instead, give your opinion of how a person SHOULD FEEL to be a GOOD SUPERVISOR. First, think of the type of person who makes a GOOD SUPERVISOR in your line of work. Second, check each proverb the way this GOOD SUPERVISOR should feel, if he were answering this survey honestly and truthfully.

EXAMPLE: Check how you think a good supervisor should feel about each proverb.

	He should nearly always disagree	He should usually disagree	He should usually agree	He should nearly always agree
Handsome is, as handsome does	☐	☐	☐	☐
Let sleeping dogs lie	☐	☐	☐	☐

NOTE: In the scoring key below the letters AA stand for "Nearly Always Agree;" A stands for "Usually Agree;" D stands for "Usually Disagree;" and AD stands for "Nearly Always Disagree."

	Score +1 for each of these answers	Score -1 for each of these answers
1. Reason rules all things...	--	A
2. A person may be educated beyond his intelligence...	AA	--
3. Too much and too little education hinders the mind...	AD	AA
4. It is better to know something about everything than all about one thing...	D	--
5. He who knows most, believes least...	AD	AA
6. It is just as well to be ignorant of many things...	AD	AA
7. Money talks...	D	--
8. The stronger more often wins...	--	AA

9.	He who demands does not command.	A	AD
10.	An increase of power brings an increase of wealth	--	AA
11.	When the end is lawful, the means are lawful	AD	AA
12.	Petty laws breed great crimes.	--	A
13.	The reasons of the strongest are often the best	D	AA
14.	A good horse should seldom be spurred.	--	AA
15.	Law is the tyrant of man	AD	AA
16.	The result justifies the deed.	AD	AA
17.	The arguments of the strongest carry the most weight.	D	AA
18.	Power passes to the best from the inferior	D	--
19.	When the cat's away the mice will play.	AD	AA
20.	A bird is known by his feathers.	--	AA
21.	You cannot change human nature	D	AA
22.	Once a gentleman, always a gentleman.	AD	AA
23.	Like father, like son.	A	--
24.	Far from eye, far from heart	D	--
25.	A man's character is revealed by his speech	D	--
26.	Necessity will teach a stupid man to be wise	A	--
27.	Dogs bark as they are reared	A	D
28.	An old dog cannot change his way of barking.	--	A
29.	An occasion lost cannot be redeemed.	--	AA
30.	People strive to give to him who already has.	AD	AA
31.	Easy come, easy go.	A	--
32.	What will be, will be.	AD	AA
33.	No pleasure without pain.	AD	AA
34.	To be poor and content is to be rich and rich enough.	--	AA
35.	Life is a battle.	D	AA
36.	Every day should be passed as if it were to be our last.	AD	--
37.	No day passes without some grief.	--	D
38.	Fate will find a way.	AD	AA
39.	There is no flying from fate.	AD	AA
40.	Nothing under the sun is accidental.	A	AD
41.	Those who cannot do, always want to do.	D	--
42.	Every man has his price	AD	AA
43.	Trust people, but not too much.	D	AA
44.	Men's faces are not to be trusted	AD	AA
45.	If you want something done well, do it yourself.	AD	AA
46.	A clean glove often hides a dirty hand.	AD	AA

47.	Make yourself into a lamb and the wolves will eat you.........	AD	A
48.	Many people kiss the hand they wish cut off.	D	AA
49.	He that praises publicly will slander privately.	AD	AA
50.	Avoid a questioner, for he is also a tattler.	D	AA
51.	A good friend never offends.	D	AA
52.	Take things as them come.	--	AA
53.	No one will get a bargain he does not ask for.	D	AA
54.	Imagination is a poor substitute for experience.	--	AA
55.	You cannot reach a high position without boldness.	D	AA
56.	Men of action are dreamers.	--	DA
57.	He who lives by hope will die of hunger.	--	AA
58.	If speech is silver, silence is golden.	AD	A
59.	"Quick" and "good" do not go well together.	AD	AA
60.	There is nothing better than being on the safe side.	D	AA
61.	Debate destroys the speed of getting things done.	AD	AA
62.	The future belongs to him who knows how to wait.	AD	AA
63.	Slow and steady wins the race	AD	AA
64.	The race is not to the swift.	AD	AA
65.	He who hesitates is lost	AD	AA
66.	He who envies others ends up poor.	A	--
67.	Each man is sorry for himself.	D	--
68.	Who is not good to himself will be good to nobody.	D	--
69.	Yourself should be the first object of charity.	AD	AA
70.	In doing what we should we deserve no praise.	--	AA
71.	The reward of a thing rightly done is to have done it.	AD	AA
72.	We always take care of number one.	AD	AA
73.	Everyone finds fault with his own trade.	AD	AA
74.	Discontent is the first step in progress.	AA	AD

NOTE: The actual scale did not present the items in the above order.

A MANAGERIAL KEY FOR THE CPI (Goodstein and Schrader 1963)

Variable

This empirically derived key yields scores which appear to show moderate to low correlation with managerial success and which distinguish between managers and men-in-general.

Description

Two hundred and six true-false items were selected from the California Psychological Inventory. The items comprised 72 percent of the Tolerance (To) subscale, 62 percent of Achievement via independence (Ai), 52 percent of Dominance (Do) and 69 percent of Femininity reversed (-Fe). Capacity for status (Cs), Self Acceptance (Sa), and Achievement via conformance (AC) also had high loadings. The 1957 version of the Inventory was used.

Sample

A total of 603 male civilians in management positions and 1748 "men-in-general" comprised the experimental sample.

Reliability/ Homogeneity

No reliability data is reported for the key. However, the CPI scales from which it is drawn are reported to show test-retest reliabilities of .60 to .71 over a one year period on a sample of high school students.

Validity

Items which discriminated between managers and men-in-general at .01 level using Chi-square were chosen for the key. The selected pool of items was not cross-validated.

Location

Goodstein, L. W. and Schrader, W. J. "An empirically derived key for the California Psychological Inventory." J. Appl. Psychol., 1963 47, pp. 42-45.

Gough, H. G. The California Psychological Inventory, Palo Alto, California: Consulting Psychologist Press, 1964.

CPI item numbers and key are available as Document #7195 from American Documentation Inst., Auxiliary Publications Project, Photo Duplication Service, Library of Congress, Washington 25, D.C. $1.25.

Administration

Self administered. Testing time should fall between one and one and half hours. Hand scoring might be suitable.

Results and Comments

Goodstein and Schrader report that their key, in addition to distinguishing between managers and men-in-general, also differentiates among top, middle, and first-line supervisors at the .01 level. Success ratings for the entire managerial group are reported to correlate +.23 with key scores, and within top management r=.25, middle management r=.27. Of course, any use of this key would require the establishment of local norms.

Item Numbers and Direction of Item Scoring for the 206 CPI Items in the

Managerial Key

Items Scored
'True'

4	224
42	239
50	259
53	320
66	326
78	359
95	376
96	403
107	410
108	412
135	413
138	432
140	448
146	451
162	453
180	464
202	475
207	
213	
221	

Items Scored
'False'

7	43	94	155	194	257	318	383	435
9	47	98	157	199	261	323	384	438
11	48	109	158	204	265	325	385	439
12	56	110	164	206	266	327	388	441
13	63	111	166	209	270	337	390	444
14	64	115	169	217	271	338	397	452
15	67	117	170	219	273	341	398	457
16	68	119	173	220	274	347	401	461
20	69	121	174	223	281	350	404	462
23	70	122	176	225	282	353	405	
24	71	124	177	226	284	358	409	
26	73	128	178	227	285	360	416	
27	75	136	181	232	286	363	417	
31	76	137	182	233	291	364	419	
32	79	139	183	236	294	365	421	
33	85	141	184	237	299	370	422	
37	90	142	186	243	300	378	423	
38	91	145	188	244	308	379	424	
40	92	149	190	252	314	381	429	
41	93	151	192	253	315	382	434	

MANAGERIAL SCALE FOR ENTERPRISE IMPROVEMENT

The stated purpose of this instrument is to measure management morale and provide an analysis of the human relations practices of a firm. The instrument is <u>NOT</u> administered as a morale scale and the assumption is made that more satisfied managers will be less critical of the firm.

The instrument contains 34 Likert scaled (five point) items for which an internal homogeneity coefficient of .89 (corrected) is reported for an unidentified sample of 213 cases.

No norms or validity data are mentioned by the publisher. The scale may be ordered from Psychometric Affiliates, Box 1625, Chicago, Illinois.

The manual for this test is deficient with regard to American Psychological Association "Standards." No references are given in the one page manual through which the potential user may evaluate previous uses of the scale. In any case local norms should be established if this scale is considered for use.

ORGANIZATIONAL CONTROL GRAPH (Tannenbaum 1966)

This is a straightforward Likert scale on which people at various levels of an organization rate the amount of influence that they and people in other levels of the organization have in the running of the organization. Tannenbaum has collected such data from a wide variety of voluntary and formal organizations, which have been found to vary both in the pattern and in general elevation of ratings given to the various organizational levels.

Ratings may be secured for both ideal and actual influence situations. One interesting finding has been that oligarchic control structures actually come to the fore even in organizations where democratic ideals are held, such as voluntary associations like the League of Women Voters or Yugoslav work groups.

For further normative and research data on this instrument see Arnold Tannenbaum's Social Psychology of the Work Organization (Belmont, California: Wadsworth 1966) and the references contained therein. The following shows how the question was asked in the League of Women Voters study:

"In general, how much influence do you think the following groups or persons actually have in determining the policies and actions of your local League"

	No Influence	A little Influence	Some Influence	A great deal of influence	A very great deal of influence
Your local president	☐	☐	☐	☐	☐
Your local board as a group (excluding the president)	☐	☐	☐	☐	☐
Your local membership as a whole (excluding the board)	☐	☐	☐	☐	☐

In this study, the board had an average just over "a great deal", the president a little short of "a great deal" and membership close to "some", in terms of actual influence.

Patchen (1962) has proposed that organizational influence can alternatively be measured by examining influence across a number of specific decision situations and then summing these into a simple index. A comparison of the two methods across three criteria shows little difference between the two approaches, although the specific decision questions had higher rates of agreement within organizational levels; that is, more managers agreed with each other on these questions, as did more rank and file. Patchen notes, however, that there is little agreement across levels for both methods. That is, managers and rank and file do not agree on the amount of influence that each other have -- which leaves this area with an interesting methodological gap.

Reference:

Patchen, M. "Alternative questionnaire approaches to the measurement of influence in organizations", American Journal of Sociology 1962, 69, 41-52.

276

PROFILE OF ORGANIZATIONAL CHARACTERISTICS (Likert 1967)

This instrument attempts to reflect empirically the concepts contained in Likert's writings on new patterns of management. In his latest work, <u>New Patterns of Management</u> (New York: McGraw-hill, in press), Likert uses the instrument in a variety of primarily business organizations to illustrate differences in the perceptions of the organizational structure as a function of the introduction of new management techniques. The data Likert presents are quite impressive in their support for the ideal decentralized system, which stresses maximal communication and interaction between participants at all levels of the organization. This "ideal" end of the continuum is fairly evident in each of the 51 items, which, therefore, might be transparent for a manager with human relations training or exposure to Likert's philosophy. The item wording would definitely have to be farmerized for use on rank-and-file samples--but there has been little data collected on non-supervisory personnel anyway. One may wonder whether the rank and file share their supervisors' general enthusiasm for the less-centralized and democratic systems of management, especially since, as we have seen in Robinson's chapter, lower-status workers expect few of these intrinsic satisfaction from their jobs. Likert feels that such practices can be appreciated by rank and file workers as much as by supervisory personnel, although it may take the former longer to adjust to the practices.

Such normative data for the instrument as exist will appear in Likert's forthcoming volume. Although full psychometric data on the instrument are as yet incomplete Likert reports split-half reliabilities over .90 for the entire scale. The scale exhibits high item homogeneity in that single management systems tend to fall in the same segment of the scale on almost all items. This effect holds true even though eight different aspects of system are tapped. The different system "aspects" are as fol

1. Leadership processes used (5 items)
2. Character of motivational forces (7 items)
3. Character of communication processes (14 items)
4. Character of interaction-influence process (6 items)
5. Character of decision-making process (8 items)
6. Character of goal-setting or ordering (3 items)
7. Character of control processes (5 items)
8. Performance goals and training (3 items)

Instructions for use of the instrument for the worker's present environment are as follows:

On the lines below each organizational variable (item), please place an <u>n</u> at the point which, in your experience, describes your organization at the present time (n=now). Treat each item as a continuous variable from the extreme at one end to that at the other.

The items are listed on a 20 point scale, split into four regions as in the sample items below.

1a. Extent to which superiors have confidence and trust in <u>subordinates</u>

| Have no confidence & trust in subordinates | Have condescending confidence & trust, such as master has in servant | Substantial but not complete confidence & trust. Still wishes to keep control of decisions | Complete confidence & trust in all matters |

2b. Manner in which motives are used

| Fear, threats, punishment, & occasional rewards | Rewards & some actual or potential punishment | Rewards, occasional punishment, & some involvement | Economic rewards based on compensation system developed through participation. Group participation & involvement in setting goals, improving methods, appraising progress toward goals, etc. |

5c. Are there forces to accept, resist, or reject goals?

| Goals are overtly accepted but are covertly resisted strongly | Goals are overtly accepted but often covertly resisted to at least a moderate degree | Goals are overtly accepted but at times with some covert resistance | Goals are fully accepted both overtly and covertly |

In addition, if one is interested in analysis of organizational change, he might ask the respondent to rate the organization as it was months ago by placing a "p" on each of the 51 scales. Alternate instructions are also available for "the kind of management you are trying to create by the management you a providing" and for "where you would like to have your organization fall" with regard to that item.

Because the items are lengthy and because the whole profile should not be used without prior experience with Likert's aim, we will merely list the items without the descriptive phrases used with the scales. Fuller data on the instrument will be given in the forthcoming volume.

1. Leadership Process Used

   a) Extent to which superiors have confidence and trust in subordinates

   b) extent to which subordinates, in turn, have confidence and trust in superiors

   c) Extent to which superiors display supportive behavior toward others

   d) Extent to which superiors behave so that subordinates feel free to discuss important things about their jobs with their immediate superior

   e) Extent to which immediate superior in solving job problems generally tries to get subordinates' ideas & opinions & make constructive use of them.

2. Character of Motivational Forces

   a) Underlying motives tapped

   b) Manner in which motives are used

   c) kinds of attitudes developed toward organization and its goals

   d) Extent to which motivational forces conflict with or reinforce one another

   e) Amount of responsibility felt by each member of organization for achieving organization's goals

   f) Attitudes toward other members of the organization

   g) Satisfaction derived

3. Character of Communication Process

   a) Amount of interaction and communication aimed at achieving organization's objectives

   b) Direction of information flow

   c) Downward communication

      (1) Where initiated
      (2) Extent to which superiors willingly share information with subordinates
      (3) Extent to which communications are accepted by subordinates

   d) Upward communication

      (1) Adequacy of upward communication via line organization
      (2) Subordinates' feeling of responsibility for initiating accurate upward communication
      (3) Forces leading to accurate or distorted upward information
      (4) Accuracy of upward communication via line
      (5) Need for supplementary upward communication system

   e) Sideward communication, its adequacy and accuracy

   f) Psychological closeness of superiors to subordinates (i.e., friendliness between superiors and subordinates)

      (1) How well does superior know and understand problems faced by subordinates?
      (2) How accurate are the perceptions by superiors and subordinates of each other

4. Character of Interaction-Influence Process

   a) Amount and character of interaction

   b) Amount of cooperative teamwork present

   c) Extent to which subordinates can influence the goals, methods, and activity of their units and departments

      (1) As seen by superiors
      (2) As seen by subordinates

   d) Amount of actual influence which superiors can exercise over the goals, activity, and methods of their units and departments

   e) Extent to which an effective structure exists enabling one part of organization to exert influence upon other parts

5. Character of Decision-making Process

   a) At what level in organization are decisions formally made?

b) How adequate and accurate is the information available for decision-making at the place where the decisions are made?

c) To what extent are decision-makers aware of problems, particularly those at lower levels in the organization?

d) Extent to which technical and professional knowledge is used in decision-making

e) Are decisions made at the best level in the organization as far as

 (1) Availability of the most adequate and accurate information bearing on the decision.

 (2) The motivational consequences (i.e., does the decision-making process help to create the necessary motivations in those persons who have to carry out the decision?)

f) To what extent are subordinates involved in decisions related to their work?

g) Is decision-making based on man-to-man or group pattern of operation? Does it encourage or discourage teamwork?

6. Character of Goal-setting or Ordering

a) Manner in which usually done

b) To what extent do the different hierarchical levels tend to strive for high performance goals?

c) Are there forces to accept, resist, or reject goals?

7. Character of Control Processes

a) At what hierarchical levels in organization does major or primary concern exist with regard to the performance of the control function?

b) How accurate are the measurements and information used to guide and perform the control function, and to what extent do forces exist in the organization to distort and falsify this information?

c) Extent to which the review and control functions are concentrated

d) Extent to which there is an informal organization present and supporting or opposing goals of formal organization

e) Extend to which control data (e.g., accounting, productivity, cost, etc.) are used for self-guidance or group problem-solving by managers and non-supervisory employees; or used by superiors in a punitive, policing manner.

8. Performance Goals and Training

a) Level of performance goals which superiors seek to have organization achieve

b) Extent to which you have been given the kind of management training you desire

c) Adequacy of training resources provided to assist you in training your subordinates

The reader may find the following shortened adaptation of the
Likert __Profile__ into 19 items a more viable instrument.

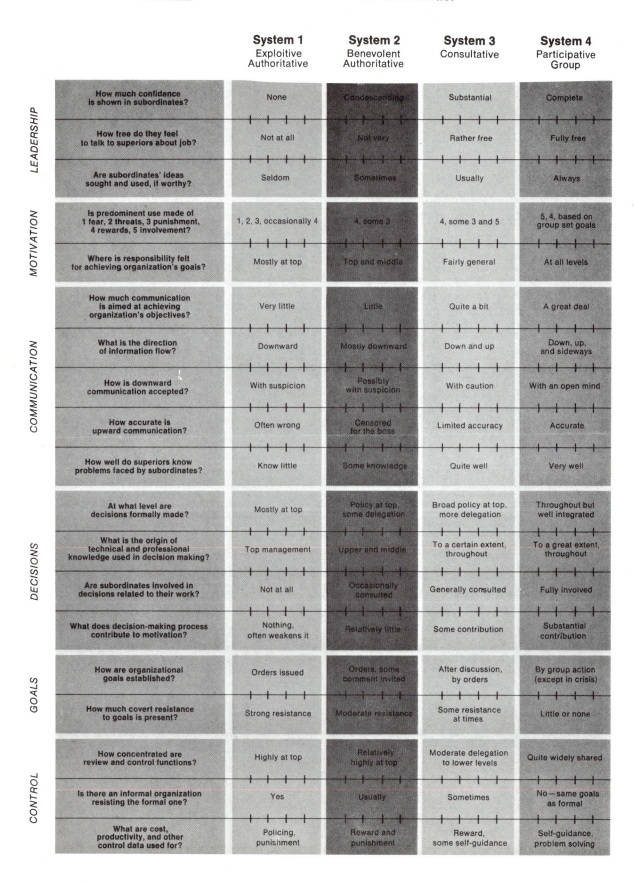

		System 1 Exploitive Authoritative	System 2 Benevolent Authoritative	System 3 Consultative	System 4 Participative Group
LEADERSHIP	How much confidence is shown in subordinates?	None	Condescending	Substantial	Complete
	How free do they feel to talk to superiors about job?	Not at all	Not very	Rather free	Fully free
	Are subordinates' ideas sought and used, if worthy?	Seldom	Sometimes	Usually	Always
MOTIVATION	Is predominent use made of 1 fear, 2 threats, 3 punishment, 4 rewards, 5 involvement?	1, 2, 3, occasionally 4	4, some 3	4, some 3 and 5	5, 4, based on group set goals
	Where is responsibility felt for achieving organization's goals?	Mostly at top	Top and middle	Fairly general	At all levels
COMMUNICATION	How much communication is aimed at achieving organization's objectives?	Very little	Little	Quite a bit	A great deal
	What is the direction of information flow?	Downward	Mostly downward	Down and up	Down, up, and sideways
	How is downward communication accepted?	With suspicion	Possibly with suspicion	With caution	With an open mind
	How accurate is upward communication?	Often wrong	Censored for the boss	Limited accuracy	Accurate
	How well do superiors know problems faced by subordinates?	Know little	Some knowledge	Quite well	Very well
DECISIONS	At what level are decisions formally made?	Mostly at top	Policy at top, some delegation	Broad policy at top, more delegation	Throughout but well integrated
	What is the origin of technical and professional knowledge used in decision making?	Top management	Upper and middle	To a certain extent, throughout	To a great extent, throughout
	Are subordinates involved in decisions related to their work?	Not at all	Occasionally consulted	Generally consulted	Fully involved
	What does decision-making process contribute to motivation?	Nothing, often weakens it	Relatively little	Some contribution	Substantial contribution
GOALS	How are organizational goals established?	Orders issued	Orders, some comment invited	After discussion, by orders	By group action (except in crisis)
	How much covert resistance to goals is present?	Strong resistance	Moderate resistance	Some resistance at times	Little or none
CONTROL	How concentrated are review and control functions?	Highly at top	Relatively highly at top	Moderate delegation to lower levels	Quite widely shared
	Is there an informal organization resisting the formal one?	Yes	Usually	Sometimes	No — same goals as formal
	What are cost, productivity, and other control data used for?	Policing, punishment	Reward and punishment	Reward, some self-guidance	Self-guidance, problem solving

12. OTHER WORK-RELEVANT ATTITUDES

The attitude scales that remain have been divided into three categories strictly on the basis of whether we encountered other scales dealing with the subjects in question. Thus, we have grouped five scales dealing with labor-management orientations, and two dealing with federal employment, but we review only one scale dealing with attitudes toward automation, one with attitudes toward the employment of older persons, and one with work opinions of the mentally ill. There doubtless exist many other scales dealing with such topics as employment of the handicapped, but we viewed these instruments as tangential to the primary purpose of this volume and did not systematically search for them. We included the scales reviewed in this section mainly because we felt it would be wasteful not at least to mention partially relevant instruments we encountered in our search of the literature. The following ten instruments are reviewed in this chapter:

1. Union and Management Attitudes toward Each Other (Stagner, et al. 1958)
2. IRC Union Attitude Scale (Uphoff and Dunnette 1956)
3. Index of Pro-Labor Orientation (Kornhauser 1965)
4. Pro-labor Attitude Error-choice Tests (Hammond 1948)
5. Attitudes toward Labor and Management (Weschler 1950)
6. Attitude toward Working for the Government (Aalto 1956)
7. Attitudes toward Working for the Government (Kilpatrick, et al. 1964)
8. Attitude toward Automation (Rosenberg 1962)
9. Attitude toward Employment of Older Persons (Kirchner 1954)
10. Opinions about Work of the Mentally Ill (Streuning and Efron 1965)

Union-management attitudes are, of course, highly important in the working world, where optimal production may depend upon adequate communication between management and labor unions, as formal representative of worker interests and dissatisfactions. Stagner, et al.'s Union-Management Attitude Scales are relevant only for the management-level personnel. The scales consist of nine statements about union leaders' view of the organization and 11 statements dealing with management's view of the union. As noted in the scale write-up, the items seem transparent and stereotyped but perhaps adequate for most measurement purposes. Internal homogeneity seems sufficient, although not high considering the transparency of the items.

The IRC Union Attitude Scale, on the other hand, taps union members' attitudes toward the union. Sampling of item content, construction procedures, sampling of respondents, reliabilities, and validation procedures all reflect a high level of methodological sophistication. The only drawbacks to the scale are its length, its applicability for the most part to only union members, and its lack of cross-validation.

Kornhauser's Index of Pro-labor Orientation taps the attitudes of the rank and file towards unions, management, government help and working-class views. The items were devised for an interview situation and depend on a number of open-ended questions, which might inhibit the responses of working-class people if given in self-administered form (i.e., if respondents would have to write in their responses). The internal structure of the questions was not empirically verified and validity data are lacking, mainly because the author was primarily interested in finding differences among various types of workers. In this sense, the Index may lay a modest claim for validity--over three times as many blue-collar workers as white-collar rate "high" on pro-labor orientation.

Two union-management "error-choice" scales, by Hammond, and Weschler, are reviewed. The items are obviously out-of-date as interest in this technique has died out since its the last application about 15 years ago. We have heard rumors that those taking the test were considerably disturbed upon hearing that the "information" test that they were taking was rigged to expose their biases.

The two scales concerning government employment have offsetting advantages and disadvantages. Aalto's instrument is strong on the psychometric desiderata of norms, reliability and validity; but the sample seems too well educated to be representative and the items may be too simple and too general. In fact, Aalto's scale is so general that it correlates quite highly with a general job satisfaction scale. Kilpatrick, et al.'s sample, on the other hand, is one of the best on which occupational data have ever been collected (see Robinson's chapter) and their instrument employs well-written items which deal with specific facets of government and private employment. However, these authors performed very few analyses of the structure of their items and limited themselves to simple analyses of single items. There is, however, a wealth of normative data on this recent and most representative sample. In addition, Kilpatrick, et al. supplemented their interviews with a number of interesting open-ended questions about federal vs. private employment.

With the growing and somewhat polemic debate about the effects of increasing automation in our society, Rosenberg's measure of <u>Attitudes toward Automation</u> may face a goodly number of competitors in the near future. Rosenberg commendably tried to examine these attitudes from a number of angles (e.g., security, wages); however, some of the sub-scale correlations were high enough to suggest that the items should have been formed into a smaller number of indices than the ten suggested. While data on test-retest reliability and validity are lacking, the scale is worth examination because item coverage of the topic appears quite comprehensive.

Another topic of growing societal concern is employment of the increasing ranks of our elderly population. Kirchner's measure of <u>Attitudes toward Employment of Older Persons</u> covers the topic adequately. Indeed, the methodology involved in the construction of this instrument is quite commendable. Its only drawbacks are item transparency, lack of substantial validity, and the response set problems inherent in straightforward Likert scales.

Streuning and Efron's measure of former mental patients' <u>Opinions About Work</u> also has a solid methodological background. The work perspectives of the mentally ill may offer basic insights into the world of work that other workers take for granted. The dimensions which emerged from the author's factor analysis, however, appear to offer more information about the perspectives of mental patients than about the structure of work attitudes. The finding that mental patients who were currently employed were just as alienated (the major factor in the item pool) as those who were not employed is worth noting.

UNION AND MANAGEMENT ATTITUDES TOWARD EACH OTHER (Stanger, et al. 1958)

Variable
Management's attitude toward labor organization within a company and union officials attitude toward upper management.

Description
The Management Attitude toward Unions scale consists of 11 Likert graded-choice type items, and the Union Attitude toward Management scale has nine items. A low score on either scale is indicative of approval. The analysis of items was carried out on data gathered from top level officials in each company and union and the scales are not recommended, therefore, for use on rank and file personnel. Both correlational and Guttman scalogram analysis techniques were used in developing these scales.

Sample
41 establishments in three southern Illinois communities provided management and union people for interviews. 76 executives and 81 union officials comprised the population of respondents. In all 41 companies, a single union bargained for the majority of the work force The range of hourly paid employees was from 73 to 2,100 and the companies represented manufacturing, utility, and service interests.

Reliability/
Homogeneity
Reliability data is not reported but the coefficient of reproducibilit' is reported as .92 for the Management scale and .90 for the Union scale.

Validity
Only face validity is assumed.

Location
Stagner, R., Chalmers, W. E., and Derber, M. L., "Guttman-type scales for union and management attitudes toward each other", J. Appl. Psycho 1958, 42, pp. 293-300.

Administration
Self-administered. Scoring is accomplished in standard Likert fashion a low score indicating a positive attitude.

Results and
Comments
Considering the nature of the validity claims for this instrument, the relative transparency of item content, and the fact that the item analysis was carried out with respect to a single union, one should be quite careful in assuming any degree of validity generalization or validity extension.

In addition to providing a measure of the general climate of union-management relations, specific item content and responses may provide data for improvement programs.

Other
References
Institute of Labor and Industrial Relations, University of Illinois, Labor-Management Relations in Illini City, Champaign, Illinois, 1954.

Derber, M. I., Chalmers, W. E. and Stagner, R. The Local Union-Management Relationship, Urbana, Illinois: Institute of Labor and Industrial Relations, University of Illinois, 1960.

285

The numbers in parentheses following the items indicate the cutting point between answers considered favorable or unfavorable.

Scale for Management Attitude Toward Union

43. Are the union officers effective leaders of their organization?

(1)---very much so
(2)---pretty good
(3)---mediocre
(4)---very poor (2.5)

35. Is the union generally reasonable or not in its claims?

(1)---very reasonable
(2)---reasonable most of the time
(3)---frequently unreasonable
(4)---extremely unreasonable (2.5)

36. Does the union interfere seriously with how the company is managed, or does the management have a reasonably free hand in running the plant?

(1)---union is no problem
(2)---it interferes a little but not seriously
(3)---it interferes quite often
(4)---it seriously interferes with management (2.0)

40. Are the union officers interested in the welfare of the rank-and-file workers?

(1)---very much so
(2)---pretty much
(3)---slightly
(4)---very little (2.0)

38. Does the union cooperate with management on production matters or not?

(1)---they are extremely cooperative
(2)---they will go along but not positively support
(3)---they do not interfere seriously but sometimes are obstructionist
(4)---they restrict production improvements quite often (2.5)

34. In general, how do you personally feel about your company's relations with the union?

(1)---very satisfied
(2)---moderately satisfied
(3)---moderately dissatisfied
(4)---very dissatisfied (2.0)

39. Has the union tended to weaken employee discipline, or has it cooperated with management on disciplinary matters?

(1)---cooperative and helpful
(2)---sometimes helps but not always
(3)---sometimes interferes with discipline
(4)---has created some serious disciplinary problems (2.5)

46. Does the union have too much power in your establishment?

(1)---not too much
(2)---too much in a few respects
(3)---too much in many respects
(4)---far too much (1.5)

44. Does the union have the support of the workers?

(1)---most of the workers are strongly behind it
(2)---only a few really active people but most workers go along
(3)---not too much feeling either way
(4)---a lot of the workers are hostile (1.0)

37. How do you feel about using the union as the main channel of communication to the workers on company policies?

(1)---strongly favor
(2)---moderately favor
(3)---moderately oppose
(4)---strongly oppose (combined with 41)

41. Are the local union officers skillful bargainers?

(1)---very much so
(2)---pretty good
(3)---mediocre
(4)---very poor (favorable if 37 + 41 = 3 or less)

Scale for Union Attitude Toward Management

43. Are the top management officials effective executives of the establishment?

(1)---very much so
(2)---pretty good
(3)---mediocre
(4)---very poor (2.0)

44. What is the top management attitude toward the union?

(1)---strongly favorable
(2)---moderately favorable
(3)---moderately unfavorable
(4)---strongly unfavorable (2.0)

47. Does the company try to live up to its agreements?

(1)---always
(2)---usually
(3)---frequently does not
(4)---rarely (2.0)

46. Does the company abuse its power in this establishment?

(1)---rarely
(2)---occasionally
(3)---frequently
(4)---very often (1.5)

34. In general, how do you personally feel about your union's relations with the company?

(1)---very satisfied
(2)---moderately satisfied
(3)---moderately dissatisfied
(4)---very dissatisfied (2.0)

36. Has the management shown any understanding of your problems as a union officer?

(1)---very understanding
(2)---understands the union situation pretty well
(3)---understanding of union problems is limited
(4)---little or no understanding of union problems (2.0)

37. Has the management tried to undermine the union position through direct dealings with the workers, or has it been careful to safe-guard the union position in such contacts?

(1)---is always careful not to hurt union
(2)---is usually careful not to hurt union
(3)---occasionally tries to weaken union
(4)---frequently tries to weaken union (2.0)

35. Is the top management generally reasonable or not when it comes to discussing union claims?

(1)---very reasonable
(2)---reasonable most of the time
(3)---frequently unreasonable
(4)---extremely unreasonable (1.5)

40. Are the top management officials interested in the welfare of the workers?

(1)---very much so
(2)---pretty much
(3)---slightly
(4)---very little (1.5)

IRC UNION ATTITUDE SCALE (Uphoff and Dunnette 1956)

iable This scale measures attitudes of union members toward unions and union administration in seven areas.

cription There are a total of 77 five-point Likert items in the scale. An original group of 121 items were both item analyzed and grouped into seven areas on the basis of expert judgments. Within the first six areas, items which met certain item analytic criteria were included. The seven areas and the questions below to which they refer are:

1) Unionism in general (item 1-20)
2) Local union in general (items 21-27)
3) Local union policies and practices (items 28-36)
4) Local union officers (items 37-48)
5) Local union administration (items 49-56)
6) National union (items 57-64)
7) General (items 65-77)

ple A total of 821 union members from nine unions responded to the original item pool. In the final sample 1,251 union members from 13 union groups were chosen to represent close to 14,000 such members.

iability/
omogeneity No test-retest data are reported. Split-half reliabilities are .96 for the first six scales combined and range from .71 to .90 for each of the six sub-scales.

lidity The scales and subscales were found to discriminate: (a) union members from non-members (b) people giving different reasons for joining the union (c) persons attending more or fewer union meetings (d) present union officers vs. past officers vs. nonofficers.

ation Uphoff, W. and Dunnette, M. Understanding the Union Member Minneapolis: University of Minnesota Press, 1956.

ministration Items are in regular Likert format. Some of the items are positive, some negative. Items to be scored negatively are indicated with a cross (+) below.

sults and
Comments The subscales show a commendable range of item content. In all, the scale reflects a proper appreciation of how attitude instruments should be constructed. Norms for each item are presented.

IRC (Industrial Relations Center) UNION
ATTITUDE QUESTIONNAIRE*

Strongly agree   Agree   Undecided   Disagree   Strongly Disagree

1 If it were not for unions, we'd have little protection against favoritism on the job.
†2 I think the best man should be kept on the job regardless of seniority.
†3 Unions impose too many restrictions on employers.
4 Charges of "racketeering" in unions are greatly exaggerated.
5 Employees of a firm have better wages and working conditions when all of them belong to unions.
6 Unions should have something to say about whom the employer hires.
7 A nonunion shop usually pays lower wages than a union shop.
†8 Union rules often interfere with the efficient running of the employer's business.
9 Every worker should be expected to join the union where he works.
†10 We need more laws to limit the power of labor unions.
†11 Labor unions hold back progress.
†12 The high wage demands of unions reduce chances for employment.
13 The growth of unions has made our democracy stronger.
14 The selfishness of employers can be fought only by strong unions.
†15 Workers should not have to join a union in order to hold a job.
†16 Labor unions should be regulated to a greater extent by the federal government.
†17 Every labor union should be required to take out a license from the U.S. government.
18 In a factory where there is a union, workers who are not members should be required to pay the regular union fees if they are getting union rates of pay.
†19 Most unions gain their membership by forcing workers to join by threats of violence.
20 If the majority of workers in a plant vote to have a union, the others should be required to join.
21 There isn't a better union than the one I belong to.
22 In case of a strike, I'm sure we'd stick together.
23 Every union member should attend at least two out of three of his local union meetings.
24 My union makes new members feel that it is worth while for them to belong.
25 My union is quick to defend any member who doesn't get a fair deal from his boss.
†26 The initiation fees for my local are too high.
†27 My union is not spending enough time telling members about what it is doing.
†28 My union is of no help when it comes to job transfer.
29 My union sees to it that overtime is given out fairly.
30 My union looks after labor's interests in the city council and the state legislature.
31 Our union dues are too low.
†32 There is not much "rhyme or reason" to the way our union votes to contribute to the various appeals for money that come to it.
†33 We give our delegates too much money to spend when they go to conventions.
34 My union doesn't show favoritism between members when it comes to settling grievances.
35 Nearly everyone in our union knows what to do when he has a grievance complaint.
36 Fines should be levied for not attending union meetings.
37 The local officers of my union are doing a good job.

39 I feel free to discuss my personal problems with my union committeeman (or steward).
40 I like the way my business agent handles our union affairs.
41 My steward (or business agent) is firm in dealing with management.
42 My union officers see to it that all reported grievances are promptly settled.
43 Our officers usually welcome suggestions from members.
44 Officers of my union are chosen because they are real leaders.
45 Our union officers know how to get the members to do things for the union.
†46 I think the president of my union is too easy going when it comes to **keeping order** at meetings.
47 Our union officers keep us informed about what they are doing.
48 Our union officers get word to us promptly when something important comes up.
49 Our union meetings are run in an efficient manner.
50 Our union meetings are over at a reasonable time.
51 There is enough discussion on motions to show what the membership really thinks.
†52 Our union meetings are dull and uninteresting.
53 We have a well-planned "order of business" at our meetings.
†54 Our union president lets a few who like to talk take too much time at meetings.
55 A member who attends our union meetings gets the feeling that he is free to speak on any issue.
56 We have enough chance to give our ideas before the bargaining committee begins negotiations with the employer.
†57 The officers of my national union are paid too much.
†58 So much of our union policy is set by our national union that there is not much point in going to our local union meetings.
†59 It is practically impossible to elect different officers in our national union.
†60 Our national union exercises too much control over the affairs of our local.
†61 Our national union takes its share of our dues but gives us very little help.
†62 Our national union interferes too much in our local affairs.
†63 We don't get enough help for our union educational program from the national union.
64 Our national union provides the necessary facts and helps at negotiation time.
65 The paid officers of my local are worth the money we pay them.
†66 I regard my union dues as a good investment.
67 My union got a "good deal" for me when the last contract was signed.
†68 My union does not keep careful enough records of all money taken in and spent.
†69 My union spends too much time and money on political action.
†70 My union officers spend too much time on things that are of no concern to my union.
71 If you read it in the union paper, you know you are getting the facts.
†72 Our union paper gives us only one side of an issue.
†73 My union does not teach us enough labor history.
†74 I feel that too many things are already decided before the union meetings are held.
75 Stewards and committeemen in my union are the choice of the rank-and-file members.
†76 If you don't agree with the officers of our union, you might as well stay home.
†77 Labor unions should be required by law to make annual public reports of the money they collect and spend.

INDEX OF PRO-LABOR ORIENTATION (Kornhauser 1965)

Variable — The total labor-orientation index combines sub-indices of working-class views, attitude toward government help, attitude toward business and its control, and attitudes toward labor unions. Scores serve as a rough measure of "liberal" socio-economic attitudes in the sense of the "New Deal" and "Fair Deal", which are generally in accord with the position of the major labor unions of the country.

Description — The index is composed of the total of scores on the four subindices, reduced to nine intervals to form the final score. The sub-indices are follows:

1. Identification with working-class views (two open-ended questions)
2. Attitudes toward government help (three agree-disagree items and one open-ended question)
3. Attitudes toward business and industry (three agree-disagree items and one open-ended questions)
4. Attitudes toward labor unions (three agree-disagree items and two open-ended questions)

Scores may vary from 0-8 on index (1), 0-10 on index (2), 0-10 on index (3) and 0-10 on index (4). Total scores then vary between 0 and 38, although, as noted above, they were reduced to nine intervals in this study.

Sample — The sample population of 407 Detroit factory workers was drawn from 13 large and medium-sized automotive manufacturing plants. Only hourly paid workers actually engaged in factory job were included. Respondents were white native-born men on payroll at least three years, aged either 20 to 29 or 40 to 49; all but 20 percent were members of the UAW-CIO. Supplementary samples were drawn the following populations: manual workers from six Detroit manufacturing companies, factory workers from eight plants in small towns outside Metropolitan Detroit, office workers (with salaries comparable to manual workers') from six Detroit automotive companies and from three manufacturing companies. Interviews were taken during 1953-54.

Reliability Homogeneity — No measures of reliability, including "coder reliability", were reported.

Validity — No quantitative measures were employed although relations with background variables were as expected (see Results).

Location — Kornhauser, A. Mental Health of the Industrial Worker New York: John Wiley and Sons, Inc., 1965, pp. 213-230.

Results and Comments — High general labor orientation was found to be related to low childhood family income, to low job skill and present income levels (even with education controlled) and to job dissatisfaction at low job levels. Size and significance of correlations were not reported.

Results and Comments (continued)

The following results were found with the sub-indices:

1. Those respondents classified as "working-class oriented" varied from 81 percent of Detroit factory workers and about 75 percent other factory workers, to 27 percent of white-collar workers. Only slight relation was observed with job satisfaction and class orientation.
2. Those respondents with lower skills and income were more favorable to government help. No relation was observed with job satisfaction.
3. A clear contrast was found between manual and white-collar attitudes toward business. Those in lower skill and income groups were especially critical of business. Unfavorable attitudes toward business was also related to job dissatisfaction.
4. Factory workers are clearly more pro-union with little difference noted by skill level. No relation was found between pro-union attitudes and job satisfaction or with attitudes toward business. This instrument, it should be noted, deals with unions in general and not with one's particular union.

The major deficiency in all these measures is that no inter-item data is given so that one can assess whether the instruments do in fact form a unidimensional scale(s) as the author assumes in his analysis.

Criteria for Coding replies to the open-ended questions are as follows:

Working-class Views		Middle-class Views
Favor greater equality of income and gains for common people	vs.	Things are pretty satisfactory as they are; no change needed
Favor government welfare and social-security measures and greater control of business	vs.	Cut governmental spending; hold down welfare measures; reduce "interferences" with business
Causes of people's getting ahead or not; emphasis on social conditions, institutions, etc.; rather than personal responsibility	vs.	Opposite emphasis
Solutions to problems through social, political, organizational means	vs.	Solutions through personal initiative, etc.

The questions making up the four subindices are as follows:

1. Index of Pro-labor Orientation re: "Working Class"
   (Rating of identification with working class versus middle-class views; each
   question scores from 0 to 4 points)

H1 a. In general, how do you feel about the way things are going in this country:
        do you want things to go along pretty much in the way they are or are there
        some important changes you'd like to see made? (What changes do you mean?)
    b. (If no change wanted) Isn't there anything at all about the way things are
        going that you would like to see changed?
    c. What other changes would you like to see?
    d. (If no one track or single topic) Well now, I have your feelings about that,
        what other kinds of changes would you like to see?

H2 a. In general, what people or group are likely to feel the same way as you
        do about how things should be in this country?
        (Get clear indication of people he has in mind, e.g., "just what people
        do you mean?" etc.)
    b. (If answer refers to specific topic) Now thinking about how a lot of others
        things--things in general--should be in this country, what people or group
        feel the same way you do?
    c. What other people or groups feel the same way you do?
    d. What people or groups are likely to feel <u>different</u> <u>than</u> <u>you</u> do about how
        things should be in this country? (Again, get clear indication of people
        he has in mind.)
    e. (If answer refers to specific topic) Now thinking about how a lot of
        other things--things in general--should be in this country--what persons
        or groups are likely to feel different than you?

H3 a. Do you think the ordinary working man can do anything to make things more
        the way he wants them?
    b. (If yes or doubtful) What can he do?
        (If no) Why is that?

H4 a. What things do you think keep people from getting ahead in the world?
    b. Who or what is to blame for this?
    c. What things do you think help people to get ahead?

H5 a. How do you feel about what the government should do to see that people have
        better housing and medical care and that old people, unemployed, and others
        like that are taken care of?
    b. Should the government do more than it's doing in helping people, or is
        it already doing too much?
    c. Why do you feel that the government (should do more) (is doing too much?)

H8 a. I'd like to ask you what you think about government control over business
        and industry. Would you say the government has too much to say about how
        business and industry are run _____, just about the right amount to say
        _____, or that the government ought to have more to say about how business
        and industry are run _____?

        Comments:

    b. Would you tell me why you think (the government has <u>too much</u> to say about how
        business and industry are run?) (the government has <u>just</u> <u>about</u> <u>the</u> <u>right</u>
        amount to say?) (the government ought to have more to say about how business
        and industry are run?)

2. <u>Index of Pro-labor Orientation re Government Help</u>
   (The first three questions score 0 to 2 points, the final one 0 to 4)

D22 The government should do more about providing low-cost housing than it has done in the past (Agree -- Disagree)

D23 The government should provide doctor and hospital care for everyone who needs it (Agree -- Disagree)

D24 Unemployment compensation payments should be larger than they are now (Agree -- Disagree)

H5 a. How do you feel about what the government should do to see that people have better housing and medical care and that old people, unemployed, and others like that are taken care of?

    b. Should the government do more than it's now doing in helping people, or is it already doing too much?

    c. Why do you feel that the government (should do more) (is doing too much)?

3. <u>Index of Pro-labor Orientation re Business and Industry</u>
   (The first 3 questions score 0 to 2 points, the final one 0 to 4)

D11 In general, the profits of business and industry are higher than they should be. (Agree -- Disagree)

D16 Working people should have more to say about how things are run in factories than they have now (Agree -- Disagree)

D17 Wealthy businessmen have too much influence in running things in this country (Agree -- Disagree)

A8 a. I'd like to ask you what you think about government control over business and industry. Would you say the government has too much to say about how business and industry are run _____, just about the right amount to say _____, or that the government ought to have more to say about how business and industry are run _____?
        Comments:

    b. Would you tell me why you think (the government has <u>too much</u> to say about how business and industry are run?) (the government has <u>just about the right amount</u> to say?) (the government ought to have <u>more to say</u> about how business and industry are run?)

4. <u>Index of Pro-labor Orientation re Unions</u>
   (The first three questions score 0 to 2 points, H6 and H7 together score 0 to 4 points)

D18 Labor unions have too much influence in running things in this country (Agree -- Disagree)

D21 Labor unions should stay out of state and national political activity altogether (Agree -- Disagree)

D25 Who would you say is more interested in the welfare of the working man--the heads of your company or the union leaders? (Heads of company -- Union leaders)

H6 Now I'd like your opinion about labor unions: Taking the unions as a whole, how do you feel about them and the things they do?

H7 a. In disputes between companies and labor unions, do you usually side with the company or the union?

    b. Why do feel this way?

    c. Why do you think companies and unions often disagree and have trouble getting along with each other?

    d. Some people say neither the union nor management cares much about the common worker -- he gets squeezed in between. What do you think about this statement?

PRO-LABOR ATTITUDE ERROR-CHOICE TESTS (Hammond 1948)

riable
The instruments attempt to measure the extent of pro-labor attitude by direction and amount of systematic error in "non-factual" information tests.

scription
The tests each consist of 20 "factual" and 20 "non-factual" forced choice items. Among the latter, one series of eight questions offers alternate answers equidistant from the truth in opposite directions, while the second series of 12 questions offers alternate answers for which the facts are indeterminable. In this study, the 20 "factual" or straight information items were used to disguise the test and were interspersed among the 20 non-factual items. A priori determined positive (or pro-) systematic errors were given a score value of 1 on each item; negative errors, no value. Selection of items was based primarily on "the writer's hunch".

To check for attitude test "set", the instrument was also administered to a different sample with an non-factual items separated from the factual items and presented as an attitude test (called ATT-INFO) A control group from the same sample was given the original test (called INFO).

ample
The experimental validation groups consisted of the following:
(1) pro-labor bias group, consisting of 18 adults employed by a major labor organization in clerical and semi-professional positions, and (2) anti-labor bias group, consisting of two businessmen's luncheon clubs, one made up of 23 middle-aged businessmen making over $10,000 a year, and one composed of 19 younger businessmen.

A third experimental population was a group of 144 students in an elementary psychology class.

eliability/
Homogeneity
The split-half reliability coefficient corrected by the Spearman-Brown formula was .78 on the labor questionnaire. The reliability sample consisted of ten cases from the union group, 40 from the two business groups, and a random sample of ten of the college students.

The reliability coefficients on the ATT-INFO test for the sample of students were .33 on the labor form as corrected by the Spearman-Brown formula.

alidity
In this "known group" validity test, the mean errors in the pro-labor and anti-labor groups were found significantly different (at the .05 level) in the direction predicted.

Response differences between the group given the ATT-INFO test and the group given the standard INFO test were not significant, leaving the possibility of attitude test set bias on the responses to the regular labor test, according to the author.

ocation
Hammond, Kenneth R., "Measuring attitudes by error-choice: an indirect method", Journal of Abnormal and Social Psychology, 1948, 43, 38-47.

Administration   Estimated administration time for each of the tests is about 30
                 minutes. Scoring requires simple summation of response codes.

Results and   Though the items appeared to discriminate fairly well between the
Comments   known groups, the ambiguous results of the attitude test "set"
                 check show these experimental instruments to be unperfected.
                 Commenting on the low reliability coefficients on the ATT-INFO forms,
                 the author suggested that the affect produced by the subjects'
                 attempting control reduced the reliability. Since an error-choice
                 form which did elicit a shift in response ("Attitudes toward Russia")
                 produced as well a higher reliability coefficient, the author remarks
                 that greater disguise and greater departure from orthodox methods "is
                 the road to more <u>meaningful</u> high reliability coefficients."

                 The author offers the following suggestions for improvement.

                 > If the items were preselected by content or symbolic analysis,
                 > the errors might provide a clue as to the prevailing set of
                 > "factual" justifications which a sample is using.

                 > The more disguised the test, of course, the better.

                 > Test constructed with four error-choices to provide for
                 > "intensity" of error might prove useful for scaling items.

                 > Factual items can provide evidence of amount of information
                 > possessed by the subject, so that the amount of error-choice
                 > should be meaningful.

                 The "information test" form of these instruments seems to limit their
                 use to a well-informed population.

Sample "Nonfactual" Questions from "Information" Test

   (6)   Financial reports show that out of every dollar

         (1) 16¢   (2) 3¢   is profit.

   (17) Man-days lost because of strikes from January to June, 1946, were

         (1) 34.5 million   (2) 98.6 million

   (20) Most unions have initiation fees

         (1) over   (2) under $35.

ATTITUDES TOWARD LABOR AND MANAGEMENT (Weschler 1950)

Variable   This test attempts to measure attitudes toward labor and management;
                 more specifically, it attempts to discover bias in either the pro-
                 labor or pro-management direction through disguised "information"
                 items about labor or management.

Description   The instrument developed into two forms. Form A consisted of 40
                 forced choice items, of which 24 were straight information (or
                 factual) and 16 "nonfactual". Form B has 45 items, of which 34 are
                 factual and 11 nonfactual.. Alternate responses are either both
                 incorrect, or controversial. Since the nonfactual items offer
                 alternate answers equidistant from the truth in alternative directions,
                 selection of one alternative or the other is assumed to indicate bias
                 in either a pro-management or a pro-labor direction.

                 In Form A, pro-labor answers were scored as 1 point each for a possible
                 total of 16, in Form B, nonfactual items received varying amounts of
                 points, depending on their former usefulness in differentiating
                 between pro-labor and pro-management groups. Maximum possible pro-
                 labor score was 25.

Sample   The sample population for Form A consisted of 155 students in economic
                 of business administration classes at UCLA, and 31 union or management
                 personnel enrolled in labor relations extension courses at the
                 University's Institute of Industrial Relations.

                 The sample population for Form B consisted of 128 upper division
                 college students at the same university, majoring in Business
                 Administration or Economics. A special validation sample included
                 67 management people, 57 union officers and members, and 62 labor
                 mediators (used as control).

Reliability/   In the first test of reliability, 90 advanced Business Administration
  Homogeneity   students were given Form A, and three weeks later, Form B; the
                 correlation coefficient between the two scores was .48. The test-
                 retest reliability coefficient on a sample of 64 advanced Business
                 Administration students with an inter-test interval of two weeks was
                 .62.

                 In a third test of reliability, the author reported a tetrachoric
                 correlation coefficient of .90 on individuals scoring above and below
                 the mean on two administrations of Form B.

Validity   As a validating criterion, respondents were asked to state (anonymously)
                 whether they felt in sympathy with labor or management. It was found
                 that the pro-labor groups attained a significantly higher (at the .01
                 level) pro-labor attitude score than the pro-management group. Eleven
                 of the 16 items were found to differentiate between the two groups.
                 These items were weighted by reference to their critical ratios and
                 the weights were utilized as the basis for rescoring the test. The
                 tetrachoric correlation between pro-labor attitude scores and pro-
                 labor declaration of sympathy was .64 for sample A and .63 for Sample B.

296

Validity (continued)	In further examinations of validity, it was found that the inventory did <u>not</u> discriminate significantly between those people having active membership in a union or a management organization, probably because most of the subjects were still in college. However, the mean score of the subgroups of active union and management personnel were significantly different in the expected direction. Parental union membership also produced significantly higher means among the subjects (all at the .01 level and below). Finally, for the validation sample using Form B, it was found that while the union officers and members obtained significantly higher scores (at the .01 level) than the management people, the intended control group of mediators attained a mean score not significantly different from that of the union group.
Location	Weschler, I. R., "An investigation of attitudes toward labor and management by means of the error-choice method: I and II", <u>J</u>. <u>Soc</u>. <u>Psychol</u>., 1950, <u>32</u>, pp. 51-62 and 63-69.
Administration	Estimated administration time is 30 minutes for Form A and 34 minutes for Form B.
Results and Comments	These items are obviously dated and would have to be revised. Althoug the tetrachoric correlations observed between scores and declared sympathy is not large enough to allow for individual prediction, the author states that the test could identify the individuals on either extreme of the range.

Noting further correlations of interest: an r of .45 was observed between the individuals who scored significantly above the mean in information (factual items) and had high pro-labor attitude scores; sex, age and income were related at a low significance level to mean score differences. The author remarks that in using the error-choice method pretesting is essential so that item analysis can be made and questions weighted in terms of their discriminating ability.

It might be expected that more than 11 items in a 16 item scale would differentiate between criterion groups.

Sample Questions from the "Labor Relations Information Inventory"

1. Factual Information Questions

_____ In 1948, the majority of strikes were caused by issues over
(a) collective bargaining terms of existing agreements
(b) union recognition
_____ Industry-wide bargaining is conducted in the
(a) Anthracite industry
(b) Automobile industry
_____ During 1948, the number of unemployed in the United States averaged
(a) 1 million
(b) 2 million

2. Sample Non-factual "Error-choice" items

_____ During April of 1948, the coal and meat strikes increased the number of
workdays lost through voluntary stoppage to
(a) 10 million workdays
(b) 6 million workdays
Correct answer: 8 million workdays.
_____ During the strike wave of April, 1948, the percent of estimated working time
lost was
(a) 1.1 percent
(b) 2.2 percent
Correct answer: 1.6 percent.
_____ The 1948 increases in the price of steel were:
(a) proportional to the union's wage gains
(b) comparatively greater than the union's wage gains.
Correct answer: not accessible
_____ After one year of operation, the Taft-Hartley Act has resulted in a trend
(a) toward successful management defenses of its rights and prerogatives
(b) toward weakening the security of even the largest unions
Correct answer: controversial
_____ During the summer of 1948, the average weekly earnings of workers in the
Bituminous Coal Industry amounted to approximately:
(a) $62
(b) $78
Correct answer: $70

ATTITUDE TOWARD WORKING FOR THE GOVERNMENT (Aalto 1956)

Variable

This scale attempts to measure general attitudes toward the federal government as an employer and the desirability of federal employment.

Description

The instrument is a 70-item 5 point Likert scale. The original pool of over 100 items was compiled from statements in political science journals, modified items from other surveys, occupational information material and other popular sources. Flesch (1948) counts of reading ease indicate that the items fall in the "standard" range (65-73) and are well within the comprehension of a high school graduate.

The original item pool was pretested on a sample of college students and then later item analyzed using criterion groups in government and industry. The possible range of scores is from 70 to 350 with 210 as the neutral or undecided point. A high score indicates a favorable attitude toward government employment. Both positive and reversed items are used to reduce the effects of response set.

Sample

Four hundred ninety three government workers and 299 private business employees returned usable questionnaires. Among the government agencies which contributed questionnaires were the Verterans Administration, Bureau of Internal Revenue, Department of Agriculture and Department of Justice. In the government sample 43% held bachelor's degrees, 23% master's and 13% doctoral degrees. Only 4% had not graduated from high school. The sample is 82% male and 4% unknown, the remainder are female.

The private sample is similar in many respects to the government sample though not as representative. It is a large group of industrial and private business employees from firms in Minnesota and other parts of the United States. Less than 1% of this sample are non-high school graduates, with 61% college graduates and 28% with advanced degrees. Ninety eight percent of the subjects in this sample are classed as managerial, semi professional, or professional with professionals accounting for 80%. 7% of this sample are female and 3% are unknown.

The private sample is younger than the government sample. The majority of the private sample is in the 26-39 year old range and the majority of the government sample is between 40-65.

Reliability/
Homogeneity

A corrected odd-even split-half internal homogeneity coefficient of .94 is reported for the government sample and .96 for the private sample.

Validity

The scale items were selected from the general pool on the basis of item analysis and cross validation using both internal and "external" criteria. To be selected an item had to show at the .01 confidence level that it discriminated between high and low scorers in both validation and cross validation samples as well as discriminating between satisfied government and satisfied private employees.

Location
: Aalto, Barbara Phillips, "A Scale Measuring Attitudes Toward Working for the Government," Ph.D. Dissertation, University of Minnesota, 1955. Ann Arbor, Michigan: University Microfilms, Inc., Pub.No. 14,514. MIC 56,244.

SEE ALSO:

Aalto, Barbara, "A Scale Measuring Attitudes Toward Working for the Government," J.Appl.Psychol., 1956 (40) 398-402.

Administration
: Self administered in less than one hour. Scoring is accomplished by summing item response category weights.

Results & Comments
: As may be reasonably assumed from the content of the items this scale also functions as an index of job satisfaction for government employees. The Hoppock Job Satisfaction Blank correlates +.45 with the responses of government employees. Since there is no correlation between scale scores and the Hoppock blank for private employees there is some evidence of discriminative validity for the scale.

This scale could be useful for counseling purposes in high school or college after predictive validity studies have been carried out. It is unlikely that the instrument could be used for selection purposes because of the transparency of the items.

The uncorrected split half coefficients reported for this scale are .89 and .92 indicating that the scale could easily be shortened or broken into parallel forms. Of course, test-retest reliability studies should be carried out to verify the stability of responses.

The following norms are presented by the author for the scores of professional and managerial government employees and all private employees.

Decile	Professional and Managerial Government Employees	All Private Employees
9	290	251
8	281	241
7	275	231
6	270	220
5	266	212
4	260	206
3	254	196
2	245	187
1	234	174

References
: Flesch, R., "A New Readability Yardstick," J.Appl.Psychol., 1948 (32) 221-233.

ATTITUDES TOWARD EMPLOYMENT IN GOVERNMENT SERVICE

Read each statement and give the answer that will show how you feel about it. Mark ON THE ANSWER SHEET (X) whether you strongly agree (SA), agree (A), are undecided (U), disagree (D), or strongly disagree (SD). Check to be sure that you answer each question in the correct place on the answer sheet. ANSWER ALL ITEMS.

Example:

```
                                        SA   A   U   D   SD
Government workers have good hours.     ( ) (X) ( ) ( ) ( )
```

Read this note carefully.

The words "government service," "government workers," and "government employees," refer to jobs and workers in the career service of the federal government. They do not include those who are elected by the people, those who are appointed by the party in power, or those who are serving in the Armed Forces.

Item No.	Statement
1	I would recommend government service as a career to my friends.
*2	In a government job it is hard to make use of one's own ideas.
3	The number of government workers should be increased.
4	If I had a son, I would be willing for him to become a government worker.
5	Government work is a "good deal."
6	Government workers are chosen with more care than workers in private industry.
7	On the whole, government workers try to do their best.
8	The government is one of the best employers to work for.
*9	As a whole, government workers are second rate.
*10	Taxes are high because we have so many government employees.
*11	Government workers get by with very little work.
*12	Government jobs are often given to friends of the political party in power.
13	In the government service, the worker who does work on his own is rewarded.
*14	In a government job there is too much "red tape" in the work you have to do.
15	There are more interesting jobs in the government service than in private industry.
*16	Government jobs are dull.
17	A young person with a government job can look forward to a bright future.
18	Given a choice between the working conditions of government and private employment, I would choose the government job.
19	There are good chances for advancement in government work.
20	"Clock-watching" occurs more in private business than among government workers.
21	In general, the pay is good in government service.
*22	In government service there is no way to get rid of workers who are doing a poor job.
*23	There is more time wasted in government work than in private work.
*24	A lot of the work that government employees do is a waste of time.
25	Government employees have high standards of honesty.
*26	In a government job a person never has to think for himself.
*27	It is who you know that counts in getting a government job.
*28	Government employees sponge off the taxpayers.
*29	Government work should be looked upon as a last resort.
30	The people of this country should be proud of their government workers.
*31	In the government service a person has to have "pull" to get ahead.
32	With a choice between the salaries of private and government employment, I would choose a government job.

33 Government workers keep trying to do a better job.

*34 The work one does in a government job is affected too much by politics.

*35 Government workers do not do an honest day's work.

*36 There are too many bosses on a government job.

37 It is an honor to work for the government.

*38 The work of the government could be done with half as much money if it were run as well as a private business.

*39 If you don't like the working conditions in a government job, there is nothing you can do about it.

*40 Government workers are paid too much money for the work they do.

*41 The best workers leave government work for other jobs.

42 You are doing important work when you work for the government.

43 The most able workers get promoted in government service.

44 On the whole, government employees are as able as those working for private companies.

*45 Government jobs are so secure that there is little desire to do good work.

46 You need more schooling for the same job in government service than in private industry.

*47 A government worker does no more work than is necessary.

48 The good points about the jobs in government service are greater than the bad points.

*49 Working for the government makes a person lazy.

*50 Government employees often get mixed up with crooks and racketeers.

*51 Government workers do not care how much of the taxpayers' money they waste.

52 Government service is only a place to get experience for a better job.

*53 The experience you get in working for a private employer is worth more than experience in a government job.

54 Most government workers are deeply interested in their jobs.

55 With a choice between the security of government and private employment, I would choose a government job.

*56 Most college students would not want to work for the government.

*57 There are too many rules to follow in doing government jobs.

*58 A government job would be all right if you couldn't get another job.

59 Government workers are doing as much that is important in science as any other group.

*60 There is too much loafing on the job in government work.

61 Given my choice of working for the government or for a private employer with equal starting salaries, I would choose government employment.

62 Good college students should be urged to enter government service.

63 Most government workers are happy with their jobs.

*64 In government jobs it is hard to mix with other workers at different job levels.

65 The quality of your work counts more toward advancement in government service than in private industry.

66 It would be fun to work for the government.

67 Government employees are noted for their courteous service.

*68 Government jobs are mostly "soft" jobs.

69 In government work you have to do a day's work for a day's pay.

70 Most government employees are hard workers.

*indicates items whose scoring must be reversed.

ATTITUDES TOWARD WORKING FOR GOVERNMENT (Kilpatrick, et al. 1964)

Variable
This instrument attempts to measure whether one's attitude toward working for the federal government is more favorable than one's attitude toward working for a large private business.

Description
Five different aspects of employment were covered: opportunity for being really successful, chance of getting ahead, chance of working up in a top-level job, security, and routine and monotony.

The five pairs of items were rated by the respondent on a ten-point agree-disagree scale. The items were distributed among 45 others dealing with occupational values (see Chapter 10.)

Sample
The sample consisted primarily of a national probability sample of 1142 employed respondents from the general public and 948 general federal employees. Special supplementary samples of scientists, executives, students and teachers were also taken. Response rates averaged between 85 and 95 percent for the various samples. (See Robinson's chapter for more detail.)

Reliability/
Homogeneity
No test-retest data were collected and no inter-item correlations are presented.

Validity
No formal tests of validity were reported although relationships with background characteristics and other attitudes may be said to bear some indirect evidence on validity.

Location
Kilpatrick, F., Cummings, M. and Jennings, M. Source Book of Study of Occupational Values and the Image of Federal Service Washington, D.C.: The Brookings Institution, 1964.

Results and
Comments
Respondents were also asked a number of open-ended questions and other ratings about federal vs. private employment; these were found to reflect the same differences found in the items, namely, that government employment is seen as offering security and private business opportunity. Government employees were rated about as high on honesty and public interest as top-level businessmen, but images are less favorable for civil servants among the better-educated.

It is truly unfortunate that inter-item analyses and analyses of relations with other questions have yet to be conducted for these data, considering the high caliber of sampling and methodological procedures

Attitudes toward working for the Government

	Average Ratings	
	Public Employed Sample	Federal Employed Sample
For a young man of ability, his best chance of being successful in life lies in working for the federal government	4.4	4.4
For a young man of ability, his best chance of being reasonably successful in life lies in working for a large private business corporation	5.4	5.0
A person who works for the federal government generally has a good chance to get ahead	6.5	6.4
A person who works for a large private business generally has a good chance to get ahead	6.7	6.1
A young man of ability who starts to work in the federal civil service has a good chance of ending up in one of the top level jobs	6.4	7.0
A young man of ability who starts to work in a large private business corporation has a good chance of ending up in one of the top level jobs	7.0	7.1
Employment with the federal government offers a high degree of security	7.4	8.1
Employment with a large private business offers a high degree of security	6.1	4.8
Most jobs in the federal government are routine and monotonous	4.9	4.2
Most jobs in private business are routine and monotonous	4.7	4.0

ATTITUDE TOWARD AUTOMATION (Rosenberg 1962)

Variable
This scale purports to measure attitude toward automation as shown by responses to ten (10) subscales. The subscales are labeled Working Conditions, Employment, Wages, Training, Job Satisfaction, Collective Bargaining, Aging Problems, Safety, Control, and Home and Family Life.

Description
The scale consists of fifty Likert scaled items. Of the fifty items thirty-three are positively stated and intermixed with 17 negatively stated items. The items' relevance to automation issues and scoring direction were determined by judges. The judging staff consisted of two psychologists, one economist, one human relations specialist, and one industrial and labor relations specialist. The range of possible scores is from 50 to 250 with a score of 150 representing the neutral point. A high score was considered to be an indication of a positive attitude toward the effects of automation. Means and standard deviations for the subscale score are presented in the Results and Comments section.

Sample
One hundred and eight respondents were secured through mail administration of 240 questionnaires. All respondents were male union members, nearly all held either an elected or appointed position with the union. The majority had spent betweeen 10 and 20 years with the company for which they worked and were in the 25 to 45 year old age range. About one-third of the sample had fewer than 10 years membership in the union and the vast majority made a salary of from $5000 to $7000. Almost all were married and more than half supported four or more persons. Four-fifths had at least a high school education.

The author does not further identify the sample except to say that, "The participants were...union members from one of the major industries faced with problems of automation in the New York Metropolitan area."

Reliability/ Homogeneity
The author gives no estimate of test-retest reliability for the scale. However, the average inter-sub-scale correlation is .26 and may give a very conservative idea of reliability based on parallel forms of a test.

Validity
No claim of other than face validity can be made for this scale.

Location
Rosenberg, Jerry M., "Perception of Automation Issues, Worker Background, and Interpersonal Behavior," Ph.D. dissertation, New York University, 1962. Ann Arbor: University Microfilms, Inc., Pub.No. 63-6675.

Administration
Self administered in less than one hour. Scoring is accomplished by summing the response category weights.

Results &
Comments

Although the author set out to construct ten 5-item subscales which were to comprise the automation questionnaire it would seem that he did not succeed. The subscale intercorrelations are sufficiently high in most cases (80% are significant at $p < .05$) to assume a reasonable degree of unidimensionality.

For each subscale the possible range of scores is from 5 to 25. The author presents the following data for the subscales:

Subscale	Mean	SD
Safety	16.19	3.86
Training	15.92	3.61
Home Life	14.34	4.39
Working Conditions	14.22	3.64
Wages	13.86	3.41
Aging Problems	13.52	2.84
Collective Bargaining	12.00	3.03
Employment	11.80	3.91
Control	10.87	3.22
Job Satisfaction	9.94	4.32

This scale may prove useful in assessing workers' attitudes toward automation issues in general. However, one may reasonably expect that opinion levels will vary with industries, unions, type of employment and sex of employee. The establishment of local norms is strongly recommended. An estimate of reliability is also a desideratum for proper use of this instrument.

All items utilized a five point answer category system. The order and response weights were as follows: (1) Disagree a great deal, (2) Disagree slightly, (3) Neither disagree nor agree, (4) Agree slightly, (5) Agree a great deal. Items marked with an asterisk (*) should be scored in reverse, i.e., 5 = Disagree a great deal, 4 = Disagree, etc.

*1. Automated plants will be noisier than the more traditional assembly lines.

2. Automated factories will be cleaner than non-automated plants.

3. Increased shift work during the night hours will be acceptable by the majority of workers.

4. Bad odors in the air within the factory will be greatly reduced because of automation.

5. Automation will lead to improved lighting in the factory.

6. Automation will lead to an expanded economy with new jobs.

*7. Those displaced by automation will have considerable difficulty in finding new jobs.

*8. Unemployed workers displaced by automation will be forced to find new opportunities in other areas of the country.

9. Automation will raise our standard of living.

*10. Automation displacement will eventually throw the country into another depression.

11. Wages under automation, will increase at an even faster rate than before automation.

12. Workers in automated plants will earn a greater salary than those doing the same type of work in non-automated plants.

*13. Under automation, wages will buy less because of increasing inflation.

*14. In an era of automation, wages will become increasingly more important to worker happiness than before automation.

*15. Part of future wages may be used for retraining programs and therefore proportionately reduce take home pay.

*16. Training may be the answer to the automation problem, but no one really knows what to train for.

17. On-the-job training will increase because of the needs created by automation.

*18. Less than half the industries that are considering automated installations will invest their money for retraining.

19. Automation will produce more semi-skilled and fewer non-skilled workers.

20. The idea of retraining will be gladly accepted by workers, especially if the company pays for it.

21. Automation will increase group morale of workers on the job.

22. Automation will improve individual job satisfaction on the job.

23. Operating an automated piece of equipment should, in general, be more interesting than operating older machines that once performed the same function.

24. Automation will require more imagination to operate the machines.

25. Automation will give the worker a greater feeling of doing something worthwhile.

*26. Automation will be a major factor in many future strikes.

27. Automation will lead to a workweek of between 32-36 hours within five years.

28. The worker will be guaranteed a "fair deal" during collective bargaining over automation.

29. Negotiations over automation will improve worker pension plans.

*30. A shorter workweek will encourage workers to find a second job for additional incomes.

31. Automation will encourage older workers to retire at an earlier age provided they receive a fair pension.

*32. Workers over fifty years of age will suffer most under automation.

*33. The worker from 20-35 years of age will almost always be chosen for retraining before someone over 40 years of age.

*34. Seniority rights will be weakened as a result of automation.

*35. Older workers operating automated equipment will find the work physically easier.

36. Operating automated equipment is usually less tiring than operating older equipment.

*37. Under automation, there may be a need for increased concentration on dials which will make the jobs more tiring.

38. Automated factories will have fewer minor accidents than in older plants.

39. Automated factories will have fewer major accidents than in older plants.

40. So called "freak accidents," i.e., getting your tie caught in the machine, will be greatly reduced in an automated plant.

41. Workers will be able to talk more during working hours in an automated plant.

*42. Automation will require increased supervisory control over the employees.

43. Automation will make it easier for the employee to advance within the company.

44. Automation will improve the relationship of mutual understanding between the employee and the employer.

*45. Under automation, workers will have less to do with making decisions in the way a job should be carried out.

46. Increased leisure time, created by automation, will lead to a closer, united family home life.

47. Automation will help reduce the rate of juvenile delinquency.

48. Automation will encourage new interest in religious activity.

49. Automation will lead and encourage communities to offer more adult education courses for workers.

50. Automation, by requiring new skills will keep children off the streets by increasing interest in their school work.

ATTITUDES TOWARD EMPLOYMENT OF OLDER PERSONS (Kirchner 1954)

Variable   This scale attempts to measure the degree of stereotyping in beliefs about the capacity and functioning of older workers (over 50).

Description   This scale is comprised of 24 Likert scaled items chosen for their ability to differentiate between upper and lower portions of several sample populations. Items were chosen which represented factual and anecdotal material about older workers, stereotyped opinions, and so on. In general, the original pool of items consisted of a group of "general items relating to opinion per se and a group of informational items concerned with the action of government, labor, and management."

The possible range of scores is from 0 to 96 with 48 as the neutral or undecided point. A high score is indicative of a positive attitude toward older employees.

Sample   A total sample of 1,460 persons provided data for the final form of the scale. This included a subgroup of 590 individual interviews with a general sample of the Minnesota population, a nationwide subgroup of personnel people, and a group of 200 psychologists members of the Minnesota Psychological Association, among others. The sample included 416 women. The age range of the subjects was from 20 years to over 60 with one subgroup (N = 13) having a mean age of 69.85 years.

Reliability   Test-retest reliability coefficients ranged from .49 to .86 with an overall coefficient of .67 (N = 36 members of a supervisory training class) over a two month period. Split half (first versus last half) coefficients ranged from .60 to .92 for various subgroups. The standard error of the true scores for each sample were, however, reasonably small and uniform indicating that the scale had adequate reliability for most purposes.

Validity   Some evidence for the validity of the scale is demonstrated by the relation between age and attitude scale score. The author estimates this coefficient as +.55 but it does not hold for all subgroups within the total sample. Groups of retired union members and rank and file employees in organizations employing older workers showed more favorable attitudes than did a general sample of the state population, personnel workers, and supervisors. The data was biased through the inclusion of persons with advanced psychological training who, in general, refused to commit themselves to a position on many questionnaire items.

Location   Kirchner, Wayne K., "Attitudes Toward the Employment of Older Persons," Ph.D. Dissertation, University of Minnesota, 1954. Ann Arbor, Michigan: University Microfilms, Inc., publication number 10,031.

Kirchner, Wayne K., et al, "Attitude Toward the Employment of Older People," J.Appl.Psychol., 1952 (36) 154-156.

Administration

This scale may be either self administered or administered through the use of individual interviews. The author used in his study mail, group, and interview types of administration.

Scoring is easily accomplished through summing the item response weights. The scale probably requires less than half an hour of a respondent's time.

Results and Comments

This scale represents a somewhat unique example of adequate psychometric procedure with regard to its construction. As will be noted by cursory perusal of the other scales in this volume the mention of test-retest reliability estimates and standard error scores is quite rare. It does, however, share with most other attitude scales a lack of clear evidence for something beyond face validity.

The author recommends that the scale be used as a diagnostic instrument to determine the need for education on the part of groups directly concerned with the employment of older persons. The relative transparency of the items may mitigate the value of the scale in this regard. The heterogeneity of the sample population indicates that the scale is applicable across a wide variety of occupational categories-- with the, possible exception of psychologists.

DIRECTIONS

On this page and the following pages you will find a number of statements.

1. Read each statement carefully.
2. Choose the word that best tells how you feel about each statement.
3. Put an "X" in the space following the word.
4. Do this for all statements.

Here is an example:

There has been too much snow in Minnesota this winter.
Strongly agree___ Agree_x_ Undecided___ Disagree___ Strongly disagree___

If you strongly agree with this statement, you would place an "X" in the space following the words "Strongly agree." If you agree with the statement you would place an "X" in the space following the word "Agree," as has been done in the sample.

There are no "right" or "wrong" answers. Just tell how you feel about each statement.

Your answers are secret.

Important: In these statements when we say "Older" we mean Over 50.

1. I think older employees have fewer accidents on the job.
Strongly agree___ Agree___ Undecided___ Disagree___ Strongly disagree___

2. Most companies are unfair to older employees.
Strongly agree___ Agree___ Undecided___ Disagree___ Strongly disagree___

3. Older employees are harder to train for jobs.
Strongly disagree___ Disagree___ Undecided___ Agree___ Strongly agree___

4. Older employees are absent more often than younger employees (under age 30)
Strongly disagree___ Disagree___ Undecided___ Agree___ Strongly agree___

5. Younger people (under age 30) act too smart nowadays.
Strongly agree___ Agree___ Undecided___ Disagree___ Strongly disagree___

6. Younger employees (under 30) usually have more serious accidents than older employees.
Strongly disagree___ Disagree___ Undecided___ Agree___ Strongly agree___

7. In a case where two people can do a job about the same, I'd pick the older person for the job.
Strongly disagree___ Disagree___ Undecided___ Agree___ Strongly agree___

8. I think that Social Security payments are too small.
Strongly disagree___ Disagree___ Undecided___ Agree___ Strongly agree___

9. Occupational diseases are more likely to occur among younger employees (those under age 30.)
Strongly agree___ Agree___ Undecided___ Disagree___ Strongly disagree___

10. The older employees usually turn out work of higher quality.
Strongly disagree___ Disagree___ Undecided___ Agree___ Strongly agree___

11. I think older employees are more grouchy on the job.
Strongly disagree___ Disagree___ Undecided___ Agree___ Strongly agree___

12. I believe that older people cooperate more on the job.
Strongly disagree___ Disagree___ Undecided___ Agree___ Strongly agree___

13. Older people seem to be happier on the job.
Strongly agree___ Agree___ Undecided___ Disagree___ Strongly disagree___

14. I feel that older people are more dependable.
Strongly disagree___ Disagree___ Undecided___ Agree___ Strongly agree___

15. Most older people cannot keep up with the speed needed in modern industry.
Strongly agree___ Agree___ Undecided___ Disagree___ Strongly disagree___

16. Supervisors find it hard to get older people to adopt new methods on the job.
Strongly agree___ Agree___ Undecided___ Disagree___ Strongly disagree___

17. Older people should get higher wages for their jobs.
Strongly disagree___ Disagree___ Undecided___ Agree___ Strongly agree___

18. You'll find that the employees who are most loyal to the company are the older employees.
Strongly agree___ Agree___ Undecided___ Disagree___ Strongly disagree___

19. Older people are too set in their ways--they don't want to change.
Strongly agree___ Agree___ Undecided___ Disagree___ Strongly disagree___

20. I think older employees have as much ability to learn new methods as other employees.
Strongly disagree___ Disagree___ Undecided___ Agree___ Strongly agree___

21. I think companies should train middle-aged employees (those aged 35-50) to handle many different jobs.
Strongly disagree___ Disagree___ Undecided___ Agree___ Strongly agree___

22. I think that older employees make better employees.
Strongly disagree___ Disagree___ Undecided___ Agree___ Strongly agree___

23. I think that most younger people are too radical in their ideas.
Strongly disagree___ Disagree___ Undecided___ Agree___ Strongly agree___

24. Pay should be based on length of service rather than on what a person does (how long a person has worked in a company should count more than the amount of work he turns out).
Strongly disagree___ Disagree___ Undecided___ Agree___ Strongly agree___

OPINIONS ABOUT WORK OF THE MENTALLY ILL (Streuning and Efron 1965)

Variable — This instrument attempts to define the dimensional structure of work attitudes of former mental patients.

Description — The domain of attitudes was conceptualized as including motivation and the value of work, the opinion climate of the social context, evaluation of self and relationships with others (especially co-workers and authority figures). Based on this conceptualization, a 103 item questionnaire of 73 Likert-type and 30 true-false items was devised, administered and factor analyzed.

Sample — The respondents were 337 male veterans who had spent some time in a mental hopital, 70 percent being classified as schizophrenics. Average age was 39 and number of average years in school was 11.

Reliability/ Homogeneity — No test-retest data were reported.

A total of seven factors emerged from a factor analysis: Alienation, Stressful existence, Authoritarian work ideology, Devaluation of work, Vocational futility, Interpersonal inadequacy and Anticipation of rejection.

Validity — In a multiple regression prediction of patients who were working compared to those not working, the five factors correlated .30, significant at the .01 level. Most of the variance was explained by the Stressful existence and Devaluation of work factors.

Location — Struening, E. and Efron, H. "The dimensional structure of opinions about work and the social context", Journal of Counseling Psychology, 12, 1965, #3.

Administration — Self-administered in about 45 to 65 minutes. Factor scoring consisted of taking those items loading over .30 on the factor and scoring them one to six (from "strongly disagree" to "strongly agree"). In order to prevent confounding factor scores, an item was scored on only one factor; this is denoted by an "a" following the items presented below.

Results and Comments — Despite the orthogonality of the factor analytic results, factor scores for Alienation, Stressful existence, and Anticipation of rejection inter-correlated so highly (well over .5) as to indicate a single factor. The author also points out the relevance of his findings to the proposition that work is essential to the recovery of mental patients: he found that those who were working were just as alienated as those who did not have a job.

Factorial Structure of Opinions About Work
and the Social Context

Loading		Item

Factor 1—Alienation from a Rejecting Environment

68	69.	In spite of what some people say, the lot of the average man is getting worse.a
64	52.	Bosses usually blame their mistakes on the workers under them.a
64	65.	These days a person doesn't really know who he can count on.a
64	57.	Bosses seldom have real respect for the workers under them.a
63	44.	Most bosses who give orders don't know any more than I do.a
60	37.	Too many people in our society are just out for themselves and don't really care for anyone else.a
59	39.	The people who work hard usually aren't rewarded for it.a
57	31.	Most bosses find it easier to complain about workers than to praise them.a
56	8.	It is hard to figure out who you can really trust these days.a
55	15.	There is not much chance that people will really do anything to make this country a better place to live in.a
55	50.	Discharged mental patients always seem to end up with the worst jobs.a
54	71.	Most people don't realize how much their lives are controlled by plots hatched in secret by others.a
53	46.	When a boss finds out that someone working for him was once in a mental hospital, he is likely to find some excuse to fire him even though his work is good.a
53	42.	Most people aren't really interested in the work they do.a
52	60.	Doctors and other people who work in mental hospitals just don't understand how hard it is for a discharged mental patient to look for and find a job.a
52	34.	People don't seem to understand my way of doing things.a
51	22.	Very few employers will hire you if you tell them you were once a patient in a mental hospital.a
49	23.	Nowadays a person has to live pretty much for today and let tomorrow take care of itself.a
46	25.	Most people do as well as they do because they are afraid of losing their jobs.
45	58.	Although most women may deny it, a wife's feeling about her husband depends upon the amount of money he earns.a
44	67.	It's not true that the harder you work the more you get.a
41	28.	One of the worse parts of work is the kidding or needling you have to take from other workers.a
41	24.	I like a job where my boss is hardly ever around.a
39	38.	I often find it hard to tell if my work pleases the boss.a
39	7.	During these times a man often can't find a job even if he really wants to work.a
38	5.	I've often felt that my fellow workers didn't understand me.a
38	124.	In the past, I had a boss who made life miserable for me.
37	47.	Employers should be required by law to hire a certain number of people who have been patients in a mental hospital, if they can do the job.
37	33.	I feel like giving up quickly when things go wrong.
36	19.	I have met very few people at work that I would like to have as close friends.a
36	70.	Mental hospitals should do much more to help patients get jobs to go to when they leave the hospital.a
35	64.	It would be foolish to give up a pension to take a job that didn't pay much more than the pension.

Factor 2—Stressful Existence

64	113.	Life is a strain for me much of the time.a
64	18.	I feel that I am not my old self.a
60	35.	It is hard for me to keep my mind on what I am doing.a
59	118.	I find it hard to keep my mind on a task or job.a
-59	40.	I usually wake up feeling well rested and full of energy.a
57	116.	There have been times when I got so upset I just couldn't do my job.a
55	123.	My sleep is fitful and disturbed.a
-54	127.	I believe I am no more nervous than most others.a
50	112.	It has always been hard for me to relax when I was working.a
48	6.	I get upset even when I make a small mistake.a
48	36.	I seem to lack the drive necessary to get as much done as other people.a
48	120.	It will be harder for me to earn a living in the future.a
-46	106.	I do not tire quickly.a
46	111.	I am easily embarrassed.a
-45	126.	I am happy most of the time.a
45	54.	Even when I am with others I feel lonely.a
42	128.	I frequently notice my hand shakes when I try to do something.a
-42	14.	I feel that I can get a good job when I want it.a
42	115.	There was a time when going to work made me so nervous that I had to quit.a
42	114.	I have always been the kind of person who worried too much.a
41	103.	My poor health has kept me from holding down a steady job.a
41	33.	I feel like giving up quickly when things go wrong.a
41	9.	I get nervous when I know my boss is watching my work.a
40	3.	A full day's work often leaves me tired and worn out.a
38	20.	While working I often worry if I am doing things right.a
34	110.	While working I often worried that I would be fired.a
33	22.	Very few employers will hire you if you tell them you were once a patient in a mental hospital.
32	108.	I have had some trouble getting along with my fellow workers.
31	5.	I've often felt that my fellow workers didn't understand me.

Factor 3—Authoritarian Work Ideology

62	73.	Obedience and respect for authority should be the very first requirements of a good citizen.a
58	63.	The most important thing to look for in a job is security.a
56	72.	Some leisure time is necessary, but it is good hard work that makes life interesting and worthwhile.a
53	1.	The best way to get along in the world is to work hard and try to forget your problems.a
47	53.	It is better to do almost any kind of work rather than do nothing.a
47	59.	Working keeps my mind off troubles.a
45	61.	The best way to get along in the world is to make careful plans for the future.a
39	16.	I usually feel like doing what I am told to do.a
39	56.	People will be honest with you as long as you are honest with them.a
38	2.	One of the nice things about work is that it gives you a chance to get together with other people.a
38	51.	Considering everything that is going on these days, things look bright for the younger generation.a
38	55.	Most of the men leaving mental hospitals are capable of holding down a job if they are given a fair chance.a
37	45.	It is hard to respect yourself if you can't do a good day's work.
37	4.	A discharged mental patient has a better chance of keeping well if he has a steady job.
36	47.	Employers should be required by law to hire a certain number of people who have been patients in a mental hospital, if they can do the job.a
34	12.	My friends think of me as a hard worker.a
29	27.	I have found that other people like to work with me.a

Factor 4—Devaluation of Work

-50   32. It's hard for an able-bodied man to really respect himself if he doesn't work.[a]

48   29. Rather than rush, it is a good idea for someone leaving a mental hospital to take a rest before starting a job.[a]

39   64. It would be foolish to give up a pension to take a job that didn't pay much more than the pension.[a]

38   48. Many discharged mental patients should never try to get a job because it upsets them and will make them sick again.[a]

-37   45. It is hard to respect yourself if you can't do a good day's work.[a]

36   11. Mental hospitals try to get too much work out of patients.[a]

-35   4. A discharged mental patient has a better chance of keeping well if he has a steady job.[a]

35   26. There is no reason to knock yourself out to do better work than the next fellow.[a]

31   66. It's best to tell your boss exactly what he wants to hear.[a]

Factor 5—Vocational Futility

50   103. My poor health has kept me from holding down a steady job.

48   101. I have had trouble getting a job.

37   120. It will be harder for me to earn a living in the future.

-35   55. Most of the men leaving mental hospitals are capable of holding down a job if they are given a fair chance.

-31   30. There are still people around these days that you know you can depend on.

30   7. During these times a man often can't find a job even if he really wants to work.

Factor 6—Interpersonal Inadequacy

62   9. I get nervous when I know my boss is watching my work.

57   20. While working I often worry if I am doing things right.

54   38. I often find it hard to tell if my work pleases the boss.

45   6. I get upset even when I make a small mistake.

45   33. I feel like giving up quickly when things go wrong.

40   28. One of the worst parts of work is the kidding or needling you have to take from other workers.

39   24. I like a job where my boss is hardly ever around.

35   21. It is better to work alone than to be bothered by having others around.

35   5. I've often felt that my fellow workers didn't understand me.

Factor 7—Anticipation of Rejection

54   122. I have often had trouble getting along with my boss or supervisor.[a]

46   108. I have had some trouble getting along with my fellow workers.[a]

46   119. I have been passed up for promotion because the boss didn't like me.[a]

43   117. Troubles at work have at times driven me to drink.[a]

41   121. I have never been well liked by any of my bosses.[a]

38   124. In the past, I had a boss who made life miserable for me.[a]

-35   62. Bosses usually find fault only when there is a good reason.[a]

33   128. I frequently notice my hand shakes when I try to do something.

31   57. Bosses seldom have real respect for the workers under them.

-30   30. There are still people around these days that you know you can depend on.[a]

29   34. People don't seem to understand my way of doing things.

[a]Item included in scoring of this factor.

13. VOCATIONAL INTEREST MEASURES

The area of vocational interest has one of the oldest and most successful histories of attitude measurement. Buros' Sixth Mental Measurement Yearbook (Gryphon Press, Highland Park, N. J.: 1965) reviews 13 occupational interest instruments and identifies over 30 others, some of which have been reviewed in earlier editions of the Buros' Yearbook. Instead of getting involved in this complex area ourselves, we have attempted to translate the reviews in Buros' Yearbook into our own rating scheme, as summarized in the table on page 315.

We have taken the liberty of disagreeing with the reviewer's ratings of some characteristics, so that the table does not represent a true "content analysis". Nevertheless, the reader will probably find the overall ratings a fairly accurate reflection of the Buros' Yearbook reviewers' overall impression. Concerning the rating of particular scale features, the question may arise of whether a "0" or a "-" is less preferable. A scale for which no information on sample characteristics or normative data is available is probably to be distrusted more than one which contains normative data on an admittedly poor sample.

It can be seen from the table that the two oldest and most popular instruments--the Strong and the Kuder--clearly are considered to be at the head of their field. The Strong is rated higher than the Kuder, and the Kuder Occupational somewhat higher than the Kuder Vocational. Only three other instruments received favorable ratings: the Gordon Occupational Check List, the Inventory of Vocational Interests, and Picture Interest Inventory.

The Strong Vocational Interest Blank (SVIB) has the most impressive research record of any psychological measure outside of intelligence tests and the leading personality inventories. The SVIB has shortcomings, as any of its reviews in Buros' Yearbooks will indicate, although the scale authors seem generally aware of them and are continually attempting improvements. For example, many of the norms are based on groups sampled ten, twenty and thirty years ago and so need to be updated. The instrument also is subject to response set--in spite of the author's contention that differing item formats are used. Again, only about 20 percent of the 399 items are not of the standard three-alternative Likert format and thus possibly the items are liable to acquiescence or social desirability response biases as well. In attempts to control this last aspect, the Kuder is preferable to the Strong, although the authors of the Strong do not feel that response set is an important problem for their instrument.

It is interesting to note that the first 100 items in the SVIB are hailed as "the most powerful section of the test in terms of separating occupations from each other" (p. 4 of the 1966 Manual). In this section, the respondent is directed to indicate whether he likes, dislikes or is indifferent to each of 100 occupations. Outside of perhaps six lower-status occupations (printer, auto mechanic, farmer, toolmaker, bankteller and bank cashier), the occupations listed all fall above or close to the top fifth of the occupational status hierarchy. Contrary to what may be implied in the Manual, therefore, it is clear from this restricted range of occupations that the scale scores might not be meaningful for those individuals not headed towards or already graduated from college, a background requisite for such high status occupations.

The remaining 299 SVIB items, which comprise the attitudinal and personality side of the instrument, may be considered as excess baggage for general purposes. These items deal with favorite school subjects (36 items), favorite amusements and hobbies (48 items), general occupational activities like "writing reports" (48 items), employable kinds of people (47 items), forced-choice preference of work activities (40 items), modified forced-choice pairings of activities (40 items), and, finally, statements of personal characteristics (39 items). Considering the vast amount of normative data collected on apparently competent samples for these latter scales, some of the scales could be quite valuable measures in their own right. The normative data, however, is available only from the publisher. The entire Strong takes only about 35 minutes to complete and the latest version gives comparative information for 52 occupations.

In addition to its advantages in the matter of response set, the Kuder Occupational (Form D) has more up-to-date normative data and a somewhat wider variety of 51 occupations. The Kuder DD, a more recent version, has norms for a more restricted sample of 23 occupations. The original Kuder Vocational did not

Feature of the Scale	Strong Vocational Interest Blank	Kuder Preference Record--Occupational	Kuder Preference Record--Vocational	Gordon Occupational Check List	Inventory of Vocational Interests	Picture Interest Inventory	Guilford Zimmerman Interest Inventory	How-Well-Do-You-Know-Your-Interests	Geist Picture Interest Inventory	Curtis Interest Scale	Fowler-Permenter Interest Record	Career Finder	Qualifications Record
Items : Sampling of content	+	++	0	0	0	+	+	+	-	0	-	0	-
Item wording & simplicity	++	++	++	++	+	P	+	+	P	+	+	0	-
Item analysis	++	++	+	++	+	0	-	0	-	-	-	0	-
Freedom from Response Set: Acquiescence	0	+	+	-	++	0	-	0	+	0	0	0	0
Social desirability	0	++	++	-	+	+	-	0	+	0	0	0	0
Statistical : Sample	++	++	++	0	-	+	0	-	0	-	-	0	0
Norms presented	++	+	+	+	-	+	0	-	-	-	-	-	0
Procedures : Reliability: test-retest	++	+	+	0	+	+	0	-	-	0	-	-	-
Homogeneity	++	++	+	0	0	+	0	0	0	0	0	0	0
Discrimination of known groups	++	++	++	0	-	+	0	-	+	+	-	-	-
Cross Validation	+	0	0	0	0	0	+	0	+	0	-	-	0
Other procedures	++	+	+	+	-	+	0	-	+	+	0	0	0
Scale itself: Overall Rating	++	++	++	+	+	+	0	0	0	-	-	--	--

The above are scored according to the following scheme:

+++ Excellent and exemplary
++ Competent
+ Adequate
- Inadequate
-- Incompetent
0 No information or not enough (or too conflicting) to make a final judgment

P= Pictorial

give the individual's rating on occupational scales but on general interest categories (computational, mechanical, etc.). This last rating plan was probably not a very useful schema with which to work. For example, a high "computational" score could indicate a potential interest in being an accountant or a mathematician yet it appears from the SVIB Manual that mathematicians have more in common with scientists and artists, while accountants seem to share the outlook of businessmen. One further advantage in the Kuder D forms is the fact that certain "redundant" items have been omitted. By redundant items we refer to the choice between "Be a dentist", "Be a chemist" and "Be an accountant", which, as one Kuder reviewer has pointed out, is what the person is taking the test to find out in the first place. The Kuder D, moreover, relies on 100 items as compared to 168 for the Kuder Vocational.

While the forced-choice character of all Kuder instruments reduces the effects of response set, the ipsative scoring method introduces certain problems in interpreting scale scores; for instance, if one scores high in one area, he must score low in others. These problems are discussed in great detail in the Kuder review article appearing in the latest edition of Buros' Yearbook (1966).

The major drawback in the both the Kuder and the Strong is their inapplicability for those heading into blue-collar work. The Minnesota Vocational Interest Inventory (1965) very nicely fills in this gap. Because it arrived on the market just recently, the MVII was not reviewed in Buros' Yearbook. The instrument is the result of 20 years of careful research, however, and undoubtedly belongs in the same league with the Strong and the Kuder. The MVII, like the Kuder, requires the respondent to pick the item he most likes and the one he most dislikes from a group of three; the instrument contains 158 such triads in all. The respondent receives scores both on 21 occupational scales--such as baker, plumber--and on nine area scores--such as mechanical and electronics. Unlike the Strong and the Kuder, the MVII reports no special norms for women.

The Gordon Occupational Check List is another instrument devised for use with people who are not likely to have the benefit of college education. The items consist of 240 short simple descriptive phrases of the job requirements for what appears to be a fairly representative sample of occupations as found in the Dictionary of Occupational Titles. The item format, which consists of the respondent underlining those job descriptions which he likes and circling those which he dislikes, is of course subject to the usual response set liabilities.

The instrument seems particularly faulty because scores apparently are given on five scales based <u>a priori</u> on Roe's categories of business, outdoor, arts, technology and service (see Chapter 16), with empirical item analyses used only as an afterthought. For example, scale norms show that women score higher in the area of "business". Most of the business items, however, refer to the clerical aspect rather than the persuasive or managerial aspect of business; it seems unlikely that these three aspects of business are seen the same way by respondents. Moreover, the correlation clustering between business-arts service and outdoor-technical are so high as to indicate that <u>two</u> areas underlie the instrument, not <u>five</u>. One important feature of the instrument is that the manual does encourage the counselor to look over the whole pattern of responses; and since the average respondent underlines only about 15 items (of 240), this scanning of responses would not seem to constitute an overly difficult job. It should also alleviate most response set objections. Another good feature of the <u>Check List</u> is that the sampling of items seems to be the most systematic and representative in the interest measurement field.

There are a few other interest scales that have special characteristics in which the researcher may be interested; we will comment on these briefly. The <u>Picture Interest Inventory</u>, as the name implies, may be used on respondents with reading problems. The <u>Inventory of Vocational Interests</u> appears to have the best safeguard against social desirability bias. The <u>Occupational Interest Inventory</u>, when combined with the <u>Vocational Interest Analysis</u>, becomes an interesting two-stage procedure, in which the Occupational form can reveal in which one of six domains (Personal-social, Natural, Mechanical, Business, Arts, Sciences) the respondent has most interest. The Vocational form, in turn, will show in which aspect of the preferred domain the respondent will most likely be interested. This is a forced-choice instrument and appears to be the most competent of the few which apply to both white-collar and blue-collar work. It is not reviewed in the latest Buros' <u>Yearbook</u>, but earlier appraisal was favorable. It is available from California Test Bureau in Los Angeles.

The <u>Strong</u>, <u>Kuder (Form D)</u> and the <u>Minnesota Vocational</u> are likely to remain the basic instruments of vocational interest measurement. In Chapter 18 of this volume, we deal with the problem of occupational similarity, and will analyze the normative data available from these vocational interest inventories to help suggest some worthwhile approximate solutions to this problem. The reader may be interested to find that a number of parallels exist among the three basic interest measures. The most important of these parallels is a common distinction drawn between the individual's desire to work with people, with ideas, or with things. For previous more theoretical attempts to isolate the major factors emerging from occupational interest research, see Roe's The Psychology of Occupations (New York: Wiley, 1956) Super's The Psychology of Careers (New York: Harper, 1957) and Super and Crites' Appraising Vocational Fitness (New York: Harper and Row, 1962).

There are four other instruments not reviewed in Buros' Yearbook which may be useful enough in a guidance or selection context to warrant separate detailed review. The first two instruments fall into the "experimental but promising" category, and the latter two qualify as "possibly of interest". None is ready to be used unless the researcher is prepared to carry out detailed checks in the analysis of his data. The four scales reviewed are:

1. Selective Word Memory Test (Edel and Tiffin 1965)

2. Job Analysis and Interest Measure (Walther 1961)

3. Sales Attitude Check List (Taylor 1960)

4. Work Attitude Key for the MMPI (Tydlaska and Mengel 1953)

The Selective Word Memory Test is certainly the most intriguing of the four instruments. The Test seems fake-proof and takes only 15 minutes to complete. Respondents are asked to read over a group of sentences and then to choose from a list of 180 words the 60 which were used in the sentences. The theory behind the test is that people sensitive to certain kinds of words (in this case those with "success" overtones) are also those most likely to be fitted to related types of work. As the reader will find in the scale write-up, the evidence collected so far is impressive.

A somewhat similar technique is employed in the Job Analysis and Interest Measure, an empirically derived forced-choice instrument designed to match the respondent with the job for which he is best suited. Like the previous instrument, the measure is best used with higher-level and supervisory personnel. Most--but not all--of its psychometric characteristics are quite impressive.

The Sales Attitude Check List, as the name implies, is confined to attempting the prediction of those who will most likely be successful in the sales field. The main advantages of the instrument are the forced-choice format and lack of complete transparency, but the Check List exhibits a number of psychometrically undesirable features such as a lack of research into internal consistency and insignificant validity correlations.

The Work Attitudes Key for the MMPI also suffers from many psychometric liabilities as we point out in the "Results and Comments" section of our review of this Key. It is unfortunate that more satisfactory data is not available for such application of this widely used and competent instrument. Still, the discriminating items isolated by the authors may be of interest to employers concerned with spotting potentially unsatisfactory employees.

Four other "promising" measures not reviewed elsewhere in this volume, should be brought to the reader's attention: the SCORES battery, Job Dimensions, The Biographical Index, and the Vocational Development Inventory. The SCORES battery consists of 19 aptitude and three interest tests which provide six composite scores for Supervision, Creativity, Organization, Research, Engineering and Salesmanship. The battery, developed for the selection and placement of higher level personnel, appears to have a competent research record. It is not available for general use, however. For further information on the SCORES battery, the reader should contact American Institutes for Research, Pittsburgh, Pennsylvania.

A vast amount of high-level research has gone into McCormick, et al.'s Job Dimensions project at the Occupational Research Center at Purdue University, West Lafayette, Indiana. A major aim of the project--as in the Job Analysis and Interest Measure--is to locate the main dimensions on which it is possible to match a worker's personal traits with his job requirements and vice versa. So far, factor analysis has revealed six replicated dimensions: Overall, Mediation, Physical Output, Communications, Situational, and Environmental. Factor scores consistent with U. S. Employment Service Job Trait Requirements have been found and some impressive validity coefficients reported.

Biographical information is undoubtedly a major untapped source of significant data about potentional job performance, but no biographical research, to our knowledge, has systematically or competently surveyed and mined the universe of information of this type. The Biographical Index is no exception. While the manual for the Index summarizes some interesting results with biographical data, little of the research reviewed refers to the present instrument itself. Data on the instrument to date appear too limited and unrepresentative to warrant general use of the Index since the item inclusion is based solely on empirical correlation. Scores are available for five sub-areas: Drive to excel, Financial status, Human relations orientation, Personal adjustment and Stability. Readers interested in possible useful biographical indices of these factors should write to Psychometric Affliates, Chicago, Illinois.

The Vocational Development Inventory was recently devised as a standardized index of vocational maturity for high-school counseling work. It is comprised of both an aptitude test and an attitude test, since an individual may at the same time be mature in one area but not the other. The aptitude section consists of thirty multiple-choice items in each of five areas: Problems, Planning, Occupational information, Self-knowledge, and Goal selection. The attitude section consists of one hundred true-false and Likert-type items dealing with the person's basis for his occupational choice, his reliance on others for decision-making, his involvement in the choice process, his planful daydreaming and fantasy, and his mean-ends congruence. Research on the instrument, as described by Brayfield and Crites in Borow's Man in a World at Work (Boston: Houghton Mifflin, 1964), seems carefully and competently executed. For further information on the Inventory, see Hall's article "The Vocational Development Inventory: a measure of vocational maturity in adolescence" in Personnel and Guidance Journal, 1963, (41), 771-775.

Holland presents a valuable survey and analysis of continuing research efforts into the determinants of occupational choice in his article "Major programs of research on vocational behavior", which also appears in Borow's Man in a World at Work. The reader may find this review of research ultimately of more benefit than the instruments outlined in this section.

SELECTIVE WORD MEMORY TEST (Edel and Tiffin 1965)

Variable

The instrument is purported "to assess 'need for success' by measuring perceptual distortion to loaded stimuli in an indirect manner."

Description

The SWMT is a short pencil and paper test which requires the examinee to read a score of sentences concerned with success and failure in a business world context. After reading the sentences the examinee is required, from memory, to choose from a list of about 180 words the 60 which were used in the sentences. This subgroup is divided into words which empirically correlate either positively or negatively with managerial success and a score is determined on the basis of the number of positively correlated words chosen minus the number of negatively correlated words chosen divided by the total number of words underlined.

Sample

Validation sample: 232 managers who were all first line supervisors in a nationwide department store chain. One hundred eighteen were assigned to a primary group and 114 to a hold out group for the purpose of cross validation.

Reliability sample: 75 seniors and graduate students in Industrial management from two midwestern universities.

Fakability sample: 49 seniors and graduate students in psychology from an unnamed university.

Reliability/ Homogeneity

Test-retest reliabilities over a six week period are reported as .83 and .81 (p $<$ .001) on the student sample cited above. Split half coefficients of .88 and .91 (using Kuder-Richardson formula #20) are reported for the managerial sample.

Validity

A Pearson coefficient of .43 (p $<$ .001) is reported between SWMT scores and paired comparison ratings of managers in the hold out group of 114 people. It must be noted that this is "concurrent validity" and that the scoring was done on the basis of an item analysis of the profiles of the primary group of 118 managers from the same company. Local norms and validity studies of both the concurrent and predictive type for individual firms should be an essential prologue to the use of this instrument.

Other validity studies using the SWMT report a phi coefficient of .61 for a cross validated study using 287 managers, a phi coefficient of .41 for a cross validated study of 57 managers from 3 companies, ϕ = .78 for 18 managers of a large chain of department stores, and ϕ = .74 for 16 airline supervisors.

Location

Information on the use of this test may be obtained from:

Eugene C. Edel, Psychological Research Branch, Personnel Management Research Division, National Security Agency, Fort George G. Meade, Maryland.

and

Joseph Tiffin, Department of Psychology, Purdue University, Lafayette, Indiana.

Administration   Self administered in about one quarter hour. Scoring may be accompli
through use of a stencil in less than two minutes per person.

Results and
Comments   That the <u>SWMT</u> is virtually unfakable seems evident from a
cursory examination of the format. A fakability study conducted by
the authors yields results which confirm this. Spearman rank-order
correlation coefficients relating "true" and "faked" scores are
reported as .86 and .85--in the same range as those found in the
reliability studies.

               The <u>SWMT</u> is a well constructed, well tested instrument and
should prove useful in future research. It is, however, still an
experimental instrument (as are most instruments in this area) and
the authors' caveat bears repeating here.

               "Although the results reported above are highly
               favorable, the <u>SWMT</u> is not yet ready for unqualified use
               in an industrial setting. The validation study reported
               provides an estimate of the <u>concurrent</u> validity of the
               SWMT. However,..., there is a great need for a long-
               range study which would assess this instrument's <u>predictive</u>
               validity over a longer time interval. Also, the faka-
               bility study, while encouraging, was conducted on relatively
               small samples and utilized the college student population.
               The fakability of this test should be assessed on larger
               samples, from actual applicant populations, under realistic
               employment conditions."

References   Edel, E.C. and Tiffin, J., "A 'motivational' measure of managerial
               success") Midwestern Psychological Association Convention,
               Chicago, Illinois, April, 1965.

               Edel, E.C. and Tiffin, J., "The reliability and fakability of a
               motivational measure of managerial success   American Psychological
               Association Convention, Chicago, Illinois, September, 1965.

Instrument   Examples of text material in the <u>SWMT</u>:

"Our most embarrassing problem is with those weak men who have established a permanent relationship with the company, but who can never be promoted.

He surrounded himself with brilliant, dominant, aggressive young men who produced or were sacrificed."

Examples from word list:

        concerning
        enemy (+)
        promising (-)
        unfit (+)
        inefficient
        aggressive (-)

The symbols in parenthesis indicate the empirically determined direction of correlation with ratings.

JOB ANALYSIS AND INTEREST MEASURE (Walther 1961)

Variable   The JAIM is a self description inventory containing items relating to interests, attitudes preferences and beliefs in a wide range of topics. The inventory provides scores on 37 subscales relating to work content, work orientation, organizational behavior, etc.

Description   The latest version of the JAIM (form 663) contains 125 items having from 2 to 5 response options. The response categories are scaled on the basis of empirically derived weights. The scores are reported as standard scores with a mean of 200 and standard deviation of 40.

      The inventory attempts to measure the fit between the individual and the job. Recognizing that personality characteristics (used in the broadest sense) may account, in large part, for success or failure on a job this inventory attempts to measure those characteristics which relate to success in a job and provide a matching description of the individual. This approach is based on the following assumptions:

1. Jobs establish behavioral requirements, and provide opportunities for personal satisfaction and feelings of value.
2. Individuals bring to the job a behavioral style, preferences, and criteria for the judgment of success; and that
3. The degree of match between job and the individual, in these dimensions, crucially influences how well the individual will perform in the job. (Walther, 1964, p. 2)

The author further states:

If the behavioral requirements of the job are within the capabilities of the individual and are also in tune with his behavioral style, he will in all probability do good work. If he has the required capabilities but the job is not particularly in line with his behavioral style, he will do good work only if he is adequately motivated by considerations extrinsic to the job and if he is not in competition with individuals whose behavioral style is consistent with the requirements of the job. If his behavioral style is antagonistic to the behavioral requirements of the job, he is likely to fail no matter how hard he tries.

A reasonably well adapted individual knows what he likes and dislikes and what works or does not work for him. Therefore, his behavioral style can be measured by a self-descriptive questionnaire administered under non-threatening circumstances.

Sample   The normative group for JAIM reports represents 4,361 applicants who took the U.S. State Department's Foreign Service Officer examination in 1963. The sample is 83% male with a modal age of 21-22 years and 94% in the age range of from 21 to 30 years. Only 12% had 3 or fewer years of college, the rest were either college seniors or degree holders. Thirty percent of the sample came from the Middle Atlantic states, 19% from East North Central states, and 15% from the Pacific states. The sample was heavily loaded (42%) with persons whose under-graduate major was History, Geography, Political Science, or Law.

Reliability/ Homogeneity

An estimate of the reliability of the final form (663) is dif-ficult to establish from the data presented by the author. Several test-retest studies on preliminary forms have yielded average test-retest reliabilities of .85 (two days) and .72 (8 months). The in-ternal homogeneity of the test is estimated at about .61.

Validity

An extended account of the validation studies using the JAIM is beyond the scope of this report. The interested reader is referred to the JAIM manual.

In brief there seems to be sufficient evidence to suggest that the JAIM might be a useful instrument in predicting performance, turnover, and promotion. Several cross-validated predictive studies are reported and a large number of concurrent validity studies are also mentioned in the manual.

Location

Walther, Regis, _Job Analysis and Interest Measurement_ (manual), Distributed for research purposes by Educational Testing Service, Princeton, New Jersey.

Administration

"The _JAIM_ may be administered either individually or to large groups. Answers are recorded on a specially prepared answer sheet for machine scoring. A soft pencil must be used and errors must be completely erased. It is desirable, but not essential, that the JAIM be given under test conditions. Useful results have been obtained by mailing it to the home of the subject with no limitations on the circumstances under which he completes it.

"It has been found that it requires about 50 minutes for the average person working in a white collar job to complete the JAIM and almost all will finish it within 60 minutes. There is no time limit, but subjects should be encouraged to work as rapidly as possible.

"Since it is important that a response be recorded for every item, effort should be made to eliminate non-responses. It is also important to emphasize strongly that no marks are to be made on the booklet it-self, and that the choices are to be recorded on the answer sheet only.

"At the present time scoring keys for the _JAIM_ are not available. Arrangements for scoring must be made through the Office of Special Tests, Educational Testing Service, Princeton, New Jersey, or through the author." (_JAIM_ manual, see above "Location")

Results and
Comments

While the <u>JAIM</u> is still an experimental instrument it appears that it may have significant potential for industrial use. The inventory seems able to distinguish between occupational groups as well as between performance levels within groups. It may prove useful in making selection and placement decisions once local norms have been established. And, it may be used for counseling high school students if it is shown to have reasonable stability over time. Like any other instrument mentioned in this volume the <u>JAIM</u> should <u>not</u> be used as the sole or primary determinant when making decisions about individuals. Further reliability, validity and fakability studies must be done before widespread usage can be recommended.

The <u>JAIM</u>'s weaknesses lie in its low face validity for the layman, and the fact that 37 scales are derived from a total of 125 items. The face validity question is not serious since many of the items do seem somewhat job related and there are only a few "personal" questions dealing with moral values. It is difficult to imagine that a testee would be offended by this test, which is sometimes the case with personality instruments.

The large number of subscales derived from relatively few items means that there are either very short subscales or considerable overlap of items from scale to scale. Factor analytic studies have shown that the apparent variables measured by <u>JAIM</u> are relation to authority, interpersonal relationships, leadership decision styles, leadership motivational styles, and reaction to aggression. Further work is required, however, before these factors should be considered to be exhaustiv

The <u>JAIM</u> is distributed only for research purposes at this time.

References

Walther, R.H., "Self-description as a Predictor of Success or Failure in Foreign Service Clerical Jobs," <u>J.Appl.Psychol</u>., 1961 (45) 16-21.

_____, "Self-description as a Predictor of Rate of Promotion of Junior Foreign Service Officers," <u>J.Appl.Psychol</u>., 1962 (46) 314-316.

Instrument   Several sample items from JAIM are presented below:

21. How lucky do you feel you have been?

   a. Almost always lucky
   b. Usually lucky
   c. Neither lucky nor unlucky
   d. Somewhat unlucky
   e. Very unlucky

38. In your work you like to

   a. Be guided by professional standards and practices
   b. Be able to use initiative and resourcefulness
   c. Have definite procedures and written instructions which you
      can follow
   d. Be told what you are expected to do and how to do it

89. It is most important to

   a. Have faith in something
   b. Be intelligent and resourceful
   c. Be kind and considerate

74. People are most likely to be influenced by

   a. Requests from people they like
   b. Orders from someone in authority
   c. Opinions of qualified experts

SALES ATTITUDE CHECK LIST (Taylor 1960)

Variable   This test claims to measure basic behavioral predelictions which are associated with success in a wide range of sales occupations.

Description   The instrument contains 31 forced choice tetrads on which the individual is asked to indicate for each tetrad, the item most descriptive and the item least descriptive of himself. The forced choice format is the usual arrangement of two desirable and two undesirable traits matched for social acceptance.

A score is based on the number of apparent success relevant items selected plus the number of apparent non-success relevant items not chosen. The possible tetrad item score ranges, therefore, from 0 to 2. Since only 27 of the 31 tetrads are actually scored the maximum possible score using the a priori key is 54. The reported range of scores is from 14 to 43.

Sample   The originial pool of items was collected from participants in a management training course at Western Reserve University. Several validi studies have been carried out and the relevant samples are described belo

Reliability   "... the authors have not attempted to determine the reliability limits of the instrument." *

Validity   In a study of 197 new car salesmen a correlation between average monthly earnings and SACL is reported as .31. The salesmen represented all cost levels of cars and were from different geographical locations. Average monthly earnings were therefore corrected for locale.

A study of 23 office equipment salesmen did not result in a significant correlation between SACL and average monthly sales or number of orders written.

In a study of Railroad Traffic salesmen only one correlation in five is significantly different from zero when SACL scores and ratings of overall performance are compared.

It would appear that at this time this instrument may best claim to have face validity on the basis of its construction method.

Location   Science Research Associates, Inc., Sales Attitude Check List, Chicago: SRA, 1960.

Administration   Self administered. No time limit is advised since most people will finish in 15 minutes. Scoring is accomplished through the use of a "self scoring" answer sheet similar to the SRA Supervisory Index. Individual raw and percentile scores may be obtained in a few minutes.

*Taylor, E. K. Manual for Sales Attitude Check List. Chicago: SRA, 1960 p.8.

**Results &
Comments**

The validity studies reported here were of the concurrent type (present employee) and it may be that predictive studies carried out on less homogeneous populations will yield better results. It is <u>not</u> recommended that this instrument be used for selection purposes until local validity studies have been completed. The assumption that a high score on the <u>a priori</u> key is better than a low one rests on shaky ground in view of the lack of significant correlations so far reported.

As may be seen from the abstracted table below, the approximate median scores vary widely across groups. This further emphasizes the need for item analysis and local validity studies.

Persons interested in conducting validity studies with this instrument are encouraged to contact the authors. Inquiries may be addressed to:

Industrial Division
Science Research Association Inc.,
259 East Erie Street
Chicago 11, Ill.

or

Personnel Research & Development Corp.,
11800 Shaker Boulevard
Cleveland 20, Ohio

NORM TABLE (abstracted)

Group	Approximate median raw score	Approximate semi-interquartile range
Automobile salesmen N = 197	26	8
Utility salesmen N = 54	29	9
Office equipment salesmen N = 141	30	8
Applicants for sales and sales managerial positions N = 180	31	7
Freight traffic salesmen N = 95	32	7

References

Taylor, E. K., et al, "A Short Forced-Choice Evaluation Form for Salesmen," <u>Personnel Psychol</u>., (6) 1953, pp. 393-401.

Taylor, E. K., and Hilton, A., "Sales Personnel Description Form: Summary of Validities," <u>Personnel Psychol</u>., (13) 1960, pp. 174-179.

Instrument   INSTRUCTIONS:

This form contains sets of phrases which are commonly used to describ
attitudes and behaviors of salesmen. Think of your own performance as a
salesman when you read them over and find the one phrase of each set of
four which describes you best. Then put an "X" in the box with an "M" in
it to indicate that this phrase is MOST DESCRIPTIVE of you. Then look for
the phrase in the set which least applies to you and put an "X" in the box
with an "L" in it to indicate that the phrase is LEAST DESCRIPTIVE. In
each set you should mark one phrase as "M" and one phrase as "L."

SAMPLE ITEMS: M   L

1.   I am emotionally disturbed at home.   ☐   ☐
      I get reports out on time, all the time.
                                                         ☐   ☐

      I have good ability in handling people.   ☐   ☐

      I have constant complaints.   ☐   ☐

2.   I enjoy life in general.   ☐   ☐

      I must be lead through new routines.   ☐   ☐

      I show sincere interest in welfare of customers.   ☐   ☐

      I will lie to my customers.   ☐   ☐

WORK ATTITUDE KEY FOR THE MMPI (Tydlaska and Mengel 1953)

Variable   This key is composed of a select sample of <u>MMPI</u> items found to discriminate ". . . between individuals whose personality organization expresses desirable attitudes toward work and good motivation toward it and individuals whose work attitude is notoriously poor."

Description   Fifty-eight items from the <u>MMPI</u> were preselected by judges on the basis of their feeling that a deviant response to a given item would give the judge an insight into the general motivational pattern and work attitude of an applicant for employment. The judges were three persons teaching industrial psychology and four personnel or employment managers with an average of 15 years experience. Of the 58 items, 37 were shown to discriminate between the good and poor workers in the sample and were retained for the scale. Many of the items retained seem to be concerned with bodily functions suggesting that hypochondriasis might be a factor in poor work attitudes.

Sample   The "good worker" sample consisted of 50 chemical company employees with two or more years of satisfactory service. The author does not mention the sex of the subjects.

The "poor work attitude" subjects were 60 white male air force personnel of whom 43 were AWOL cases, eight malingerers, seven disciplinary problems, and two miscellaneous cases.

The samples were matched on age, education, general occupational level, marital status and I.Q. "The typical subject was about 27 years old, average I.Q., completed the eleventh grade and was more likely to be married than single."

Reliability/   The author reports no estimate of reliability or homogeneity.
Homogeneity
Validity   The 37 items selected for the final scale are reported to distinguish between "good" and "poor" employees at at least the .01 level using χ^2. The derived key was then folded back and the two groups were rescored for the purposes of establishing a cutting score.

Location   Tydlaska, Mary and Robert Mengel, "A Scale for Measuring Work Attitude for the MMPI," <u>J.Appl.Psychol.</u>, 1953 (37) pp. 474-477.

Administration   The scale can be self administered separately or scored as part of the whole <u>MMPI</u>. The 37 item scale should not take the average person more than 20 minutes to complete. Scoring is accomplished by adding the number of deviant responses.

Results and Comments

Notwithstanding the authors' efforts to identify their key as an "experimental" instrument, this scale hardly follows recommended procedures.

Many knowledgeable psychologists have remarked that scores on a scale should tell us at least as much as we already know. In the case of this work attitude key the items were preselected on the basis of their probable diagnostic ability. This study merely confirmed that about 2/3 of the items were able to discriminate between populations. This, of course, is desirable but offers little in the way of new insights.

The samples chosen by the authors leave a great deal to be desired. The value in being able to differentiate poor air force personnel from good civilian workers is not immediately apparent. How much variance in the subjects' scores is due to the radically different environments in which they work? It is also not clear whether or not the two populations were matched for sex. The "good" and "poor" nature of the samples raises some interesting questions. For example, would it be legitimate to equate AWOL offenses (2/3 of the military sample) with incidental absence in the industrial sample? To say the least, the authors were not clear in their statement of the validity and comparability of their criteria measures.

The technique of item analyzing a test and then rescoring it using only those items which were found to discriminate between the criterion groups is not only logically invalid but misleading. When a scoring key or the selection of items is based on a tryout sample, a validity coefficient must be based on one or more separate cross validation samples--<u>not</u> on the tryout group or a larger group of which the tryout sample is a part.

Since more than 78% of the items on the scale are scored in the "true" direction the questions of response set and fakability are raised. The authors investigated neither of these questions.

The lack of an estimate of the reliability for this scale in addition to the many other insufficiencies mentioned above serve to preclude its use in any but the most experimentally oriented applications

Instrument   MMPI booklet number of items   MMPI booklet number of items
for which the deviant response   for which the deviant response
is "TRUE"   is "FALSE"

13, 16, 32, 35, 40, 41, 59, 84,   3, 9, 88, 164, 207, 257, 318,
109, 112, 170, 244, 250, 259,   407
272, 301, 312, 331, 335, 343,
389, 395, 404, 406, 435, 487,
507, 526, 549

     A three-page table listing the 37 items, MMPI booklet number,
proportions of good and poor workers/question, etc., may be ordered
as Document 4080 from Chief, Photoduplication Service
                     ADI Aux Publishing Project
                     Library of Congress
                     Washington 25, D.C. $1.25

14. OCCUPATIONAL STATUS MEASURES

For a long time, occupational status has been the backbone of empirical sociology. Factor analytic investigations into the various scales that have been proposed have invariably found such scales to be measuring essentially the same underlying dimension (Stefflre 1959, Haer 1957, Kahl and Davis 1955). Status gradations have held up so well that some recent authors have suggested that ratio-scaling procedures may be as applicable as the usual approach using ordinal or interval scale indices (Hamblin and Smith 1967). We still find the six interval-scale and three ordinal-scale measures reviewed below to be more than sufficient for most purposes. As each measure has advantages and disadvantages peculiar to the research problem at hand, it may be worthwhile first to discuss these qualities comparatively. The nine scales considered in this section are:

1. Socio-Economic Status Scale (Duncan 1961)

2. Socio-Economic Status Scores (Bureau of Census 1963)

3. Occupational Ratings (North and Hatt 1947, 1965)

4. Index of Status Characteristics (Warner, et al. 1949)

5. Index of Social Position (Hollingshead and Redlich 1958)

6. Index of Class Position (Ellis, et al. 1963)

7. Class Identification (Centers and others 1949-1966)

8. Facets for Job Evaluation (Guttman 1965)

9. Occupation Scale (Warner, et al. 1949: part of the Index of (4) above)

We find the standard Duncan Socio-Economic Status Scale to be superior for most survey and large sample situations. The scale was devised from 1950 Census aggregate data on the average income and education level of persons in each Census occupational category. Weights for these two variables were based on regression equations relating North-Hatt ratings (see below) with 1950 Census income and education figure for 45 of the 90 North-Hatt occupations. Because the scale was compiled solely from these two objective characteristics, certain anomalies appear. For example, since clergymen typically earn small salaries, their Duncan score is considerably below that found by the more subjective procedures.

In the blue-collar world, large differences are found among semi-skilled workers in various industries. Although this "situs" factor has been found to reflect important differences between workers (see Chapter 16), much of the difference might be considered as spurious regional variation. For example, factory workers in such Southern industries as the tobacco and textile industries have lower levels of education and income than workers in such Nothern industries as the printing and photographic industries. On the other hand, the researcher may want to retain these distinctions in his analysis. Another anomaly appears in certain occupations where apprentices have higher status ratings than those regularly employed in the same occupations. For these reasons, Duncan does not recommend that the scale be used for comparisons within certain regions of the country or within certain segments of the status hierarchy, like skilled workers. Not only are scores available for overall ratings (running from 0 for a laborer in the tobacco industry to 96 for a dentist), but decile score are also available whic tell in what tenth of the population the person's occupational group fell in 1950.

The Bureau of the Census itself has devised <u>Socio-Economic Status Scores</u> for occupations based on 1960 Census income and educational material without resort to weightings based on occupational prestige ratings. The reader will notice that these Census Bureau scores would seem to correlate highly with the Duncan scores, despite apparent differences in their derivation. For the Census scores, percentile ratings for income and educational ranking in the population were averaged to determine the score for each occupation group. The computation of an individual's total score depends on his average percentile rating for income, occupation and education. Thus, while ten percent of the population falls in each tenth score range for each of the three characteristics, the overall distribution of status scores is more normal (i.e., bell-shaped) than uniform. Hence, three and a half percent of the population scores between 90 and 99 (high status), but over 15 percent of the population scores between 50 and 59. Because of gradual changes in income and education distributions in the United States, it seems to us that the suggested total socio-economic status ratings will become less and less useful than the ratings which are given to occupations. Even more important in this Census Bureau work may be the procedures for identifyin status inconsistency (see Chapter 15), and the data which Nam and Powell (1965) present showing the usually unwanted effects of race, rural-urban location, and stage in the life cycle, on socio-economic status scores.

In contrast to the Census scores, the North-Hatt Occupational Ratings rely solely on subjective occupational ratings of representative samples of respondents to measure occupational status. The respondents are asked to rate their "own personal opinion of the general standing that a job has" on a five category scale: excellent, good, average, somewhat below average, and poor. Scores can range from 100 (all "excellent" ratings) to 20 (all "poor" ratings), although the obtained ratings range from 33 (shoe shiner) to 96 (Supreme Court Justice). The Occupational Ratings are somewhat limited by the fact that scores are available on only 90 occupations as compared to the over 500 occupation scores available in the Duncan SES Scale. In addition, the average rating of 70 indicates a bias toward over-sampling high status occupations. In further qualification, it should be noted that the respondent's own social status and familiarity with various occupations have been found to affect scores. Lowered reliability has also been found for occupations in the middle of the status scale. Although Guttman scale analysis of Hatt's (1950) data failed to generate the hypothesized single overall prestige dimension, Hatt did find internally homogeneous scales within the following eight occupational "situs" groups: Political, Professional, Business, Recreation, Agriculture, Manual, Military and Service. Thus, within political occupations, for example, Hatt reported that people in national positions rated higher than these in local positions, while within the recreation and aesthetics area people in the "high" arts rated higher than journalists, who in turn rated higher than recreation workers.

Overall occupational ratings have been found to be highly stable over time (r=.99 from 1947 to 1963) and across social systems (see Hodge, Treiman and Rossi 1965 and Hodge, Siegel and Rossi 1965). Compared to the Duncan scores, however, the restricted range of occupations severely limits general survey analysis usage at present. However, Robert Hodge (personal communication) at NORC is currently analyzing prestige ratings collected on over 400 occupational titles, although final results are not expected before 1969. Still, one may prefer to substitute some of current North-Hatt ratings which are discrepant from Duncan corresponding ratings. For example, the Duncan scale seems to underrate clergymen, farmers, and certain blue collar workers (e.g., machinist, carpenter) while overrating entertainers, newspaper personnel and sanitation workers. No satisfactory answers to the problem of rating farmers—who earn much of their income in kind—seem to have been proposed in any of the systems reviewed in this chapter; special notice should be given to income, farm size, farm condition, etc., before assignment of status scores to farmers.

Warner, et al.'s Index of Status Characteristics and Hollingshead and Redlichs' Index of Social Position undoubtedly would intercorrelate highly, although we know of no empirical comparison between the two. Warner, et al.'s ISC is based on weighted seven-point scales for the following characteristics (with weights in parentheses): occupation (4), source of income (3), type of house (3) and dwelling area (2). Hollingshead and Redlich's ISP uses education (a seven-point scale, weighted 5) and two of the same variables used by Warner, et al.--residential area (a six-point scale weighted 6) and occupation (a seven-point scale weighted 9). Scores on ISC vary from 12 to 84 and on ISP from 20 to 134, although both sets of authors ultimately reduce their schemes to five classes. Due to the fact that both indices rely on familiarity with the person's residential area, their applicability may be limited to surveys of single communities. One important feature of the Warner Index is its seven-point occupation scale, probably the most sophisticated short classification available.

Also highly correlated (r=.86) with Hollingshead and Redlich's measure is the Index of Class Position suggested by Ellis, et al. The index is based on two factors: the person's occupation (rated on the seven-point Hollingshead and Redlich scale) and his response to a two-part question regarding his subjectively perceived social class (see the reference to Centers below). Scores vary from 2 to 12. Ellis, et al. present a number of empirical relations in which their measure usually emerges as a slightly better predictor than Hollingshead and Redlich's index. As a cautionary note, it should be mentioned that the sample on which their study was based was a small and atypical one and that the Index has yet to be extended to more representative samples. In contrast to the indices reviewed in the previous paragraph, the ICP is applicable to multi-community research. We would suggest that the seven-point Warner, et al. occupational scale be substituted for that of Hollingshead and Redlich if one decides to use the Index of Class Position.

As the range of possible score values decreases (the Ellis, et al., Index has only 11 possible values), we appear close to crossing the arbitrary and nebulous boundary between interval and ordinal scales. Indeed, one of the first steps that Warner, et al. and Hollingshead and Redlich took with their scale scores was to reduce them to five ordered categories.*

---

*Hence, as Landecker (1960) points out, these are hardly to be thought of as five distinct social classes, as classifications across adjacent classes are subject to a great deal of unrelaibility. Landecker finds it more appropriate to talk of "class" distinctions only at the top of the occupational status structure.

There exist three further status scales which seem to us to be more appropriately called ordinal scales. One is the Warner, et al. seven-point ordinal scale, which is described as part of their Index of Status Characteristics. The other two status scales are not based on occupation per se but on subjective evaluations of one's class position (Center's question) or on characteristics of one's present occupational responsibilities (Guttman).

Center's inclusion of the term "working class" represented a major advance in measuring class identification. Up to this time (1945), only three class alternatives (upper, middle and lower) had been presented to respondents, and the "middle" response was chosen by almost 90 percent of those interviewed. A more equitable distribution between working and middle class resulted from Center's innovation. There is some question as to the representativeness of Center's original sample; noticeable differences are apparent between his distribution and that obtained from more recent Survey Research Center studies which use more refined sampling methods. Changing single words or phrases in class identification questions appears to affect resulting responses seriously (Hamilton 1966). Landecker (1963) maintains that the Center's question taps only one of six possible aspects of "class consciousness". He proposes a typology that could be used to generate more complex and more adequate indices of class identification.

Guttman's Facets for Job Evaluation were devised for the purpose of setting up in Israel equitable civil service salaries that were not basically dependent on factors conceived of as extraneous, such as perceived importance of the occupation, scarcity of people in the occupation, the number of people one supervised, and level of education. In this instrument, either the respondent or an outside judge rates the respondent's occupational duties on four three-alternative items and one four-alternative item. The cutting point for each item alternative defines a total of 12 steps along a Guttman multi-category scale. The items are short and appear to represent basic and reliably rated job features which do not depend on a person's line of work, as the author intended. Unfortunately, we do not have any quantitative data on the construction of the index.

There have been countless other indices and schemes designed to reflect occupational class but, to our knowledge, the instruments reviewed here represent those most widely used and widely applicable. We have chosen not to present one particular genre of indices--those based on household characteristics and possessions. While there is little, if anything, objectionable in attempting to index status by noting the characteristics of the respondent's dwelling unit, living standards and possessions change so radically over time that Chapin's revised 1952 scale seems rather outdated today, as does Sewell's Farm Status Scale (both measures are described in Miller, 1964).

The same obsolescence factor may also be inherent in a 55 interval scale devised for West Germany by Scheuch and Ruschemeyer (1960) which depends on rating of personal possessions. This scale laudably considers many other diverse status characteristics, such as theatre attendance and type of books read. The scoring scheme is weighted as follows:

I	Income of main provider	9	points maximum
	Per capita income of household	6	" "
	Ratio room-per-person	3	" "
	Index of possession of valued goods	3	" "
II	Occupation of main provider	12	" "
III	Level of education	9	" "
	Reading level	6	" "
	Concert attendance	3	" "
	Theatre attendance	3	" "
		54	points maximum

The following distribution of status was found for a sample of 420 respondents in West Germany.

		C	
11.9%	Lower lower stratum	0-13 points	
41.0%	Upper lower stratum	14-20	"
		B	
22.4%	Lower middle stratum	21-26	"
15.9%	Middle middle stratum	27-34	"
4.3%	Upper middle stratum	35-40	"
		A	
3.1%	Lower upper stratum	41-48	"
0.0%	Upper upper stratum	49-54	"
1.4%	No classification possible		

(n = 420)

REFERENCES

Hamilton, R., "Reply to Tucker", American Sociological Review, 1966, 31, 857.

Haer, J., "Predictive utility of five indices of social satisfaction", American Sociological Review, 1957, 22, 541-6.

Hamblin, R. and Smith, Carole "Values, status and professors", Sociometry, 1966, 24, 183-197.

Kahl, J. and Davis, J., "A comparison of indices of socio-economic status", American Sociological Review, 1955, 20, 317-325.

Hatt, P., "Occupation and social stratification", American Journal of Sociology, 1950, 55, 538-43.

Hodge, R., Siegel, P. and Rossi, P., "Occupational prestige in the United States: 1925-1963" in Bendix, R. and Lipset, M. (eds.), Class Status and Power New York: Free Press, 1965.

Hodge, R., Treiman, D. and Rossi, P., "A comparative study of occupational prestige", in Bendix and Lipset op. cit.

Landecker, W., "Class boundaries", American Sociological Review, 1960, 25, 868-877.

Landecker, W., "Class crystallization and class consciouness", American Sociological Review, 1963, 28, 219-229.

Miller, D., Handbook of Research Design and Social Measurement New York: David McKay, 1964.

Nam, C. and Power, Mary, "Variations in socio-economic structure by race, residence and life cycle", American Sociological Review, 1965, 30, 97-103.

Scheuch, E. and Ruschemeyer, D., "Scaling social status in Western Germany", British Journal of Sociology, 1960, 11, 151-168.

Stefflre, B., "Analysis of the inter-relationship of ranking of occupations", Personnel Guide J., 1959, 37, 435-8.

SOCIO-ECONOMIC STATUS SCALE (Duncan 1961)

On the following pages we present the abridged Census occupational code (United States Bureau of Census 1960) together with the corresponding occupational titles. Preceding these two listings is a new, simplified, three-digit identification number which has been recently instituted for Survey Research Center studies. Occupations are grouped under the familiar eight-category Census Bureau system devised by Alba Edwards over 30 years ago.

Following this identification information are four socio-economic status ratings: the original Duncan scores, the Duncan decile score, the Census Bureau SES score, a four-category class score devised by the Survey Research Center. We will briefly comment on the Duncan scores in this section; in the section following the listings we present some brief information on the Census Bureau scores.

The final three columns report further Census Bureau population information that may be of interest and use to researchers: the percentage of the total working population codable into each occupation in the 1960 census, the percentage of women employed in each occupation, and the total percentage increase or decrease in membership of each occupational grouping between 1950 and 1960. These figures are derived from pages 425-430 of Wattenberg and Scammon (1965).

In our introductory remarks we briefly described how the Duncan score was derived. Readers interested in more detail should consult the original source (Reiss, et al. 1961). Duncan scores are not available for members the armed forces, live-in laundresses and those not employed.

We caution readers against using the Census code which follows for occupational coding purposes. One can not master occupation coding overnight as there are many subtleties in this art, especially for blue-collar occupations; certainly, one should reserve adequate time for training and cross-checking. Anyone planning any sort of detailed occupation coding should heed a number of sound recommendations made by McTavish (1964). The introduction to the Census Bureau's publication (1960) is also strongly recommended for a number of occupational distinctions that we have omitted from the following abridged code. The Survey Research Center is planning to print a shortened set of occupational coding instructions for the Census occupational index in the near future; it is our understanding, however, that the Census publication is currently out-of-print.

In addition to the basic two-digit code, we have listed the Duncan Decile Score. This score puts the original score in perspective regarding the rest of the population. Hence, the top tenth of the population (that is, decile 9) range in occupational scores from 66 to 96, while the next tenth ranges only from 55 to 65. Those in the 70-79th percentile have an even smaller range, 40 to 49.

The modified white-collar, blue-collar code was developed at the Survey Research Center by Richard Rice in order to correct intuitive notions that there are some misclassifications in the broad Census Bureau categories (for instance, "newsboy"does qualify as a white-collar job) and in order more adequately to reflect real status differences in the white-collar vs. blue-collar distinction.

The following categories are used:

1. High status white-collar
2. Low status white-collar
3. High status blue-collar
4. Low status blue-collar
5. Farm occupations

The devision between high and low status was determined by finding the median score separately within the white-collar domain and within the blue-collar domain. Those occupations falling above their respective medians were coded "high" and those falling below were coded "low".

References

McTavish, D., "A method for more reliably coding detailed occupations into Duncan's socio-economic categories" American Sociological Review, 1964, 29, 402-406.

Reiss, A., Duncan, O. Hatt, P. and North, C., Occupations and Social Status New York: The Free Press of Glencoe, 1961.

United States Bureau of the Census, 1960 Census of Population, Alphabetical Index of Occupations and Industries Washington; U. S. Government Printing Office, 1960

Wattenberg, B. and Scammon, R., This USA New York: Doubleday, 1965.

I. PROFESSIONAL, TECHNICAL, AND KINDRED WORKERS

Census Book Code	ISR Code	Occupation	Duncan Socio-Economic Index	Duncan Popula-tion Decile	Census Socio-Economic Index	Rice Modified White-Blue Collar	1960 Census Data		
							Percent Popula-tion	Percent Women	Percent Increase 1950-60
000	001	Accountants & auditors	78	9	92	1	.74	17	24
010	002	Actors & actresses	60	8	84	1	.02	38	-26
012	003	Airplane pilots & navigators	79	9	96	1	.04	01	91
013	004	Architects	90	9	98	1	.05	03	28
014	005	Artists & art teachers	67	9	88	1	.16	35	30
015	006	Athletes	52	8	60	1	.01	08	-63
020	007	Authors	76	9	93	1	.04	25	77
021	008	Chemists	79	9	94	1	.13	09	11
022	009	Chiropractors	75	9	89	1	.02	10	10
023	010	Clergymen	52	8	67	1	.31	02	20
030-060	012	College presidents, prof's, instructors (n.e.c.)	84	9	96	1	.25	22	42
070	013	Dancers & dancing teachers	45	7	61	1	.03	81	26
071	014	Dentists	96	9	99	1	.13	02	10
072	015	Designers	73	9	91	1	.11	13	133
073	016	Dieticians & nutritionists	39	6	64	1	.04	93	17
074	017	Draftsmen	67	9	87	1	.34	06	61
075	018	Editors & reporters	82	9	95	1	.16	37	41
		Engineers, technical					1.35	01	63
080	020	Aeronautical	87	9	97	1	.08	02	194
081	021	Chemical	90	9	98	1	.06	01	25
082	022	Civil	84	9	96	1	.24	01	25
083	023	Electrical	84	9	97	1	.29	01	72
084	024	Industrial	86	9	95	1	.15	02	140
085	025	Mechanical	82	9	96	1	.25	*	39
090	026	Metallurgical, meta'ts.	82	9	97	1	.03	01	49
091	027	Mining	85	9	97	1	.02	*	-15
092-093	028	Not elsewhere classified (Inc. kind not reported)	87	9	96	1	.14	01	106
101	029	Entertainers (n.e.c.)	31	5	48	2	.01	23	-26
102	030	Farm & home management advisors	83	9	94	1	.02	47	9
103	031	Foresters & conserva-tionists	48	7	78	1	·05	02	24
104	032	Funeral directors & embalmers	59	8	83	1	·06	06	-7
105	033	Lawyers & judges	93	9	98	1	·33	04	17
111	034	Librarians	60	8	64	1	·13	86	51
120	035	Musicians & music teachers	52	8	72	1	·31	56	22
130-145	036	Natural scientists (n.e.c)	80	9	95	1	·10	11	27
150	037	Nurses, professional	46	7	71	1	·92	98	46
151	038	Nurses, student professional	51	8	50	1	·09	99	-25
152	039	Optometrists	79	9	96	1	·02	04	9
153	040	Osteopaths	96	9	99	1	·01	12	-24
154	041	Personnel & labor-relations workers	84	9	96	1	·15	31	87
160	042	Pharmacists	82	9	95	1	·14	08	4
161	043	Photographers	50	8	73	1	·08	12	-4
162	044	Physicians and surgeons	92	9	99	1	·36	07	19
163	011	Public relations men & publicity writers	82*	9	95	1	·05	23	64
164	045	Radio operators	69	9	90	1	·05	10	71
165	046	Recreation & group workers	67	9	84	1	·06	43	127
170	047	Religious workers	56	8	63	1	·09	62	35
171	048	Social & welfare workers,	64	8	85	1	·15	72	27
172-175	049	Social scientists	81	9	96	1	·09	25	59
180	050	Sports instructors & officials	64	8	87	1	·12	32	70
181	051	Surveyors	48	7	71	1	·07	04	74
182-184	052	Teachers (n.e.c.)	72	9	89	1	2.60	72	50
185	053	Technicians, med. & dent.	48	7	73	1	·22	63	80
190-191	054	Technicians, testing	62	8	80	1	·44	10	295
192	055	Technicians,(n.e.c.)	62	8	85	1	·10	24	256
193	056	Therapists & healers (n.e.c)	58	8	81	1	·06	54	49
194	057	Veterinarians	78	9	95	1	·02	02	10
195	058	Professional, technical, & kindred workers (n.e.c.)	65	8	86	1	·49	20	251
		TOTAL					11.36	38	47

* Less than .01

Census Book Code	ISR Code	Occupation	Duncan Socio-Economic Index	Duncan Population Decile	Census Socio-Economic Index	Rice Modified White-Blue Collar	1960 Census Data		
							Percent Population	Percent Women	Percent Increase 1950-60
250	061	Buyers & dept. heads, store	72	9	92	1	.37	23	64
251	062	Buyers & shippers, farm prod.	33	6	51	2	.03	02	-39
252	063	Conductors, railroad	58	8	73	1	.07	*	-21
253	064	Credit men	74	9	92	1	.07	25	43
254	065	Floormen & floor mgrs., store	50	8	79	1	.02	48	01
260	066	Inspectors, public admin. (incl. not rep.)	63	8		1	.12	03	32
260(906+J)	067	Federal public admin. & postal service	72	9	89	1	.06	04	46
260(926)	068	State public admin.	54	8	81	1	.02	04	41
260(936)	069	Local public admin.	56	8	82	1	.03	05	09
262	070	Mgrs. & super's, buildings	32	6	41	2	.08	36	-20
265	071	Officers, pilots, pursers, & engineers, ship (other than navy or coastguard)	54	8	79	1	.06	*	-11
270	072	Officials and administrators	66	0		1	.31	19	29
270(906 & J)	073	Federal pub. admin. & postal service (incl. not reported)	84	9	94	1	.11	12	35
270(926)	074	State pub. admin.	66	9	90	1	.06	13	58
270(936)	075	Local pub. admin.	54	8	79	1	.15	27	16
275	076	Officials - lodge, society, union, etc.	58	8	82	1	.05	10	24
280	077	Postmasters	60	8	82	1	.06	41	-05
285	078	Purchasing agents & buyers (n.e.c.)	77	9	92	1	.16	10	63
		TOTAL					1.40		

III B: MANAGERS, OFFICIALS, & PROPRIETORS (N.E.C.) SALARIED ONLY

Census Book Code	ISR Code	Occupation	Duncan Socio-Economic Index	Duncan Population Decile	Census Socio-Economic Index	Rice Modified White-Blue Collar	Percent Population	Percent Women	Percent Increase 1950-60
R-SALARIED = 290		If NA industry - see "All Other Industry" below. For Agriculture, Forestry, Fisheries, & Mining - See "All Other Industries" below.							
R(C)	080	Construction	40	8	84	1	.23	03	66
R(206-459 B,M)	081	Manufacturing	79	9	95	1	1.01	07	54
R(507-526 L)	082	Transportation	71	9	87	1	.18	04	22
R(536-579)	083	Communications, utilities & sanitary services	76	9	93	1	.16	11	31
R(606-629)	084	Wholesale trade	70	9	90	1	31	07	27
	085	Retail trade (if NA kind see "Other Retail Trade")	56	8		1	96	16	19
R(637 & F)	086	Food & dairy products stores & milk retg.	50	7	78	1	.16	09	10
R(639 & G)	087	Gen. Mchdse. - 5 & 10 store	68	9	90	1	.14	25	47
R(646 + 647)	088	Apparel & access. stores & shoe stores	69	9	89	1	.08	33	19
R(648 + 649)	089	Furniture, home furn, & equipment stores	68	9	89	1	.05	11	13
R(656)	090	Motor vehicles & access., retail	64	8	88	1	.13	04	52
R(657)	091	Gasoline service stations	31	6	63	2	.07	01	23
R(658)	079	Drugstores	59	8					
R(D)	092	Eating and drink places	39	7	70	1	.12	39	05
R(666 + 676)	093	Hardware, farm implements, & building material, retail	64	8	87	1	.08	04	24
R(678-696)	094	Other retail trade (incl. not rep.)	59	8	84	1	.12	18	-01
R(706 & 716)	095	Banking & other finance	85	9	96	1	.32	13	71
R(726 & 736)	096	Insurance & other real estate	84	9	96	1	.22	17	100
R(806 & 807)	097	Business services	80	9	96	1	.10	21	151
R(808)	098	Auto repair & garages	47	7	76	1	.03	04	-11
R(809)	099	Misc. repair services	53	8	81	1	.01	07	67
R(826-839)	100	Personal services	50	8	78	1	.12	35	18
R(999 & 017-156, 846-898, A,H,E)	101	All other ind. (incl. not rep.) Incl. Agric. (for farm mgr. see code 222) Forestry, Fisheries, & Mining	62	8	89	1	.36	31	64
		TOTAL (SALARIED)		9			4.02	13	43

*Less than .01

II C: MANAGERS, OFFICIALS, & PROPRIETORS (N.E.C.) SELF-EMPLOYED ONLY

Census Book Code	ISR Code	Occupation	Duncan Socio-Economic Index	Duncan Population Decile	Census Socio-Economic Index	Rice Modified White-Blue Collar	1960 Census Data		
							Percent Population	Percent Women	Percent Increase 1950-60
R-SELF-EMPLOYED=291		(If NA ind. see "All Other Indus." below) For Agriculture, Forestry, Fisheries, & Mining, see "All Other Ind." below.							
R(C)SE	103	Construction	51	8	79	1	·36	01	13
R(206-459, B,M)SE	104	Manufacturing	61	8	88	1	·27	07	-30
R(507-526,L) SE	105	Transportation	43	7	73	1	·06	06	-24
R(536-579)SE	106	Communications & utilities, & sanitary services	44	7	72	1	·01	08	-26
R(606-629)SE	107	Wholesale trade	59	8	85	1	·21	05	-24
		Retail trade (If NA kind see "Other retail trade"	43	7		1	1.57	18	-29
R(637+F)SE	109	Food & dairy products stores & mild ret'g.	33	6	54	2	·34	19	-45
R(639+G)SE	110	Gen. Mchdse.-5&10 store	47	7	72	1	·07	23	-42
R(646+647)SE	111	Apparel & access. stores	65	8	88	1	·09	34	-34
R(648+649)SE	112	Furn., home furn., & equipment stores	59	8	86	1	·08	09	-28
R(656) SE	113	Motor vehicles & acc.	70	9	89	1	·09	03	-07
R(657)SE	114	Gasoline serv. stations	33	6	63	2	·24	03	03
R(D)SE	115	Eating & drink places	37	6	71	1	·33	31	-28
R(666+676)SE	116	Hardware, farm impl., & building mat., retail	61	8	90	1	·10	05	-21
R(678-696+ 658)SE	117	Other retail trade (inc. not rep.)	49	7	75	1	.23	21	-28
R(706&716)SE	118	Banking & other finance	85	9	97	1	.03	05	02
R(726&736)SE	119	Insurance & other real estate	76	9	95	1	·08	16	10
R(806+807)SE	120	Business services	67	9	91	1	·06	16	12
R(808)SE	121	Auto repair serv. & gar.	36	6	68	1	·06	03	-37
R(809) R(826-839) SE	122	Misc. repair services	34	6	60	2	·03	05	-33
	123	Personal services	41	7	68	1	.20	33	-10
R(999&017 -156,846- 898,A,H,E) SE	124	All other ind. (incl. not rep.) Incl. Agric. (for farmer see Code N), Forestry, Fisheries, & Mining	49	7	76	1	.15	22	-01
		TOTAL (SELF-EMPLOYED)		7			3.09	15	-22
		TOTAL (SALARIED)					4.02	13	43
		TOTAL (IIA)					1.40		
		TOTAL MANAGERS, OFFICIALS PROPRIETORS (NON-FARM)					8.51	14	8

Census Book Code	ISR Code	Occupation	Duncan Socio-Economic Index	Duncan Population Decile	Census Socio-Economic Index	Rice Modified White-Blue Collar	1960 Census Data		
							Percent Population	Percent Women	Percent Increase 1950-60
301	125	Agents (n.e.c.)	68	9	90	1	.25	17	29
302	126	Attendents & assis., Library	44	7	50	1	.05	77	157
303	127	Att's., Physicians & dentists office	38	6	56	1	.11	97	73
304	128	Baggagemen, transportation	25	5	54	2	.01	03	-30
305	129	Bank tellers	52	8	75	1	.20	69	102
310	130	Bookkeepers	51	8	73	1	1.45	84	27
312	131	Cashiers	44	7	69	1	.76	79	106
313	132	Collectors, bill & acct.	39	7	66	1	.05	22	32
314	133	Dispatchers & starters, vehicle	40	7	73	1	.09	12	86
315	134	Express messenger & railway mail clerks	67	9	85	1	.01	04	-64
320	085	File clerks	44	7	73	1	.22	86	27
321	173	Insur. adjusters, examiners, & investigators	62	8	89	1	.09	12	75
323	135	Mail carriers	53	8	80	1	.31	02	20
324	136	Messenger & office boys	28	5	43	2	.10	18	07
325	137	Office machine operators	45	7	69	1	.49	74	118
333	102	Payroll & timekeepers	44	7	73	1	.17	59	68
340	108	Postal clerks	44	7	73	1	.34	19	17
341	153	Receptionists	44	7	73	1	.22	98	129
Z	507	Secretaries	61	8	82	1	2.31	97	80
343	138	Shipping & rec. clerks	22	5	58	2	.46	08	-01
345	139	Stenographers	61	8	82	1	.43	96	-36
350	501	Stock clerks & storekeepers	44	7	73	1	.54	15	45
351	140	Telegraph messengers	22	5	33	2	.01	05	-42
352	141	Telegraph operators	47	7	75	1	.03	23	-41
353	142	Telephone operators	45	7	72	1	.58	96	01
354	143	Ticket, station & exp. agt.	60	8	82	1	.11	22	08
360	506	Typists	61	8	82	1	.84	93	48
Y	144	Clerical & kind. workers (n.e.c.)	44	7	73	1	4.68	59	28
		TOTAL					14.91	77	35

IV: SALES WORKERS

Census Book Code	ISR Code	Occupation	Duncan Socio-Economic Index	Duncan Population Decile	Census Socio-Economic Index	Rice Modified White-Blue Collar	1960 Census Data		
							Percent Population	Percent Women	Percent Increase 1950-60
380	145	Ad. agents & salesmen	66	9	90	1	.05	14	03
381	146	Auctioneers	40	7	67	1	.01	03	-24
382	147	Demonstrators	35	6	62	2	.04	93	83
383	148	Hucksters & peddlers	08	1	08	2	.09	57	140
385	149	Ins. agents & brokers & underwriters	66	9	89	1	.57	10	34
390	150	Newsboys	27	5	20	2	.31	04	98
393	151	Real estate agents & brokers	62	8	86	1	.30	24	37
S S=394 S(206-459		Salesmen & sales clerks (n.e.c.) (If ind. NA see "Other Ind.")	47	7		1	6.03	41	14
B,M)	154	Manufacturing	65	8	88	1	.74	11	42
S(606-629) S(637-696	155	Wholesale trade	61	8	85	1	.78	04	22
D,F,G)	156	Retail trade	39	6	61	1	4.22	54	07
S(999 & all not above)	157	Other ind. (incl. not rep.)	50	8	77	1	.22	26	37
395	152	Stock & bond salesmen	73	9	94	1	.04	06	157
		TOTAL					7.44	36	19

Census Book Code	ISR Code	Occupation	Duncan Socio-Economic Index	Duncan Population Decile	Census Socio-Economic Index	Rice Modified White-Blue Collar	1960 Census Data		
							Percent Population	Percent Women	Percent Increase 1950-60
401	158	Bakers	22	5	50	4	.17	16	-10
402	159	Blacksmiths	16	3	31	4	.03	01	-53
403	160	Boilermaker	33	6	59	4	.04	*	-31
404	161	Bookbinders	39	6	69	3	.04	57	-13
405	162	Brickmasons, stonemasons, & tile-setters	27	5	50	4	.32	*	18
410	163	Cabinetmakers	23	5	48	4	.11	01	-10
Q	164	Carpenters	19	4	35	4	1.43	03	-07
413	165	Cement & concrete finishers	19	4	34	4	.07	*	45
414	166	Compositors & typesetters	52	8	79	3	.28	09	02
415	167	Cranemen, derrickmen & hoistmen	21	4	52	4	.20	01	23
420	168	Decorators & window dressers	40	7	67	3	.08	46	17
421	169	Electricians	44	7	74	3	.55	01	09
423	170	Electrotypers & stereotypers	55	8	81	3	.01	01	-24
424	171	Engravers, exc. photoengravers	47	7	75	3	.02	18	16
425	172	Excavating, grading, & road machinery operators	24	5	57	4	.35	*	103
430		Foremen (n.e.c.) (If ind. NA see "Other Ind.")	49	7		3	1.86	07	40
430(C)	174	Construction	40	7	65	3	.16	*	69
		Manufacturing (If mfg. but NA kind see "Other non-dur. goods" below)	53	8			1.17	08	46
430(237-249)	176	Metal industries	54	8	76	3	.20	02	56
430(256-259,M)	177	Machinery, incl. elec.	60	8	82	3	.21	05	66
430(267-276)	178	Transportation equip.	66	9	84	3	.13	01	63
430(286-296,206-236)	179	Other durable goods	41	7	71	3	.16	06	34
430(346-367,B)	180	Textiles, textile products & apparel	39	7	66	3	.12	32	09
430(386-459,306-329)	181	Other non-dur. goods (incl. not spec. mfg.)	53	8	79	3	.36	08	46
430(L)	182	Railroads & railway exp. services	36	6	61	3	.06	*	-33
430(536-579)	184	Telecommunications & utilities & sanitary services	56	8	79	3	.09	02	43
430(999+017-156,606-936,A,D,E,F,G,H,J)	185	Other ind. (incl. not rep)	44	7	73	3	.34	09	36
431	186	Forgemen & hammermen	23	5	51	4	.02	04	-10
432	187	Furriers	39	6	66	3	.01	15	-71
434	188	Glaziers	26	5	57	4	.02	02	49
435	189	Heat treaters, annealers, & temperers	22	5	58	4	.03	02	12
444	190	Inspectors, scalers, & graders, log & lumber	23	5	48	4	.03	04	06
450		Inspectors (n.e.c.) (If NA ind. see "Other Ind." below)	41	7		3	.16	06	05
450(C)	192	Construction	46	7	76	3	.02	01	86
450(L)	193	Railroads & railway exp. serv.	41	7	65	3	.05	*	-19
450(507-579)	194	Transport., exc. rr comm. & other pub. utilities	45	7	74	3	.02	02	16
450(999 & all not above, except J, K, 906-936)	195	Other non-mfg. ind. (incl. not rep.)	38	6	71	3	.06	15	05
451	196	Jewelers, watchmakers, goldsmiths, & silversmiths	36	6	63	3	06	06	-21
452	197	Job-setters, metal	28	5	64	4	06	01	62
453	198	Linemen & servicemen, telegraph, telephone, & power	49	7	76	3	43	02	28

* Less than .01

V : Craftsmen, Foremen, & Kindred Workers (continued)

Census Book Code	ISR Code	Occupation	Duncan Socio-Economic Index	Duncan Popula-tion Decile	Census Socio-Economic Index	Rice Modified White-Blue Collar	1960 Census Data		
							Percent Popula-tion	Percent Women	Percent Increase 1950-60
450	199	Locomotive engineers	58	8	68	3	.09	*	-21
460	200	Locomotive firemen	45	7	76	3	.06	*	-30
461	201	Loom fixers	10	1	32	4	.04	01	-21
465	202	Machinists	33	6	68	4	.80	01	-04
		Mechanics & repairmen	25	5		4	3.57	01	28
470	203	Airconditioning, heating & refrigeration	27	5	61	4	.10	*	45
471	204	Airplane	48	7	79	3	.18	02	60
472	205	Automobile	19	4	52	4	1.09	03	03
473	206	Office machine	36	6	66	3	.05	01	-06
474	207	Radio & television	36	6	62	3	.16	02	35
475	208	Railroad & car shop	23	5	52	4	.06	*	-16
480	209	Not elsewhere classified (incl. NA type)	27	5	61	4	1.92	02	49
490	210	Millers, grain, flour, feed, etc.	19	4	39	4	.01	01	-05
491	211	Millwrights	31	6	62	4	.11	*	13
492	212	Molders, metal	12	1	41	4	.08	03	-18
493	213	Motion picture projec-tionists	43	7	73	3	.03	02	-32
494	214	Opticians & lens grinders & polishers	39	6	72	3	.03	15	06
495	215	Painters, const. & maint.	16	3	37	4	.64	02	-04
501	216	Paperhangers	10	1	22	4	.02	14	-51
502	217	Pattern & model makers, exc. paper	44	7	74	3	.06	02	08
503	218	Photoengravers & lithog's	64	8	84	3	.04	05	-12
504	219	Piano & organ tuners & repairs	38	6	54	3	.01	03	-23
505	220	Plasterers	25	5	46	4	.08	*	-18
510	221	Plumbers & pipefitters	34	6	64	4	.51	*	11
512	222	Pressmen & plate printers, printing	49	7	77	3	.12	04	50
513	223	Rollers & roll hands, metal	22	5	54	4	.05	03	01
514	224	Roofers & slaters	15	3	34	4	.09	*	13
515	225	Shoemakers & repairers, exc. factory	12	1	22	4	.06	04	-38
520	226	Stationary engineers	47	7	72	3	.43	01	26
521	227	Stone-cutters & carvers	25	5	44	4	.01	02	-28
523	228	Structural metal workers	34	6	66	4	.07	22	-51
525	230	Tinsmiths, coopersmiths, & sheet metal workers	33	6	68	4	.23	01	12
530	231	Tool & die makers & setters	50	8	77	3	.29	01	19
535	232	Upholsterers	22	5	53	4	.10	10	-03
545	233	Craftsmen & kind. workers, n.e.c.	32	6	62	4	.17	02	52
555	428	Members of the armed forces: Enlisted men							
555	429	Officers	"						
555	244	N.A. whether enlisted or officer	"						
		TOTAL					14.30	03	13

* Less than .01

VI: OPERATIVES & KINDRED WORKERS

Census Book Code	ISR Code	Occupation	Duncan Socio-Economic Index	Duncan Population Decile	Census Socio-Economic Index	Rice Modified White-Blue Collar	1960 Census Data		
							Percent Population	Percent Women	Percent Increase 1950-60
		Apprentices (If trade NA) see trade)	35	6		3	.14	03	-27
601	236	Auto mechanics	25	5	46	4	*	01	-51
602	237	Bricklayers & masons	32	6	57	4	.01	*	-51
603	238	Carpenters	31	5	50	4	.01	01	-44
604	239	Electricians	37	6	61	3	.01	01	03
605	240	Machinists & toolmakers	41	7	59	3	.02	01	-01
610	241	Mechanics, exc. auto	34	6	60	4	.01	02	-43
612	242	Plumbers & pipefitters	33	6	60	4	.01	01	-33
613	243	Building trades (n.e.c.)	29	5	49	4	*	02	-38
614	245	Metalworking trades (n.e.c.)	33	6	55	4	.01	02	-16
615	246	Printing trades	40	7	57	3	.02	02	-25
620	247	Other specified trades	31	5	51	4	.01	08	-33
621	248	Trade not specified	39	6	55	3	.02	06	-32
630	249	Asbestos & insulation workers	32	6	63	4	.03	04	30
631	451	Assemblers	17	4	61	4	1.06	45	73
632	250	Attendants, auto serv. & parking	19	4	44	4	.03	04	30
634	251	Blasters & powdermen	11	1	33	4	.01	01	-37
635	252	Boatmen, canalmen, & lock keepers	24	5	50	4	.01	01	-14
640	253	Brakemen, railroad	42	7	71	3	.10	*	-19
641	254	Bus-drivers	24	5	65	4	.29	10	17
642	256	Chainmen, rodmen, axemen, survey	25	5	47	4	.02	04	43
643	500	Checkers, examiners, & inspectors, manual	17	4	61	4	.80	46	47
645	257	Conductors, bus & street rw	30	5	61	4	.01	02	-62
650	258	Deliverymen & routemen	32	6	59	4	.68	03	76
651	259	Dressmakers & seamstresses, exc. factory	23	5	35	4	.19	97	-16
652	260	Dyers	12	1	36	4	.03	04	-24
653	261	Filers, grinders & polishers, metal	22	5	57	4	.25	06	02
654	262	Fruit, nut & veget. graders, & packers, exc. factory	10	1	19	4	.04	71	-18
670	263	Furnacemen, smeltermen, pourers	18	3	45	4	.09	02	-01
671	299	Graders, sorters, manuf.	17	4	14	4	.06	68	-08
672	264	Heaters, metal	29	5	56	4	.01	02	-17
673	300	Knitters, loopers, toppers, textile	21	4	47	4	.07	68	-43
674	265	Laundry & dry cleaning oper.	15	3	37	4	.64	72	-09
675	266	Meatcutters, exc. slaughter & packing house	29	5	60	4	.29	03	05
680	267	Milliners	46	7	73	3	.01	91	-67
685	268	Mine operators & laborers (n.e.c.) (If NA which below)	10	1		4	.51	*	-45
685(136)	269	Coal mining	02	0	18	4	.22	*	-63
685(146)	270	Crude petrol & nat gas	38	6	70	3	.16	*	-06
685(156+126)	271	Mining & quarrying, exc fuel	12	1	36	4	.14	01	-24
690	272	Motormen, mine, factory, logging camp, etc.	03	0	28	4	.02	01	-40
691	273	Motormen, street, subway, etc.	34	6	64	4	.01	01	-40
692	274	Oilers & greasers, exc auto	15	3	44	4	.09	01	-09
693	235	Packers & wrappers n.e.c.	18	4	38	4	.76	61	43
694	275	Painters, exc. const. & maint.	18	4	47	4	.23	10	21
695	276	Photographic process workers	42	7	65	3	.07	44	49
701	277	Power-station operators	50	8	78	3	.04	05	25
703	278	Sailors & deck hands	16	3	40	4	.06	01	-22
704	255	Sawyers	05	0	10	4	.15	03	-04
705	279	Sewers & stitchers, manuf.	17	4	39	4	.96	94	24
710	280	Spinners, textile	05	0	20	4	.08	79	-39
712	281	Stationary firemen	17	3	40	4	.14	01	-28
713	282	Switchmen, railroad	44	7	72	3	.09	*	-04

* Less than .01

Census Book Code	ISR Code	Occupation	Duncan Socio-Economic Index	Duncan Population Decile	Census Socio-Economic Index	Rice Modified White-Blue Collar	1960 Census Data Percent Population	Percent Women	Percent Increase 1950-60
714	283	Taxi drivers & chauffers	10	1	37	4	.26	03	-20
T	284	Truck & tractor drivers	15	3	40	4	2.58	01	19
720	285	Weavers, textile	06	0	27	4	.10	42	-36
721	286	Welders & flame cutters	24	5	62	4	.60	05	40
W		Operatives & Kindred Workers N.E.C.					7.74	30	05
W=775		Non-Manufacturing					1.07	17	02
W(C)	363	Construction (For other non-mfg. ind. see after mfg. ind. see after mfg. industries below)	18	4	38	4	.16	01	43
		Manufacturing (If NA what kind of mfg. see under "Manufacturing")	18	3		4	6.67	32	06
		Durable goods	17	3		4	3.17	21	11
		Lumber & wood products, exc. furniture							
W(206)									
W(207)	290	Sawmills, planing mills, & millwork	07	1	12	4	.16	04	-28
W(208)	291	Misc. wood products	09	1	25	4	.06	21	-01
W(209)	292	Furniture & fixtures	09	1	27	4	.17	15	-04
W(216-236)	293	Stone, clay & glass prod. (If NA which below)	17	3		4	.26	16	05
W(216)	294	Glass & glass products	23	5	50	4	.08	16	-02
W(217)	295	Cement, concrete, & gypsum prod. & plaster	10	1	29	4	.05	01	24
W(218)	296	Structural clay products	10	1	31	4	.03	12	-02
W(219)	297	Pottery & related products	21	4	49	4	.03	40	-34
W(236)	298	Misc. nonmetallic mineral & stone products	15	3	41	4	.06	16	57
		Metal Industries	16	3		4	.84	13	15
W(237)	301	Blast furnaces, steel works & rolling mills	17	3	49	4	.16	02	-17
W(238)	302	Other primary iron & steel industries	12	1	39	4	.10	04	-01
W(239)	303	Primary nonferrous ind.	15	3	47	4	.13	11	29
W(246)	304	Cutlery, hand tools, & other hardware	16	3	48	4	.05	38	14
W(247)	305	Fabricated structural met. products	16	3	48	4	.10	07	14
W(248)	306	Misc. Fab. metal prods.	15	3	48	4	.29	21	47
W(249)	307	Not spec. metal industries	14	2	47	4	*	23	-58
W(256 + 257, M)	308	Machinery, exc. elec. (If NA which below)	22	5		4	.43	12	23
W(256)	309	Agricultural machinery	21	4	59	4	.04	05	-34
W(257)	310	Office & store machines & devices	31	5	67	4	.04	34	-08
W(M)	311	Misc. machinery	22	5	57	4	.36	11	40
W(259)	312	Elec. mach., & equip. & supp.	26	5	62	4	.48	49	44
W(267-276)	313	Trans. equip. (If NA which below)	23	5		4	.45	11	04
W(267)	314	Motor veh. & equip.	21	4	61	4	.27	11	-19
W(268)	315	Aircraft & parts	34	6	71	4	.12	14	154
W(269)	316	Ship & boat bldg. & repairing	16	3	41	4	.03	05	34
W(276)	317	Railroad & misc. trans. equipment	23	5	56	4	.03	08	04
W(286-289)	318	Professional & photographic equip. & watches (If NA which below)	29	5		4	.10	39	18
W(286)	319	Prof. equip. & supplies	23	5	57	4	.07	39	49
W(287)	320	Photo equip. & supplies	40	7	73	3	.02	23	20
W(289)	321	Watches, clock, & clock-work operated devices	28	5	62	4	.01	58	-41
W(296)	322	Misc. mfd. ind.	16	3	42	4	.22	48	-01

* Less than .01

Census Book Code	ISR Code	Occupation	Duncan Socio-Economic Index	Duncan Population Decile	Census Socio-Economic Index	Rice Modified White-Blue Collar	1960 Census Data		
							Percent Population	Percent Women	Percent Increase 1950-60
		Non-durable goods					3.48	41	02
		Food & kindred products (If NA which see Not Spec. Food Ind. below)	16	3		4	.73	31	20
W(306)	324	Meat products	16	3	43	4	.21	27	44
W(307)	325	Dairy products	22	5	53	4	.09	07	-02
W(308)	326	Canning & preserving fruits, veg., & sea foods	09	1	26	4	.14	62	41
W(309)	327	Grain mill products	14	3	36	4	.05	07	03
W(316)	328	Bakery products	15	3	38	4	.07	36	36
W(317)	329	Confectionary & related products	12	1	34	4	.04	50	-06
W(318)	330	Beverage industries	19	4	48	4	.07	13	-07
W(319)	331	Misc. food prep. & kindred products	11	4	32	4	.05	22	07
W(326)	332	Not spec. food ind.	19	4	46	4	.01	49	-06
W(329)	333	Tobacco mfg.	02	0	13	4	.06	62	-25
W(346-356)	334	Textile mill prod. (If NA which below)	06	0		4	.58	48	-21
W(346)	335	Knitting mills	21	4	47	4	.10	78	142
W(347)	336	Dyeing & finishing textiles, exc. knit goods	08	1	38	4	.04	18	-04
W(348)	337	Carpets, rugs, floor cov.	14	3	44	4	.02	43	-39
W(349)	338	Yarn, thread, & fab. mills	02	0	14	4	.39	45	-33
W(356)	339	Misc. tex. mill prod.	10	1	33	4	.03	38	-23
W(367&B)	340	Apparel & other fabricated textile prod. (If NA which below)	21	5		4	.68	73	04
W(B)	341	Apparel & access.	22	5	39	4	.61	75	03
W(367)	342	Misc. fab. tex. prod.	17	3	36	4	.06	61	14
W(386-389)	343	Paper & allied products (If NA which below)	19	4		4	.35	23	10
W(386)	344	Pulp, paper, & paperbd. mills	19	4	51	4	.17	09	11
W(387)	345	Paperboard containers, boxes	17	3	37	4	.11	33	19
W(389)	346	Misc. paper & pulp prod.	19	4	52	4	.07	41	-03
W(396+398)	347	Printing, publishing, & allied industries	31	5	60	4	.15	38	36
W(406-409)	348	Chemical & allied prod. (If NA which below)	20	4		4	.30	15	15
W(406)	349	Synthetic fibres	09	1	51	4	.04	34	-13
W(407)	350	Drugs & medicines	26	5	57	4	.03	37	36
W(408)	351	Paints, varnishes, & related prod.	15	3	51	4	.03	08	07
W(409)	352	Misc. chem. & allied prod.	23	5	55	4	.21	10	20
W(416+419)	353	Petroleum & coal prod. (If NA which below)	51	8		3	.08	02	.00
W(416)	354	Petroleum refining	56	8	79	3	.07	01	02
W(419)	355	Misc. pet. & coal prod.	14	2	44	4	.01	06	-15
W(426&429)	356	Rubber prod. & misc. plastic products	22	5		4	.25	28	20
W(436-438)	357	Leather & leather prod. (If NA which below)	16	3		4	.31	48	-17
W(436)	358	Leather: tanned, curried & finished	10	1	37	4	.03	14	-39
W(347)	359	Footwear exc. rubber	09	1	31	4	.23	51	-12
W(438)	360	Leather prod. exc. footwear	14	2	36	4	.05	53	-20
W(459)	361	Not spec. mfg. ind. (Incl. MFG. but NA kind)	16	3	44	4	.02	41	-46
		Other non-manufacturing					.91	19	-04
		Construction-see before mfg industries (If NA what kind see Not. Spec. Ind. below)							
W(L)	364	Railroads & railway express services	15	3	42	4	.09	01	-40
W(507-526)	365	Transportation, exc. rail	23	5	53	4	.06	07	17
W(536-579)	366	Communications & utilities & sanitary services	21	4	52	4	.08	03	-05
W(606-696, D.F.G)	367	Wholesale & retail trade	17	3	38	4	.34	28	-02
W(806-809)	368	Business & repair services	19	4	45	4	.11	12	45
W(826-839 K)	369	Personal services	11	1	29	4	.02	50	-24
W(906-936 J)	370	Public administration	17	3	50	4	.07	10	-10
W(999-non manuf.)	362	Not spec. non-mfg. ind. (Incl. non-mfg. but NA kind)	18	3		4	.14	30	.12
W(999 & 017-018, 706-736, 846-898, A.E.H)	371	All other industries	20	4		4			
		TOTAL					19.91	28	09

* Less than .01

Census Book Code	ISR Code	Occupation	Duncan Socio-Economic Index	Duncan Popula-tion Decile	Census Socio-Economic Index	Rice Modified White-Blue Collar	1960 Census Data Percent Popula-tion	Percent Women	Percent Increase 1950-60
810	380	Attendants, institutions, hosp.	13	1	38	4	.63	73	92
812	381	Attendants, prof. & per. serv. n.e.c.	26	5	46	4	.12	70	73
813	382	Att's. rec. & amusement	19	4	26	4	.10	13	-02
814	383	Barbers	17	3	37	4	.28	03	01
815	384	Bartenders	19	4	46	4	.29	11	-12
820	386	Bookblacks	08	1	02	4	.02	04	-31
821	385	Boarding & lodg. housekeepers	30	5	35	4	.05	88	02
823	287	Chambermaids & maids, exc. private household	11	1	18	4	.28	98	40
824	387	Charwomen & cleaners	10	1	15	4	.30	67	54
825	388	Cooks, exc. priv. h.h.	15	3	31	4	.93	64	28
830	389	Counter & fountain workers	17	3	41	4	.26	71	79
831	390	Elevator operators	10	1	28	4	.12	32	-19
832	939	Housekeepers & stewards, exc. private households	31	6	61	4	.24	80	38
834	394	Janitors & sextons	09	1	18	4	.96	13	31
835	502	Kitchen workers n.e.c. exc. private households	11	1	18	4	.52	58	54
840	396	Midwives	37	6	51	3	*	78	-45
841	400	Porters	04	0	16	4	.24	02	-11
842	401	Practical nurses	22	5	32	4	.34	96	50
843	288	Hairdressers, cosmetologists	17	3	37	4	.47	89	45
850	391	Firemen, fire protection	37	6	73	3	.22		25
851	392	Guards, watchmen, doorkeepers	18	4	38	4	.40	03	03
852	395	Marshalls & constables	21	5	44	4	.01	04	-09
853	397	Policemen & detectives (If NA which below)	39	7		3	.40	03	31
853(All others)	399	Private	36	6	67	3	.03	08	-17
853(906-936,J)	398	Government	40	7	74	3	.37	02	36
854	402	Sheriffs & bailiffs	34	6	66	4	.04	05	30
860	405	Watchmen (crossing) & bridge tenders	17	3	39	4	.04	45	195
874	403	Ushers, recreation & amuse-ment	25	5	34	4	.02	31	-37
875	404	Waiters & waitresses	16	3	39	4	1.39	87	25
890	406	Service workers except private household (n.e.c.)	11	1	18	4	.30	43	-02
		TOTAL					8.94	53	28

* Less than .01

VIII: PRIVATE HOUSEHOLD WORKERS

Census Book Code	ISR Code	Occupation	Duncan Socio-Economic Index	Duncan Popula-tion Decile	Census Socio-Economic Index	Rice Modified White-Blue Collar	1960 Census Data Percent Popula-tion	Percent Women	Percent Increase 1950-60
801	175	Baby sitters, priv. house-holds	07	1	07	4	.54	97	367
802	372	Housekeepers, priv. h.h. (If NA which below)	19	4		4	.23	99	04
802(L,O)	374	Living out	21	4	32	4	.15	98	03
802(LI)	373	Living in	10	1	25	4	.09	99	05
803	375	Laundress, priv. h.h. (If NA which below)	12	1		4	.06	98	-44
803(LO)	376	Living out	12	1	09	4	.06	98	-44
803(LI)	505	Living in	—	—	09	4	*	100	-65
P	377	Priv. h.h. workers n.e.c. (If NA which below)	07	1	07	4	1.99	96	07
P(LO)	379	Living out	06	0	07	4	1.83	96	14
P(LI)	378	Living in	12	1	26	4	.16	94	-36
		TOTAL					2.83	96	22

* Less than .01

IX: FARMERS AND FARM MANAGERS (NOT LABORERS & FOREMEN)

Census Book Code	ISR Code	Occupation	Duncan Socio-Economic Index	Duncan Popula-tion Decile	Census Socio-Economic Index	Rice Modified White-Blue Collar	1960 Census Data		
							Percent Popula-tion	Percent Women	Percent Increase 1950-60
N(self owner)	019	Farmers (farm owners)	14	2		8			
N(ten, share)	059	Farmers (tenants & share-croppers)	14			8	3.88	05	-42
N(NA type)	191	Farmers (NA which type)	14	2		8			
222	060	Farm managers	36	6		8	04	03	-30
		TOTAL					3.92	05	-42

X: FARM LABORERS AND FOREMEN

Census Book Code	ISR Code	Occupation	Duncan Socio-Economic Index	Duncan Popula-tion Decile	Census Socio-Economic Index	Rice Modified White-Blue Collar	1960 Census Data		
							Percent Popula-tion	Percent Women	Percent Increase 1950-60
901	407	Farm Foremen	20	4		8	.04	02	38
U	408	Farm laborers, wage workers	06	0		8	1.93	12	-21
V	409	Farm lab., unpaid family workers	17	3		8	.44	44	-69
905	410	Farm service lab., self-emp.	22	5		8	.01	02	-43
		TOTAL					2.42	17	-38

Census Book Code	ISR Code	Occupation	Duncan Socio-Economic Index	Duncan Population Decile	Census Socio-Economic Index	Rice Modified White-Blue Collar	1960 Census Data		
							Percent Population	Percent Women	Percent Increase 1950-60
960	323	Carpenters helpers, exc. logging & mining	07	0	16	4	.07	01	-30
962	411	Fishermen & oystermen	10	1	11	4	.06	01	-47
963	412	Garage laborers, car washers & greasers	08	1	24	4	.14	03	32
964	413	Gardeners, exc. farm and groundskeepers	11	1	19	4	.33	02	38
965	414	Longshoremen & stevedores	11	1	25	4	.09	01	-16
970	415	Lumbermen, raftsmen, woodchoppers	04	0	04	4	.21	01	-28
971	416	Teamsters	08	1	13	4	.03		-03
972	417	Truck drivers' helper	09	1	28	4	.05	01	-32
973	503	Warehousemen n.e.c.	08	1	28	4	.19	01	60
		Laborers, n.e.c. Non-manufacturing	07	1		4	2.79	03	-03
X(C)	491	Construction (for other non-mfg. ind. see after mfg. Industries below)	07	1	16	4	1.16	01	08
X(985)		Manufacturing (If NA what kind see not spec. ind. under manufacturing below)	08	1		4	1.49	07	-17
		Durable goods					.96	04	-15
X(206)		Lumber & wood prod. exc. furn. Logging							
X(207)	419	Sawmills, planing mills, & millwork	03	0	04	4	.15	02	-34
X(208)	420	Misc. wood products	02	0	09	4	.02	09	-27
X(209)	421	Furniture & Fixtures	05	0	19	4	.03	08	-08
X(216-236)	422	Stone, clay & glass prod. (If NA which below)	07	1		4	.13	03	01
X(216)	423	Glass & glass products	14	2	31	4	.02	07	-02
X(217)	424	Cement, concrete, gypsum, plaster products	05	0	22	4	.04	01	18
X(218)	425	Structural clay products	05	0	19	4	.04	03	-08
X(219)	426	Pottery & related prod.	07	1	30	4	.01	16	-31
X(236)	427	Misc. nonmetallic mineral & stone products	05	0	23	4	.02	02	14
		Metal Industries	07	1		4	.39	03	-11
X(237)	430	Blast furnaces, steel works, rolling mills	09	1	35	4	.19	01	-15
X(238)	431	Other primary iron & steel ind.	04	0	18	4	.07	01	-19
X(239)	432	Primary nonferrous ind.	06	0	34	4	.04	02	-04
X(246)	433	Cutlery, hand tools & other hardware	07	1	27	4	.01	18	-48
X(247)	434	Fabricated structural metal products	07	1	27	4	.03	03	15
X(248)	435	Misc. fab. met. prod.	10	1	27	4	.06	11	16
X(249)	436	Not spec. metal ind.	09	1	28	4	*	11	-57
X(256+257)M	437	Machinery, exc. elec. (If NA which below)	11	1		4	.07	04	-16
X(256)	438	Agric. mach., tractors	14	2	38	4	.01	03	-47
X(257)	439	Office & store machines & devices	17	3	45	4	*	08	05
X(M)	440	Miscellaneous machinery	10	1	32	4	.06	03	-07
X(259)	441	Electrical machinery, equipment and supplies	14	2	45	4	.05	18	-02
X(267-276)	442	Transportation equipment (If NA which below)	11	1		4	.10	03	-17
X(267)	443	Motor vehicles & motor vehicle equipment	13	1	42	4	.06	03	-27
X(268)	444	Aircraft and parts	15	3	51	4	.01	06	65
X(269)	445	Ship & boat bldg. rpr.	02	0	19	4	.02	02	-09
X(276)	446	Railroad & misc. transportation equipment	08	1	31	4	.01	04	-03

* Less than .01

Census Book Code	ISR Code	Occupation	Duncan Socio-Economic Index	Duncan Population Decile	Census Socio-Economic Index	Rice Modified White-Blue Collar	1960 Census Data		
							Percent Population	Percent Women	Percent Increase 1950-60
X(286-289)	447	Professional & photographic equipment & watches (If NA which below)	11	1		4	.01	19	-07
X(286)	448	Profess. equip. & supp.	10	1	37	4	*	18	17
X(287)	449	Photo. equip. & supp.	16	1	41	4	*	18	17
X(289)	504	Watches, clock, & clock-work operated devices	11	1	29	4	*	32	-62
X(296)	450	Misc. Mfg. industries	12	1	28	4	.02	18	-22
		Non-durable goods					.53	10	-18
	451	Food & kind. prod. (If NA which see Not. Spec. Food Ind. below)	09	1		4	.21	08	-16
X(306)	452	Meat products	08	1	32	4	.05	10	-18
X(307)	453	Dairy products	13	1	34	4	.03	03	-23
X(308)	454	Canning & preserv. fruits vegetables & sea foods	06	0	15	4	.04	17	02
X(309)	455	Grain-mill products	06	0	23	4	.03	02	-07
X(316)	456	Bakery products	10	1	30	4	.01	12	78
X(317)	457	Confect., & related prod.	10	1	33	4	.01	17	-17
X(318)	458	Beverage industries	16	3	34	4	.03	03	-19
X(319)	459	Misc. food prep. & kind. prod.	05	0	17	4	.03	05	-41
X(326)	460	Not spec. food ind.	14	2	40	4	*	20	-20
X(329)	461	Tobacco Manufacturers	00	0	10	4	.01	31	02
X(346-356)	462	Textile mill products (If NA which below)	03	0		4	.06	16	-33
X(346)	463	Knitting mills	04	0		4	*		
X(347)	464	Dyeing & finishing textiles except knit goods	09	1		4	*		
X(348)	465	Carpets, rugs, floor covering	14	2		4	*		
X(349)	466	Yarn, thread, & fabric mills	01	0	12	4	.05	16	-34
X(356)	467	Misc. textile-mill products	06	0	14	4	*		
X(367&B)	468	Apparel & other Fab. textile products	09	1	21	4	.02	40	-02
X(B)	469	Apparel & accessories	11	1		4			
X(367)	470	Misc. fab. textile products	06	0		4			
X(386-389)	471	Papers & allied prod. (If NA which below)	07	1		4	.06	06	-15
X(386)	472	Pulp, paper, & paperbd. mills	06	0	27	4	.04	02	-13
X(387)	473	Paperbd. containers & boxes	10	1	31	4	.01	12	-01
X(389)	474	Misc. paper & pulp products	08	1	30	4	.01	17	-39
X(396&398)	475	Printing, publishing, allied industry	23	5	50	4	.02	13	09
X(406-409)	476	Chemicals & allied products (If NA which below)	08	1		4	.07	02	-13
X(406)	477	Synthetic fibers	04	0	30	4	*	06	-22
X(407)	478	Drugs & Medicines	22	5	48	4	*	08	03
X(408)	479	Paints, varnishes and related products	08	1	42	1	*	05	-34
X(409)	480	Misc. chemicals & allied products	08	1	18	4	.06	03	-10
X(416 & 419)	481	Petroleum & Coal products (If NA which below)	22	5		4	.03	01	-36
X(416)	482	Petroleum refining	26	5	59	4	.02	01	-40
X(419)	483	Misc. petroleum and coal products	03	0	26	4	*	02	-03
X(426&429)	484	Rubber products	12	1	41	4	.03	13	-14
X(436-438)	485	Leather & leather products (If NA which below)	06	0	27	4	.02	22	-28
X(436)	486	Leather; tanned, curried & finished	02	0		4	*		
X(437)	487	Footwear, except rubber	10	1		4	*		
X(438)	488	Leather products, except footwear	12	1		4	*		
X(459)	489	Not Specified manufacturing industries (Incl. Manuf. but NA kind)	08	1	26	4	*	11	-77
X(L)	492	Railroads & railway express service	03	0	20	4	.21	02	-52
X(507-526)	493	Transportation, except rail-roads	09	1	28	4	.14	01	04
X(536-579)	494	Telecommunications and utili-ties & sanitary service	06	0	18	4	.19	01	-06
X(606-696)	495	Wholesale & retail trade	12	1	28	4	.58	05	38
X(806-809)	496	Business & repair services	26	1	09	4	.04	04	54
X(K,826-839)	497	Personal services	09	0	01	4	.12	07	-03
X(906-936 J)	498	Public administration	29	1	07	4	.12	03	-22
X(999-non manuf.)	490	Non-manufacturing (incl. non-manuf. NA kind)	07	1		4	.23	09	-16
X(999+017-018,706-499,736,A)	499	All other industries (incl. not reported.)	07	0	06	4			
		Total					5.47	04	-07

* Less than .01

SOCIO-ECONOMIC STATUS SCORES (Bureau of Census 1963)

As noted in the introduction to this section, the Census Bureau scores are based on 1960 percentile data on income and education for the general population. Occupational scores based on the average income and education percentiles have been listed in the immediately preceeding tables. The following average scores for the general Census Bureau categories are given:

Scores for Categories of Major Occupation Groups

Score	Category	Score	Category
90	Professional, technical, and kindred workers	45	Operatives and kindred workers
81	Managers, officials, and proprietors, except farm	34	Service workers, including private household
71	Clerical, sales, and kindred workers	20	Laborers, except farm and mine
58	Craftsmen, foremen, and kindred workers		

The percentile norms on which these scores are based are interpreted as follows: Only two percent of the population has had more than four years of college training and only six percent of the population reported a family income over $10,000 in 1960. Thus, a person having both characteristics would score 98 on education and 94 on income. His average score of 96 would be added in with those of other people in his occupation to determine the overall status score for that occupation. The complete norms for education and income are as follows:

Scores for Categories of Years of School Completed

Score	Category	Score	Category	Score	Category
98	College: 5 or more	67	High school: 4	23	Elementary: 8
93	4	49	3	13	7
89	3	42	2	08	5 and 6
86	2	34	1	04	3 and 4
83	1			02	1 and 2
				01	None

Scores for Categories of Family Income (or Income of Persons Not in Families)

Score	Category	Score	Category	Score	Category
100	$25,000 or more	74	$7,000 to 7,499	21	$3,000 to $3,499
98	$15,000 to $24,999	69	$6,500 to $6,999	17	$2,500 to $2,999
94	$10,000 to $14,999	63	$6,000 to $6,499	12	$2,000 to $2,499
89	$9,500 to $9,999	57	$5,500 to $5,999	08	$1,500 to $1,999
87	$9,000 to $9,499	49	$5,000 to $5,499	05	$1,000 to $1,499
84	$8,500 to $8,999	41	$4,500 to $4,999	03	$500 to $999
81	$8,000 to $8,499	34	$4,000 to $4,499	01	Loss, none, or
78	$7,500 to $7,999	27	$3,500 to $3,999		less than $500

In addition to the preceding information, the basic descriptive document from the Census Bureau (1963) contains variations in status by region. For instance, Southerners score much lower than people from other regions, as one might expect. Similar variations by race, residence and stage in the life cycle are presented by Nam and Powers (1965), who point out the importance of taking these factors into account in assigning a person a single status score.

Another important feature of this research is that scores of status inconsistency have been calculated as well. In the national population, however, less than 30 percent of job-holders have scores on all three variables that are status consistent (roughly a 20-point difference across the three indices). As Hodge (1962) pointed out, it is probable that members of certain occupations, such as clergymen, are more likely to be status inconsistent than others.

References

Hodge, R., "The status consistency of occupational groups", American Sociological Review, 1962, 27, 336-343.

Nam, C. and Powers, M., "Variations in socio-economic structure by race, residence and the life cycle" American Sociological Review, 1965, 30, 97-103.

U. S. Bureau of the Census, Methodology and Scores of Socio-Economic Status Working Paper #15, Washington, D. C., 1963.

OCCUPATIONAL RATINGS (North and Hatt 1947, 1965)

Ratings were obtained by NORC from nearly 3,000 nationwide respondents in 1947 and again obtained in 1963, this time drawn from a sample less than a quarter the original size. Complete breakdown of percentages with each of the five response alternatives (plus "don't know") for each occupation in both samples is given in Hodge, et al. (1965). As noted in the introduction to the chapter, scores on the following occupations can vary from 20 (poor) to 100 (excellent).

In addition to the sets of ratings we have contrasted what appears to be the corresponding Duncan scale value. Major discrepancies were listed in the introduction to this section although the reader may want to check them for himself.

Gusfield and Schwartz (1963) have criticized the NORC scale as being evaluative or affective rather than descriptive or analytic. Although this is probably the case, it is hard to imagine any set of judges who would not rely on "good-bad" judgments in assessing occupational prestige.

References

Gusfield, J. and Schwartz, M., "The meanings of occupational prestige: reconsideration of the NORC scale", American Sociological Review 1963, 28, 265-270.

Hodge, R., Siegel, P. and Rossi, P., "Occupational prestige in the United States", in Bendix, R. and Lipset, S., (eds.) Class Status and Power New York: Free Press, 1965.

OCCUPATIONAL RATINGS

Paul K. Hatt and C. C. North

Occupation	1947	1963	Duncan*
U. S. Supreme Court Justice	96	94	93
Physician	93	93	92
State Governor	93	91	66(?)
Cabinet member in the federal government	92	90	84
Diplomat in the U. S. Foreign Service	92	89	84
Mayor of a large city	90	87	54(?)
College professor	89	90	84
Scientist	89	92	81
United States Representative in Congress	89	90	84
Banker	88	85	85
Government scientist	88	91	80
County judge	87	88	93
Head of a department in a state government	87	86	66
Minister	87	87	52
Architect	86	88	90
Chemist	86	89	79
Dentist	86	88	96
Lawyer	86	89	93
Member of the board of directors of a large corporation	86	87	62(?)
Nuclear physicist	86	92	80
Priest	86	86	52
Psychologist	85	87	81
Civil Engineer	84	86	84
Airline pilot	83	86	79
Artist who paints pictures that are exhibited in galleries	83	78	67
Owner of factory that employs about 100 people	82	80	79
Sociologist	82	83	81
Accountant for a large business	81	81	78
Biologist	81	85	80
Musician in a symphony orchestra	81	78	52
Author of novels	80	78	76
Captain in the regular army	80	82	54
Building contractor	79	80	51
Economist	79	78	80
Instructor in the public schools	79	82	72
Public school teacher	78	81	72
County agricultural agent	77	76	83
Railroad engineer	77	76	58
Farm owner and operator	76	74	36
Official of an international labor union	75	77	58
Radio announcer	75	70	65
Newspaper columnist	74	73	82
Owner-operator of a printing shop	74	75	49(?)
Electrician	73	76	44
Trained machinist	73	75	33

* For many of these occupations there is no precise Duncan equivalent. The most obvious cases of lack of equivalence are listed with a question mark (?).

Occupational Ratings (continued)

Occupation	1947	1963	Duncan
Welfare worker for a city government	73	74	64
Undertaker	72	74	59
Reporter on a daily newspaper	71	71	82
Manager of a small store in a city	69	67	62
Bookkeeper	68	70	51
Insurance agent	68	69	66
Tenant farmer--one who owns livestock and machinery and manages the farm	68	69	20
Traveling salesman for a wholesale concern	68	66	61
Playground director	67	63	67
Policeman	67	72	40
Railroad conductor	67	66	58
Mail carrier	66	66	53
Carpenter	65	68	19
Automobile repairman	63	64	19
Plumber	63	65	34
Garage mechanic	62	62	19
Local official of a labor union	62	67	58
Owner-operator of a lunch stand	62	63	37
Corporal in the regular army	60	62	(?)
Machine operator in a factory	60	63	16
Barber	59	63	17
Clerk in a store	58	56	39
Fisherman who owns his own boat	58	58	10
Streetcar motorman	58	56	34
Milk routeman	54	56	32
Restaurant cook	54	55	15
Truck driver	54	59	15
Lumberjack	53	55	04
Filling station attendant	52	51	19
Singer in a nightclub	52	54	52
Farmhand	50	48	06
Coal miner	49	50	02
Taxi driver	49	49	10
Railroad section hand	48	50	03
Restaurant waiter	48	49	16
Dock worker	47	50	11
Night watchman	47	50	18
Clothes presser in a laundry	46	45	15
Soda fountain clerk	45	44	17
Bartender	44	48	19
Janitor	44	48	09
Share cropper--one who owns no livestock or equipment and does not manage farm	40	42	14
Garbage collector	35	39	06
Street sweeper	34	36	06
Shoe shiner	33	34	08
AVERAGE	69.8	71.0	

INDEX OF STATUS CHARACTERISTICS (Warner, et al. 1949)

This index is composed of four status characteristics: occupation, source of income, type of house and type of residential area. The objective index which is based on weightings of these characteristics was found to correlate .97 with a more cumbersome Evaluated Participation method. This latter measure required that six sets of ratings be collected from socially aware persons from every stratum of society and then be checked and evaluated in terms of their consistency. Of the four status measures, the seven-point occupation scale alone correlated .91 with Evaluated Participation; the other three measures all correlated between .82 and .85. As mentioned previously, Warner, et al.'s sophisticated occupation scale may be adequate enough to be used alone.

For the total Index proposed by Warner, et al., however, occupation is not weighted much more heavily than the other status characteristics. The suggested weights are 4 for occupation, 3 for source of income, 3 for house type and 2 for dwelling area. The rating schemes for each characteristic are given on the following pages. Warner, et al. used the following boundaries for classifying respondents into one of the five classes with the percentage of respondents falling in each category listed in parentheses:

Upper class (3%)	12-22
Upper-middle class (11%)	23-37
Lower-middle class (31%)	38-51
Upper-lower class (41%)	52-66
Lower-lower class (14%)	67-84

An example of how this scheme works is shown by the following, a high-school student from Warner, et al.'s text:

Evelyn's father is a "clerk out at the mill" which gives him a rating of 3 for occupation. Since a clerk receives a salary, her father's rating for source of income is 4. She lives "with her parents in an average house", giving a rating of 3 for house type. For dwelling area, Evelyn receives a 3; she lives "in a fairly nice street in the Southeast region".

Occupation rating	3 (X4) =	12
Source of Income	4 (X3) =	12
House type	3 (X3) =	9
Dwelling area	3 (X2) =	6
		42 (Lower-middle class)

As a precautionary note, it should be mentioned that the weights given to the status characteristics were determined from a single regression equation instead of being calculated on the half of the sample and then cross-validated with the other half. Despite the competent research that went into their work, Warner, et al. have been rightly criticized for generalizing their results from small communities. Some of the rating scales making up the ISC might be much more difficult to apply to residents of metropolitan areas. The Index does have the advantage of not being dependent on shifting educational and income standards.

References: Warner, W., Meeker, M. and Eels, K., Social Class in America Chicago: Science Research Associates 1949.

Source of income was classified as follows and weighted 3:

1--Inherited wealth. Families were so classified who lived on money made by a previous generation. This includes money derived from savings and investments or business enterprises inherited from an earlier generation. Inherited wealth is frequently referred to as "old money" in contrast to "new money". This source of income has the highest prestige since it implies that there has been money in the family for several generations.

2--Earned wealth. Families or individuals were so classified if they lived on savings or investments earned by the present generation. This category implies considerable wealth, for the individual lives on interest from capital and has amassed sufficient money so that he does not need to work. This source of income applies most frequently to men who have made a large amount of money and are able to retire and live comfortably on their earnings. They differ from individuals who are retired because of old age and live on pensions, etc. In the present case, it is not that they are too old to work, but that they no longer need to work. One gains prestige in American society by being a successful business man and making a large fortune. Therefore, these individuals are given a higher rating than those who work for a living.

3--Profits and fees. This includes money which is paid to professional men for services and advice. It also includes money made by owners of businesses for sale of goods and royalties paid to writers, musicians, etc.

4--Salary. This is a regular income paid for services on a monthly, or yearly, basis. This category also includes the commission type of salary paid to salesmen.

5--Wages. This is distinguished from salary since the amount is determined by an hourly rate. It is usually paid on a daily or weekly basis.

6--Private Relief. This includes money paid by friends or relatives for the sake of friendship or because of family ties. It also includes money given by churches, associations, etc., when the agency does not reveal the names of those getting help. People receiving this form of income usually have no money themselves and only through this help are saved the shame of asking for public relief.

7--Public relief and non-respectable income. This includes money received from a government agency or from some semi-public charity organization which does not mind revealing the names of those getting help. A non-respectable income includes money made from illegal occupation as gambling, prostitution, and bootlegging (during prohibition).

People living on life insurance policies, social security benefits, or old age pensions were assigned the source of income on which they were dependent while they were working.

In general, if a person received income from more than one source, the chief source of income was used. However, there were some cases in which it was known that an individual's income was derived equally from two sources. In such cases it was possible to split the difference between the value assigned for two sources. This was done chiefly for members of the upper class who were working but were known to have inherited considerable wealth. It was also applied to business men who had a salary (4) and also had invested considerable money and derived part of their income from interest on earned wealth (2).

Type of housing (weighted 3) is given on a seven-point scale as follows:

1--Excellent houses. This includes only houses which are very large single-family dwellings in good repair and surrounded by large lawns and yards which are landscaped and well cared for. These houses have an element of ostentation with respect to size, architectural style, and general condition of yards and lawns.

2--Very good houses. Roughly, this includes all houses which do not quite measure up to the first category. The primary difference is one of size. They are slightly smaller, but still larger than utility demands for the average family.

3--Good houses. In many cases they are only slightly larger than utility demands. They are more conventional and less ostentatious than the two higher categories.

4--Average houses. One-and-a-half to two-story wood-frame and brick single-family dwellings. Conventional style, with lawns well cared for but not landscaped.

5--Fair houses. In general, this includes houses whose condition is not quite as good as those houses given a 4 rating. It also includes smaller houses in excellent condition.

6--Poor houses. In this, and the category below, size is less important than condition in determining evaluation. Houses in this category are badly run-down but have not deteriorated sufficiently that they cannot be repaired. They suffer from lack of care but do not have the profusion of debris which surrounds houses in the lowest category.

7--Very poor houses. All houses which have deteriorated so far that they cannot be repaired. They are considered unhealthy and unsafe to live in. All buildings not originally intended for dwellings, shacks, and over-crowded buildings. The halls and yards are littered with junk, and many have an extremely bad odor.

Using this classification, houses intended for one family but converted into multiple-family dwellings were handled as they had been in the first case; each dwelling unit was given a rating one point lower than the rating arrived at one the basis of the total structure. Apartments in regular apartment buildings were not limited to one rating but ranged from good housing to bad housing. It should be emphasized that in ranking apartments the total size of the structure is less important than the condition and the way the building is kept up, for the single fact that an apartment building is large does not make it a desirable place to live; a small apartment building may be considered a very good place to live. The best way to rank apartments seemed to be on the basis of the size of living unit per individual family and the building's exterior condition.

As is to be expected, the areas at the two extremes of the scale are most clearly defined and easiest to rank. Most of the areas defined fall in a general category of average or slightly below. A description of the levels and each category is given below and weight of 2 was given:

1--Very high. In Jonesville, as in most towns and small cities, this includes but one area. Residents, aware that this area has a high status reputation, remark that "no one can live here unless his family has lived in the community for

at least three generations." The best houses in town are located in such an area.
The street are wide and clean and have many trees.

2--High. Dwelling areas felt to be superior and well above average but a
little below the top. There are fewer mansions and pretentious houses in such
districts than in the first. However, the chief difference is one of reputation.

3--Above average. A little above average in social reputation and to the
eye of the scientific observer. This is an area of nice but not pretentious
houses. The streets are kept clean and the houses are well cared for. It is
known as a "nice place to live" but "society doesn't live here."

4--Average. These are areas of workingmen's homes which are small and
unpretentious but neat in appearance. In these areas live "the respectable people
in town who don't amount to much but never give anybody any trouble."

5--Below average. All the areas in this group are undesirable because they
are close to factories, or because they include the business section of town, or
are close to the railroad. There are more run-down houses here because there are
people living in these areas who "don't know how to take care of things." They
are more congested and heterogeneous than those above. It is said that "all
kinds of people live here, and you don't know who your neighbors will be."

6--Low. These areas are run-down and semi-slums. The houses are set close
together. The streets and yards are often filled with debris, and in some of the
smaller towns, like Jonesville, some of the streets are not paved.

7--Very low. Slum districts, the areas with the poorest reputation in town,
not only because of unpleasant and unhealthy geographical positions--for example,
being near a garbage dump or a swamp--but also because of the social stigma
attached to those who live there. The houses are little better than shacks.
The people are referred to by such terms as "squatters along the canal," and are
said to be lazy, shiftless, ignorant, and immoral. This general reputation is
assigned to most people living in such sections regardless of their abilities or
accomplishments.

Revised Scale for Rating Occupation (Weight 9)

Rating Assigned to Occupation	Professionals	Proprietors and Managers	Business Men	Clerks and Kindred Workers, Etc.	Manual Workers	Protective and Service Workers	Farmers
1	Lawyers, doctors, dentists, engineers, judges, high-school superintendents, veterinarians, ministers (graduated from divinity school), chemists, etc. with post-graduate training, architects	Businesses valued at $75,000 and over	Regional and divisional managers of large financial and industrial enterprises	Certified Public Accountants			Gentleman farmers
2	High-school teachers, trained nurses, chiropodists, chiropractors, undertakers, ministers (some training), newspaper editors, librarians (graduate)	Businesses valued at $20,000 to $75,000	Assistant managers and office and department managers of large businesses, assistants to executives, etc.	Accountants, salesmen of real estate, of insurance, postmasters			Large farm owners, farm owners
3	Social workers, grade-school teachers, optometrists, librarians (not graduate), undertaker's assistants, ministers (no training)	Businesses valued at $5,000 to $20,000	All minor officials of businesses	Auto salesmen, bank clerks and cashiers, postal clerks, secretaries to executives, supervisors of railroad, telephone, etc., justices of the peace	Contractors		
4		Businesses valued at $2,000 to $5,000		Stenographers, bookkeepers, rural mail clerks, railroad ticket agents, sales people in dry goods store, etc.	Factory foremen, electricians { own plumbers { business carpenters { ness watchmakers	Dry cleaners, butchers, sheriffs, railroad engineers and conductors	
5		Businesses valued at $500 to $2,000		Dime store clerks, hardware salesmen, beauty operators, telephone operators	Carpenters, plumbers, electricians (apprentice), timekeepers, linemen, telephone or telegraph, radio repairmen, medium-skill workers	Barbers, firemen, butcher's apprentices, practical nurses, policemen, seamstresses, cooks in restaurant, bartenders	Tenant farmers
6		Businesses valued at less than $500			Moulders, semi-skilled workers, assistants to carpenter, etc.	Baggage men, night policemen and watchmen, taxi and truck drivers, gas station attendants, waitresses in restaurant	Small tenant farmers
7					Heavy labor, migrant work, odd-job men, miners	Janitors, scrubwomen, newsboys	Migrant farm laborers

INDEX OF SOCIAL POSITION (Hollingshead and Redlich 1958)

Weightings on the three characteristics comprising this scale--residence, occupation and education--were determined by correlating the three scale values with class position as judged by two sociologists familiar with the community. There was 96 percent agreement between judges, using five categories. As was the case for Warner, et al.'s ISC, occupation correlated highest (r=.88) with judged class position. Weights of 9 for occupation, 6 for residence and 5 for education were finally chosen on the basis of multiple regression analysis in which the total correlation between the index and estimated class was .94. Again, as in Warner, et al.'s study, proper cross-validation was not used in the determination of weights.

Boundary scores across the five classes employed by the authors were as follows:

Class	I	Highest	(3%)	20-31
	II	High	(10%)	32-55
	III	Middle	(19%)	56-86
	IV	Low	(48%)	87-115
	V	Lowest	(20%)	116-134

It will be noted that distribution by class is essentially similar to that found in Warner, et al.'s study.

To give an example of Index scoring: the score of a family whose head works at a clerical job, is a high school graduate, and lives in a middle-rank residential area would be:

Residence	3	(X6)	= 18
Occupation	4	(X9)	= 36
Education	4	(X5)	= 20
			74 (Class III)

Reference

    Hollingshead, A. and Redlich, F. Social Class and Mental Illness New York: Wiley, 1958.

1. <u>The Residential Scale</u>. The residential scale was based upon ecological research carried on by Maurice R. Davie and his associates in the New Haven community over a 25-year span. In the early 1930s, Davie mapped the city of New Haven ecologically, and ranked residential areas on a six-position scale that ranged from the finest homes to the poorest tenements. Jerome K. Myers brought Davie's data up to data as of 1950, within the city of New Haven, and mapped the suburban towns in the same way that Davie had mapped New Haven in earlier years. This work provided a uniform scale for the evaluation of addresses. Weight=6

2. <u>The Occupational Scale</u>. The occupational scale is a modification of the Alba Edwards system of classifying occupations into socioeconomic groups used by the United States Bureau of the Census. The essential differences between the Edwards system and the one used is that Edwards'does not differentiate among kinds of professionals or the size and economic strengths of businesses. The scale used in the <u>Index of Social Position</u> ranks professions into different groups and business by their size and value. Without further discussion of similarities and differences between the Edwards system and ours, we will proceed to characterize each of the seven positions on the scale we used: (1) executives and proprietors of large concerns, and major professionals, (2) managers and proprietors of medium-sized businesses and lesser professionals, (3) administrative personnel of large concerns, owners of small independent businesses, and semiprofessionals, (4) owners of little businesses, clerical and sales workers, and technicians, (5) skilled workers, (6) semiskilled workers, and (7) unskilled workers. Weight = 9.

3. <u>The Educational Scale</u>. The educational scale is premised upon the assumption that men and women who possess similar educations will tend to have similar tastes and similar attitudes, and they will also tend to exhibit similar behavior patterns.

The educational scale was divided into seven positions:

(1) Graduate professional training. (Persons who completed a recognized professional course which led to the receipt of a graduate degree were given scores of 1.)

(2) Standard college or university graduation. (All individuals who had completed a four-year college or university course leading to a recognized college degree were assigned the same scores. No differentiation was made between state universities or private colleges.)

(3) Partial college training. (Individuals who had completed at least one year but not a full college course were assigned this position.)

(4) High school graduation. (All secondary school graduates whether from a private preparatory school, public high school, trade school, or parochial high school were given this score.)

(5) Partial high school. (Individuals who had completed the tenth or eleventh grades, but had not completed high school were given this score.)

(6) Junior high school. (Individuals who had completed the seventh grade through the ninth grade were given this position.)

(7) Less than seven years of school. (Individuals who had not completed the seventh grade were given the same scores irrespective of the amount of education they had received.) Weight = 5.

INDEX OF CLASS POSITION (Ellis, et al. 1963)

This index grew out of a need for a measure of social class in a college student setting where neither the Hollingshead and Redlich nor Warner, et al. schemes were applicable because residential information was not readily available. The proposed index uses two pieces of information: occupation and subjective class identification. Occupation is coded on the Hollingshead and Redlich scale, and the class identification question is based on Kahl and Davis's (1955) modification of the Center's question.

The arguments advanced for consideration of this index are based on interviews with 200 Stanford freshmen. The Index of Class Position was found to be a better predictor of upper class respondents than Hollingshead and Redlich's scale alone, although the differences do not appear dramatic enough to warrant unqualified recommendation. The combination of subjective and objective measures, however, seems a good direction for research, although Haer (1955) found objective and subjective indices to differ depending on the size and heterogeneity of the city. In the present study, the two indices correlated .70.

Boundary scores across six classes were as follows:

I	Upper	2
II	Upper-middle	3-4
III	Middle	5-7
IV	Lower-middle	8-9
V	Upper-lower	10
VI	Lower-lower	11-12

References

Ellis, R., Lane, W. and Olesen, V., "The index of class position: an improved intercommunity measure of stratification", American Sociological Review, 1963, 28, 271-277.

Haer, J. "A comparative sutdy of the classification technique of Warner and Centers", American Sociological Review, 1955, 20, 689-692.

Kahl, J. and Davis, J. "A comparison of indices of socio-economic status", American Sociological Review, 1955, 20, 317-325.

1. An American social scientist has made a study of the United States which indicated that in this country there are four major social classes: the Middle, the Lower, the Working and the Upper social classes. In which of these social classes would you say your family belongs?
(If Middle) Would you say your family belonged to the upper-middle, middle-middle or lower-middle social class?

1. Upper
2. Upper-middle
3. Middle-middle
4. Lower-middle
5. Working

2. Occupation (after Hollingshead and Redlich):

1. Executives and proprietors of large concerns; major professionals
2. Managers and proprietors of large concerns: lesser professionals
3. Administrative personnel of large concerns: owners of small, independent businesses; semiprofessionals
4. Owners of little businesses; clerical and sales workers; technicians
5. Skilled workers
6. Semi-skilled workers
7. Unskilled workers.

CLASS IDENTIFICATION (Centers and others 1949-1966)

In 1945, Centers (1949) asked a national sample of 1100 white male adults the following question, which was asked again in the 1952 Survey Research Center election study:

If you were asked to use one of the four names for your social class which would you say belonged in: the middle class, lower class, working class or upper class?

The following distributions were obtained:

	Centers	SRC (1952)
Upper class	3%	2%
Middle class	43	35
Working class	51	59
Lower class	1	2
Don't believe in classes	1	1
Dont't know	1	1

It is generally conceded that the Survey Research Center results are more representative of the population as a whole. The SRC sample also includes both men and women.

As part of its continuing studies of electoral behavior, the Survey Research Center has asked a class identification question of samples of between 1250 and 2000 respondents regularly for the past 15 years. Since slightly different wording has been employed since 1952, comparability to the responses to Center's question is limited. However, the major wording difference is the omission of the choices of "upper" and "lower" class, which did not seem to be very popular. In 1956 a three-part question was instituted, in which the respondents first indicated whether they thought of themselves as belonging to a certain class or not (about two-thirds do). All respondents, whether or not they had answered the first part affirmatively, were asked to which class they belonged. The question and its distribution for national samples in 1956, 1958 and 1966 are as follows:

There's quite a bit of talk these days about different social classes. Most people say they belong either to the middle class or to the working class. Do you ever think of yourself as being in one of these classes?

	1956	1958
Yes	63%	65%
No	36	34
Other	1	1

Which class? Would you say that you are about an average (Class Selected) person or that you are in the upper part of the (Class Selected)? (All respondents, whether answering YES or NO to the above)

	1956	1958	1966
(Average working class	51%	51%	46%
(Working class, NA average			
(or upper part	2	1	2
(Upper part of working class	8	7	10
(Average middle class	29	29	30
(Middle class, NA average or upper	1	1	2
(Upper middle class	7	9	8
(Rejects idea of class	1	1	1
(Don't know, other	1	1	1

The final part of this latter series of questions was dropped in the 1960 and 1964 elections with the following results:

There's quite a bit of talk these days about different social classes. Most people say they belong either to the middle class or to the working class. Do you ever think of yourself as being in one of these classes?

	1960	1964
Yes	72%	61%
No	25	37
Other	3	2

Which one? (All respondents)

	1960	1964
Middle	32%	40%
Working	64	56
Does not accept idea	2	2
DK, other	2	2

The same question was asked in 1962 with one important exception: that those answering "no" to the first part of the question were not asked the second. Hence, the 1962 figures are not comparable to those obtained earlier or later.

Summarizing across the years produces the following distribution:

	1952	1956	1958	1960	1964	1966
Middle class	35%	37%	39%	32%	40%	40%
Working class	59	61	59	64	56	58
Upper or lower	4	-	-	-	-	-
Does not accept idea	1	1	1	2	2	1
DK; other	1	1	1	2	2	1

Outside of 1960, the results show only a slight increase in middle-class identification of the population over the years, in spite of the rapid rise in number of people in higher-status occupations. Most interesting are the differential results by occupational level. As expected, those respondents in higher level and white-collar occupations identify more with the middle classes, and those respondents in blue-collar occupations identify more with the working classes. The relation is not perfect, however; Hamilton (1966) has noted that roughly half of the clerical and sales group[*] identify themselves as working class. Tucker (1966), on the other hand, found the following distribution by occupation in a 1963 national sample:

If you were asked to describe your social class, to which class would you say you belonged--working, lower, lower-middle, middle, upper-middle or upper?

	Clerical & Sales	Craftsmen & Operatives
Lower and working	18%	42%
Lower-middle	11	10
Middle	52	38
Upper-middle and upper	19	10
	(N=62)	(N=190)

While there are some serious problems in comparing Tucker's six-alternative question with the simpler Survey Research Center question, it is obvious that respondents find the "working" response less appealing in a context offering more alternatives. As the above table shows, a greater number of alternatives also leads to greater discrimination by occupation, in line with theoretical expectations. Only future investigations using a number of approaches (see Landecker 1963) will determine which type of question is the more accurate indicator of class identification. Hamilton (1966) reports an interesting finding in favor of the SRC question: 91 percent of the working-class identifiers as opposed to only 30 percent of middle-class identifiers report their family background as working-class. The contiguity of the two questions in the interview schedule may be spuriously boosting this relation, however. Future research on class identification should be directed both at a multiple-indicator approach and at a special examination of people who hold strong, weak and inconsistent attitudes on class identification questions.

For some comparative data on class identification across nine countries, the reader is referred to Buchanan and Cantril (1953)

---

[*]It will be remembered from Robinson's chapter that this group showed inconsistent work attitudes _vis-a-vis_ other white-collar jobs.

References

Buchanan, W. and Cantril, H. How Nations See Each Other Urbana: University of Illinois Press, 1953.

Centers, R. The Psychology of Social Classes Princeton, N. J.: Princeton University Press, 1949.

Hamilton, R. "The marginal middle class: a reconsideration" American Sociological Review, 1966, 31, 192-199.

Reference (continued)

Landecker, W. "Class crystallization and class consciousness" American Sociological Review, 1963, 28, 219-229.

Tucker, C. "On working-class identification" American Sociological Review 1966, 31, 856-857 (See also Hamilton's "Reply to Tucker" on p.857)

FACETS FOR JOB EVALUATION (Guttman 1965)

As mentioned in the introduction, this instrument is not intended to be a measure of stratification, although it effectively performs this function. Each of the five items is intended to rank one's job "with respect to level of advancement of work specified by the job and without reference to line of work". Each item deals with restrictions on the job.

Guttman suggests that there twelve ordered levels defined by the five items. These are:

1. $a_1\ b_1\ c_1\ d_1\ e_1$ (low)

2. $a_1\ b_1\ c_1\ \underline{d_2}\ e_1$

3. $a_1\ b_1\ \underline{c_2}\ d_2\ e_1$

4. $\underline{a_2}\ b_1\ c_2\ d_2\ e_1$

5. $a_2\ \underline{b_2}\ c_2\ d_2\ e_1$

6. $a_2\ b_2\ c_2\ d_2\ \underline{e_2}$

7. $a_2\ \underline{b_3}\ c_2\ d_2\ e_2$

8. $a_2\ b_3\ c_2\ \underline{d_3}\ e_2$

9. $a_2\ b_3\ c_2\ d_3\ \underline{e_3}$

10. $\underline{a_3}\ b_3\ c_2\ d_3\ e_3$

11. $a_3\ b_3\ \underline{c_3}\ d_3\ e_3$

12. $\underline{a_4}\ b_3\ c_3\ d_3\ e_3$ (high)

Outside of a couple of newspaper articles, there is no formal citation to give for the present scale. We were introduced to the scale in a seminar on facet theory conducted by Professor Guttman, and we understand that it will appear in his forthcoming publication on this topic. Readers intrigued with the scheme should contact Professor Guttman at Hebrew University in Jerusalem, Israel for more of the complex background of the items. Item E, by the way, is considered optional.

A. <u>Specificity of Guidelines</u>

    a_1 Detailed instructions

    a_2 General instructions

    a_3 Policy

    a_4 Creates policy

B. <u>Subordination to Supervision</u>

    b_1 Receives instructions

    b_2 Consults

    b_3 Independent (selects consultants)

C. <u>Time of Supervision</u>

    c_1 Constant and direct

    c_2 At completion of each task

    c_3 At fixed intervals

D. <u>Freedom to Change Matters Received</u>

    d_1 Transmit as is

    d_2 Modify

    d_3 Create

(Optional) E. <u>Level of Receiver</u>

    e_1 Mixed

    e_2 High

    e_3 Very high

15. STATUS INCONSISTENCY:

SOME CONCEPTUAL AND METHODOLOGICAL CONSIDERATIONS

Stanislav V. Kasl
Institute for Social Research
The University of Michigan

This chapter has five aims: 1) to note the several types of status incon-sistency which can be distinguished and to suggest differing labels for these; 2) to outline the theoretical significance of the status inconsistency variable and thereby to justify our interest in it; 3) to indicate the range of empirical studies which have investigated the correlates of status inconsistency; 4) to consider some conceptual problems which surround the notion of status inconsistency and which have tended to detract from the clarity and significance of past findings; 5) to examine some methodological issues in data analysis; specifically, those attendant upon attempts to construct an index of status inconsistency and to establish its correlates.

1) Types of status inconsistency

It is rather clear that a typology of status inconsistency can be generated out of an enumeration of the individuals or units on whom two or more status ranks are measured. Thus, status inconsistency can be a property of:

a) a single individual, such as when we are comparing education of the family head with his occupation.

b) a "natural" pair of individuals, such as comparing husband's education with wife's education. (When such a pair of individuals spans two generations, as in the case of father's occupation and son's occupation, the usual term "mobility" is certainly appropriate. Chapter 17 will consider some theoretical and research issues dealing with mobility.)

c) a group of interacting individuals, such as Air Force crews (Adams, 1953) or task-oriented groups (Burnstein and Zajonc, 1965; Exline and Ziller, 1959). A group may be considered high on status inconsistency if: (1) it has many individuals for each of whom the investments or contributions are out of line with his rewards; (2) if it consists of individuals homogeneous with respect to investments, but heterogeneous in rewards; (3) if it consists of individuals heterogeneous with respect to investment, but homogeneous in rewards.

d) a collection of individuals, such as those belonging to the same occupational groups. Hodge (1962) has recently argued that occupations are meaningful social units and that one should not neglect investigations of the status inconsistency of different occupational groups.

Given then the fact that there are at least four distinguishable types of status inconsistency, and that, moreover, a plethora of terms exists labelling the same phenomenon--status incongruence, discrepancy, imbalance, equilibrium, crystallization and inconsistency--one is tempted to offer the suggestion that different terms be used to designate the different types. Since the author is aware that stipulations for new linguistic conventions are notorious in their failure to achieve the desired goal, he offers the following labelling rules for the more limited purpose of clarity and convenience in the present report: a) Status incongruence as property of a single individual; b) Status discrepancy as a property of a pair of individuals; c) Status equilibrium as property of an interacting group; d) Status crystallization as property of a collective, such as an occupational group. That still leaves status inconsistency as a general term representing all of the subtypes.

2) Theoretical considerations

Let us now turn to a brief consideration of the theoretical significance of status inconsistency. The long standing interest of social scientists in status variables stems, in large part, from the symbolic interactionist position of Cooley (1902) and Mead (1934), and from role theory (e.g., Biddle and Thomas, 1966; Gross, et al. 1958; Sarbin, 1954). This broad theoretical orientation asserts that an individual's rank or position on a status dimension is important because it partly determines certain expectations about his behavior. Specifically, an individual's rank affects his expectations about the behavior of others toward him, his expectations of himself and others' expectations of him. The total pattern of these interacting expectations will influence the individual's concept of himself and the concept others have of him, that is, his self-identity and public identity, respectively (French & Kahn, 1962; Miller, 1963).

Recently, it has been argued that the averaging of the various status indicators in order to arrive at a single index is not always a satisfactory procedure and that one should also consider the congruence or the discrepancies among them (Benoit-Smullyan, 1944; Fenchel, et al. 1951; Lenski, 1954). If an individual's rank on one status dimension is out of line with his rank on another, then, according to role theory, there is the strong possibility of conflicting expectations about the behavior of others and uncertainty about appropriateness of one's own behavior. This, in turn, should lead to role conflict, unsatisfactory social relationships, social ambiguity, unstable or inconsistent self-identity, a more favorable orientation toward social change and attempts to establish a better costs-rewards balance (Broom, 1959; Goffman, 1957; Homans, 1961; Jackson, 1962; Lenski, 1954; Sampson, 1963). In short, when there is an inconsistency among the several status indicators which are used to characterize an individual, he is presumed to be under stress which is then predicted to have adverse effects on his physical and mental health.

It is possible that future developments and refinements of status inconsistency theory will lead to three somewhat different positions deriving from: a) role theory (e.g., Jackson, 1962; Lenski, 1954); b) a Thibaut and Kelley (1959) kind of analysis of interpersonal relationships with emphasis on cost-reward matrices (e.g., Homans, 1961; Hodge, 1962); and c) a general cognitive consistency orientation (e.g., Sampson, 1963). At the moment it would seem important to remember two points. One is that we can distinguish at least four types of status inconsistency (as outlined above), and the other is that the effects of status inconsistency need not be investigated on the selfsame individual(s) on whom status inconsistency is assessed. Thus, for example, one can study the effects of the husband's status incongruence on his wife, or the effects of parents' status discrepancy on the offspring. This would seem to imply that future theory needs extension, as well as refinements. At present it is strongest in characterizing effects of status incongruence on the person's own health and behavior and additional theoretical formulations will have to be developed to cover effects of other types of status inconsistency on other individuals. For example, a recent report (Kasl and Cobb, 1967) offers a theoretical explanation of the effects of parents' status discrepancy on physical and mental health of the adult offspring.

Also worth noting is the fact that in current work these distinctions are not clearly recognized. As Mitchell (1964) notes, Lenski (1954) uses all the characteristics of husbands in classifying their wives, whereas Jackson (1962) uses only the husbands' occupation, together with wives' own education and racial-ethnic orgin, to classify the wives. Similarly, a report offering a status inconsistency index based on national norms (U. S. Bureau of the Census, 1963) uses <u>total</u> family income to characterize the family head, while in another study it is stated the "since the only income data available were on total family income, this dimension was omitted" (Jackson, 1962, p.471).

3) <u>Some empirical findings</u>

Keeping the above points in mind, let us now turn to a brief examination of the major relevant studies. Individuals whose status indices are incongruent report more psychophysiological symptoms (Jackson, 1962; Jackson and Burke, 1965), have more rheumatoid arthritis (King and Cobb, 1958), are more likely to be liberal in their political attitudes (Lenski, 1954) and to be dissatisfied with the power distribution in our society (Goffman, 1957), and tend to show less social participation (Lenski, 1956). Members of interacting workgroups show greater mutual trust, intimacy, congeniality and agreement when they are characterized by high status equilibrium (Adams, 1953; Exline and Ziller, 1959). Negative evidence, however, is reported by Kornhauser (1965) who studied men coming from a rather restricted range of occupations and found no relationship between an index of mental health and several measures of incongruence.

Notable are also a few studies which pay attention to the direction of status incongruence. Thus, some writers have interpreted high education-low occupation incongruence as a discrepancy between aspirations and achievement and have related such incongruence to job dissatisfaction (Mann, 1953) and to higher rates of first admissions to hospital for schizophrenia among urban Negroes (Parker and Kleiner, 1966). In one study (Jackson and Burke, 1965) to direction of status incongruence was important in one of the two alternative regression models which could be chosen.

The effects of parental status discrepancy on the offspring have also been investigated. Several studies report that when mother's education (or occupational status prior to marriage) exceeds father's, the offspring's attained or aspired education will be higher (Floud, et al. 1954; Krauss, 1964; Morgan, et al. 1962). In these studies, however, the effects of vertical status do not seem to have been fully eliminated. A recent report indicates that parental status incongruence and discrepancy can have strong effects on the physical and mental health of the adult offspring (Cobb and Kasl, 1966; Kasl and Cobb, 1966).

4) <u>Methodological considerations</u>

Let us now turn to the general problem: What conceptual distinctions and clarifications need to be made in order to evaluate past work on status inconsistency and to plan future studies? It would seem that one needs to consider the following points:

1) What dimensions (status ranks) should be used?
2) What population and environmental characteristics will enhance or attenuate the predicted effects of status inconsistency?
3) Should one expect different types of status inconsistency to have differential effects?

The problem of choice of status ranks to be used in deriving a measure of status inconsistency is one which different authors face with varying degrees of thoroughness. A recent report from the Census Bureau (U. S. Bureau of the Census, 1963; see also Nam and Powers, 1965) offers this rather skimpy justification for its choice of variables: "The component items of the measures (occupation, education and income) were selected because they represent somewhat different aspects of socioeconomic status...An ethnic characteristic (e.g., race or nationality) was not included because it was felt that such an item can be more properly treated as a correlate of, rather than as a component of, socioeconomic status" (p.3). Many other writers (e.g., Landecker, 1963; Lenski, 1954 and 1956; Jackson, 1962) would presumably disagree, since they did include racial-ethnic origin in their measure of status incongruence. On the other hand, there are social scientists like Goffman (1957) who consider the problem of choice more thoroughly and offer an explicit theoretical rationale for their choice of status dimensions. That such a choice will affect the comparability of results should not be doubted. Lenski (1956a) argues that Kenkel's (1956) failure to replicate the original (Lenski, 1954) findings stems, in part, from the use of different components in Kenkel's status incongruence index. Lenski's justification for his own choice of status dimensions is nothing more than the assertion that "they seemed to be the four basic components of status in contemporary American life" (1956, p.368). Jackson and Burke (1965) obtained somewhat different reuslts, depending on whether or not their analytical model assumed that racial-ethnic status per se has an additive effect. Demerath (1962), Kenkel (1956) and Mitchell (1964) have all suggested that much of the effect attributed by Lenski (1959) to incongruence may, in fact, be due to a difference between high and low ethnic status.

What, then, should be our choice of the status dimensions that will make up the status inconsistency index? What guidelines should we use in this choice? No firm answer to these questions seems possible inasmuch as: 1) different theoretical orientations suggest somewhat different dimensions, and 2) different population and environmental characteristics may make different dimensions more suitable for a particular study.

Irrespective of the theoretical orientation used, the following would seem to be basic requirements in choosing appropriate status dimensions (they are based on Goffman's (1957) analysis of the problem).

1) Adequate agreement in the population, or relevant subpopulation, on the ordering of the units of the heirarchical dimension.

2) Evidence that the dimension is an adequate indicator of some orientation or expectation on the part of the office holder and/or the role senders.

3) Evidence that the two orientations or expectations deriving from the two status dimensions being paired are to some degree, and in sone sense, consistent or inconsistent with each other.

4) Evidence that the life situations in which the respondent typically finds himself arouse at the same time both sets of orientations or expectations.

The above four criteria, however, should not be seen as more than approximate and incomplete guides. Consider, for example, a comparison of husband's education with wife's education. If the husband has a college degree and the wife only a high school degree, then their marriage might reasonably be characterized as status discrepant, using role theory (e.g., Jackson, 1962) and the above criteria. On the other hand, a Homans-type analysis of their relationship might reveal that no status discrepancy exists because the husband's higher "investment", higher education, is accompanied by higher "rewards", higher power and respect. Or consider the hypothetical case of a Negro doctor, a combination of low racial-ethnic status and high occupational status. If such an individual lives in a segregated neighborhood, treats only Negro patients, and belongs to a segregated medical association, then his incongruence should be near a minimum. Racial-ethnic status, in any case, is difficult to fit into Homans' theoretical framework; that is, it is not quite clear why, in a work situation for example, being a Negro is comparable to other forms of low "investment", such as poor education or poor skills, and why it should lead to differential expectations about "commensurate rewards". A final comment on the inadvisability of using routinely racial-ethnic status as one of the components of indices of status inconsistency: it is such a powerful, all-pervasive characteristic of an individual that to treat it in an undifferentiated way as one of a number of status variables may tend to dilute its effects and obscure its true role (see also Demerath (1962) and Mitchell (1964) for an expression of a similar viewpoint).

The national data on correlates of status inconsistency (U. S. Bureau of the Census, 1963; Nam and Powers, 1965) raise additional questions. For one, there is a strong association between types of status inconsistency and the life cycle: in those family heads under 35 the most common types of inconsistency are those reflecting low income and high education. With increasing age, up to 64, the reverse types of inconsistency become more common: low education and high income. Part of this effect, presumably, is due to the historical trend in educational attainment. There also appear to be regional differences: in the West those types of inconsistency reflecting high occupation are especially infrequent, and those reflecting high income are especially frequent, while in the South the pattern is reversed. However, the racial-urban correlates appear to be largely an artifact: the excess of status consistency in non-white family heads in rural areas seems to be primarily due to the fact that a majority of those respondents belong to the lowest category of overall socioeconomic status. And, of course, being in an extreme category makes it difficult to be also very inconsistent on the separate status indicators.

Now if these findings indicate that, for example, a certain type of inconsistency is typical for a certain stage of life cycle, then are we not facing somewhat of a dilemma: calling something incongruous even though it is really

382

something typical, expected? But what about occupational differences? Is it not
possible that the effects of the life cycle are more powerful in some occupations,
like college professors or business managers, than in others, such as semi-
skilled laborers, where increases in income may hardly keep up with the pace set
by inflation? And what about regional differences? Should the Southern high
school teacher be necessarily classified as status inconsistent because, in part,
the rest of the country pays its teachers more? These considerations suggest that
inconsistency should be viewed as a departure from the norms characterizing
the respondent's own reference group, rather than as a departure from national
norms. Minimally, this would demand controls for age, sex, race, possibly also
geographical region, urban-rural difference, and occassionally, occupational
groups. Of course, the controls have to be instituted at the point of construction of the inconsistency index, rather than only during analysis of its correlates.
That is, it would not be carrying out the intent of the above suggestion if we
were to use a single set of cut-off points for computing consistency for all
subjects, but then to split up the subjects according to age in order to see if
the correlates of inconsistency vary with age.

In concluding the discussion of choice of status dimensions, we need to raise
one more question: what role should a factor analysis of the intercorrelations
of an exhaustive set of status dimensions play in our decisions? The answer here
would seem to depend partly on how much we want to be guided by the pattern of
obtained intercorrelations, rather than by theoretical considerations. Stauts
inconsistency theory, of course, does not state how well the various status
indicators should be correlated; however, implicitly it seems to suggest that the
two status variables being paired should be moderately correlated. If the
correlation is too high, only a very small fraction of the cases can be classified
as inconsistent, while if the correlation is very low, then it is probable that
a position on one dimension does not arouse expectations about a commensurate
position on the other one. It then follows from this kind of a viewpoint that
factor analysis is not highly useful here since in using factor-based status
dimensions we would be picking those dimensions which are minimally correlated
with each other. The usefulness of factor analysis would also depend on the clarity
of a particular set of results. Thus, in the study by Kahl and Davis (1955),
only two factors were obtained, one of which was a mixture of house-residential
area values and of parental status. Moreover, income could not be clearly placed
with either factor. A status incongruence index derived from these two factors
would thus be an ambiguous mixture of mobility and consistency.

The next question to be considered is: Should we expect different types of
status incongruence to have differential effects? The general position which will
be offered here is that given the imperfect articulation of the status inconsistency theory and given the uncertainty surrounding the choice of status
variables, our data analysis methods must be detailed enough to detect relationships
other than a global inconsistency effect. This would suggest that status variables
need to be considered in pairs and the direction of inconsistency also noted. Some
crucial variables, as racial-ethnic origin, ought to be treated alternatively
both as status dimensions and as control variables.

This position of openness to new or divergent relationships is an obvious,
sensible research strategy (though just as obviously ignored in a number of past
studies). However, it can be also justified on theoretical grounds. Broom (1959),
in an programmatic article, strongly suggests that variations in profiles of

status inconsistency may have important implications for role conflict, upward mobility and mental health. The work of Parker and Kleiner (1966) also argues strongly for asymmetrical effects of education-occupation incongruence. If education and occupation indicate level of aspiration and achievement, respectively, then the combination of high education and low occupation creates but temporary dissonance which can be easily "resolved" with an additional perception, like "I am a failure" or "They discriminate against me." On the other hand, low education and high occupation may be associated with high self-evaluation, as well as some of the adverse effects predicated from role theory (e.g., Jackson, 1962). Even Homans' (1961) theoretical analysis in terms of investments and commensurate rewards seems to suggest asymmetry of inconsistency effects. If the rewards are seen as too low, for a given level of investment, the person may seek to have his rewards raised and, if unsuccessful, may lower in some way his investments. But, if the rewards are seen initially as too high, the person may react by striving to increase his investment or possibly by changing his notion about what is commensurate.

5) Methods of statistical analysis

Let us now turn to some methodological and statistical issues, most of which revolve around the problem of the relationship of vertical status to status inconsistency, and the association of both of these to selected dependent variables. We may begin by noting some necessary consequences of the computational procedures which yield the inconsistency indices. One consequence is that if overall status is a simple average of the various status components, then individuals who are very high or very low on overall status cannot be very incongruent. This is by virtue of the arithmetic involved and should not be claimed either as an important theoretical point or as a meaningful empirical finding, as some have done (e.g., Freedman, et al. 1956). Another consequence is that if occupation, education and income are used in deriving an incongruence index, then presenting the results for high, medium and low occupational levels, as Goffman (1957) does, may not be enough of a control for overall status. That is, subjects who are high on occupation but are classified as incongruent, because of their relatively low education and/or income, must necessarily have an overall status rank which is lower than the rank of subjects who are high on occupation and are classified as congruent. Finally, we may note that if a group of status congruous subjects is compared with incongruous subjects and they are found to be equal on mean overall status, the two groups must still be different with respect to the distribution of overall status scores. Specifically, the congruous subjects will have more cases who are at the extremes of the distribution, while the incongruous subjects will have more cases in the middle of the distribution. Thus, if the relationship between overall status and some dependent variables is non-linear--U-shaped, inverted U-shaped, positively accelerated or negatively accelerated--then the comparability of the two groups on mean status still does not rule out all effects of overall status.

When the dependent variable is not related to the separate status dimensions, then the major issue is how to construct an index of status incongruence. When two status dimensions, like education and occupation are being paired, three possibilities exist: 1) to form a two-by-two table by splitting each variable at the median, with the high-high and low-low quadrants yielding the congruous cases; 2) to group the subjects into a number of categories according to educational level, and then for each educational category find the median level of occupation and select some predetermined proportion of subjects around the median as the congruous cases; 3) to obtain the correlation between education and occupation and then use the regression equation (e.g., Guilford, 1956, pp. 366-368) to compute for each level of education the occupational level. The amount of difference between predicted and actual occupational level reflects the amount of incongruence. It should be apparent that these three methods yield progressively more refined scores. In the analysis of the data we want to carry out two orthogonal comparisons: 1) congruous vs. incongruous and 2) education $>$ occupation vs. education $<$ occupation. When the dependent variable is measured on an interval scale, the appropriate analysis of variance procedure may be found in Hays (1963) or Winer (1962). However, when we are dealing with a dichotomous variable or a nominal scale, the procedures for partitioning contingency tables suggested by Bresnahan and Shapiro (1966) or Castellan (1965) may be used.

When the dependent variable is associated with one or more of the status variables, a number of possibilities exist. If the dependent variable is measured on an interval scale, one may simply dichotomize the two status variables at the median and treat the problem as a two way analysis of variance where the inter-action term reflects the incongruence effects. Winer, (1962) discusses the least-square and unweighted-means solutions for the case of unequal cell frequencies and the appropriateness of each. It must be noted, in addition, that when the cell frequencies are highly variable, the resultant interaction term is underestimated. When the number of cases is sufficiently large, we may want to split the status variables into more than two categories. In that case the main effects should be also tested for linear and non-linear components; similarly, the interaction effect should be broken down into linear and residual components since we are specifically interested in demonstrating that as status incongruence increases, the interaction effect is stronger. An alternative procedure would be to use regression analysis in which the status dimensions are converted to dummy variables (Suits, 1957). It is this procedure which Jackson and Burke (1965) chose to reanalyze the old Jackson (1962) data.

It should be also possible to deal with the problem of an association of the dependent variable with the status variables by first computing corrected scores on the former. Here, we should avoid an overall status score since as Demerath (1962) and Mitchell (1964) have argued, this tends to dilute the effects of that status dimension which is particularly strongly related to the dependent variable. Instead, a multiple regression procedure should be used to compute a predicted score on the dependent variable, and the difference between the predicted and obtained score is then our adjusted score. From here on the analysis would proceed as outlined above for dependent variables uncorrelated with vertical status.

When the dependent variable which is correlated with status is a dichotomous one or measured on a nominal scale, we face a somewhat different problem. If our two status variables are dichotomized at the median, we can generate a 2 x 2 x 2 frequency table (the third dimension being presence vs. absence of the dependent variable) which can then be analyzed for the 2 main effects and an interaction effect by two comparable procedures: partitioning of Chi-square (Yule and Kendall, 1950; Winer, 1962) or the likelihood ratio test (McGill, 1954; Mood, 1950). Both methods furnish a straightforward analogy to analysis of variance. However, the likelihood ratio test is to be preferred when some of the expected cell frequencies are quite small. Moreover, the likelihood ratio test is both a test of significance, when the ratio is coverted into a Chi-square, as well as a measure of association, when information theory units are used to indicate rate of transmission of information (reduction in uncertainty). And because of the similarity of these procedures to analysis of variance, it again holds that when expected cell frequencies are highly unequal, the interaction term is underestimated.

When the status vairables are each divided into several categories, then the problem is how to compute expected cell frequencies which reflect only the additive effect of the two status dimensions, and then how to test for the significance of the departure from these expected frequencies, where such a departure reflects effects of incongruence. Lenski (1964) and Demerath (in press) offer a model for generating expected cell values, but both agree that the problem of significance testing is not yet solved. It would seem that in the two procedures discussed above, partitioning of Chi-square and the likelihood ratio test, the interaction term offers an adequate approximation to a test of significance of departure from additivity. Strictly speaking, such an interaction simply reflects the differences between obtained and expected cell frequencies which are not due to the main effects. As such, the test is not sensitive to the ordinal nature of the two status scales; moreover, it simply lumps all departures from main effects into a single interaction term without being sensitive to degrees of incongruence. However, it should be possible to use the Lenski (1964) or Demerath (in press) model to compute cell frequencies expected from simple additive effects, order these along the dimension of degree of status incongruence, and compare these with obtained frequencies by using a measure like the gamma (Goodman and Kruskal, 1954) which reflects the degree to which the relation between two variables is a monotone one.

Conclusions

This completes the discussion of the five issues listed in the introduction as the substance of this report. We may conclude with a brief consideration of future research. First of all, it would seem that we need to include in our future thinking a historical-developmental orientation as well. Is the meaning of status incongruence the same for the man who at 40 goes to night school to further his education as it is for the man whose educational level is the same but who completed his education in his teens? Does it make a difference if a person achieves an "inappropriately" high income level because he has two jobs, because he is self-employed and works hard, or simply because his pay on his job is usually high? Has the person experienced fluctuations in his position on a particular status dimension, and, therefore, in his status incongruence? Secondly, we need to be more differentiated about the settings in which the effects of status inconsistency are being investigated: at work, at the home within the family, in leisure activities with friends, etc. The measurement convenience of global demographic status variables should not obscure the need for assessing more relevant status dimensions in particular research settings. Finally, it would seem that since past work has largely concentrated on relating the pattern of status interrelationships, status inconsistency, directly to selected dependent variables, the next step in this area is to begin to explore some of the intervening processes postulated by the status inconsistency theory. Chief among these is the notion of conflicting expectations. It should be possible to integrate status inconsistency theory more fully with role conflict theory (as outlined, for example, in Kahn, et al. 1964) and thereby enlarge and strengthen its conceptual base. Thus, we need to know which type of role conflict listed by Kahn, et al.--intra-role sender, inter-sender, inter-role, person vs. role, and role ambiguity--is associated with what type of status inconsistency, and what differential consequences they may have.

REFERENCES

Adams, S.: Status Congruency as a Variable in Small Group Performance, Social Forces, 32:16-22, 1953.

Benoit-Smullyan, E.: Status, Status Types, and Status Interrelations, American Sociological Review 9:151-161, 1944.

Biddle, B.J. and Thomas, E.J. (eds.): Role Theory: Concepts and Research, New York: Wiley, 1966.

Bresnahan, J.L. and Shapiro, M.M.: A General Equation and Technique for the Exact Partitioning of Chi-Square Contingency Tables, Psychological Bulletin, 66:252-262, 1966.

Broom, L.: "Social Differentiation and Stratification," in Norton, R.K., Broom, L. and Cottrell, L.S., Jr. (eds.): Sociology Today, New York: Basic Books, 1959, pp. 429-441.

Burnstein, E. and Zajonc, R.B.: The Effect of Group Success on the Reduction of Status Incongruence in Task-Oriented Groups, Sociometry, 28:349-362, 1965.

Castellan, N.J. Jr.: On the Partitioning of Contingency Tables, Psychological Bulletin, 64:330-338, 1965.

Cobb, S. and Kasl, S.V.: The Epidemiology of Rheumatoid Arthritis, American Journal of Public Health, 56:1657-1663, 1966.

Cooley, C.H.: Human Nature and the Social Order, New York: Scribner's, 1902.

Demerath, N.J., III: Status Discrepancy and Vertical Status: Criticisms and Suggested Remedies, in paper read at the American Sociological Association meeting, Washington, D. C., 1962.

-----, Social Class in American Protestantism, Chicago: Rand McNally, in press

Exline, R.V. and Ziller, R.C.: Status Congruency and Interpersonal Conflict in Decision-Making Groups, Human Relations, 12:147-162, 1959.

Fenchel, G.E., Monders, J.H., and Hartley, E.L.: Subjective Status and the
Equilibration Hypothesis, Journal of Abnormal and Social Psychology,
46:476-479, 1951.

Floud, J.E., Martin, F.M., and Halsey, A.H.: "Educational Opportunity and Social
Selection in England," in Transactions of the Second World Congress of
Sociology, London: International Sociological Association, Vol. II, 1954,
pp. 194-208.

Freedman, R., Hawley, A.H., Landecker, W.S., Lenski, G.E., and Miner, H.M.:
Principles of Sociology, New York: Holt, Rinehart & Winston, 1956.

French, J.R.P., Jr., and Kahn, R.L.: A Programmatic Approach to Studying the
Environment and Mental Health, Journal of Social Issues, 18:1-47, 1962.

Goffman, I.W.: Status Consistency and Preference for Change in Power Distribution,
American Sociological Review, 22:275-281, 1957.

Goodman, L.A. and Kruskal, W.H.: Measures of Association for Cross-Classifications,
Journal of American Statistical Association, 49:732-764, 1954.

Gross, N.C., Mason, W.S., and McEacherm, A.W.: Exploration in Role Analysis,
New York: Wiley, 1958.

Guilford, J.P.: Fundamental Statistics in Psychology and Education, New York:
McGraw-Hill, 1956.

Hays, W.L.: Statistics for Psychologists, New York: Holt, Rinehart & Winston, 1963.

Hodge, R.W.: The Status Consistency of Occupational Groups, American Sociological
Review, 27:336-343, 1962.

Homans, G.C.: Social Behavior: Its Elementary Forms, New York: Harcourt, Brace &
World, 1961.

Jackson, E.F.: Status Consistency and Symptoms of Stress, American Sociological
Review, 27:469-480, 1962.

388

Jackson, E.F., and Burke, P.J.: Status and Symptoms of Stress: Additive and Interaction Effects, American Sociological Review, 30:556-564, 1965.

Kahl, J.A., and Davis, J.A.: A Comparison of Indexes of Socio-economic Status, American Sociological Review, 20:317-325, 1955.

Kahn, R.L., Wolfe, D.M., Quinn, R.P., Snoek, J.D., and Rosenthal, R.A.: Organizational Stress: Studies in Role Conflict and Ambiguity, New York: Wiley, 1964.

Kasl, S.V. and Cobb, S.: The Health Effects of Parental Status Incongruence, Psychosomatic Medicine, 28:770-771 (abstract), 1966.

------, The Effects of Parental Status Incongruence and Discrepancy on Physical and Mental Health of Adult Offspring, submitted to Journal of Personality and Social Psychology, 1967.

Kenkel, W.F.: The Relationship Between Status Consistency and Politico-economic Attitudes, American Sociological Review, 21:365-368, 1956.

King, S.H., and Cobb, S.: Psychosocial Factors in the Epidemiology of Rheumatoid Arthritis, Journal of Chronic Diseases, 7:466-475, 1958.

Kornhauser, A.: Mental Health of the Industrial Worker, New York: Wiley, 1965.

Krauss, I.: Sources of Educational Aspirations among Working-Class Youth, American Sociological Review, 29:867-879, 1964.

Landecker, W.S.: Class Crystallization and Class Consciousness, American Sociological Review, 28:219-229, 1963.

Lenski, G.: Status Crystallization: A Non-Vertical Dimension of Social Status, American Sociological Review, 19:405-413, 1954.

Lenski, G.E.: Comment on Kenkel's Communication, American Sociological Review, 21:368-369(a), 1956.

Lenski, G.: Social Participation and Status Crystallization, American Sociological Review, 21:458-464(b), 1956.

Lenski, G.: Comment, Public Opinion Quarterly, 28:326-330, 1964.

Mann, F.C.: A Study of Work Satisfaction as A Function of the Discrepancy Between Inferred Aspirations and Achievement, unpublished doctoral dissertation, University of Michigan, 1953.

McGill, W.J.: Multivariate Information Transmission, Psychometrika, 19:97-115, 1954.

Mead, G.H.: Mind, Self and Society, Chicago:University of Chicago Press, 1934.

Miller, D.R.: "The Study of Social Relationships: Situation, Identity, and Social Interaction," in Koch, S. (ed.), Psychology: A Study of A Science, New York: McGraw-Hill, 1963, Vol. 5, pp. 639-737.

Mitchell, R.E.: Methodological Notes on A Theory of Status Crystallization, Public Opinion Quarterly, 28:315-325, 1964.

Mood, A.M.: Introduction to the Theory Statistics, New York: McGraw-Hill, 1950.

Morgan, J.N., David, M.H., Cohen, W.J., and Brazer, H.E.: Income and Welfare in the United States, New York: McGraw-Hill, 1962.

Nam, C.B., and Powers, Mary G.: Variations in Socioeconomic Structure by Race, Residence, and the Life Cycle, American Sociological Review, 30:97-103, 1965.

Parker, S., and Kleiner, R.J.: Mental Illness in the Urban Negro Community, New York: the Free Press, 1966.

Sampson, E.E.: Status Congruence and Cognitive Consistency, Sociometry, 26:146-162, 1963.

Sarbin, T.R.: "Role Theory," in Lindzey, G. (ed.), Handbook of Social Psychology, Cambridge: Addison-Wesley, Vol. I, 1954, pp. 223-258.

Suits, D.B.: Use of Dummy Variables in Regression Equations, Journal of the American Statistical Association, 52:548-551, 1957.

Thibaut, J.W., and Kelley, H.H.: The Social Psychology of Groups, New York: Wiley, 1959.

U.S. Bureau of the Census: Methodology and Scores of Socioeconomic Status,
    Working Paper No. 15, Washington, D. C., 1963.

Winer, B.J.: Statistical Principles in Experimental Design, New York: McGraw-Hill, 1962.

Yule, G.V., and Kendall, M.G.: An Introduction to the Theory of Statistics,
    New York: Hafner, 1950.

SOME MEASURES OF STATUS INCONSISTENCY

The preceding text has offered several suggestions for constructing an index of status inconsistency and it is our intention here to describe these procedures in greater detail. We shall first discuss three examples where the index is based on the relationship between a pair of status variables and then two examples where the index is based on the inter-relationships among three or more status variables. The reader is reminded that because of the conceptual and methodological complexities of status inconsistency, as discussed in the text, the examples to be described below are simplified procedures with their own inherent limitations.

Let us suppose that the two status variables being paired are education and occupation. The first and crudest index of status inconsistency which can be constructed is simply to dichotomize the two status variables at the median and to construct a 2 by 2 table. The high-high and low-low cells are then, of course, the status consistent cases.

The second possible approach is illustrated by Figure 1: the level of education is broken down into a number of ordered categories and within each educational category, the median occupational level is found, using a coding schema such as Duncan's (see Chapter 14) to order the occupations. Then one selects a predetermined proportion (say 30 percent, as in Figure 1) of cases above and below the median for each educational category and designates these "status consistent" cases. For the categories at the extremes of educational level, it seems reasonable to include all cases below the median at the "less than grade school end" and all cases above the median for the "postgraduate training" category among the status consistent cases. All respondents in the

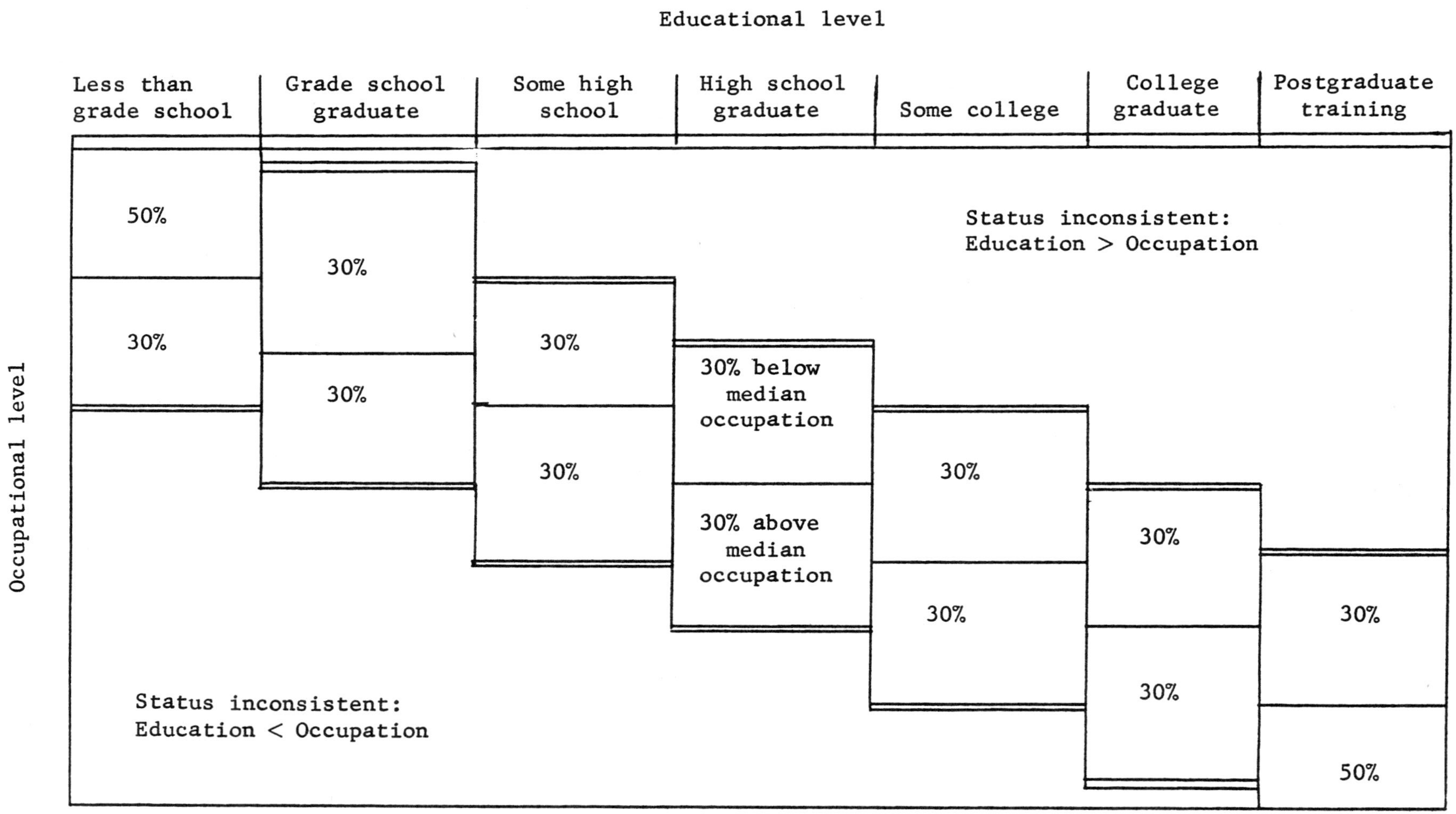

Educational level

	Less than grade school	Grade school graduate	Some high school	High school graduate	Some college	College graduate	Postgraduate training
	50%	30%	30%	30% below median occupation	30%	30%	30%
	30%	30%	30%	30% above median occupation	30%	30%	50%

Status inconsistent: Education > Occupation

Status inconsistent: Education < Occupation

Occupational level

Figure 1. An illustration of a method for obtaining a classification with regard to status consistency.

lower left-hand area of Figure 1 (education $<$ occupation) are then the "over-achievers," while those in the upper right-hand area (education $>$ occupation) are the "underachievers."

The third approach utilizes a linear regression equation and derives a status inconsistency score for each individual from the difference between predicted and actual (obtained) score. This approach assumes interval scale measurement on X and Y, with the inconsistency score = $X - X^1$, where

$X^1 = r_{xy}\left(\dfrac{\sigma_x}{\sigma_y}\right)(Y - \bar{Y}) + \bar{X}$ = predicted occupational level,

X = obtained (actual) occupational level, and

Y = educational level used to predict occupational level.

A positive inconsistency score would thus indicate an individual's occupational level higher than is predicted on the basis of his education. The "status consistent" cases will be then some proportion of cases above and below the zero point of the inconsistency scale.

The next two procedures are applicable when more than two status variables are involved. One procedure is quite general and is due to Lenski (1954). Basically, the scores on each status dimension are converted into normalized percentile scores, and then an index of the distance between all pairs of scores is obtained. Suppose that we are dealing with three status dimensions: x = education, y = occupation, and z = income. Then the index is given by the formula $\sqrt{(x-y)^2 + (x-z)^2 + (y-z)^2}$, where x , y, and z are the aforementioned normalized percentile scores. An alternative is to compute the mean status score and obtain the index by taking the square root of the sum of the squared deviations from this mean. This index will reflect the amount of status inconsistency (really, variability in status scores) and scores below an arbitrary cutoff point designated the "status consistent" cases. This index weights all status scores equally and disregards the types of inconsistency involved. See text for a discussion of the reasons why such a global index may not be appropriate.

An alternative approach which does keep track of the type of inconsistency involved has been suggested in the U.S. Bureau of Census (1963) document. After converting occupational, educational and income data into percentile-like scores, they coded the subjects into 13 status consistency types according to the following rules (reproduced verbatim):

a. If the range between the highest and lowest scores was 20 or less, recode 1 was assigned.

b. If the range between the highest and lowest scores exceeded 20, and the range between the medium and lowest scores was 20 or less and less than the range between the highest and medium scores--
   (1) Recode 2 was assigned if the income score was highest
   (2) Recode 4 was assigned if the education score was highest
   (3) Recode 6 was assigned if the occupation score was highest

c. If the range between the highest and lowest scores exceeded 20 and the range between the highest and medium scores was 20 or less and equal to or less than the range between the medium and lowest scores--
   (1) Code 3 was assigned if the income score was lowest
   (2) Code 5 was assigned if the education score was lowest
   (3) Code 7 was assigned if the occupation score was lowest

d. If the range between the highest and medium scores and the medium and lowest scores each exceeded 20--
   (1) Code 8 was assigned if the occupation score was highest and income score lowest
   (2) Code 9 was assigned if the occupation score was highest and education score lowest
   (3) Code 10 was assigned if the education score was highest and occupation score lowest
   (4) Code 11 was assigned if the education score was highest and income score lowest
   (5) Code 12 was assigned if the income score was highest and occupation score lowest
   (6) Code 13 was assigned if the income score was highest and education score lowest.

The resulting status consistency types may be described as follows:

Status Consistency Type	Characteristics
1	All three components consistent
2	Occupation and education consistent; income high
3	Occupation and education consistent; income low
4	Occupation and income consistent; education high
5	Occupation and income consistent; education low
6	Education and income consistent; occupation high
7	Education and income consistent; occupation low
8	All inconsistent; occupation highest, income lowest
9	All inconsistent; occupation highest, education lowest
10	All inconsistent; education highest, occupation lowest
11	All inconsistent; education highest, income lowest
12	All inconsistent; income highest, occupation lowest
13	All inconsistent; income highest, education lowest

As discussed in the text, the main advantages of this index is that it keeps track of the type and direction of inconsistency, and that because it is based on recent national norms it permits a standardized operationalization. The disadvantages are: a) the income data are total family income; b) the score on occupation is not a prestige score but simply the score assigned to the occupation category because of the average income and education for all members of that category; c) it may require adjustments for age (life cycle), geographical region or some other variable pertinent to a particular study setting.

16.   OCCUPATIONAL SITUS

Contrary to what might be inferred from a survey of the sociological literature, there exist other aspects of a person's occupation than status which can
be useful in uncovering significant variation in behaviors and attitudes. One of
the most intriguing is "situs", the horizontal counterpart of the vertical dimension
of status. A situs is a category of individuals or positions placed on a level
with other categories, all of which are given the same evaluation. Situs
differentiations are usually made on a functional basis, for example, on the basis
of the psychological functions of dealing with things, data or people or the
sociological function of the occupation in the social system. The following five
situs category systems are discussed:

1. Situs Categories (Morris and Murphy 1959)

2. Occupational Groups (Roe 1956)

3. Occupational Classification (Super 1957)

4. Census Bureau Industry Groupings (1960)

5. Data, People, Things (Dictionary of Occupational Titles 1965)

Morris and Murphy, in the fullest exposition of the development and utility
of the situs dimension, differentiate occupations into ten situs categories on the
basis of societal function. Because these authors present not only a clear
exposition but also a valuable situs typology, we recommend their article to
interested readers. The authors review a number of previous occupational category
systems which have incorporated a situs dimension. The Warner, et al. and North-
Hatt systems, reviewed in the previous section, use somewhat incomplete situs
codes, while the systems of two psychologists, Roe and Super, are more comprehensive
and more in line with the situs categories proposed in this review. Morris and
Murphy next discuss the wide applicability of situs analysis. "Situs ambiguity"
could be used as an important cue to the dynamics of changing occupations, role
conflict within an occupation, and the problems of marginality and occupational
mobility. Different situs categories could also "form characteristic sub-cultures"
which would underlie important sources of common values, norms, understandings and

attitudes. The authors' situs scheme, which is outlined and illustrated in Table 1, is based on student ratings.

In a subsequent article, Murphy and Morris (1961) present impressive evidence to substantiate their earlier claims. Their sample was small and not cross-sectional (701 white males in four San Francisco census tracts), but the variables were of definite sociological import--political affiliation and class identification. Sample sizes were sufficient for only four of the ten situs categories, but the following dramatic differences were obtained:

	Commerce	Finance & Records	Manufacturing	Building & Maintenance
Republican	69%	60%	36%	26%
Democrat	31	40	64	74
Middle Class Identification	81%	71%	38%	24%
Working Class Identification	19	29	62	76

Most important, these differences remained essentially unaffected when controlled for two leading status indicators, income and education--except at the college level where situs made only slight or moderate differences, but still in direction indicated above. The authors suggested other variables that should vary by situs as well--such as mobility and alienation--and speculated on the origins of the observed differences (historical, entrepreneurial-bureaucratic etc.) One problem with the above figures is that the observed differences may be due to a "collar" distinction, i.e., the distinction between lower clerical and sales workers in commerce, finance, and records vs. skilled and semi-skilled workers in business, maintainence and construction. Nevertheless, the dimension deserves more attention than it has received since this article appeared and it is hoped that exposure here will resurrect some interest in what would appear to be a important occupational background variable.

While Morris and Murphy point out the major distinctions made by Roe and Super, they do not present the two schemes in detail. For the readers' interest, the total systems of Roe and Super are outlined in Tables 2 and 3.

In Roe's chart, occupational groups are ordered so that contiguous ones are more closely related than non-contiguous ones (with the exception of the arbitrarily placed "outdoor" group). In Roe's book, this chart is used as a general introduction to a detailed description of the hypothesized interests, values and developmental experiences of people who enter these eight areas of

TABLE 1

SITUS SCHEME OF MORRIS AND MURPHY

(From "The Situs Dimension in Occupational Structure
American Sociological Review 1959 (24) 231-239)

THEORETICAL SITUS LOCATION OF SELECTED OCCUPATIONS AND EMPIRICAL LOCATION MADE BY SAMPLE OF STUDENT RATERS

SITUSES

PRESTIGE RANK QUARTILES (Student Ratings)	1 Legal Authority	2 Finance & Records	3 Manufacturing	4 Transportation	5 Extraction	6 Building & Maintenance	7 Commerce	8 Aesthetics & Entertainment	9 Education & Research	10 Health & Welfare
1	Supreme Court Justice Lawyer	City Manager	Owner of a Large Factory	President of a Railroad			Architect	Conductor of a Symphony Orchestra	College President	Physician Minister
2		Banker	Biologist for a Pharmaceutical Company	Airline Pilot	Geologist in an Oil Company	Building Contractor	Advertising Executive Commercial Artist		Philosopher County Agricultural Agent	Welfare Worker
3	Policeman	Bookkeeper	Machinist		Farmer Forest Ranger		Manager of a Hardware Store	Radio Announcer Singer in a Night Club	Music Teacher	Fireman
4	Prison Guard	Cashier in a Restaurant	Restaurant Cook	Mail Carrier Truck Driver	Coal Miner	Waiter in a Restaurant Garbage Collector	Milk Route Man	Barber		

STRATA

NOTE: Arrows indicate that over 25 per cent of the students placed the occupation in a situs other than that theoretically expected on the basis of situs definitions supplied. For those interested, the authors have available a list of a large number of occupations classified by theoretically appropriate situs categories.

1. Legal authority -- All occupations primarily concerned with the formulation, arbitration, interpretation, or enforcement of the law, including those primarily concerned with the custody of law-breakers.

2. Finance and Records -- All occupations primarily concerned with the handling of monetary affairs or the processing of records, accounts, or correspondence.

3. Manufacturing -- All occupations primarily concerned with the fabrication of articles or the processing of raw materials on a production-line basis.

4. Transportation -- All occupations primarily concerned with the movement of persons or goods from one location to another.

5. Extraction -- All occupations primarily concerned with the extraction, procurement, or production of raw materials.

6. Building and Maintenance -- All occupations primarily concerned with the construction of buildings or other non-massproduced units, or the installation, maintenance, or repair of equipment, property or facilities.

7. Commerce -- All occupations primarily concerned with the buying, selling, exchange, or marketing of goods or persons.

8. Arts and Entertainment -- All occupations primarily concerned with the creation of art forms or with the provision of entertainment, recreation, information, or aesthetic satisfaction for the public.

9. Education and Research -- All occupations primarily concerned with formal instruction or training or with the acquisition of knowledge as an end in itself.

10. Health and Welfare -- All occupations primarily concerned with the detection, prevention, or alleviation of illness, hazard, or distress.

TABLE 2

ROE'S OCCUPATIONAL CLASSIFICATION SYSTEM

(Source: Roe, A., *The Psychology of Occupations*
New York: Wiley 1956 p. 151)

Vertical dimension roughly represents status; horizontal dimension, situs.

Level	Group							
	I. Service	II. Business Contact	III. Organization	IV. Technology	V. Outdoor	VII. Science	VII. General Cultural	VIII. Arts and Entertainment
1	Personal therapists Social work supervisors Counselors	Promoters	United States President and Cabinet officers Industrial tycoons International bankers	Inventive geniuses Consulting or chief engineers Ships' commanders	Consulting specialists	Research scientists University, college faculties Medical specialists Museum curators	Supreme Court Justices University, college faculties Prophets Scholars	Creative artists Performers, great Teachers, university equivalent Museum curators
2	Social workers Occupational therapists Probation, truant officers (with training)	Promoters Public relations counselors	Certified public accountants Business and government executives Union officials Brokers, average	Applied scientists Factory managers Ships' officers Engineers	Applied scientists Landowners and operators, large Landscape architects	Scientists, semi-independent Nurses Pharmacists Veterinarians	Editors Teachers, high school and elementary	Athletes Art critics Designers Music arrangers
3	YMCA officials Detectives, police sergeants Welfare workers City inspectors	Salesmen: auto, bond, insurance, etc. Dealers, retail and wholesale Confidence men	Accountants, average Employment managers Owners, catering, dry-cleaning, etc.	Aviators Contractors Foremen (DOT I) Radio operators	County agents Farm owners Forest rangers Fish, game wardens	Technicians, medical, X-ray, museum Weather observers Chiropractors	Justices of the Peace Radio announcers Reporters Librarians	Ad writers Designers Interior decorators Showmen
4	Barbers Chefs Practical nurses Policemen	Auctioneers Buyers (DOT I) House canvassers Interviewers, poll	Cashiers Clerks, credit, express, etc. Foremen, warehouse Salesclerks	Blacksmiths Electricians Foremen (DOT II) Mechanics, average	Laboratory testers, dairy products, etc. Miners Oil well drillers	Technical assistants	Law clerks	Advertising artists Decorators, window, etc. Photographers Racing car drivers
5	Taxi drivers General houseworkers Waiters City firemen	Peddlers	Clerks, file, stock, etc. Notaries Runners Typists	Bulldozer operators Deliverymen Smelter workers Truck drivers	Gardeners Farm tenants Teamsters, cowpunchers Miner's helpers	Veterinary hospital attendants		Illustrators, greeting cards Showcard writers Stagehands
6	Chambermaids Hospital attendants Elevator operators Watchmen		Messenger boys	Helpers Laborers Wrappers Yardmen	Dairy hands Farm laborers Lumberjacks	Nontechnical helpers in scientific organization		

TABLE 3

SUPER'S OCCUPATIONAL CLASSIFICATION SYSTEM

(Source: Super, D., The Psychology of Careers
New York: Harper 1957 p. 48)

Dotted lines and other symbols are references for locating a "civil
engineer employed in conservation work for the National Park Service"
or in "a mining company" or "the telephone company".

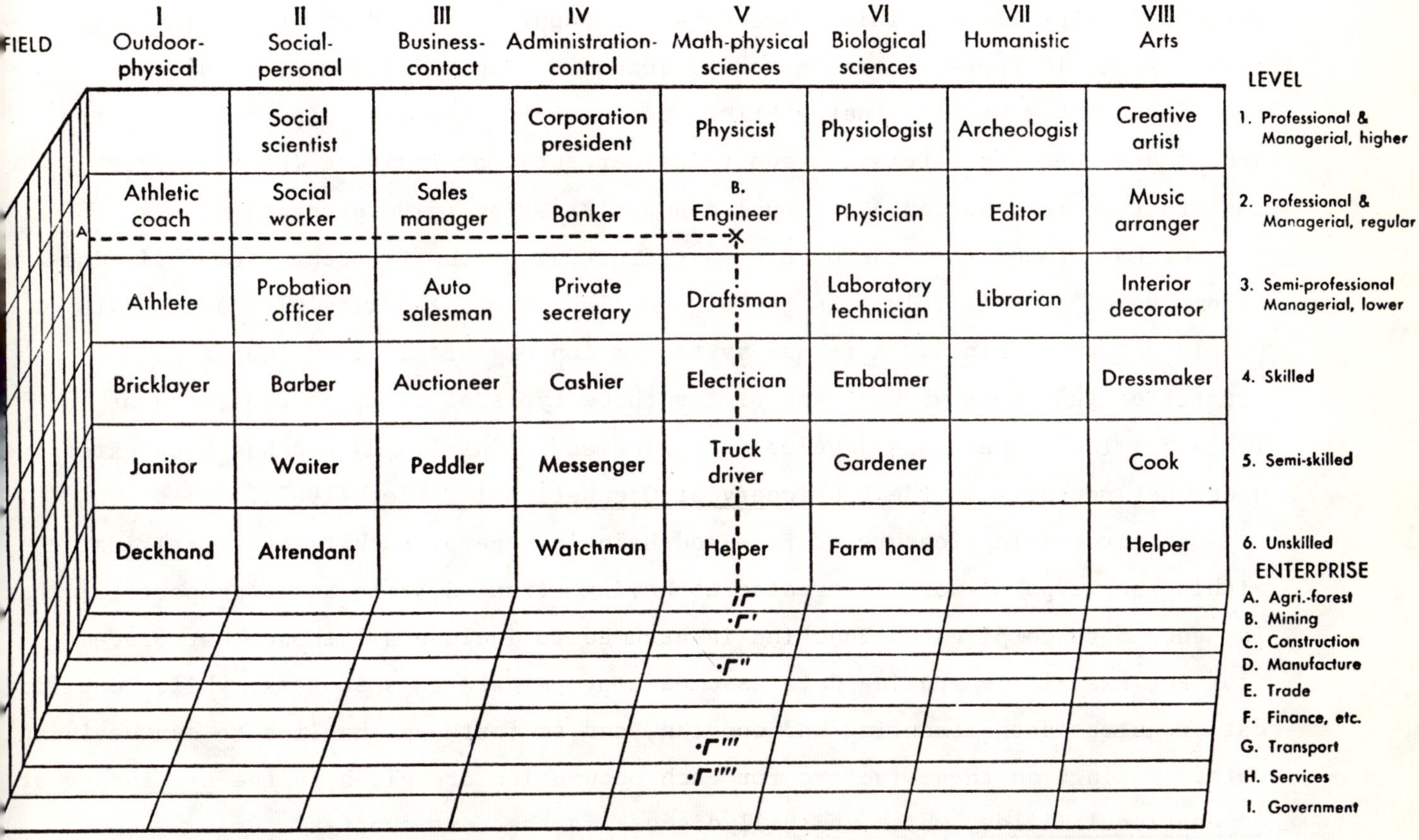

FIELD	I Outdoor-physical	II Social-personal	III Business-contact	IV Administration-control	V Math-physical sciences	VI Biological sciences	VII Humanistic	VIII Arts	LEVEL
		Social scientist		Corporation president	Physicist	Physiologist	Archeologist	Creative artist	1. Professional & Managerial, higher
	Athletic coach	Social worker	Sales manager	Banker	B. Engineer	Physician	Editor	Music arranger	2. Professional & Managerial, regular
	Athlete	Probation officer	Auto salesman	Private secretary	Draftsman	Laboratory technician	Librarian	Interior decorator	3. Semi-professional Managerial, lower
	Bricklayer	Barber	Auctioneer	Cashier	Electrician	Embalmer		Dressmaker	4. Skilled
	Janitor	Waiter	Peddler	Messenger	Truck driver	Gardener		Cook	5. Semi-skilled
	Deckhand	Attendant		Watchman	Helper	Farm hand		Helper	6. Unskilled

ENTERPRISE

A. Agri.-forest
B. Mining
C. Construction
D. Manufacture
E. Trade
F. Finance, etc.
G. Transport
H. Services
I. Government

FIG. 1. A SCHEME FOR CLASSIFYING OCCUPATIONS BY LEVEL, FIELD, AND ENTERPRISE

work. Super's "Field" dimension represents a slight revision of Roe's eight groups, and his "Enterprise" dimension overlaps to a great extent with the Morris-Murphy situs dimension and the Census Bureau Industry Code.

The Census Bureau Industry Code and the proportion of the 1960 population engaged in each industry is presented as Table 4. Certain occupational sociologists would argue that the Census Code is the most useful situs code because of the vast accumulation of research experience that has gone into its construction. Manufacturing appears as the most populated of the twenty-five major industry codes, with over a quarter of United States working population employed in the field. This segment of the population is distributed rather evenly among 14 types of manufacturing concerns (e.g., furniture, food). If the distinctions within manufacturing are retained, the most populated industry groups are then other retail trade (nine percent), agriculture (seven percent), construction (six percent) and public administration (five percent).

We have found that one of the most fruitful of the frequently-used distinctions covered in this volume is the distinction between working with data, with people and with things. A formal systemization of this distinction, with stratified functions within each of the three types of work, is presented as Table 5. This scheme was developed by Fine and Heinz (1958) and has been extensive used most recently in the Dictionary of Occupational Titles (1965).

An interesting feature of Fine and Heinz's scheme is that the stratification within each type of work is treated as having "true" Guttman scale properties; that is, each more complicated function is assumed to include all those that precede it. For example, computing data assumes copying data as a subtask, while compiling data requires both computing and copying, and so forth up the line to synthesizing data. Ratings on these factors for each occupation are given in the Dictionary of Occupational Titles, which we shall discuss in the next chapter.

It will be noted that four of the five situs schemes take into account status differences within each situs. This is also true of the Warner, et al. and Hatt systems which we reviewed with status measures.

The finding of Murphy and Morris that situs differences were minimal within the college-educated segment of the population may indicate an important generalization about behavioral and attitudinal differences between occupational groups. Among the college educated, maximal differences may be expected between people-oriented, object-oriented and idea-oriented occupations as noted by Rosenberg (1957) as well as by other research reviewed in the following chapter.

TABLE 4

INDUSTRY GROUP OF EMPLOYED PERSONS, FOR THE UNITED STATES: 1960

ISR Code	Industry group	Percent distribution	
0	Agriculture	6.6%	
1	Forestry and fisheries	0.1	
1	Mining	1.0	
1	Construction	5.9	
2	Manufacturing	27.1	
	Furniture, and lumber and wood products		1.7
	Primary metal industries		1.9
	Fabricated metal industries (incl. not spec. metal)		2.0
	Mechinery, except electrical		2.4
	Electrical machinery, equipment, and supplies		2.3
	Motor vehicles and motor vehicle equipment		1.3
	Transportation equipment except motor vehicle		1.5
	Other durable goods		2.1
	Food and kindred products		2.8
	Textile mill products		1.5
	Apparel and other fabricated textile products		1.8
	Printing, publishing and allied products		1.8
	Chemical and allied products		1.3
	Other nondurable goods (incl. not spec. mfg.)		2.7
3	Railroad and railway express service		1.5
3	Trucking service and warehousing		1.4
3	Other transportation		1.4
3	Communications		1.3
3	Utilities and sanitary services		1.4
4	Wholesale trade	3.4	
5	Food and diary products store		2.6
5	Eating and drinking places		2.8
5	Other retail trade		9.4
6	Finance, insurance and real estate	4.2	
6	Business services	1.2	
7	Repair services		1.3
7	Private households		3.0
7	Entertainment and recreation services		0.8
9	Educational services: Government	3.9	
8	Private		1.3
8	Welfare, religious and nonprofit membership organs.		1.3
8	Hospitals		2.6
8	Other professional and related services		2.5
9	Public administration	5.0	
-	Industry not reported	4.0	

EMPLOYED TOTAL = 64,639,247 =   100%

TABLE 5

STRUCTURE OF WORKER FUNCTION

(From: Dictionary of Occupational Titles Washington, GPO, 1965 Volume II)

	THINGS		DATA		PEOPLE		
A	Observing	A	Observing	A	Observing		
B	Learning	B	Learning	B	Learning		
C	Handling	K	Comparing	R	Taking Instructions-Helping		
D	Feeding-Offbearing	L	Copying	S	Serving		
E	Tending	M	Computing	T	Speaking-Signalling		
F	Manipulating	N	Compiling	U	Persuading,	V	Diverting
G	Operating-Controlling	O	Analyzing	W	Supervising,	X	Instructing
H	Driving-Operating	P	Coordinating	Y	Negotiating		
I	Precision Working	Q	Synthesizing	Z	Mentoring		
J	Setting Up						

Notes:

1. Each successive function reading down usually or typically includes all those that procede it.

2. Feeding-Offbearing and Tending, Operating-Controlling and Driving-Operating, and Setting Up are special cases involving machines and equipment of Handling, Manipulating, and Precision Working, respectively, and hence are indented under them.

3. The hyphenated factors Feeding-Offbearing, Operating-Controlling, Driving-Operating, Taking Instructions-Helping, and Speaking-Signalling are single functions.

4. The factors separated by a comma are separate functions on the same level separately defined. They are on the same level because although excluded from the one above it, usually one or the other and not both are included in the one below.

5. A more detailed description of each function is given in Appendix B to Chapter 18.

Perhaps the fact that there are so few people-oriented and idea-oriented occupations in the four occupational groupings (which were mainly business occupations) used by Murphy and Morris accounts for the greater homogeneity of viewpoints among the college-educated membership of these industries.

Once one moves out of ranks of the college-educated, professionals, and managers, situs can be expected to play a more important role, for the reasons proposed by Murphy and Morris. Studies of occupational mobility (see Chapter 17) have uncovered a parallel finding that working-class sons tend to move up or down in the same types of industries that employed their fathers. That is, the upwardly mobile son of a automobile assembly-line worker is more likely to remain in a manufacturing industry as, for instance, an automobile mechanic than to move into construction as, perhaps, a carpenter. This finding may have important implications for studies of subjective stratification measures such as prestige ratings as well as for the application of reference group theory to occupational attitudes.

References

Fine, S. and Heinz, C., "The functional occupational classification structure", Personnel and Guidance Journal, 1958, 37, 168-174.

Morris, R. and Murphy, R., "The situs dimension in occupational literature", American Sociological Review, 1959, 24, 231-239.

Murphy, R. and Morris, R., "Occupational situs, subjective class identification, and political affiliation", American Sociological Review, 1961, 26, 383-392.

Rosenberg, M., Occupations and Values, Glencoe, Illinois: Free Press, 1957.

U. S. Department of Labor, Dictionary of Occupational Titles, Washington: U. S. Government Printing Office, 1965, Volume II.

17. SOCIAL MOBILITY

There exists a large sociological literature dealing with social mobility and its correlates. Most social mobility studies largely consist of the comparison of a son's occupation with that of his father according to some stratification scheme, usually some variant of the simple eight Census Bureau occupational categories devised by Edwards. However, the term "social mobility" may also refer to changes in the same person's occupation over a certain time period. As there are a number of methodological problems in the analysis of social mobility, before undertaking any extended analyses in this area, the reader should consult Duncan's (1966) definitive review, "Methodological Issues in the Analysis of Social Mobility" (in Smelser, N. and Lipset, S., <u>Social Structure and Social Mobility in Economic Development</u>, Chicago: Aldine Press, 1966).

A summary of the extent of one major aspect of social mobility, the congruence of father's and son's occupation, is given in the following table. The figures listed are the proportions of those currently employed in an occupation whose fathers were employed in a particular occupation. These data are based on a 1962 special study by the Census Bureau of nearly 40,000 male employees. Permission to use these figures was given by O. Dudley Duncan, whose detailed analysis of information of this sort will appear in Blau and Duncan's forthcoming <u>The American Occupational Structure</u> to be published by Wiley.

There are a number of interesting findings summarized in the table. First of all, an indication of an underlying status factor is provided by evidence that to a considerable extent one's present occupational status is determined by the status of the occupation of one's father. In the next chapter, "Occupational Similarity", this same relationship is revealed in a multidimensional analysis of these data. At the same time, it is clear that the status factor does not completely determine occupational choice.

Further comparisons of interest can be drawn from the table. For example, persons in self-employed rather than salaried professions were more likely to have fathers who were self-employed professionals or managers; while those in other sales rather than retail sales were more likely to have fathers in white-collar occupations. Those in a blue-collar occupation in manufacturing were more likely to have fathers in the manufacturing area than at another blue-collar level, like craftsman or operative. The interested reader would be well advised to read Blau and Duncan's account of the variations summarized in this and other such tables.

We present one procedure for measuring an individual's social mobility that has been several times in the literature: the method devised by Tumin and Feldman. Following a description of the method, we include a number of its advantages and disadvantages cited by the authors. The procedure seems applicable to any occupational rating scheme, but its use requires knowledge of respondent's occupation, his father's occupation and the occupation of all the respondent's brothers.

Mobility from Father's Occupation to Occupation in 1962, for Males 25 to 64 Years Old: Distribution by Origins

Derived from tables appearing in Blau and Duncan's The American Occupational Structure, Wiley (in press)

Father's Occupation		Respondent's Occupation in 1962																		Total
		(1)	(2)	(3)	(4)	(5)	(6)	(7)	(8)	(9)	(10)	(11)	(12)	(13)	(14)	(15)	(16)	(17)	(18)	
(1)	Prof. SE	14.5	3.9	1.5	.8	3.8	1.1	.8	.3	.6	.3	.3	.3	.4	.2	.6	.5	.6	.8	1.2
(2)	Prof. Sal.	7.0	9.5	4.9	2.1	5.8	3.4	3.8	1.6	.6	1.9	2.1	2.1	1.9	1.4	.4	.5	.3	2.0	3.0
(3)	MOP, Sal.	8.7	7.9	8.7	4.0	7.0	2.6	4.4	2.7	2.2	2.6	1.4	1.2	1.0	1.8	.7	.3	.3	3.5	3.5
(4)	MOP, SE	18.5	9.6	16.5	16.3	13.2	15.2	7.1	3.5	5.7	5.2	3.7	3.4	3.7	1.6	2.0	1.5	1.6	5.4	7.1
(5)	Sales, Oth.	5.6	3.4	5.2	2.6	8.1	4.4	1.7	.8	.8	1.5	.5	1.0	.6	.0	.4	.4	.3	1.6	1.9
(6)	Sales, Ret.	.9	2.3	3.0	2.8	4.7	2.9	1.8	1.4	1.1	.8	1.5	1.1	1.4	.1	1.2	.7	.0	1.4	1.7
(7)	Cler.	4.9	7.3	4.4	2.3	5.9	2.6	4.5	2.9	1.2	3.1	1.2	1.9	3.2	1.5	1.3	.8	.0	3.7	3.1
(8)	Craft, Mfg.	3.8	8.3	6.1	5.1	4.3	6.3	5.7	12.0	5.1	5.1	6.2	4.7	4.8	4.5	3.2	.5	.4	5.2	5.7
(9)	Craft, Con.	3.0	3.2	4.4	5.8	4.1	2.6	6.2	6.9	13.7	5.5	3.6	3.9	4.6	2.6	4.9	.8	1.8	4.9	4.8
(10)	Craft, Oth.	4.0	7.0	7.4	6.0	7.9	6.1	8.0	6.9	5.8	11.0	5.3	7.8	5.4	3.8	4.1	1.2	1.2	6.9	6.4
(11)	Oper., Mfg.	5.2	6.4	5.1	6.1	6.5	7.1	7.5	12.9	4.9	7.7	13.7	6.9	7.1	14.5	6.3	1.2	2.8	8.2	7.6
(12)	Oper., Oth.	2.8	7.5	4.2	6.2	5.4	6.0	6.7	6.5	6.6	8.6	6.9	10.9	7.1	6.5	6.4	1.2	4.4	6.9	6.6
(13)	Service	2.3	3.7	4.0	3.7	4.8	5.3	6.3	4.8	4.7	3.9	5.1	4.6	8.2	5.4	3.3	.8	.6	3.3	4.3
(14)	Lab., Mfg.	.0	1.0	1.2	.8	.4	.8	1.3	2.6	1.0	1.5	3.2	2.2	3.0	5.9	2.4	.6	.9	1.9	1.8
(15)	Lab., Oth.	1.0	2.0	1.9	2.1	3.3	4.7	6.0	4.5	4.8	4.8	5.3	5.9	6.2	6.7	9.6	.7	2.8	3.9	4.2
(16)	Farmers	11.2	10.8	13.3	24.3	10.1	17.6	18.3	20.1	30.4	24.4	26.6	29.4	22.8	29.5	32.6	82.0	59.7	28.8	25.9
(17)	Farm Lab.	.3	.5	.9	1.5	.5	2.1	1.5	2.3	3.1	2.4	3.4	3.7	3.6	3.9	5.6	2.9	14.5	2.9	2.6
(18)	NA	6.3	5.7	7.3	7.5	4.4	9.2	8.5	7.4	7.7	9.7	9.9	9.0	15.0	10.2	14.9	3.5	7.8	8.7	8.5
	Total	100.0	100.0	100.0	100.0	100.0	100.0	100.0	100.0	100.0	100.0	100.0	100.0	100.0	100.0	100.0	100.0	100.0	100.0	100.0
N =		573	4065	3127	2786	1252	619	2449	2881	1959	2853	3974	3024	2184	851	1711	2069	678	2869	39969

SE = Self-Employed

Sal = Salaried

MOP = Manager, Official, Proprietor

Oth = Other

Ret = Retail

Mfg = Manufacturing

Con = Construction

Lab = Laborer

STEPS IN MEASURING OCCUPATIONAL MOBILITY (Tumin and Feldman 1957)

1. Divide the sample into the different fathers' occupational groups

2. For each of the father's occupational groups in turn, compute:

    (a) The mean occupational score ($\bar{x}$) of <u>all</u> their sons, i.e., the mean occupational score of all respondents and borthers whose fathers share a common occupation
    (b) The standard deviation (σ) of this distribution, i.e., the   of the occupation distribution of all respondents and brothers whose fathers have the same occupation

3. <u>F</u>or each respondent compute the deviation of his occupational score from the $\bar{x}$ occupational score of all respondents and brothers whose fathers have the same occupation, i.e., the deviation of the respondents' occupational score from the mean computed in 2(a) above.

4. Divide the deviation computed in 3 above by the σ (computed in 2(b) above) of that distribution. The resulting z score is the GOMS. Ten is added to make all scores positive.

5. The procedure may be stated as follows:

    $$\text{GOMS} = \frac{\bar{x} - x + 1}{\sigma} = z$$

    Where $\bar{x}$ = mean occupational score of all respondents and brothers of occupationally-similar fathers
          x = respondent's individual occupational score
          σ = standard deviation of the distribution of occupational scores of all respondents and their brothers within the same fathers' occupational group

Possible advantages of the GOMS are:

1. Changes in occupational position that are nominal and not consequential are less likely to introduce differential bias into the measurements, since the GOMS measures mobility in terms of the extent to which the respondent deviates from the average achievement of all others whose fathers had the same occupational rank. Thus, whatever new meanings may be inherent in the occupational shift simultaneously and without differential bias apply to all concerned.

2. Both father's and peers' statuses are built into the measures, since father's occupation is used as the base line, and the GOMS is itself a function of the occupational distribution of all sons of these fathers. Such a measure may correspond more closely than estimates based on divergence from father with the subjective estimates of mobility made by the actors themselves. This is not meant to be taken as a demonstrated advantage of the GOMS. Rather, it is a specification of the conditions under which the GOMS would be more useful than measures that do not use the peer group as the reference group.

3. Individuals can be assigned mobility scores with the GOMS since in fact

the averages have to be computed from such individual scores. Thus, respondents can be resorted on the basis of their mobility experience, which can then be used as an independent or intervening variable in a research design.

4. The full weight of the experiences of the sons of highest-and lowest-rated fathers enters into the scores, since, for instance, the son of a professional can be scored as upwardly mobile if he exceeds the average of all other sons of professionals, and the son of an agricultural day-laborer can be scored as downwardly mobile if he scores lower than the average of all other sons of day-laborers.

5. Birth order, birth spacing and number of siblings are controlled for by randomizing their effects through the technique of taking an average of all the sons of any family (i.e., the respondent and all his brothers) who are in the labor force and using their average score as the one assigned to the respondent.

We may now cite the possible disadvantages of the GOMS:

1. Since the GOMS is calculated in standard scores, there is no way of measuring the concrete distance moved by any respondent, nor of tracing the concrete places in the division of labor into and out of which he has moved in his occupational history.

2. Because the GOMS is standard score, persons within more dispersed distributions receive lower mobility scores even when normality exists. And if the distributions are skewed rather than normal, a serious bias may occur. For example, a jump of two occupational categories may be equal to only one standard deviation interval (s.d.i.) in some distributions but as much as three s.d.i.'s in other distributions.

These handicaps may be so substantial under some conditions that the use of the GOMS would be contraindicated. However, when the necessary conditions can be met the GOMS suggests itself as a powerful tool of analysis. The GOMS is offered not as a substitute for other measures but as a corollary measure of other aspects of the large and complex set of experiences called social mobility. The extent to which this proves to be a useful measure depends upon the extent to which (a) the specified conditions are met, (b) the requisite data are available, and (c) the comparison with peer groups is important in the theory with which one is working.

All of the above material is taken from: Tumin, M. and Feldman, A., "Theory and measurement of social mobility" American Sociological Review 1957 (22) 281-288.

18. OCCUPATIONAL SIMILARITY

A fundamental aim of attitude measures is the meaningful location of those population groups which are maximally different from other groups. In this sense, occupational similarity is the major occupational feature that the various measures reviewed in this volume attempt to assess. The proposed grouping of occupations by occupational status and situs should reveal important and interesting differences in attitude and behavior. These two promising schemes, however, represent incomplete efforts toward the goal of a comprehensive taxonomy of occupations which would encode the occupational distinctions most likely to reflect the largest differences in work attitudes or behavior.

We base our interest in the occupational similarity problem on the assumption that a person's occupation conveys quite a bit of information about the respondent. While we cannot believe that all people are likely to find their way into occupations in which their personal requirements are optimally matched with the job requirements, we would agree that there exist strong pressures on the individual in this direction. Even in those less skilled occupations which use only a portion of a person's talents and which may not reflect any sort of personal choice at all (i.e., the person may take the job because it is the only one he can get), there exist social pressures and norms which are important sources of homogeneity in the attitudes and behavior of those who are employed in such occupations.

It appears that socio-economic status has provided the most important guidelines along the road toward an adequate taxonomy, as is shown by the large status differences found in a number of attitude structures reviewed in Robinson's chapter. However, as Robinson noted, the broad status categories hide such important distinctions as insurance and real-estate salesmen vs. sales clerks, and protective workers vs. other service workers. To be sure, the omitted distinctions are included in the abridged Census Code of over 500 categories, for which Duncan and Census socio-economic scores are available, but 500 is surely a unwieldy number of categories for most analytic purposes. At the present stage of occupational research from representative samples, between eight and 500 categories would be optimal. More specifically, we recommend the use of between 20 and 100 categories, in each of which substantial proportions--over one percent--of the working population are found.

We will present in this chapter three bodies of data bearing on the topic of occupational similarity. We first cover certain sociological studies of occupational similarity which seem to indicate the predominance of the social status factor in similarity. These studies are based on the following kinds of data: occupations of friends, neighbors, or fathers, as well as occupational differences based on attitude and leisure activity variables. Next, we turn to the substantial body of psychological studies dealing with occupational interests. Since these studies are usually confined to restricted samples of either blue-collar or white-collar workers, normative data on the vocational interest measures yield interesting occupational differences on attitudinal variables which are at least partially controlled for social status differences. In addition, we shall point out the major occupational similarities which appear prevalent in the Dictionary of Occupational Titles, probably the largest research effort directed toward a comprehensive taxonomy of occupations.

Finally, we shall present a tentative two-digit code which incorporates some of the major differences found in the three previous chapters as well as those found in earlier chapters of this volume. For the interested reader, this scheme can be contrasted with the standard Survey Research Center code which has been used in studies of Political Behavior.

We hasten to point out that the considerations reviewed in this chapter hardly exhaust all considerations that would be relevant in a concerted enterprise to construct a taxonomy of occupations. Wilensky (1964) notes that most of the myriad job descriptive labels can be more fruitfully grouped under three general headings. While none of the three is specifically covered in the following analyses, it should be noted that Wilensky presents considerable evidence (see Robinson's chapter) that the three headings do point to major sources of job satisfaction or job discontent. The headings are:

1) Freedom: discretion in choice of tools, techniques, pacing and timing of work

2) Authority-responsibility and skill

3) Organizational context (e.g., democratic vs. authoritarian, private vs. public)

The first category primarily covers physical variables such as spatial movement, repetitiveness of mental attention, but also includes closeness of supervision and opportunity for self-expression. The second includes responsibility for men or equipment, together with abilities and training required for the job. The final category includes factors on which least information is usually available: in addition to factors listed under (3) above, it covers size of the organization, organizational diversity, hierarchical structure and organizational integration.

Ratings on most of the variables under the first and second headings are given in the Dictionary of Occupational Titles for a large number of occupations. Application of the multidimensional analysis procedures used in following sections would seem a most profitable further step toward the goal of a more adequate taxonomy. Unfortunately, such a project could not be handled within the scope of the present volume. For those interested, the complete list of over thirty job variables available for over one hundred occupational groupings in the Dictionary of Occupational Titles [1]/ is given in Table 1.

Even when these variables are added to or subsumed under Wilensky's headings, most social scientists would undoubtedly consider the list incomplete. Psychologists might want to include aspects of personality or cognitive styles required for the job. The social psychologist might want an indication of the job holder's role requirements and role expectations, as well as, perhaps, the types of relations one has with those he deals with (exploitative, coercive, socioemotional, etc.) The sociologist might be interested in the percentage of females in the occupation or whether the number of people in the occupation are declining or increasing relative to the rest of or certain portions of the work force.

Moreover, even when these and untold other variables are added into the multidimensional analysis, there will be arguments on the appropriateness of certain groupings. Occupants of certain groupings will surely object to their fellows, in line with the abundant psychological and sociological evidence to the effect that people make greater distinctions between themselves and those they are close to than they do between themselves and those less similar (see Hovland

_____

[1]/ Shartle (1964) lists a number of limitations of functional classification systems like the DOT. For example, entrance requirements vary with general social conditions, specific locales or specific "in house" requirements.

Table 1: Variables rated in the <u>Dictionary of Occupational Titles</u>, Volume II

1. GED. General Educational Development (length of time)

2. SVP. Specific Vocational Preparation (length of time)

3. Aptitudes: G--intelligence; V--verbal; N--numerical; S--spatial; P--form perception; Q--clerical perception; K--motor coordination; F--finger dexterity M--manual dexterity; E--eye-hand-foot coordination; and C--color perception. Except for E and C, these categories correspond to the aptitudes measured by the subtests of the General Aptitude Test Battery.

4. Interests (or preferences) in five bipolar pairs
    1. Things and objects vs. people and communication of ideas
    2. Business contact vs. scientific and technical
    3. Routine, concrete vs. abstract and creative
    4. Social welfare vs. non-social
    5. Prestige (or esteem) vs. tangible, productive satisfaction

5. Temperaments: indicating adjustments to:
    1. Variety and change
    2. Repetitive, short cycle
    3. Work under specific instructions
    4. Direction, control, planning
    5. Dealing with people
    6. Isolation
    7. Influencing people
    8. Performing under stress
    9. Seniority or judgment criterion; arriving at generalizations
    0   Measurable or verifiable criteria
    X   Feelings, ideas, facts
    Y   Set limits, tolerance or standards

6. Physical demands
    1. Lifting, carrying, pushing and/or pulling
    2. Climbing and/or balancing
    3. Stooping, kneeling, crouching and/or crawling
    4. Reading, handling, fingiring and/or feeling
    5. Talking and/or hearing
    6. Seeing

7. Working condition
    1. Inside, outside or both
    2. Extremes of cold plus temperature changes
    3. Extremes of heat plus temperature changes
    4. Wet and humid
    5. Noise and vibration
    6. Hazards
    7. Fumes, odors etc.

and Sherif 1952, among others). The problem is that every person is unique, as
is the way he fulfills his occupational duties, so that any decision to group
one person with another is somewhat arbitrary. Hence, research into occupational
similarity is bound to take on the overtones of a fundamentally thankless task.

However, we know from the abundant literature on social status that large and
reliable differences between occupations do exist. We have also seen much evidence
in this volume that social status does not describe all the available variance
and that situs distinctions (such as different industries, or working with data,
people or things) have led to further interesting sources of variance. The
problem becomes one of finding in what context such distinctions do make a difference. Toward this goal, the application of a relatively recent tool in the
social sciences, Smallest Space Analysis (SSA), will be employed.

Perhaps a few descriptive words on SSA would be appropriate. The general
philosophy underlying SSA is far simpler than that of its closest counterpart,
factor analysis. The input for SSA is treated as being indices of similarity,
while the input for factor analysis is treated as being fundamentally dependent
on some underlying "factor structure". For illustration, we will look at a hypothetical case of three variables A, B and C, for which the following correlation
matrix is found:

	A	B	C
A			
B	.81		
C	.81	.81	

A factor analysis might describe the factor structure as dependent on a single
factor, where A, B and C have the following correlations with that factor:

A	.9
B	.9
C	.9

On the other hand, in two dimensions, SSA would generate an equilateral
triangle as follows:

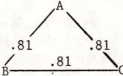

The reader should not infer from this somewhat misrepresentative example that
the two methods generate widely different results. Surprisingly, despite the
vastly different assumptions underlying the two methods, they often arrive at quite
convergent multidimensional structures. However, on balance thus far, SSA has often

uncovered more plausible and simplified structures than has factor analysis. Unfortunately, we do not have in hand at this time any formal citations that can be given for this claim. In fact, outside of the Laumann and Guttman article discussed below, there is little in the way of adequate description and illustration of the technique in the literature. One can only say that the simplified assumptions underlying SSA many times seem more appropriate to the kinds of analysis problems that one currently encounters in the social sciences. Certainly, SSA seems the most appropriate tool for examining the problem of occupational similarity, the first step towards an adequate taxonomy of occupations.

1. Sociological Evidence of Occupational Similarity

The sociological evidence we shall review generally points to social status as the major factor determining occupational similarity.[2] This finding holds over a fairly wide selection of variables: the occupations of friends, neighbors and fathers, as well as work attitudes, attitudes about various aspects of one's life space, and participation in various leisure time activities. The first published study on this topic was Laumann and Guttman's (1966) Smallest Space Analysis of the occupational similarities of respondents with those of their father, father-in-law, three closest friends and two neighbors. The sample consisted of 422 white male residents of Cambridge and Belmont, Massachusetts, who were asked to list their occupations along with the occupations of the three closest friends they saw regularly, the occupations of people who lived in either side of their homes and the occupations of their fathers and fathers-in-law. For each Duncan score of the respondents' occupation, the percentage of occupations falling in each Duncan score interval of the seven other persons named by the respondent was calculated. When these indices of similarity were fed into the Smallest Space Analysis program, the authors interpreted the results as indicating that three dimensions were needed for an acceptable fit. The coefficient of alienation,[3] a measure of goodness-of-fit for the program, was .13 for three

---

[2] Moreover, we understand that one study found that status emerged as the major factor when students were asked to judge the "similarity" of various occupations; unfortunately we know of no formal reference to this study.

[3] The Coefficient of Alienation is defined as $(1-(1-\emptyset)^2)^{\frac{1}{2}}$ where $\emptyset$ is the ratio of the sum of the squared differences between the distances as calculated from the coordinate system and the same distances permuted to maintain the rank-order of the original coefficients, divided by twice the sum of the squared distances. For more details, see the original article.

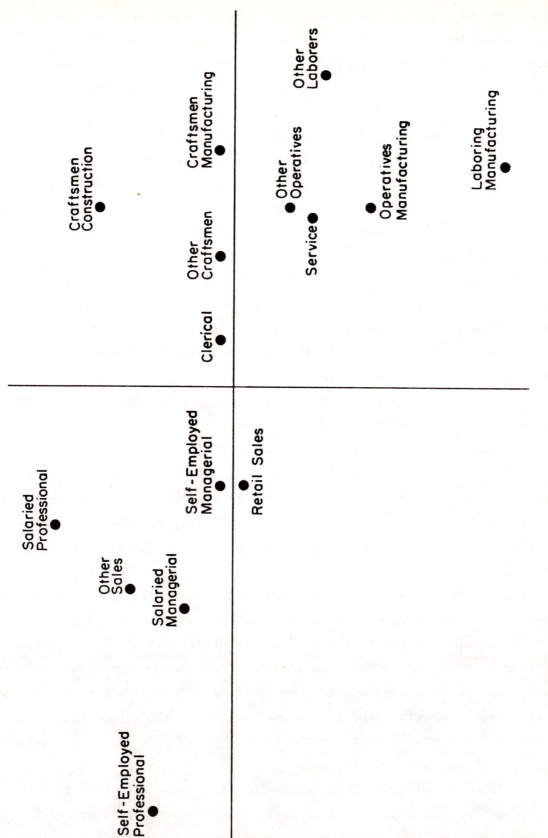

FIGURE 1: SMALLEST SPACE ANALYSIS PLOT OF 1962 INTERGENERATIONAL OCCUPATIONAL MOBILITY DATA. DATA FROM BLAU AND DUNCAN (IN PRESS)

dimensions vs. .26 for two dimensions where .00 denotes a perfect fit. The major dimension was found to correlate .82 with the Duncan code, indicating the importance of the status factor, but Laumann and Guttman felt that far more than just a status factor was indicated in their findings. However, outside of a possible entrepreneurial-bureaucratic distinction for the third dimension, the authors were unable to place a convenient label on these final two dimensions.

Hauser (1965) pointed out a number of problems with the Laumann and Guttman analysis, the most critical of which was the authors' use of the full range of Duncan scores rather than score intervals. By collapsing to 10 or 20 scores intervals, (vs. the 55 intervals used in the Laumann-Guttman article), Hauser was able to find single-dimensional status factors for the Laumann-Guttman data which never exceeded an alienation coefficient of .15, no matter how the data were grouped. Again, the second and third dimensions were uninterpretable, but this time they seemed so unimportant as not to matter.

Hauser further analyzed the 1962 Census occupational mobility data (see previous chapter on occupational mobility) via Smallest Space Analysis. The coefficient for the 16 non-farm occupations diagrammed in Figure 1 was .12 for one dimension, again clearly related to status. Blau and Duncan (1967) present a slightly more complete analysis of the mobility data and find that a hint of a bureaucratic-entrepreneurial factor is indicated in some of their analyses. Figure 1 also reveals a trace of a situs factor among the 16 occupations, in that craftsmen, operatives and laborers tend to cluster together within manufacturing as much as they cluster by separate occupational categories across industries.

The final body of data on occupational similarity comes from the study of Americans' Use of Time by Converse and Robinson (1967). In Robinson's chapter we saw how a Smallest Space Analysis of work attitudes and behaviors also generated a major status factor with the coefficient of alienation .41. A second factor, differentiating entrepreneurial- people-oriented respondents such as sales personnel and the self-employed from the data-oriented such as scientists, bookkeepers and engineers, lowered the coefficient of alienation to .25, and a third "masculine-feminine" factor lowered it to .14. The first two dimensions are mapped in Figure 2 in Chapter 3.

Additional data from the Converse-Robinson study is mapped in Figure 2 of this chapter. The input for this analysis is average scale scores for 28 occupational categories on a number of variables described below. A national urban sample of 500 men interviewed in late 1965 and early 1966 supplied the basic sources of the data. The men indicated their yearly participation in 18 types of

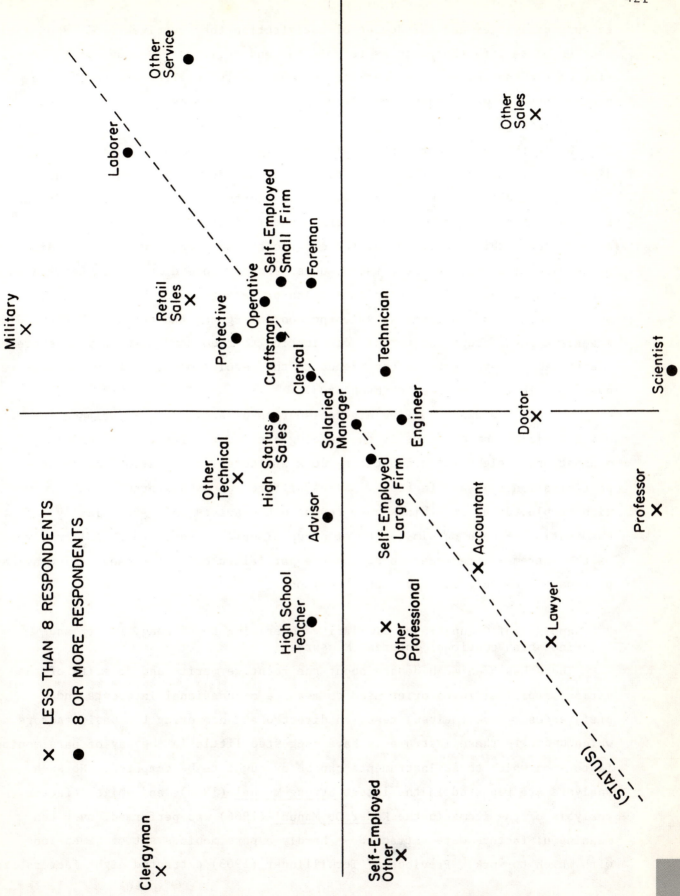

FIGURE 2: SMALLEST SPACE ANALYSIS PLOT OF LEISURE TIME ATTITUDES AND BEHAVIORS. DATA FROM CONVERSE AND ROBINSON, THE STRUCTURE AND MEANING OF TIME USE (IN PRESS)

× LESS THAN 8 RESPONDENTS

● 8 OR MORE RESPONDENTS

leisure activities and the degree of satisfaction they received from 18 possible sources of satisfaction, such as television and children. Because of the small size of the sample, some occupations were naturally underrepresented; those occupations for which there were less than eight respondents are indicated with an "X" in Figure 2.

While the major (horizontal) dimension in Figure 2 has the flavor of a status dimension, it has a coefficient of alienation of .36. A more satisfactory status factor is revealed in the rotated dimension (dotted line) which can be drawn from the two dimensional solution with a coefficient of alienation of .19 (an additional third factor drops the coefficient only down to .11.) The dimension perpendicular to this rotated factor does disclose some distinction between such data-oriented occupations as scientist and professor and such entrepreneurial-people-oriented occupations as sales-person, clergyman and teacher, but the dimensio reveals enough exceptions to this distinction to recommend viewing with extreme skepticism the apparent correspondence to the results obtained from the work-related questions in the Converse-Robinson study.

We have now examined five diverse sources of sociological variance for which socio-economic status is the leading predictor: father's occupation, friends' occupations, neighbors' occupations, work attitudes and behavior, and leisure participation and satisfactions. Situs differences or differences between working with people, data, or things have revealed themselves only sporadically. In the examination of data on similarity of occupational interests which follows, most of the extreme differences in status are partialled out beforehand, allowing us perhaps to see more clearly these "horizontal" sources of variance.

2. Mappings of Occupational Similarity Underlying the Strong, Kuder, and Minnesota Vocational Interest Measures

There has been much debate about the relative merits and demerits of the various empirical inventories used to measure occupational interests and preferences. Nevertheless, research directed at uncovering the basic factors which underlie these instruments have suggested little in the way of parsimonious factors on which these instruments can be or ought to be compared. No such analyses are reported in the latest Strong Manual (1966), and while a factor analysis of the items in the Kuder DD Manual (1966) was performed, over ten meaningful factors were extracted -- hardly a parsimonious set of dimensions with which to work. Previously, Terwillinger (1963) extracted eight factors from analyses of <u>Kuder Preference Record</u>, value questions and occupational preference rankings, while Schutz and Baker (1962) had found seven occupational factors in a factor analysis of the <u>Kuder D</u> (occupational). Both studies, however, used college students and not people employed in relevant occupations.

In an earlier research effort, Cottle (1948) had investigated the dimensions underlying the <u>Kuder Preference Record</u>, the <u>Strong Vocational Interest Blank</u> and <u>Bell Interest Inventory</u> on a single sample of adult males. However, in this study, the emphasis was on the dimensions common to all three inventories and not on dimensions peculiar to each individually. Subsequent to Cottle's investigation, five of his basic occupational interest factors--work with things and objects vs. people and ideas; business contact vs. scientific-technical activities; routine, concrete and organized work vs. abstract and creative work; social situations vs. non-social; desire for prestige or esteem vs. tangible or productive rewards--were used to form the basis of interest ratings for occupational classification in Volume II of the latest Dictionary of Occupational Titles (1965).

Super and Crites (1962), attempting to synthesize research into basic vocational interest dimensions, proposed that eight headings be used: scientific, social welfare, literary, material (working with tangibles), systematic, contact (with people for material gain), aesthetic appreciation and aesthetic expression. Roe (1956) had suggested that her eight category classification system could be used to compare the factors apparently underlying six vocational interests tests, including the <u>Strong</u> and the <u>Kuder</u>. For example, she matched her "business contact" category with a "business contact" factor on the <u>Strong</u> and the "persuasive" cluster in the Kuder, and made her "science" category encompass the <u>Strong</u> "things vs. people" distinction and the <u>Kuder</u> "scientific" cluster. Some of her comparisons, however, such as "service occupations", are quite arbitrary while others, such as "outdoor", appear in few interest tests.

While all the above factors and factor schemes provide ample clues regarding major expected differences between occupations, at least as the differences are defined by the item content of the most popular occupational interest inventories, they do not distinguish the dimensions unique to each instrument. Again, the factors do not convey much information about the contiguity of occupations, that is, they do not reveal whether a physician is more similar to an accountant, an artist, or minister, across a representative sample of characteristics. Such information would be an addition to information visible in clients' empirical scores that would be extremely useful to counselors both in

describing most likely alternative occupations and in gaining understanding of
the normal differences expected from the constitution of the inventories.
Deviations from normal patterns may reveal complex occupational interests that no
single job could fulfill. For example, if doctors and dentists tend to have
more in common than either profession does with accountants, then a person who
scores high on the dentist and accountant scales but low on the doctor scale
may well have interests that neither occupation could easily satisfy.

Those familiar with the earlier Strong Manuals may remember the spheres of
occupational distances which conveyed so much interesting information about the
contiguity of occupations. Using a forerunner of the current MVII, Norman (1960)
found four dimensions which described 80 percent of the variance between 115
occupational and reference groups. Mapping of occupations on these four dimensions
provided basic insights into the structure of occupations not otherwise easily
visible. We will similarly attempt to portray maps of occupational similarity.
However, it is our contention that comparatively simple mappings portrayable in
two dimensions exist which explain the bulk of variance in occupational inventories,
and that these mappings reflect important features and weaknesses of the various
instruments.

The mappings are based on Smallest Space Analyses of correlations between
members of various occupations as given in the manuals for the three of the most
useful vocational interest inventories--the Strong (SVIB), the Kuder DD and
Minnesota Vocational Interest Inventory (MVII). There are some conceptual
problems in using the correlation coefficients that are based on multiply-keyed
items. Despite the fact that this procedure leads to spuriously high or low
correlation coefficients, the Smallest Space Analysis uses only the ordinal
properties of these coefficients. The correlation coefficients appears to the
author to be a reasonable distance measure for the purposes of the Smallest Space
Analysis, although future research of this type should concentrate on using
cleaner distance measures. It has been the author's experience, however, that the
use of gross similarity measures like the correlation coefficient does not radically
affect the results emerging from Smallest Space Analyses.

For the Strong Blank, the mean scores for each of the 37 male occupational
criterion groups as found on pages 38 and 39 of the 1959 Manual were inter-
correlated and the resulting correlation matrix was fed into the Smallest
Space Analysis program. The solution for the two major dimensions is seen in
Figure 3. The spacing in Figure 3 yields a coefficient of alienation of .17 with th

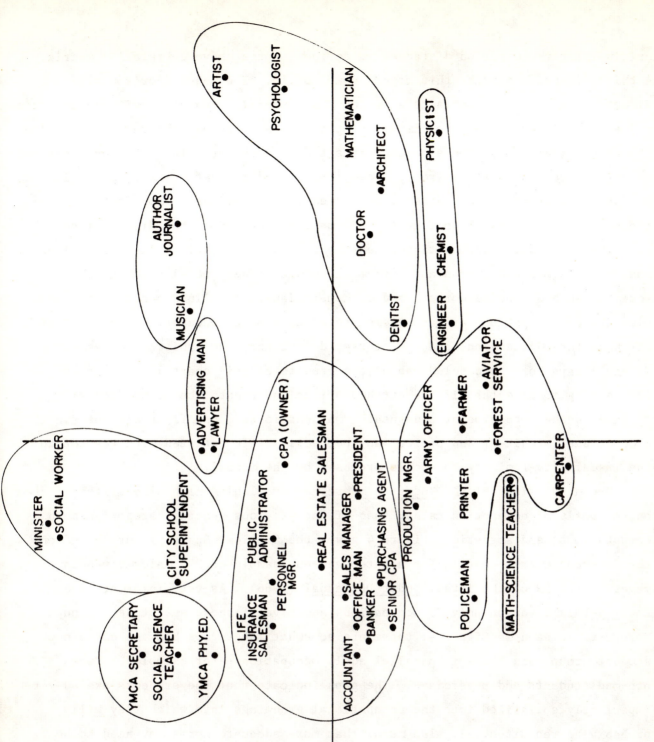

FIGURE 3 : SMALLEST SPACE ANALYSIS PLOT OF RELATIONSHIPS BETWEEN OCCUPATIONAL GROUPS ON SVIB (1959). Lines represent arbitrarily defined clusters.

original inter-occupation distances as defined by the above correlation matrix. A third dimension brought this figure down to .10. The major (horizontal) dimension in Figure 3 contrasts a business and social orientation with an artistic and scientific outlook--more simply, it provides a doers vs. thinkers distinction; the second (vertical) dimension contrasts the more object-oriented occupations such as carpenters and aviators from the people-oriented occupations such as ministers and social workers. These dimensions, however, are obviously imperfect descriptions of the richness of contiguity information conveyed by the diagram itself.

The third dimension distinguished those with commercial or business values, such as salesmen and accountants, from those who valued social or abstract activity such as social workers and mathematicians. The lines surrounding the clusters of occupations are an attempt to group similar occupations on the basis of these three dimensions and, of course, do reflect some arbitrary decisions. We shall have more to conclude about the results of this chart later. It is interesting to note that if one extends a line underneath the point "social science teacher" to a point underneath "mathematician", one finds all but two occupations (architect and office man) perfectly differentiated with respect to the masculinity-feminity sub-scale proposed by the manual.

Recent versions of the Kuder Form are now available which also differentiate on the basis of occupation rather than of the previous general categories such as computational and artistic. Figure 4 gives the Smallest Space picture based on the intercorrelation matrix for a heterogeneous sample of 276 males given on pages 58 and 59 of the latest Kuder DD Manual (1966). As yet, information on the Kuder is given on only 23 occupations and five of these are student groups. Moreover, as seen in Figure 4, there are somewhat large gaps between certain student groups and those in parallel adult occupations--for example, between pre-med students and physicians. The gaps indicate that the students are as yet imperfectly socialized into the occupational groupings into which they will probably be recruited. It also means that more adequate norms may need to be devised to bring the Kuder occupational norms up to Strong standards. The two dimensional solution has a coefficient of alienation of .20 with the original input matrix; the third dimension brings the figure down to .09. The first (horizontal) dimension in Figure 4 is similar to the second factor for the Strong Blank, the people- vs. object-oriented distinction, while the second dimension contrasts scientists--especially students--with people dealing with more tangible products,

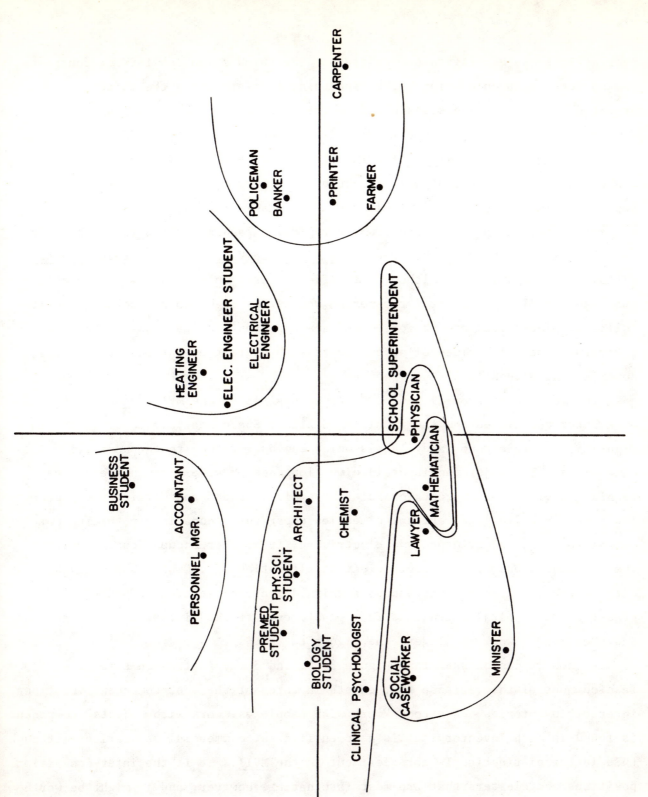

FIGURE 4: SMALLEST SPACE ANALYSIS PLOT OF RELATIONSHIPS BETWEEN OCCUPATIONAL GROUPS
ON KUDER DD (1966). Lines represent arbitrarily defined clusters.

such as bankers, architects and printers. The third dimension further contrasts the object- vs. people-oriented, by including chemists among the object-oriented. The group lines again define the major groupings suggested by the distances found in the three-dimensional solution.

Both the Strong and Kuder instruments suffer from a noticeable bias toward higher white-collar occupations. Since over half of the present United States population is employed in blue-collar occupations--although the white-collar segment of the occupational spectrum is rapidly expanding--the Strong and Kuder bias leaves a large area uncovered. The Minnesota Vocational Interest Inventory (1965) fills in this gap, although it differentiates only within the blue-collar domain and still does not tell the person whether he ought to be looking at white-collar or blue-collar occupations. Perhaps a person's educational background determines the white-blue-collar choice to such a great extent that test items covering the dimension are not needed.

The mean scores for 21 groups given on page 18 of the MVII Manual (1965) were inter-correlated and the resulting Smallest Space Analysis is presented in Figure 5. There are no handy labels which can be attached to the underlying dimensions. The major (horizontal) dimension does provide a rough "person vs. machine" division which contains "clean vs. dirty hands" and "office vs. factory" overtones as well. The vertical dimension separates occupations entailing complex manual work such as printer and electrician, from other occupations. Together the two dimensions yield a coefficient of alienation of .10 with the original inter-correlation matrix distances; a third dimension, separating printers, pressman and hospital attendants from plasterers, truck drivers, electricians and sheet metal workers, lowers the figure to .04.

By now it can be seen that Figure 3, 4, and 5 may portray in simplified fashion most of the variance that exists in three of the most competent vocational interest inventories. A strong "work with people vs. work with objects" component is found in each inventory, as is a scientific vs. commercial separation--although this latter distinction is not clear cut in the MVII. It is the inter-occupation positions and clusters that are most fascinating, however, and it might be worth-while to comment on them.

There would appear to be about nine clusters of occupations in the sample for the Strong criterion groups:

1. Commercial: accountants, bankers, salesmen, administrators, etc.
2. Manual: production managers, carpenters, aviators, etc.

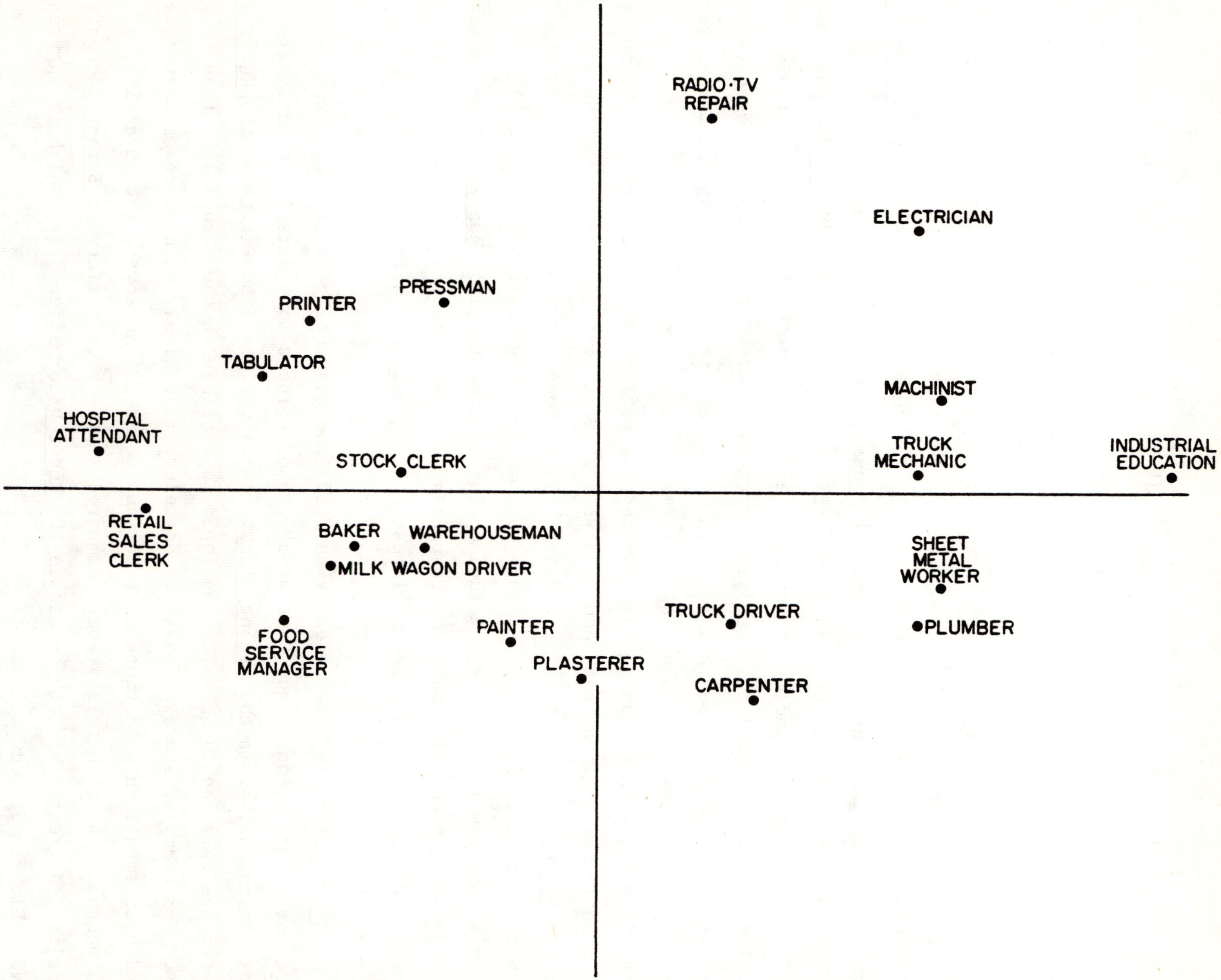

FIGURE 5: SMALLEST SPACE ANALYSIS PLOT OF RELATIONSHIPS BETWEEN OCCUPATIONAL GROUPS ON MVII (1965).

3. Art-science: artists, doctors, etc., and perhaps psychologists and mathematicians
4. Physical science: engineers, chemists and physicists
5. Social: (YMCA secretary, physical education instructors and social science teachers
6. Social-administrative: social workers, ministers, school superintendents
7. Arts: musicians, authors
8. ?: Advertising men, lawyers
9. Math-science teachers

In the latest Strong Manual, normative information according to occupation is broken down into 11 categories, most of which overlap with the nine we have suggested, as well as with the nine categories suggested in the 1959 Strong Manual. There are some groupings in the present Manual, however, which could be questioned on the basis of mean score differences given in the Manual on pages 40 and 41. Pharmacists and morticians, for example, have high scores on certain health science occupations, more similar to the scores of veternarians or osteopaths than of the commercial businessmen with whom they are grouped. Again, math-science teachers have more in common with scientists and mathematicians than they do with farmers, printers and other assorted occupations with which they are combined. Application of the Smallest Space Analysis program to the latest normative data on the Strong would certainly be desirable, although it would be surprising to see the structure in Figure 3 change very much, since two-thirds of the 52 occupations now listed have remained unchanged from the 1959 Manual. Some of the Strong scales are still based on responses well over ten years old and need to be updated on new groups, as the latest scale Manual has already done for some occupations.

Kuder materials have recently shifted from presenting general area scores, such as "computational" and "artistic", to offering a more direct occupational categorization, as in the Strong Blank. As is obvious from Figure 4, the Kuder DD normative data should be better equipped to distinguish the occupations than it is. For example, scores of bankers correlate more highly with scores of carpenters and policemen than with those of other businessmen. Moreover, the total list of 23 occupations is certainly scant compared to the rich variety of Strong occupational scales. A greater variety exists in the Kuder D normative data, which is apparently available for 51 occupations.

Nevertheless, there are essential parallels in the overall structure of the occupational groupings of Figures 3 and 4, the Strong and the Kuder DD. There are roughly five groupings for the Kuder DD:

1. Scientist: chemists, architects, student science majors, etc.; possibly physicians and clinical psychologists
2. Social administrative: ministers, social workers, lawyers, school superintendents
3. Manual: farmers, printers, carpenters, policemen and bankers
4. Commercial: business students, personnel managers, accountants
5. Engineering: electrical engineers, heating engineers, engineering students

Three of these groups compare directly with the Strong groups: commercial, manual and social administrative. The science grouping for the Strong combines the engineering cluster and part of the scientist cluster in the Kuder; the other part of the Kuder scientist cluster forms the art-science grouping for the Strong. What about the spatial relationship among these clusters? In the case of the seven definable Strong clusters, Figure 3 essentially reduces to:

Social-Administrative

Social   Arts

Commercial   Physical   Art-Science
                        Science
Manual

For the six groupings of the Kuder, rotating Figure 4 about 180° results in the following pattern:

Social-Administrative

Manual   Art-Science

Engineers   Science

Business

Outside of the necessity of interchanging the business and manual clusters and moving engineers somewhat to the right, there is a reasonable resemblance between the two diagrams. A plot of the second and third dimensions of the Kuder results in:

Social-Administrative

Manual   Art Science
                            Science

Business   Engineer

Here only the business and manual clusters need be inter-changed to make the Kuder and Strong plots line up.

Occupational similarity data can have a number of important applications in both industrial and survey research. For instance, the analyst must always make decisions on what kinds of employees to include in each group or how to subdivide his sample so as to maximize differences between groups. At present, he has to work from such sketchy guidelines as the Bureau of the Census occupational categories. The problem is especially acute for survey researchers, who often overlook or are unaware of the fact that the eight broad Census categories of professional, service, sales and so on, group ministers with strip-teasers, policemen with gardeners, and sales clerks with real estate agents.

Occupational similarity data could also be used to help solve the research problems resulting from the fact that there are job attitudes unique to certain types of jobs. While almost all research has shown that people in higher status jobs like their work more, some professional-technical occupational groups (like technicians and male school teachers) show levels of discontent equivalent to those of certain groups of factory machine operators. A further research problem is obvious from Figure 3, 4 and 5: numbers of various occupational groups differ widely in the things that they expect from their work, a fact which makes the search for single determinants of job satisfaction across all occupations quite fruitless. It is best to conduct such a search on single homogeneous groupings at a time. But how can we determine what are homogeneous occupations and what are not?

The "work with objects vs. work with people" dimension, which has cropped up so often in this volume, has been found to show dramatic differences in child-rearing practices (Pearlin and Kohn 1966). Obedience was stressed far more and self-control far less by the "work with things" parents, a finding which held true for both white-collar and blue-collar workers. These differences are undoubtedly linked with role requirements at work and suggest that the objects vs. people distinction may be a crucial one in the world of work.

There remain a host of occupational status distinctions that cannot be made with the present normative data on interest inventories because the inventories offer so little in the way of cross-collar comparison. In relation to our review of the sociological similarity analyses in the previous section, it is interesting to note that the distinctions mapped in Figures 3, 4 and 5 do tend to show up (but usually are dwarfed by) differences on the basis of occupational status. One further body of data that might help us decide whether class or job content factors distinguish more of the variance between occupations is the extensive rating system provided in Volume II of the latest Dictionary of Occupational Titles. It would take a major research effort, however, to codify all these data on a representative sample of occupational groups for purposes of Smallest Space Analysis. We shall look at some of the major distinctions in the following section.

Three final words of caution about the simplicity of Figures 3, 4 and 5: first, as suggested above, purer measures of similarity need to be used in future efforts. Second, analyses of the normative data for the 52 occupations in the latest Strong Manual and the 51 occupations for the occupational Kuder D still need to be performed. Finally, the diagrams are designed as summary figures like a mean or average, and as such they disguise important sources of variation in which the researcher may be interested. The world is prettier in two dimensions than it is real.

3. Some Similarity Assessments Implicit in the Dictionary of Occupational Titles.

The Dictionary of Occupational Titles (DOT) is considered the world's most widely used occupational document. It was first published in 1939 by the U. S. Employment Service and has been updated and expanded a number of times since then. The latest (1965) edition comes in two volumes, the first dealing with occupational definitions, the second with similarity groupings. While thousands of occupations are defined in Volume I, these are reduced to somewhat over 100 "Worker Trait Groups" which are in turn placed into one or more of 22 "Areas of Work" in Volume II. Clearly, these categories are of prime interest in our search for a comprehensive occupational taxonomy.

Each occupation in the DOT is given a six digit identification number, [2] of which the first three digits refer to straightforward occupational categories, and the fourth, fifth, and sixth digits refer to ratings of level of relation to data, to people, and to things. Appendix A to this chapter defines the first two occupational code digits, omitting the further differentiation of the third digit. Appendix B presents the second three digits, or descriptive codes, which we examined briefly in the chapter on "Occupational Situs". The "relation to data" scale (fourth digit) will serve here to explain the rating scheme employed in the descriptive codes: at the highest levels (code 0 or 1), the person is involved in synthesizing data, while at the lowest level (code 6) the person is merely comparing data; in codes 7 and 8 are people who have nothing to do with data. While the descriptive codes are based on judgments and ratings rather than test measures, they can provide rough guidelines.

---

[2] A major limitation of this identification number is that it is not linked up in any way with the Census Bureau occupation code. It is our understanding that a governmental committee has been established to bring about such a correspondence between the DOT identification code and the Census code.

As we do not have the resources to deal with the thousands of original occupations in the DOT, we will examine the 22 work areas and present the manner in which the 114 worker trait groups fit under these headings. We understand that both classification schemes were devised on the basis of somewhat arbitrary operations using a counter-sorter rather than more objective computer procedures, such as factor analysis. This may be a reflection more of the failure of psychometricians to have provided workable multidimensional procedures than of the shortcomings of procedures used by the DOT researchers.

In this short section we will deal with two superficial summarizations of the DOT groupings. The first summarization, given in Table 2, is a chart showing how the 22 major work areas generally fit into the hierarchies of data, people and things. The placements represent group averages, which conceal a certain amount of variation within the work areas. Where more than one or two of the worker trait groups under a work area depart radically from the general patterns for that work area, the work area is classified in two or more cells of Table 2. Thus, some trait groups under "Business Relations" involve low level contact with people, while other require medium to high contact; a similar pattern exists for groups in "Crafts" where some craftsmen (especially foremen) have far more personal contact than others.

While there are some interesting and plausible groupings appearing in Table 2, the chart merely serves to show similarity between occupations at the grossest level of all the information in the DOT. A more refined method involves looking at the similarity between the 22 work areas by counting the number of two digit occupational titles they have in common. Even this method, however, represents a farily monumental task, with the large number of trait groups falling under each heading. The quick tally that we were able to conduct suggested that the 22 work areas can be further regrouped under the following five headings:

MANUAL   : Elemental work, Machine work, Crafts, Farming/fishing etc., Transportation

COMMERCIAL: Business relations, Clerical, Merchandising, Managerial-supervisory

SERVICE   : Personal service, Legal and law enforcement, Investigating/inspecting

ARTS   : Entertainment, Music, Photography and communications, Writing

SCIENTIFIC: Engineering, Mathematics and science, Medicine and Health, Counseling/guidance, Education and training

TABLE 2: Groupings of 22 Major Occupational Headings Used in <u>DOT</u>
on the basic of Data, People and Things Hierarchies

DATA

THINGS		Very High	High	Medium	Low
High 0,1,2	High 0,1,2		Farming, fishing etc. Medicine & health		
	Medium 3,4,5				
	Low 6,7,8	Counseling & guidance	Education & teaching Farming, fishing etc Legal & law enforcement Medicine & health		
Medium 3,4,5,6	High 0,1,2	Arts	Crafts	Merchandising	Crafts
	Medium 3,4,5	Mangerial & supervisory	Transportation		
	Low 6,7,8	Music Managerial & supervisory Counseling & guidance Writing	Business relations Managerial & supervisory Transportation	Entertainment Merchandising	
Low 7,8	High 0,1,2	Engineering Math & science	Farming, fishing etc. Crafts Medicine & health	Photography etc. Investigating etc.	Crafts
	Medium 3,4,5			Clerical	Machine work
	Low 6,7,8	Engineering Math & science	Business relations Medicine & health Farming, fishing etc. Legal & law enforcement	Clerical Investigating etc.	Elemental Personal service

Again, there is a certain amount of arbitrariness involved in squeezing the work areas under these five rubrics; the classifications are presented in decreasing similarity to the heading employed. Thus, elemental work most clearly falls under MANUAL, machine work less clearly, with farming/fishing, and transportation least clearly. Transportation has a number of occupations in common with clerical, managerial/supervisory, and investigating/inspecting.

The reader may or may not find these five headings helpful in deciphering the extensive material in the DOT. In order to convey a greater sense of the wealth of data contained in the DOT, we have presented the complete list of 114 worker trait groups in Appendix C under their appropriate "Area(s) of Work". As noted earlier, some trait groups fall under more than one work area. For each worker trait group, the reader will also find the appropriate rating(s) for the data-people-things hierarchies, as well as the occupational codes. Where five or more occupational titles under the two-digit code are found, that occupational code is listed under "Major", with the remaining occupations listed under "Minor". Thus, for the first worker trait group in Appendix C--signaling, etc.--there are only three occupational titles listed under protective services (occupational code 37), two under transportation work (code 91) and one each under construction work (code 86) and logging (code 94).

All in all, the DOT research offers far greater discrimination at the higher white-collar occupational levels than at the blue-collar level. As noted earlier, this unequal coverage also occurs in the two most popular vocational interest tests, the Strong and the Kuder. What becomes most critical in our search for an optimal set of occupational categories for survey research analysis is some way of finding more refined methods of classifying blue-collar workers than dividing them into skilled, semi-skilled and unskilled.

4. A Tentative Revised Occupation Code for Survey Research

Compelled by no particular impetus other than some shortcomings of the Survey Research Center Political Behavior Code (Appendix D) we perceived in our own analysis of work attitudes, we have taken this opportunity to suggest the occupation code presented in Appendix E. This code was constructed by subjectively weighting, in order: (1) status and situs differences noted in the previous chapter (2) the differences found in the previous three sections of this chapter, and (3) the differences in job satisfaction found in Robinson's chapter. The code was constructed so that the 500+ category system used by the Census Bureau could

be collapsed into a two digit code in which substantial portions--generally
not less than one percent--of the working population would be included under each
category.

Status differences, especially as defined by Duncan decile scores, were
treated as offering the most crucial differentiations within the white-collar
domain. Within the professional-technical area of this domain, the working with
data vs. working with people distinction offered the most viable source of
differentiation, although many occupations can only arbitrarily be placed in
one or the other of these two categories. In contrast to the status differences
used in the white-collar area, situs differences were used as the major source
of variance within blue-collar occupations. It is not likely that situs differences
will always lead to attitudinal or behavioral differences as large as those
reported by Murphy and Morris (see Chapter 16). However, outside of the skilled-
semiskilled-unskilled distinction, there is almost no other empirical distinction
developed for differentiating within the blue-collar domain.

The situs categories used in the revised code were selected mainly on the
basis of convenient Census industrial codes and not on the basis of such more
empirically important criteria as the presence or political affiliations of a
labor union. Nevertheless, some of these latter differences are undoubtedly
present in the Census categories we have collapsed, as in differences among
construction vs. manufacturing vs. wholesale or retail trade.

It will be noted that lower-status workers are largely separated into the
general code headings of Appendix E according to the working with data, people or
things distinction. Thus, with some exceptions, lower-status workers dealing
with data are listed under "Clerical workers", those dealing with people under
"Service workers" and those dealing with things under "Skilled, Semi-skilled or
Unskilled workers".

By making situs differentiations only among blue-collar workers, we do not
mean to imply that situs differences (as defined by type of industry) are not
important within the white-collar or professional domain. Kilpatrick, et al.
(see Robinson's chapter) among other investigators, have noted basic differences
among white-collar and professional people working for the government, those
working for industry, and those working in the academic world. Unfortunately,
data are not yet available from which we can determine whether such situs differences
are more pervasive than the basic professional, managerial, clerical and sales
distinctions we have made here. More important, we cannot yet determine what

segments of these basic groupings are most affected by type of industry.

The above features cover the major considerations that went into the construction of the occupation code in Appendix E. There are a number of other considerations which are more appropriately discussed within the context of the ten headings used in the code. These headings, like the categories which comprise them, are placed in rough order by socio-economic status; we say "rough" because, in many instances, such ordering may be nearly impossible to determine with any satisfactory degree of reliability. Where possible, we have included the ISR classification numbers to define clearly the occupations covered (see Chapter 14 to find the exact occupations included under each code in Appendix E). Unfortunately, we found it impossible to match the more detailed ISR blue-collar classification system of skilled, semi-skilled, and unskilled categories with our blue-collar code, based as it is on Census Industries.

The first decision on the composition of the ten headings was to attempt to divide the Professional-Technical heading into data-oriented and people-oriented headings. Although some of the code categories contain fairly low proportions of the population, the fact that the Professional-Technical area was the largest growing portion of the working population between 1950 and 1960 indicates that some of these rather sparsely populated entries may fill out in the years ahead. The people- vs. data-orientation led to some difficult coding decisions about doctors, artists and entertainers; some readers may wish to arrange the 18 code categories differently. It will be noted that the people-oriented professions contain a much higher proportion of women than the data-oriented professions, with notable exceptions such as lawyers and clergymen among the people-oriented and dieticians and medical technicians (in the "other medical" code) among the data-oriented.

Within the Managers, Officials and Proprietors heading, the Census occupation code could not be used to separate the self-employed precisely from the salaried-- which is perhaps the most important distinction to be made under this heading. For the most part, the Appendix E code achieves the separation of the salaried from the self-employed, although some of the latter may be scattered in salaried codes 23, 24, 25 and especially 26. The self-employed code categories are designed to distinguish owners of larger firms such as manufacturing plants or department stores from owners of smaller businesses such as gas stations or small repair shops. A more satisfactory differentation might be obtained from other data on the self-employed on the volume of business, profits, or number of employees of the firm.

Within the heading of Sales Workers, it is most important to separate in-surance or real estate salesmen and stock or bond brokers from retail sales clerks. It would also appear that salesmen in manufacturing and wholesaling are more likely to have higher status positions (and to be male) than retail sales clerks. On the other hand, it is clear that retail sales clerks are in more prestigeous occupations than newsboys, home demonstrators, and so on.

As the male-female distinction is extremely important within Clerical Workers, we have divided the occupations under this heading into three "male" and five "female" categories. It is fairly obvious that business agents and insurance adjusters, together with postal employees, should be separated from the other clerical occupations.

Within each of the three blue-collar headings (Craftsmen, Operatives, and Laborers), we have separated the following five industry groupings:

1) Manufacturing, durable goods
2) Manufacturing, non-durable goods
3) Transportation, communication and utilities
4) Construction, mining and agriculture (except laborers)
5) Trade

In addition, within each of the major three blue-collar headings, we have distinguished one special industrial group which contains a large bloc of workers: repair services, especially automotive repair, for Craftsmen (Skilled Workers); personal service, especially laundry workers, for Operatives (Semi-Skilled); and services and public administration for Laborers. The most important group to be distinguished within the heading of Skilled Workers is foremen, along with any self-employed craftsmen who may be identified, for they are likely to have higher status positions. Along the same line, apprentices are separated from other Semi-Skilled Workers.

While we felt constrained by the lack of guidelines for differentiating blue-collar workers, we found even less information by which to distinguish Service Workers. Two groups definitely stand out: protective (and armed) service workers, and private household workers. We have further differentiated "personal care" service (barbers, practical nurses etc.), resturant workers (cooks, bartenders etc.) and attendants (watchmen, elevator operators etc.). Finally, we split non-household cleaning personnel into male occupations (janitors, porters, bootblacks) and female occupations (charwomen, chamber maids).

The final general heading, Farm Workers, is split into only three categories: owner-tenants, wage laborers, and other. The owner-tenant category could be

usefully further differentiated with auxilliary information on the value or
size of the farm, last year's profits, or even the type of farming done.
Distinguishing farm owners from tenant farmers would probably be useful for
analytic purposes.

Briefly then, this is the rationale behind the Appendix E code: it is
meant as a first approximation to a more adequate description of the United States
working population than is available from the broad Census categories, which
constitute the ten headings of the Appendix E code. Surely, far more than the
one week's labor that went into the construction of the code would be required
before a truly satisfactory category system could be devised. It is in the
spirit of offering some tentative distinctions that would be useful in the
implementation of such an endeavor that the Appendix E code is proposed.

It is well to remember that there are numerous background occupational
factors that the research analyst should keep in mind in addition to the occupation
itself. For example, age is an important consideration: the blue collar worker
who becomes a foreman at age 35 should differ from the worker who becomes a
foreman at age 55; similarly, the person who graduates from college at age 35
should differ from one who graduates at age 22. Other biographical features may
be important as well, such as history of self-employment, or employment in many
jobs or in few jobs.

Blau, P. and Duncan, O. The American Occupational Structure. New York: Wiley
     (in press).

Clark, K. E. Manual: Minnesota Vocational Interest Inventory. New York:
     Psychological Corporation, 1965.

Cottle, W. C. "A factorial study of selected instruments for measuring personality
     and interest". Abstract American Psychologist 3 300 July 1948.

Guttman, L. "A general nonmetric technique for finding the smallest Euclidean
     space for a configuration of points" Psychometrika, 1967 (in press).

Hauser, R. "The pattern of occupation stratification: a substantive and methodo-
     logical critique" (Mimeo) University of Michigan, 1965.

Kuder, G. F. General Manual: Occupational Interest Survey (Kuder DD) Chicago:
     Illinois: Science Research Associates, 1966.

Laumann, E. and Guttman, L. "The relative associational contiguity of occupations
     in an urban setting", American Sociological Review, 36, 1966, 169-178.

Lingoes, J. C. "An IBM-7090 program for Guttman-Lingoes Smallest Space Analysis
     III" Behavioral Science, 11 (1966), 75-6.

Norman, W. "A spatial analysis of an interest domain" Educational and Psycho-
     logical Measurement, 20, 347-361, 1960.

Pearlin, B. and Kohn, M. "Social class, occupation, and parental values: a
     cross-national study" American Sociological Review, 31, 466-479, August, 1966.

Roe, A. The Psychology of Occupation, New York: Wiley, 1956.

Strong, E. and Campbell, D. Manual: SVIB, Stanford, California: Stanford
     University Press, 1966.

Schutz, R. and Baker, R. "A factor analysis of the Kuder Preference Record-
     Occupational Form D" Educational and Psychological Measurement, 22:
     97-104 Spring 1962.

Super, D. and Crites, J. Appraising Vocational Fitness. New York: Harper and
     Row, 1962

Terwillinger, J. "Dimensions of occupational preference" Educational and
     Psychological Measurement 23: 525-542, August, 1963.

Dictionary of Occupational Titles: Volume II Washington: U. S. Government
     Printing Office, 1965.

APPENDIX A

DICTIONARY OF OCCUPATIONAL TITLES
OCCUPATIONAL CATEGORIES, DIVISIONS, AND GROUPS
OCCUPATIONAL CATEGORIES (FIRST DIGIT)

0
1 } Professional, technical, and managerial occupations

2 Clerical and sales occupations
3 Service occupations
4 Farming, fishery, forestry, and related occupations
5 Processing occupations
6 Machines trades occupations
7 Bench work occupations
8 Structural work occupations
9 Miscellaneous occupations

TWO-DIGIT OCCUPATIONAL DIVISIONS (FIRST AND SECOND DIGITS)

PROFESSIONAL, TECHNICAL, AND MANAGERIAL OCCUPATIONS

00
01 } Occupations in architecture and engineering

02 Occupations in mathematics and physical sciences
04 Occupations in life sciences
05 Occupations in social sciences
07 Occupations in medicine and health
09 Occupations in education
10 Occupations in museum, library, and archival sciences
11 Occupations in law and jurisprudence
12 Occupations in religion and theology
13 Occupations in writing
14 Occupations in art
15 Occupations in entertainment and recreation
16 Occupations in administrative specializations
18 Managers and officials, n.e.c.
19 Miscellaneous professional, technical, and managerial occupations

CLERICAL AND SALES OCCUPATIONS

20 Stenography, typing, filing, and related occupations
21 Computing and account-recording occupations
22 Material and production recording occupations
23 Information and message distribution occupations
24 Miscellaneous clerical occupations
25 Salesmen, services
26
27 } Salesmen and salespersons, commodities
28
29 Merchandising occupations, except salesmen

SERVICE OCCUPATIONS

30 Domestic service occupations
31 Food and beverage preparation and service occupations
32 Lodging and related service occupations
33 Barbering, cosmetology, and related service occupations
34 Amusement and recreation service occupations
35 Miscellaneous personal service occupations
36 Apparel and furnishings service occupations
37 Protective service occupations
38 Building and related service occupations

FARMING, FISHERY, FORESTRY, AND RELATED OCCUPATIONS

40 Plant farming occupations
41 Animal farming occupations
42 Miscellaneous farming and related occupations
43 Fishery and related occupations
44 Forestry occupations
45 Hunting, trapping, and related occupations
46 Agricultural service occupations

PROCESSING OCCUPATIONS

50 Occupations in processing of metal
51 Ore refining and foundry occupations
52 Occupations in processing of food, tobacco, and related products
53 Occupations in processing of paper and related materials
54 Occupations in processing of petroleum, coal, natural and manufactured gas, and related products
55 Occupations in processing of chemicals, plastics, synthetics, rubber, paint, and related products
56 Occupations in processing of wood and wood products
57 Occupations in processing of stone, clay, glass, and related products
58 Occupations in processing of leather, textiles, and related products
59 Processing occupations, n.e.c.

MACHINE TRADES OCCUPATIONS

60 Metal machining occupations
61 Metalworking occupations, n.e.c.
62
63 } Mechanics and machinery repairmen
64 Paperworking occupations
65 Printing occupations
66 Wood machining occupations
67 Occupations in machining stone, clay, glass, and related materials
68 Textile occupations
69 Machine trades occupations, n.e.c.

BENCH WORK OCCUPATIONS

70 Occupations in fabrication, assembly, and repair of metal products, n.e.c.
71 Occupations in fabrication and repair of scientific and medical apparatus, photographic and optical goods, watches and clocks, and related products
72 Occupations in assembly and repair of electrical equipment
73 Occupations in fabrication and repair of products made from assorted materials
74 Painting, decorating, and related occupations
75 Occupations in fabrication and repair of plastics, synthetics, rubber, and related products
76 Occupations in fabrication and repair of wood products
77 Occupations in fabrication and repair of sand, stone, clay, and glass products
78 Occupations in fabrication and repair of textile, leather, and related products
79 Bench work occupations, n.e.c.

STRUCTURAL WORK OCCUPATIONS

80 Occupations in metal fabricating, n.e.c.
81 Welders, flame cutters, and related occupations
82 Electrical assembling, installing, and repairing occupations
84 Painting, plastering, waterproofing, cementing, and related occupations
85 Excavating, grading, paving, and related occupations
86 Construction occupations, n.e.c.
89 Structural work occupations, n.e.c.

MISCELLANEOUS OCCUPATIONS

90 Motor freight occupations
91 Transportation occupations, n.e.c.
92 Packaging and materials handling occupations
93 Occupations in extraction of minerals
94 Occupations in logging
95 Occupations in production and distribution of utilities
96 Amusement, recreation, and motion picture occupations, n.e.c.
97 Occupations in graphic art work

Explanation of Relationships Within Data, People, Things Hierarchies Used in DOT

Much of the information in this edition of the Dictionary is based on the premise that every job requires a worker to function in relation to Data, People, and Things, in varying degrees. These relationships are identified and explained below. They appear in the form of three hierarchies arranged in each instance from the relatively simple to the complex in such a manner that each successive relationship includes those that are simpler and excludes the more complex. The identifications attached to these relationships are referred to as worker functions, and provide standard terminology for use in summarizing exactly what a worker does on the job by means of one or more meaningful verbs.

A job's relationship to Data, People, and Things can be expressed in terms of the highest appropriate function in each hierarchy to which the worker has an occupationally significant relationship, and these functions taken together indicate the total level of complexity at which he must perform. The last three digits of the occupational code numbers in the Dictionary reflect significant relationships to Data, People, and Things, respectively. These last three digits express a job's relationship to Data, People, and Things by identifying the highest appropriate function in each hierarchy to which the job requires the worker to have a significant relationship, as reflected by the following table:

DATA (4th digit)	PEOPLE (5th digit)	THINGS (6th digit)
0 Synthesizing	0 Mentoring	0 Setting-Up
1 Coordinating	1 Negotiating	1 Precision Working
2 Analyzing	2 Instructing	2 Operating-Controlling
3 Compiling	3 Supervising	3 Driving-Operating
4 Computing	4 Diverting	4 Manipulating
5 Copying	5 Persuading	5 Tending
6 Comparing	6 Speaking-Signaling	6 Feeding-Offbearing
7 } No significant relationship	7 Serving	7 Handling
8 }	8 No significant relationship	8 No significant relationship

DATA: Information, knowledge, and conceptions, related to data, people, or things, obtained by observation, investigation, interpretation, visualization, mental creation; incapable of being touched; written data take the form of numbers, words, symbols; other data are ideas, concepts, oral verbalization.

0 **Synthesizing:** Integrating analyses of data to discover facts and/or develop knowledge concepts or interpretations.

1 **Coordinating:** Determining time, place, and sequence of operations or action to be taken on the basis of analysis of data; executing determinations and/or reporting on events.

2 **Analyzing:** Examining and evaluating data. Presenting alternative actions in relation to the evaluation is frequently involved.

3 **Compiling:** Gathering, collating, or classifying information about data, people, or things. Reporting and/or carrying out a prescribed action in relation to the information is frequently involved.

4 **Computing:** Performing arithmetic operations and reporting on and/or carrying out a prescribed action in relation to them. Does not include counting.

5 **Copying:** Transcribing, entering, or posting data.

6 **Comparing:** Judging the readily observable functional, structural, or compositional characteristics (whether similar to or divergent from obvious standards) of data, people, or things.

PEOPLE: Human beings; also animals dealt with on an individual basis as if they were human.

0 **Mentoring:** Dealing with individuals in terms of their total personality in order to advise, counsel, and/or guide them with regard to problems that may be resolved by legal, scientific, clinical, spiritual, and/or other professional principles.

1   **Negotiating:** Exchanging ideas, information, and opinions with others to formulate policies and programs and/or arrive jointly at decisions, conclusions, or solutions.

2   **Instructing:** Teaching subject matter to others, or training others (including animals) through explanation, demonstration, and supervised practice; or making recommendations on the basis of technical disciplines.

3   **Supervising:** Determining or interpreting work procedure for a group of workers, assigning specific duties to them, maintaining harmonious relations among them, and promoting efficiency.

4   **Diverting:** Amusing others.

5   **Persuading:** Influencing others in favor of a product, service, or point of view.

6   **Speaking-Signaling:** Talking with and/or signaling people to convey or exchange information. Includes giving assignments and/or directions to helpers or assistants.

7   **Serving:** Attending to the needs or requests of people or animals or the expressed or implicit wishes of people. Immediate response is involved.

THINGS: Inanimate objects as distinguished from human beings; substances or materials; machines, tools, equipment; products. A thing is tangible and has shape, form, and other physical characteristics.

0   **Setting Up:** Adjusting machines or equipment by replacing or altering tools, jigs, fixtures, and attachments to prepare them to perform their functions, change their performance, or restore their proper functioning if they break down. Workers who set up one or a number of machines for other workers or who set up and personally operate a variety of machines are included here.

1   **Precision Working:** Using body members and/or tools or work aids to work, move, guide, or place objects or materials in situations where ultimate responsibility for the attainment of standards occurs and selection of appropriate tools, objects, or materials, and the adjustment of the tool to the task require exercise of considerable judgment.

2   **Operating-Controlling:** Starting, stopping, controlling, and adjusting the progress of machines or equipment designed to fabricate and/or process objects or materials. Operating machines involves setting up the machine and adjusting the machine or material as the work progresses. Controlling equipment involves observing gages, dials, etc., and turning valves and other devices to control such factors as temperature, pressure, flow of liquids, speed of pumps, and reactions of materials. Setup involves several variables and adjustment is more frequent than in tending.

3   **Driving-Operating:** Starting, stopping, and controlling the actions of machines or equipment for which a course must be steered, or which must be guided, in order to fabricate, process, and/or move things or people. Involves such activities as observing gages and dials; estimating distances and determining speed and direction of other objects; turning cranks and wheels; pushing clutches or brakes; and pushing or pulling gear lifts or levers. Includes such machines as cranes, conveyor systems, tractors, furnace charging machines, paving machines and hoisting machines. Excludes manually powered machines, such as handtrucks and dollies, and power assisted machines, such as electric wheelbarrows and handtrucks.

4   **Manipulating:** Using body members, tools, or special devices to work, move, guide, or place objects or materials. Involves some latitude for judgment with regard to precision attained and selecting appropriate tool, object, or material, although this is readily manifest.

5   **Tending:** Starting, stopping, and observing the functioning of machines and equipment. Involves adjusting materials or controls of the machine, such as changing guides, adjusting timers and temperature gages, turning valves to allow flow of materials, and flipping switches in response to lights. Little judgment is involved in making these adjustments.

6   **Feeding-Offbearing:** Inserting, throwing, dumping, or placing materials in or removing them from machines or equipment which are automatic or tended or operated by other workers.

7   **Handling:** Using body members, handtools, and/or special devices to work, move, or carry objects or materials. Involves little or no latitude for judgment with regard to attainment of standards or in selecting appropriate tool, object, or material.

NOTE: Included in the concept of Feeding-Offbearing, Tending, Operating-Controlling, and Setting Up, is the situation in which the worker is actually part of the setup of the machine, either as the holder and guider of the material or holder and guider of the tool.

The 144 worker trait groups and the 22 major areas of work
under which they fall in the DOT. Ratings on data, people,
things hierarchies (see Appendix B) are given at left and
occupational categories covered (see Appendix C) are given
at right. "Major Occupation" means that five or more occupations of this type are grouped under the title in question.

DATA PEOPLE THINGS		TITLE	OCCUPATIONS Major	Minor
		ELEMENTAL WORK (EW)		
868		Signaling etc.		37,86,91,94
886	*MA	Feeding-offbearing	50,52,53,55,57 58,61,64,66,67 68,69,92	36,40,41,42,51,54 56,59,60,65,71,78 80,81,84,86,93,94 95,97
887		Handling	22,31,36,40,51 52,54,55,56,57 58,59,61,68,70 71,72,73,74,75 76,77,78,79,80 84,85,86,91,92 93,94,95,97	23,24,29,30,32,33 34,35,37,38,41,42 43,44,46,50,53,60 62,63,64,65,66,67 69,81,82,89,90,96

*Also classified under Machine Work

		MACHINE WORK (MA)		
280,380		Set-up and/or all-round machine operating	55,60,61,68,69	00,01,02,50,51,54 57,58,59,65,66,67 80,81,92,93,95,97
780		Set-up and adjustment		34,50,51,52,53,55 61,62,63,64,65,66 68,69,81,92
782		Operating-controlling	50,51,52,53,54 55,57,58,60,61 64,65,66,67,68 69,78,81,91,95 97	19,20,21,36,37,42 43,56,59,62,63,80 84,85,86,89,92,93 94,96
883	TR	Driving-operating	40,85,86,90,91 92,93,94	35,38,42,43,51,55 57,59,66,80,89,95
885		Tending	36,50,51,52,53 54,55,56,57,58 59,60,61,64,65 66,67,68,69,78 92,95,97	19,20,21,23,35,40 41,42,44,46,62,80 81,82,84,85,86,89 91,93,96

Classified elsewhere

886	EW	Feeding-offbearing		

DPT		TITLE	Major	Minor

CRAFTS (CR)

DPT		TITLE	Major	Minor
130,131,132 133,134,137	MS TR FF	Supervisory work (Farming logging, manufacturing etc.)	31,40,50,51,52 54,55,57,58,60 61,62,63,66,68 69,70,71,72,73 74,75,77,78,80 82,86,91,92,95	19,32,36,38,41,42 43,44,46,53,56,59 64,65,67,76,81,84 85,89,90,93,94,96 97
138	MC TR FF	Other supervisory work (similar to above)	54,82,91,95	40,41,46,50,52,53 55,57,58,62,65,66 71,72,73,78,80,84 85,86,89,90,92,93 94,96,97
261,361		Costuming, tailoring etc.		78,96
281,381		Cooking etc.	31	30
281,381		Craftsmanship etc.	60,61,62,63,70 71,72,73,75,76 77,78,80,82,86 96,97	29,33,34,35,36,37 38,46,50,51,52,53 55,56,57,58,64,65 66,69,74,79,81,84 85,89,91,93,95
781	FF	Precision working	62,63,70,71,72 73,78,80,82,84 86,97	31,36,38,45,46,50 52,57,58,65,68,74 75,76,77,81,85,93 94,95,96
884	FF	Manipulating	36,40,43,51,52 55,57,58,62,63 70,71,72,73,74 75,76,77,78,79 80,81,82,85,86 93,95,97	20,22,24,29,31,37 38,41,42,44,45,46 50,54,59,60,61,67 84,89,91,92,94,96

FARMING, FISHING, FORESTRY (FF)

DPT		TITLE	Major	Minor
181		Cropping, animal farming etc.	40,41	42,43,45
384	SC	Related technical work		02,04,19,42,44,46

Classified elsewhere

DPT		TITLE	Major	Minor
128,228	ET	Vocational education		
130,131,132 133,134,137	TR MS CR	Supervisory work (farming, logging etc.)		
138	TR MS CR	Supervisory work (farming etc.)		
188,288	EN	Surveying, prospecting etc.		
781	CR	Precision working		
884	CR	Manipulating		

TRANSPORTATION (TR)

DPT		TITLE	Major	Minor
363,364,463		Transportation service work	91	

Classified elsewhere

DPT		TITLE	Major	Minor
130,131,132 133,134,137	MS FF CR	Supervisory work (farming, logging etc.)		
138	MS FF CR	Supervisory work (farming etc.)		
168	CL	Scheduling, dispatching etc.		
168,228,268	ET	Flight and related training		
268,383	II	Transporting and test driving		
368	CL	Facilities, services etc.		
383	ME	Delivery and service work (nec)		
868	EW	Signaling and related work		
883	MA	Driving-operating		

DPT		TITLE	Major	Minor
		BUSINESS RELATIONS (BR)		
118,168		Administration	07,09,16,18	04,05,10,15,19,37
118,168		Contract negotiation etc.	18,19	15,16
228		Business training		16,23
138		Supervisory work (clerical, sales etc.)	20,21,22,23,91	10,18,24,29,37,93 95,96,97
168		Managerial work	16,18,19	07,09,10,11,14,15 29,31,35,37,40,41 44,46,91,96
168,268		Consultative and business services	16,18	09
168,268		Interviewing, information-giving etc.	16	15,18,19,20,24
188,288		Accounting, auditing etc.	16	18,19
288		Title and contract search etc.		10,11,16,18,20
288,388		Corresponding etc.		20,24
368		Information processing	24	09,10,15,16,19,20 21,22,23,34,35,91 96
		CLERICAL (CL)		
168	TR	Scheduling, dispatching etc.	91,95	16,18,19,20,22,23 24,35,37,52,93,96
268,368		Secretarial etc.		20,96
368	TR	Facilities, services etc.	91	21,22,24,29,34,35 37,30,93,95
368		Paying and receiving		21,23
382,384,387 484,487	II	Inspecting and stock checking	22,71,72,73,78 80,91,94,95	07,16,19,24,29,36 37,41,46,50,51,52 53,54,55,57,58,59 60,61,62,63,64,67 68,69,70,75,76,77 82,85,86,92,93,96 97
382,582		Typesetting, reproducing etc.		20,21,23,65
388		Classifying, filing etc.	20,22,91	10,13,15,16,18,19 21,23,24,29,37,41 57,95,97
388		Stenographic etc.		20
388,488		Computing and related recording	21,22	15,16,18,20,24,29 36,52,58,86,91,94
484,485,487 584,585,587 683,684,685 687	II	Sorting, inspecting, measuring etc.	22,52,55,57,68 70,71,72,73,75 76,78,80,91,92 97	00,01,10,16,20,21 23,24,29,34,35,36 37,40,41,43,44,51 53,54,56,58,59,60 61,62,63,64,65,66 67,69,74,77,79,82 85,86,92,94,96
588		Typing and related recording	20	15,21,23
588,688		Routine checking and recording	20,22,23	07,16,19,21,24,37 52,65,79,90,91,92 95,96,97
862	PC	Switchboard service		23
Classified elsewhere				
368	BR	Information processing		
288,388	BR WR	Correspondence etc.		
138	ME MS BR	Supervisory work (clerical, sales)		

DPT		TITLE	Major	Minor

MERCHANDISING (ME)

DPT		TITLE	Major	Minor
068	WR	Promotion and publicity		16
158,168		Purchase and sales work	16	18,19,25,26,27,28 29,46,96
251		Sales and service work		27,63,71,82
258,358,458		Demonstration and sales work	25,26,27,28,29	
383,483	TR	Delivery and service work (nec)		29
858		Selling and related work	29,34	14

Classified elsewhere

DPT		TITLE	Major	Minor
118,168	LE BR	Contract negotiating		
138	MS BR CL	Supervisory work (clerical, sales etc.)		
151	EN	Sales engineering		

MANAGERIAL AND SUPERVISORY WORK (MS)

DPT		TITLE	Major	Minor
138	PS	Supervisory work (service etc.)	31	18,30,32,33,34,35 36,38

Clissified elsewhere

DPT		TITLE	Major	Minor
118,168	BR	Administration		
128	MH ET	Supervising and instructing (nursing)		
130,131,132	FF TR CR	Supervisory work (farming logging etc.)		
138	ME CL BR	Supervisory work (clerical etc.)		
138	FF TR CR	Other supervisory work (farming etc.)		
168	BR	Managerial work		

DPT		TITLE	Major	Minor

PERSONAL SERVICE (PS)

DPT		TITLE	Major	Minor
271,371		Beautician, barber	33	
468,478		Customer service work (nec)	29	22,24,28,31,32,36 65,91
863,864,865		Miscellaneous customer	34	14,29,31,35,36,91
867,873 874,877		Service work		
868		Accomodating work		31,34,35,45
868,878		Miscellaneous personal service work	30,31,33,34,35	32,36,38,91
868,878		Usher, messenger etc.	34,35	23,24,29,32,91
874,877		Animal care	35	15

Classified elsewhere

DPT		TITLE	Major	Minor
138	MS	Supervisory work (services)		
868,878	LE	Protecting and related work		
878	MH	Child and adult care		
108,118,168		Legal and related work	11	16
868,878	PS	Protecting and related work	37	24,40

Classified elsewhere

DPT		TITLE	Major	Minor
118,168	ME BR	Contract negotiating etc.		
168,268	II	Investigating, protecting etc.		
187,284,287	II LI	Appraising, investigating etc.		
288	BR	Title, contract search etc.		

WRITING (WR)

DPT		TITLE	Major	Minor
018,038,068		Journalism and editorial work	13	05
088		Creative writing	13	
268		News reporting etc.		13
288		Translating, editing etc.	13	10,15,16,19,96

Classified elsewhere

DPT		TITLE	Major	Minor
068	ME	Promotion and publicity		
188,288	EN	Technical writing etc.		
288,388	CL BR	Corresponding etc.		

INVESTIGATING, INSPECTING AND TESTING (II)

DPT		TITLE	Major	Minor
168,268	LE	Investigating, protecting etc.	16,37	09,15,19,24,44
181,281,381	MH SC	Materials analysis etc.	01,02,07	04,19,46,52,97
187,284,287	LE	Apprasing, investigating	16	14,15,18,19,29,31 44,77,82,86,91,95
283,383	TR	Transporting and test driving		19,80,91

Classified elsewhere

DPT		TITLE	Major	Minor
288	LE BR	Title and contract search etc.		
382,384,387 484,487	CL	Inspecting and stock checking		
484,485,487 584,585,587 683,684,685 687	CL	Sorting, inspecting, measuring and related work		

DPT			TITLE	Major	Minor
			ART (AR)		
028	EN	ET	Instructive work (Fine arts etc.)	15	14
031,051,061			Decorating and art work	14	
062	PC		Photographic work		14
081			Art work	14	29,97
281,381			Artistic restoration etc.	14	05,10,19,29,31,52
			ENTERTAINMENT (EN)		
028			Creative entertainment		15
048			Dramatics		15
048	MU		Instrumental music		15
048	MU		Rhythmics		15
148,268	PC		Radio announcing etc.		13,15
248,348			Physical amusement etc.	15	19,34
268,368,468			Miscellaneous amusement	15	18,34
848			Speciality entertainment	15	29
868			Modeling etc.		29,96

Classified elsewhere

DPT			TITLE	Major	Minor
028	ET	MU	Instructive work (fine arts)		
			MUSIC (MU)		
088			Musical work, creative		15

Classified elsewhere

DPT			TITLE	Major	Minor
028	AR		Instructive work (fine arts)		
048	EN		Instrumental music		
048	EN		Vocal music		
048	EN		Rhythmics		
			PHOTOGRAPHY AND COMMUNICATIONS (PC)		
282,382			Photographic machine work	14,97	19,96
282,382			Radio, TV transmitting	19,95	

Classified elsewhere

DPT			TITLE	Major	Minor
068	ME		Promotion and publicity		
188,288	EN		Technical writing etc.		
288,388	CL	BR	Corresponding etc.		

DPT		TITLE	Major	Minor
		ENGINEERING (EN)		
081,088		Engineering research and design	00,01	02
151	ME	Sales engineering		00,01
168	SC	Technical coordination	00,01	02,04,07,16,18,19
181,281		Drafting etc.	00,01	24
181,281		Technical work etc.	00,01	19
187		Engineering etc.	00,01	
188,288		Industrial engineering etc.	01	00,07,16,18,19,22
188,288	FF	Surveying, prospecting etc.	01,02	19,24,93
188,288	WR	Technical writing		
		MATHEMATICS AND SCIENCE (SC)		
021	MH	Health physics		07
081		Scientific research	02,04,07	
088,081		Mathematics and physical science	02	01

Classified elsewhere

DPT		TITLE	Major	Minor
088	CG	Social sciences		
168	EN	Technical coordination		
181,281,381	MH II	Materials analysis etc.		
188,288	BR	Accounting, auditing		
384	FF	Technical work		
		MEDICINE AND HEALTH (MH)		
101		Surgery		07
108		Medical services (veterinary)	07	
128,228		Therapeutic and related work		07
368,378		Nursing and medical services	07	
878		Child and adult care	35	30,34

Classified elsewhere

DPT		TITLE	Major	Minor
021	SC	Health physics		
128	MS ET	Supervisory and instructive (nursing)		
182,281,381	SC II	Materials analysis etc.		
228	ET	Physical education		

PT		TITLE	Major	Minor

COUNSELING, GUIDANCE ETC (CG)

PT		TITLE	Major	Minor
088	SC	Social sciences	05	04,16
108,208	ET	Guidance and counseling	19	04,09,12

Classified elsewhere

PT		TITLE	Major	Minor
168,268	BR	Interviewing, information-giving etc.		

EDUCATION AND TRAINING (ET)

PT		TITLE	Major	Minor
128	MH	Supervisory and instructive (Nursing etc.)	07	
128,228		Industrial training		09,16,23,37,44,62 68,71,78,90,91,94
128,228	FF	Vocational education	09	42
168,228,268	TR	Flight training etc.	19	09
228		Education (high school and above)	09	
228		Miscellaneous instructive		09,15,19,43
228	MH	Physical education	15	09
228		Training services		16
228,328		Animal training	15	34

Classified elsewhere

PT		TITLE	Major	Minor
028	EN	Instructive work (fine arts etc.)		
108,208	CG	Guidance and counseling		
228	BR	Business training		

APPENDIX D

STANDARD OCCUPATION CODE FOR POLITICAL BEHAVIOR PROGRAM

Survey Research Center
Inter-University Consortium for Political Research

Below is the revised occupation code to be used for all political behavior studies. Insofar as possible, studies now processed into the ICPR archive have been or will be recorded to conform with these conventions.

Occupation Code

Code

3-digit Codes from Department of Commerce Census of Occupations, 1960 Edition

Professional and Technical (000-195)

01. Accountants and Auditors (000)
02. Clergymen (023)
03. Teachers - secondary and primary (182-184)
04. Teachers - college, librarians, principals (030-060, 111)
05. Dentists (071)
06. Physicians and Surgeons (162)
07. Engineers (080-093)
08. Lawyers and Judges (105)
09. Social and Welfare Workers (165, 171)
10. Other Medical and Paramedical - Chiropractors, Optometrists, Osteopaths, Pharmacists, Veterinarians, Nurses, Therapists, and Healers (022, 152, 153, 160, 194, 150, 151, 193)
11. Scientists, Physical and Social - e.g., Chemists, Physical and Biological Scientists, Statisticians, etc. (021, 130-145, 171-175)
12. Technicians - Airplane Pilots and Navigators, Designers, Dieticians and Nutritionists, Draftsmen, Foresters and Conservationists, Funeral Directors, Embalmers, Photographers, Radio Operators, Surveyor, Technicians (medical, dental, testing, n.e.e.) (012, 072, 073, 074, 103, 104, 161, 164, 181, 185, 190-192)

Code

13.   Public Advisors - Editors and Reporters, Farm and Home Management Advisors, Personnel and Labor Relations Workers, Recreation and Group Workers, Religious Workers (075, 102, 153, 165, 175)

17.   Other Semi-Professional or Professional (with college degree) - e.g., Architects

18.   Other Semi-Professional (no college degree)

19.   Professional, NA what type

Self-employed Businessmen. Managers and Officials (R. 250-289)

21.   Self-employed Businessman, Owner or Part-owner, "Large" Business (earned more than $10,000 in 1963)

22.   Self-employed Businessman, Owner or Part-owner, "Small" Business (earned less than $10,000 in 1963)

23.   Self-employed Business, NA what size

28.   Other Managers, Officials, and Proprietors

29.   Manager, Official or Proprietor, NA what type

Clerical and Sales (Y, Z, 301-360, S, 380-395)

30.   Bookkeeper (310)

31.   Stenographers, Typists, and Secretaries (345, 360, Z.)

32.   Other Clerical (Y, 301-360)

33.   Sales, Higher-status traveling or 'outside' goods (381, 382)

34.   Sales, Higher-status traveling or "outside" services (380, 385, 393, 395)

35.   Sales. "Inside" Sales. Salesman, Clerk (S)

36.   Sales. Lower-status "outside sales. Hucksters, Peddlers, Newsboys (383, 390)

37.   Other Sales

38.   Clerical, NA what type (Y, Z, 301-360)

39.   Sales, NA what type (S, 380-395)

Skilled Workers (Q, 401-554)

41.   Self-employed Artisans and Craftsmen

42.   Foremen (430)

48.   Other Craftsmen and Kindred Workers

49.   Skilled Workers, NA what type

Semi-skilled. Operatives and Kindred Workers (T, W, 601-721)

51.   Operatives and Kindred Workers

Code

Service Workers (555, 801-890, P)

61. Protective Service Workers - Firemen, Marshalls and Constables, Policemen and Bailiffs (850-854)
62. Other Protective Service (860)
63. Members of Armed Service - Enlisted men, NA whether enlisted or officer (555)
64. Members of Armed Service - Officers (555)
65. Private Household Workers (P, 801-803)
68. Other Service Workers (810-842, 874-890)
69. Service Worker, NA what type

Unskilled Laborers (U, V, X, 901, 905, 960-973)

71. Farm Laborers (U, V, 901, 905)
78. Other Laborers (X, 960-973)
79. Unskilled, NA what type

Farm Operators (N, 222)

81. Farm Managers (222)
82. Farm Owners and Tenants (N)
89. Farmers, NA what type

Unemployed and Students

91. Unemployed with private income (Rentier)
92. Student (IF R is a part-time day student, classify here rather than by occupation. If R is studying nights, classify by occupation)
93. On Strike (code occupation and unemployment times as for general unemployed)
94. Other general unemployed

Retired

95. Retired

Housewife

96. Housewife (If R works part-time outside home, R should be classified according to part-time occupation)
99. NA

NOTE: Coding of part-time farmers. Depends on classification of head. (1) If land was farmed part-time but only non-farm job was mentioned, non-farm job was coded. (2) Apparent workers who had picked up small farms while maintaining non-farm jobs were coded non-farm. (3) Farm heads who appeared to be picking up non-farm work on side were coded "farm". In general, depended on coder estimate of primacy. Where all else was equal (or unknown) coded by first mention.

APPENDIX E

TENTATIVE REVISED OCCUPATION CODE

(ISR Identification Number Used: See Duncan Code Column 2)

		% 1960 Population
Professional - Technical (Data Oriented) -- 5.4%		
01	Physicians, surgeons, dentists, osteopaths (014,040,044)	.50
02	Engineers, programmers (020-028)	1.35
03	Physical and social scientists (008,036,049)	.32
04	Accountants and auditors (001)	.74
05	Artistic (004,005,007,015,043)	.44
06	Other medical (009,016,032,039,042,053,056,057)	.58
07	Draftsmen, surveyors (017,051)	.41
08	Technicians, except medical (054,055)	.54
09	Other, not classified above (033,031,045)	.14
10	Professional - technical (n.e.c.) (058)	.49
Professional - Technical (People Oriented) -- 6.0%		
11	Lawyers and judges (033)	.33
12	College teachers, librarians, principles (012,034)	.41
13	Public advisors (011,018,030,041,046,048)	.64
14	Teachers: secondary grades and n.e.c. (052)	1.04
15	Teachers: primary grades (052)	1.56
16	Clergymen and religious workers (010,047)	.40
17	Entertainers (002,006,013,029,035,050)	.60
18	Nurses, professional and student (037,038)	1.01
		11.40

Managers, Officials, Proprietors -- 8.5%

(Salaried)

21	Financial (095,096,097)	.64
22	Manufacturing (081)	1.01
23	Public administration and transportation (063,066,067,068, 069,071,072,073,074,075,077)	.62
24	Retail trade, repair, housing and services (086) (except under 25) (070,079,086-094,098,099,100)	1.20
25	All other industries (080,082,083,084,101)	1.24

(NA Self-Employed or Salaried)

26	Buyers etc. (061,062,064,065,076,078)	.70

(Self-Employed)

27	Construction and manufacturing (103,104)	.63
28	Higher profit trade (107,111,112,113,116,118,119)	.74
29	Lower retail trade and other (105,106,109,110,114,115,117, 121-124)	1.72
		8.50

Sales Workers -- 7.5%

41	Insurance, real estate etc. (145,149,151,152)	.96
42	Manufacturing, wholesale trade etc. (154,155,157)	1.81
43	Retail trade (156)	4.22
44	Newsboys, demonstrators etc. (146,147,148,150)	.46
		7.45

Clerical Workers -- 14.9%

31	Agents etc. (125,132,133,134,173,141,143,501)	1.17
32	Postal clerks and mail carriers (108,135)	.65
33	Messengers etc. (128,136,138,140)	.58
35	Secretaries (507)	2.31
36	Bookkeepers (130)	1.45
37	Cashiers, bank tellers and payroll (102,129,131)	1.13
38	Telephone and office machine operators (137,142)	1.07
39	Other office workers (126,127,085,153,139,506)	1.87
30	Clerical (n.e.c.)	4.68
		14.91

Craftsmen, Foremen (Skilled Workers) -- 14.3%

51	Foremen	1.86
52	Transportation, communication and utilities	1.37
53	Manufacturing (durable goods)	2.94
54	Manufacturing (non-durable goods)	1.35
55	Construction, mining, agriculture	3.30
56	Trade	.67
57	Repair services	1.37
58	All other	1.43
		14.30

Operatives (Semi-Skilled) -- 19.9%

61	Apprentices	.14
62	Transportation, communication and utilities	2.06
63	Manufacturing (durable goods)	6.27
64	Manufacturing (non-durable goods)	6.07
65	Construction, mining, agriculture	1.31
66	Trade	2.38
67	Personal services	.79
68	All other	.83
		19.91

Service Workers -- 11.8%

71	Protective and armed services (391,395,397,398,399,402)	.67
72	Personal care (288,383,384,385,396,401)	1.42
73	Restaurant workers (388,389,404)	2.58
74	Attendants (380-382,390,392,403,405)	1.43
75	Private household (175,372-379,505)	2.83
76	Other cleaning work, male (386,394,400,502)	1.74
77	Other cleaning work, female (287,387,393)	.82
78	Service workers (n.e.c.) (406)	.30
		11.79

Laborers (Except Farm) -- 5.4%

81	Construction (323,491)	1.22
82	Manufacturing durable goods (419-450)	.96
83	Manufacturing, non-durable goods (452-489)	.53
84	Transportation, communication, utilities (493,494,495,414, 416,417)	.71
85	Trade (503,495)	.77
86	Services and public administration (412,413,496,497,498)	.75
87	Laborers (n.e.c.) (411,415,499)	.44
		5.44

Farm Workers -- 6.3%

91	Owners, tenants and managers (019,059,060,191)	3.92
92	Unpaid family workers, foremen, self-employed (407,409,410)	.49
93	Laborers, wage workers	1.93
		6.34